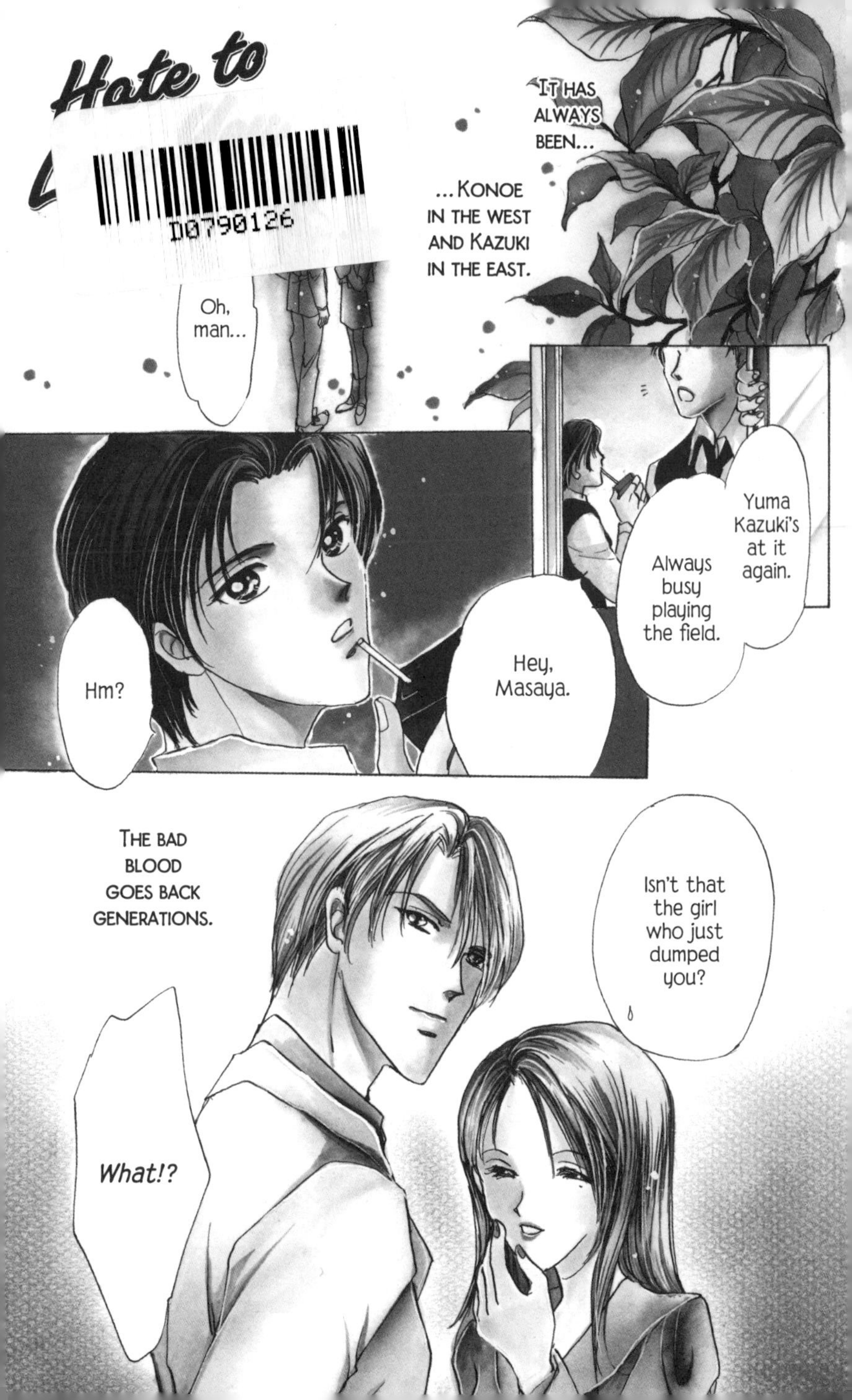
Hate to
It has always been...
...Konoe in the west and Kazuki in the east.
Oh, man...
Yuma Kazuki's at it again.
Always busy playing the field.
Hey, Masaya.
Hm?
Isn't that the girl who just dumped you?
The bad blood goes back generations.
What!?

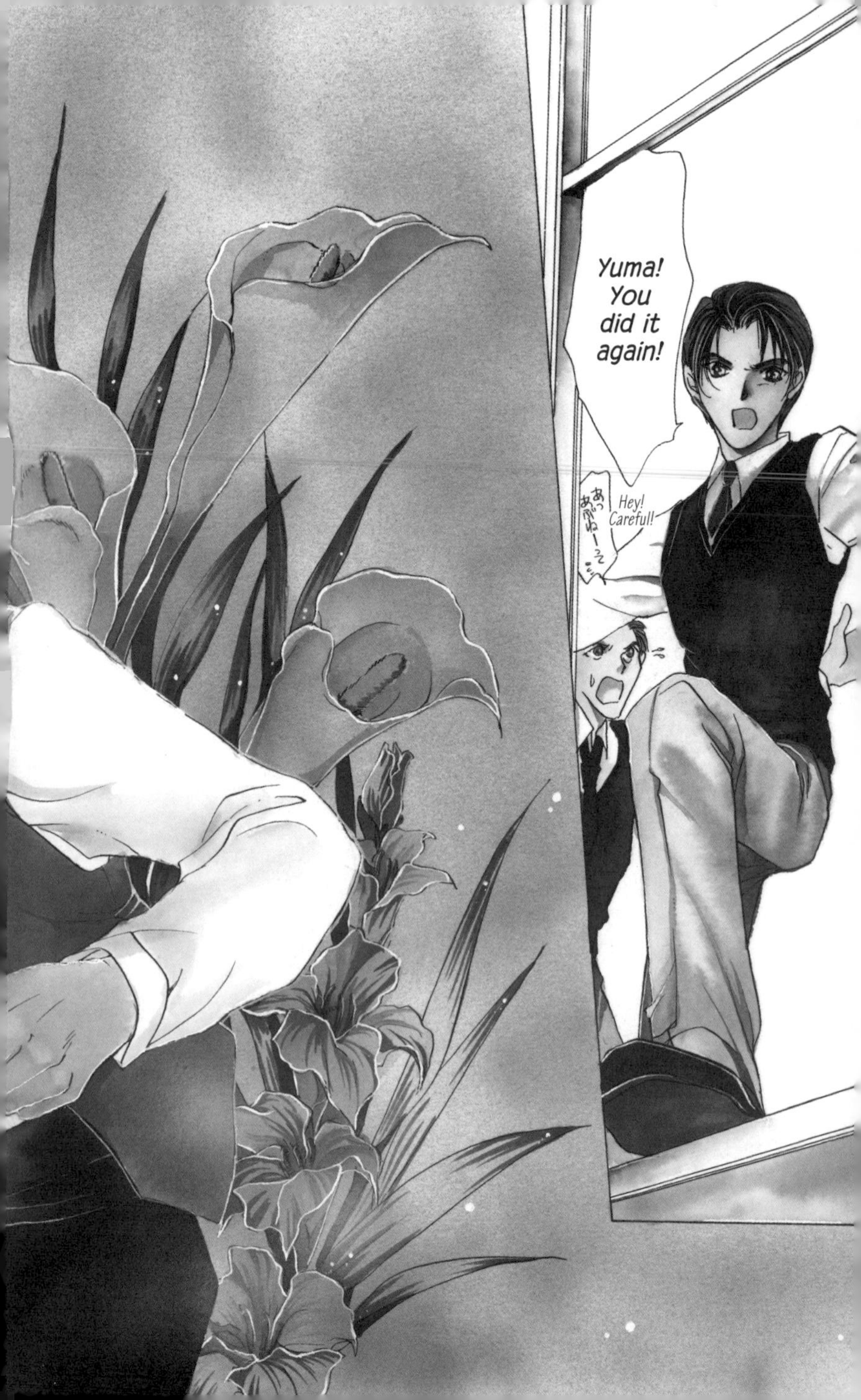
Yuma! You did it again!
Hey! Careful!

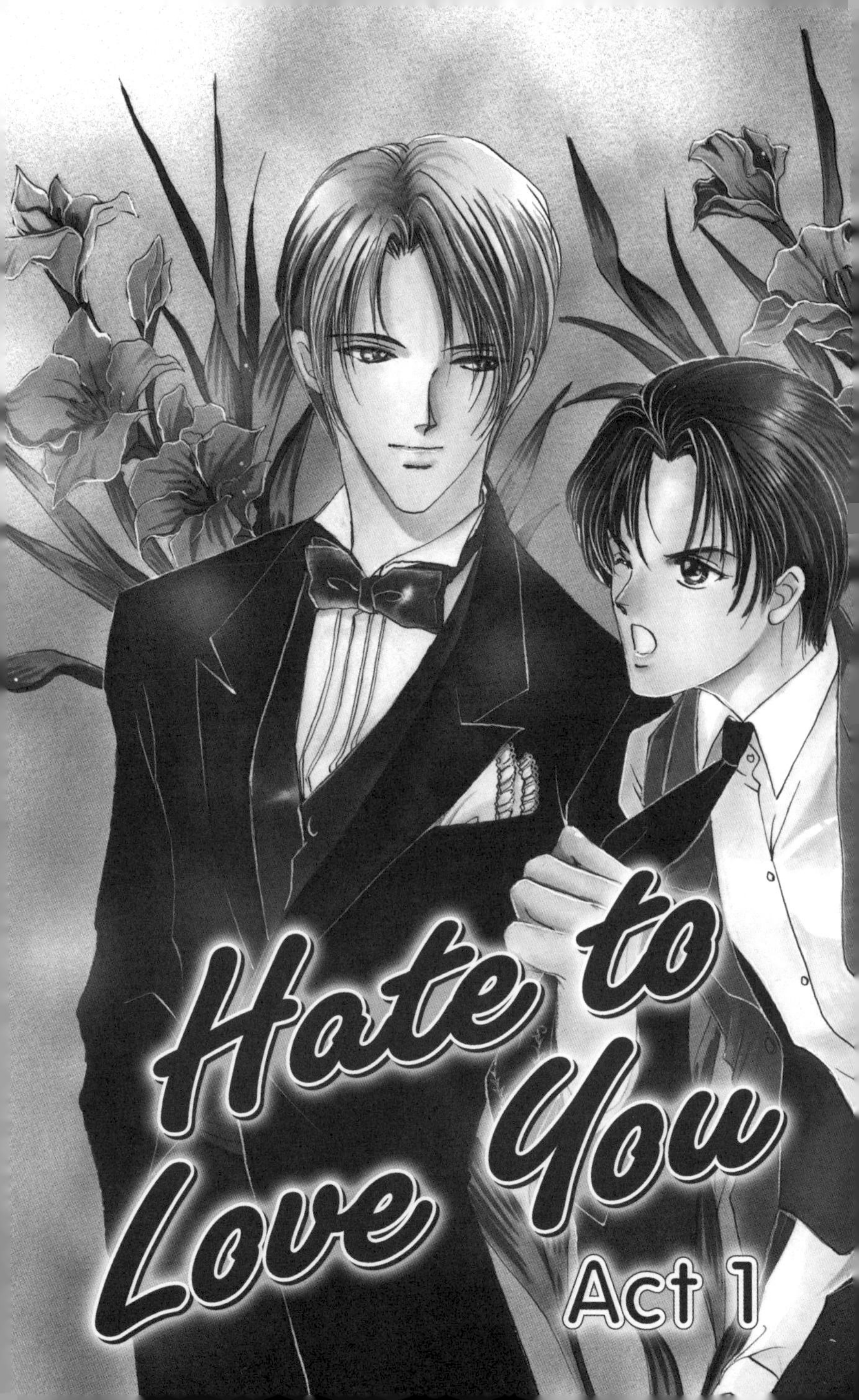
Hate to Love You
Act 1

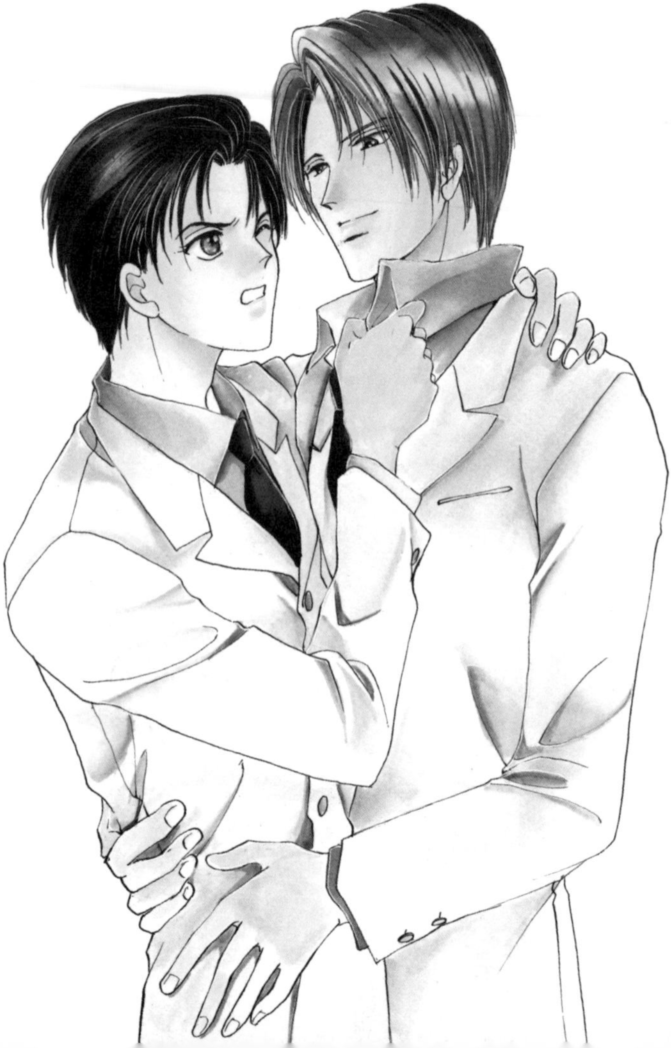

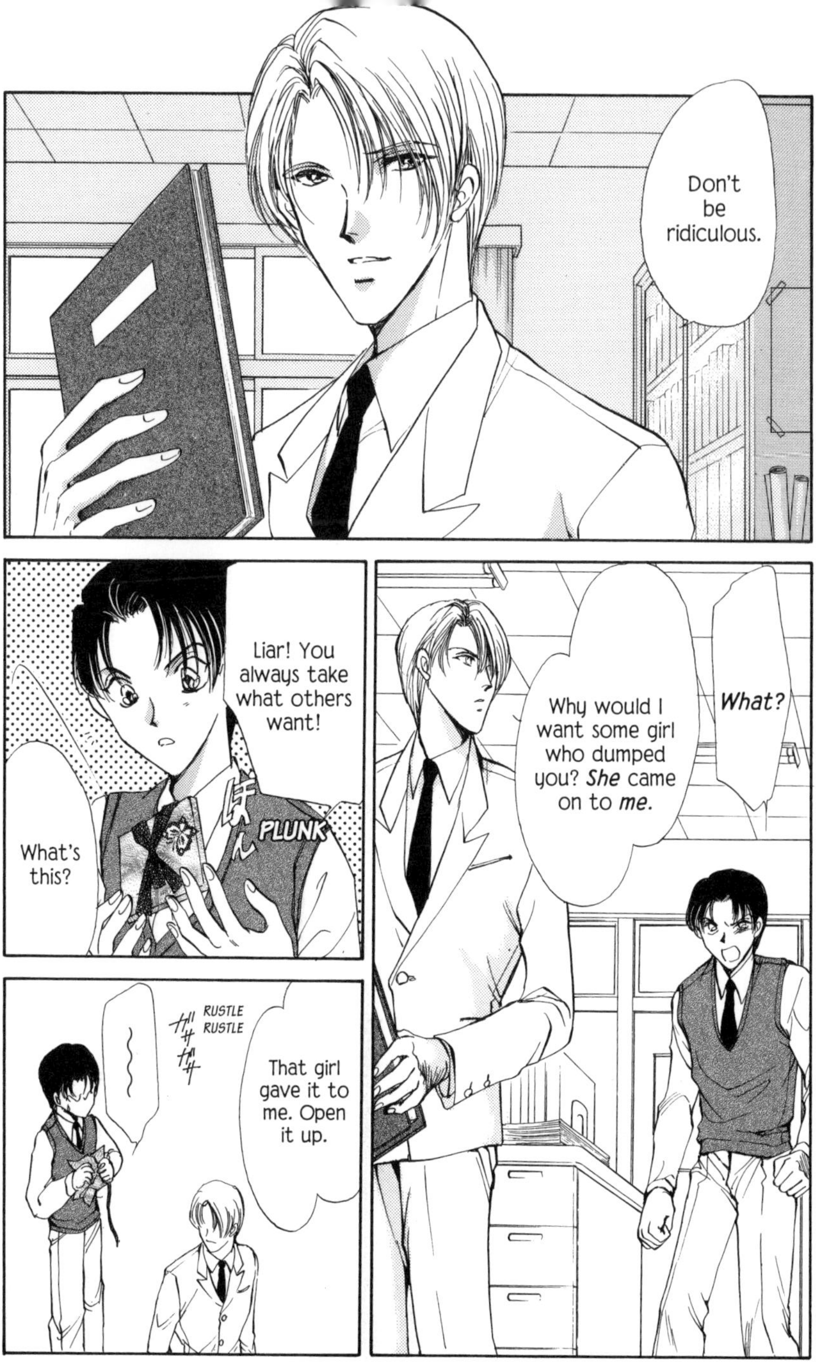
Don't be ridiculous.
What?
Why would I want some girl who dumped you? *She* came on to *me.*
Liar! You always take what others want!
ぽん
PLUNK
What's this?
That girl gave it to me. Open it up.
RUSTLE RUSTLE

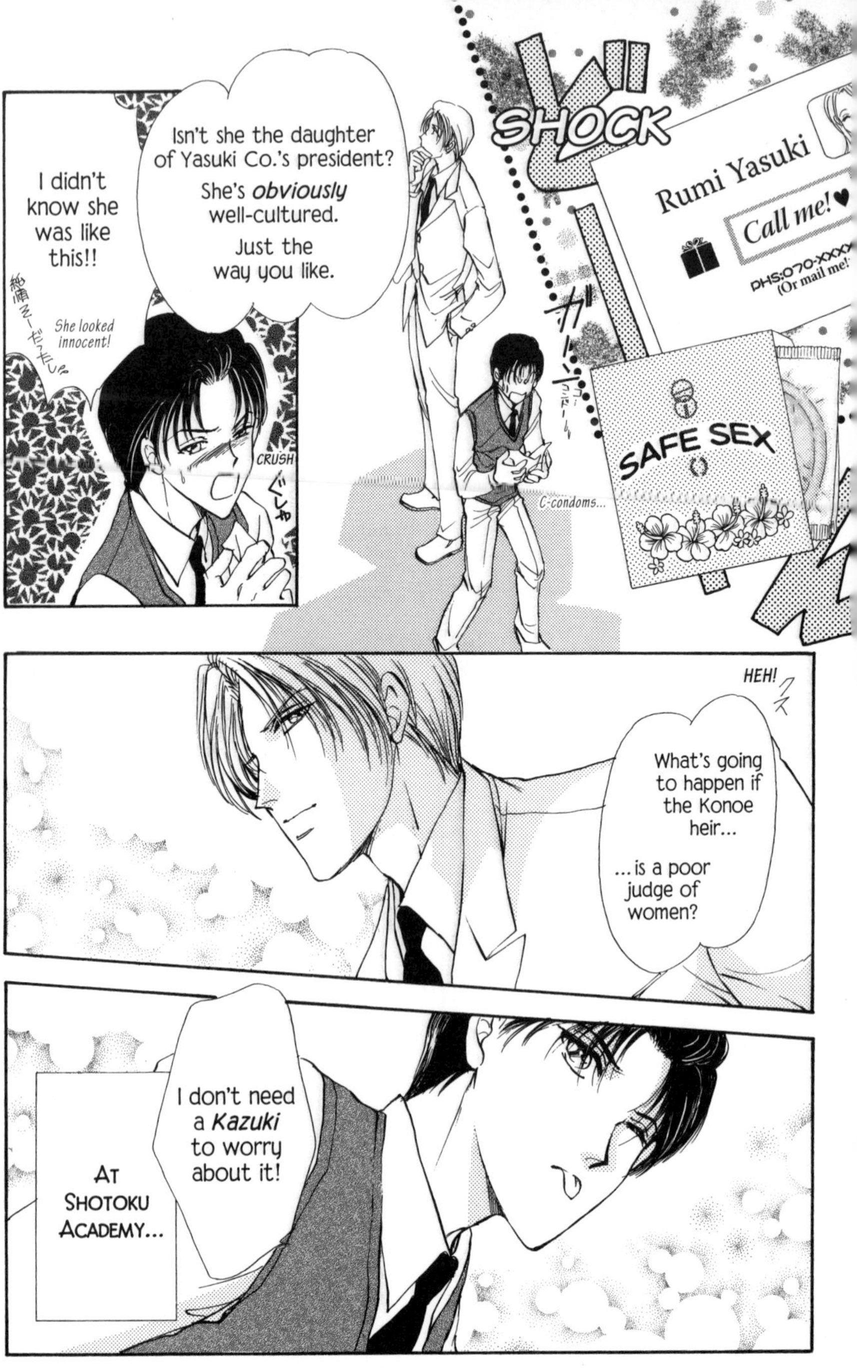
SHOCK
Rumi Yasuki
Call me!♥
PHS:070-XXXX
(Or mail me!
SAFE SEX
C-condoms...
Isn't she the daughter of Yasuki Co.'s president? She's *obviously* well-cultured. Just the way you like.
I didn't know she was like this!!
She looked innocent!
CRUSH
HEH!
What's going to happen if the Konoe heir...
...is a poor judge of women?
I don't need a *Kazuki* to worry about it!
AT SHOTOKU ACADEMY...

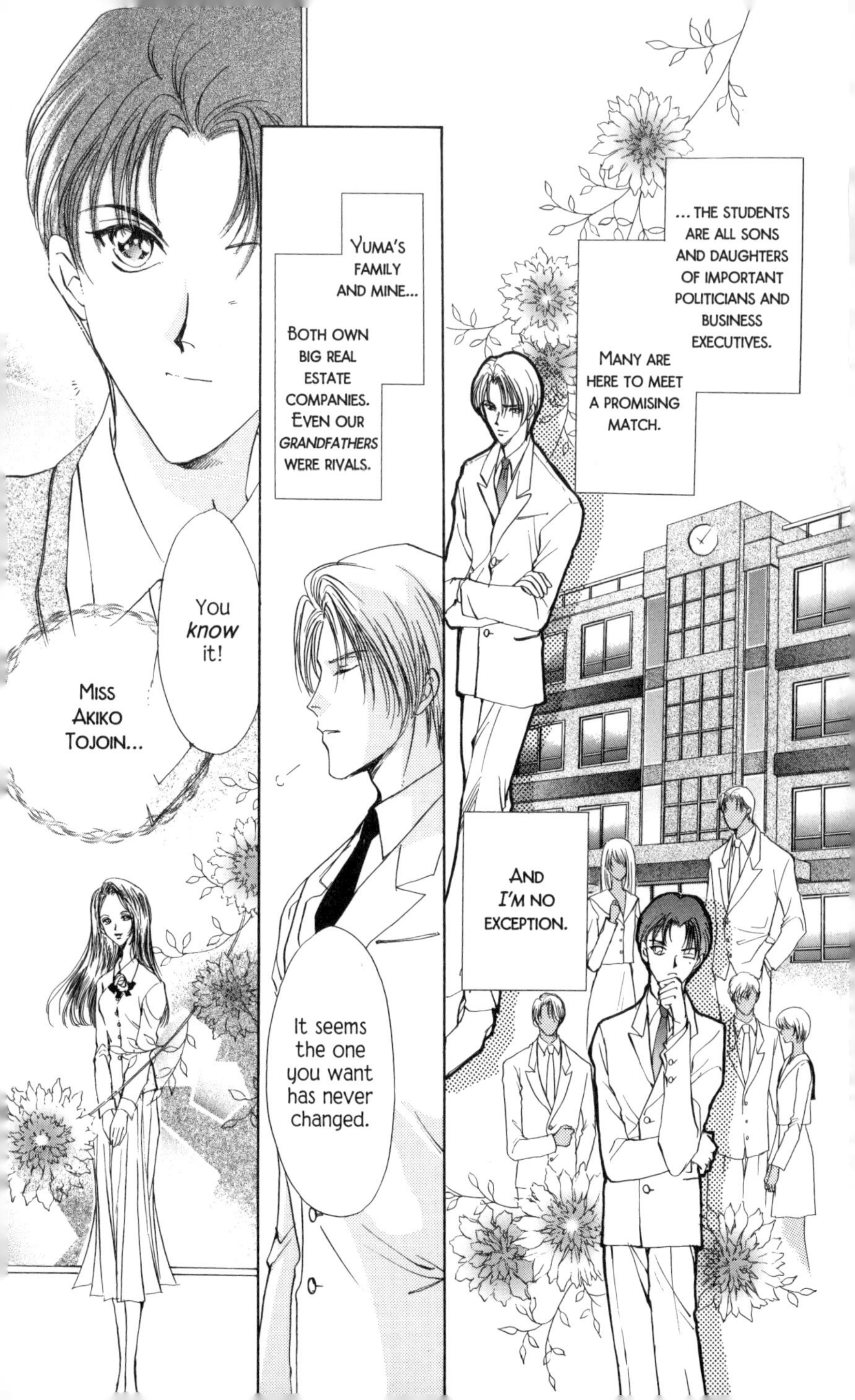
... THE STUDENTS ARE ALL SONS AND DAUGHTERS OF IMPORTANT POLITICIANS AND BUSINESS EXECUTIVES.
MANY ARE HERE TO MEET A PROMISING MATCH.
AND *I'M* NO EXCEPTION.
YUMA'S FAMILY AND MINE...
BOTH OWN BIG REAL ESTATE COMPANIES. EVEN OUR *GRANDFATHERS* WERE RIVALS.
It seems the one you want has never changed.
You *know* it!
MISS AKIKO TOJOIN...

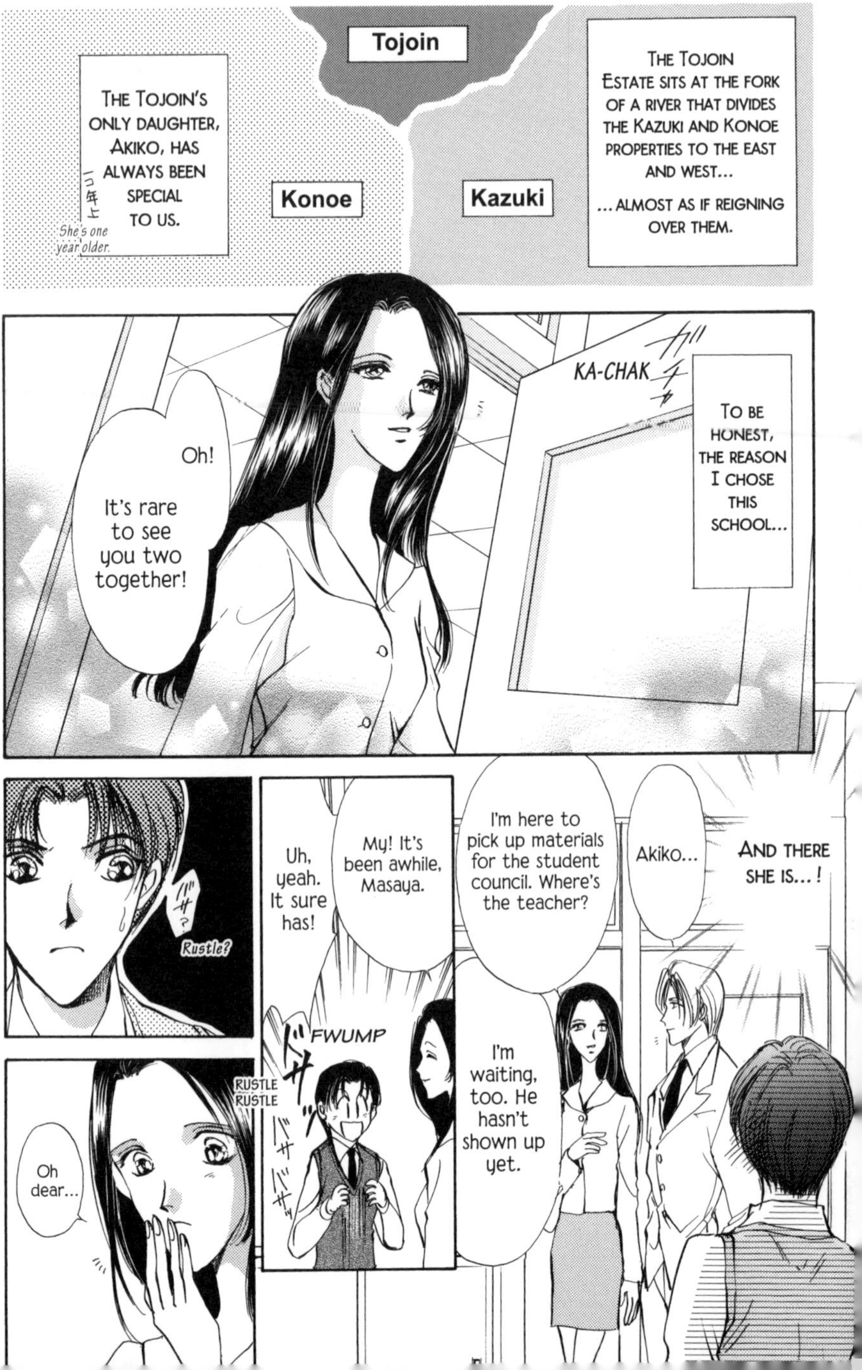
THE TOJOIN ESTATE SITS AT THE FORK OF A RIVER THAT DIVIDES THE KAZUKI AND KONOE PROPERTIES TO THE EAST AND WEST...
...ALMOST AS IF REIGNING OVER THEM.
Tojoin
Kazuki
Konoe
THE TOJOIN'S ONLY DAUGHTER, AKIKO, HAS ALWAYS BEEN SPECIAL TO US.
She's one year older.
KA-CHAK
TO BE HONEST, THE REASON I CHOSE THIS SCHOOL...
Oh!
It's rare to see you two together!
AND THERE SHE IS...!
Akiko...
I'm here to pick up materials for the student council. Where's the teacher?
I'm waiting, too. He hasn't shown up yet.
My! It's been awhile, Masaya.
Uh, yeah. It sure has!
FWUMP
RUSTLE RUSTLE
Rustle?
Oh dear...

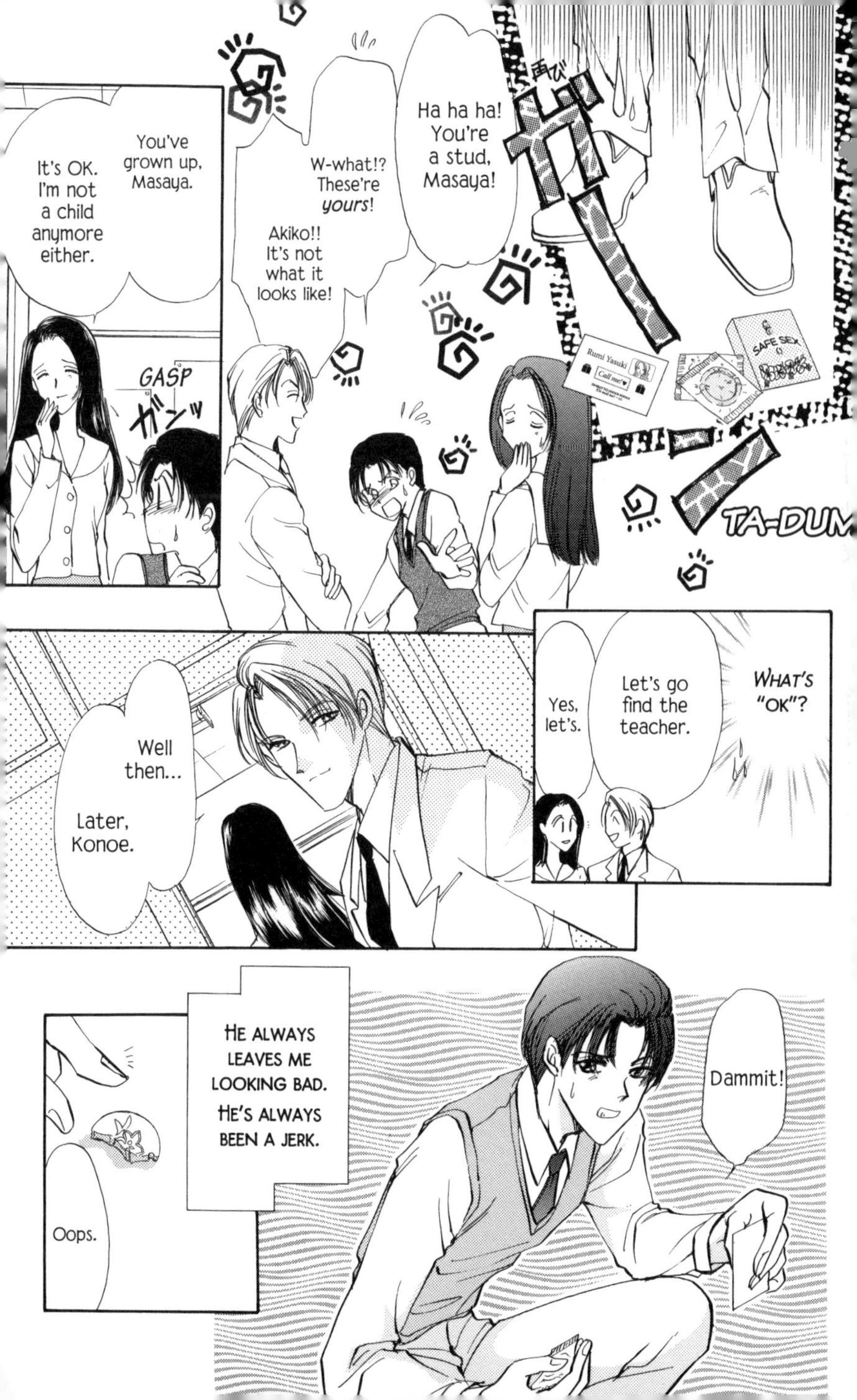
再び
SAFE SEX
Rumi Yasuki
Call me!♥
Ha ha ha! You're a stud, Masaya!
W-what!? These're *yours*!
Akiko!! It's not what it looks like!
TA-DUM
You've grown up, Masaya.
It's OK. I'm not a child anymore either.
GASP
ガンッ
WHAT'S "OK"?
Let's go find the teacher.
Yes, let's.
Well then...
Later, Konoe.
Dammit!
HE ALWAYS LEAVES ME LOOKING BAD.
HE'S ALWAYS BEEN A JERK.
Oops.

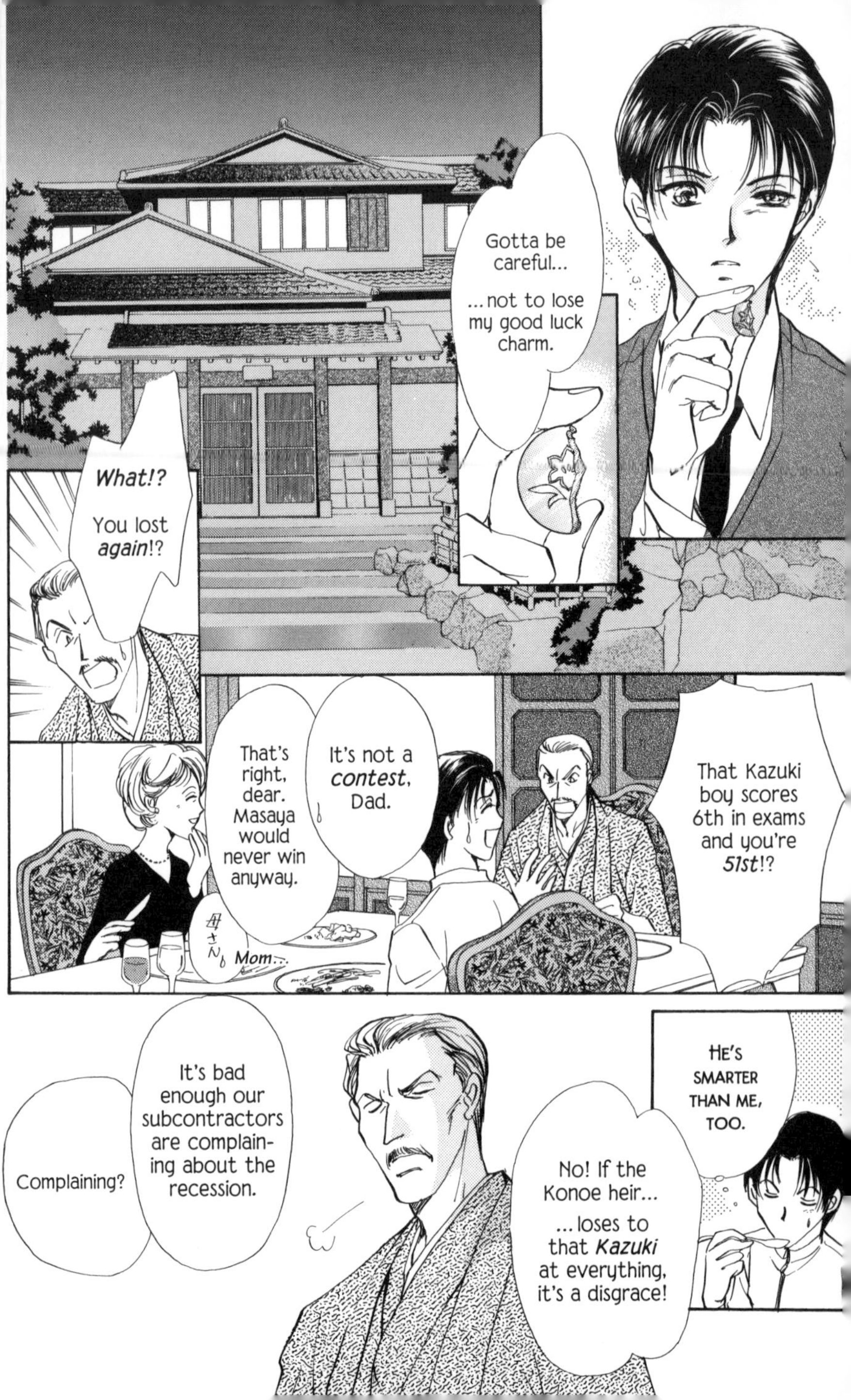
Gotta be careful...
...not to lose my good luck charm.
What!? You lost *again*!?
That Kazuki boy scores 6th in exams and you're *51st*!?
It's not a *contest*, Dad.
That's right, dear. Masaya would never win anyway.
母さん。 *Mom...*
HE'S SMARTER THAN ME, TOO.
No! If the Konoe heir...
...loses to that *Kazuki* at everything, it's a disgrace!
It's bad enough our subcontractors are complaining about the recession.
Complaining?

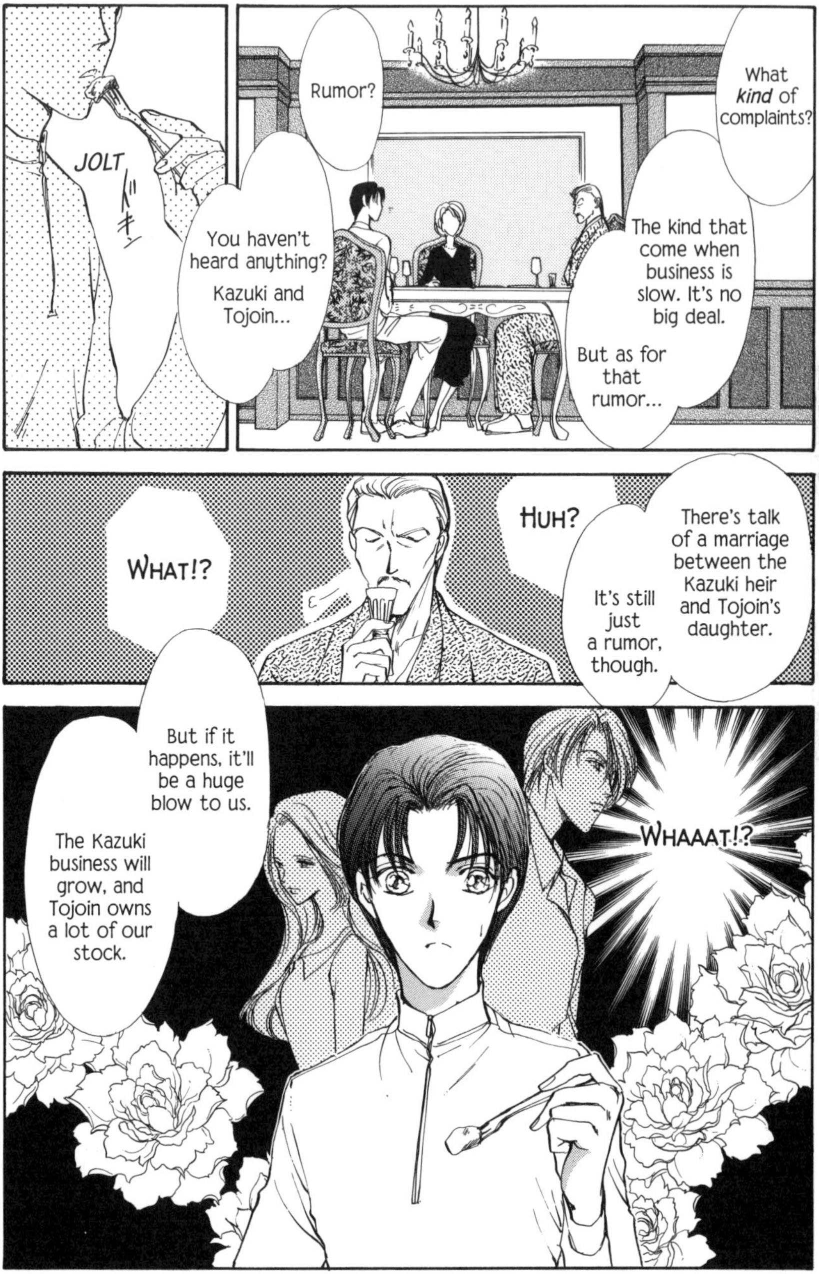

What *kind* of complaints?
The kind that come when business is slow. It's no big deal.
But as for that rumor...
Rumor?
You haven't heard anything?
Kazuki and Tojoin...
JOLT
There's talk of a marriage between the Kazuki heir and Tojoin's daughter.
It's still just a rumor, though.
HUH?
WHAT!?
WHAAAT!?
But if it happens, it'll be a huge blow to us.
The Kazuki business will grow, and Tojoin owns a lot of our stock.

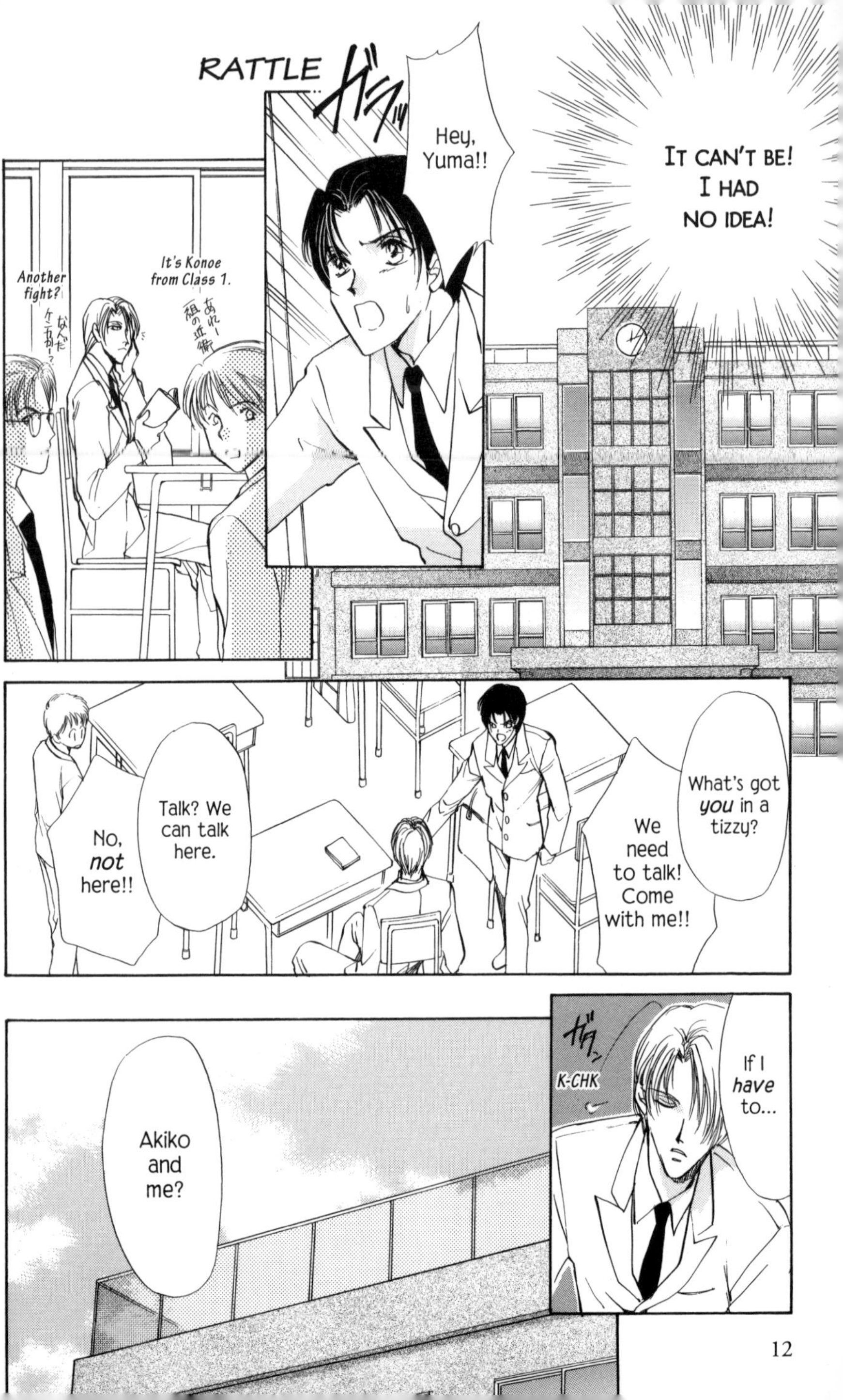
It can't be! I had no idea!
RATTLE ガラッ
Hey, Yuma!!
It's Konoe from Class 1.
あれー一組の近衛
Another fight?
なんだケンカかー?
What's got *you* in a tizzy?
We need to talk! Come with me!!
Talk? We can talk here.
No, *not* here!!
ガタン
K-CHK
If I *have* to...
Akiko and me?

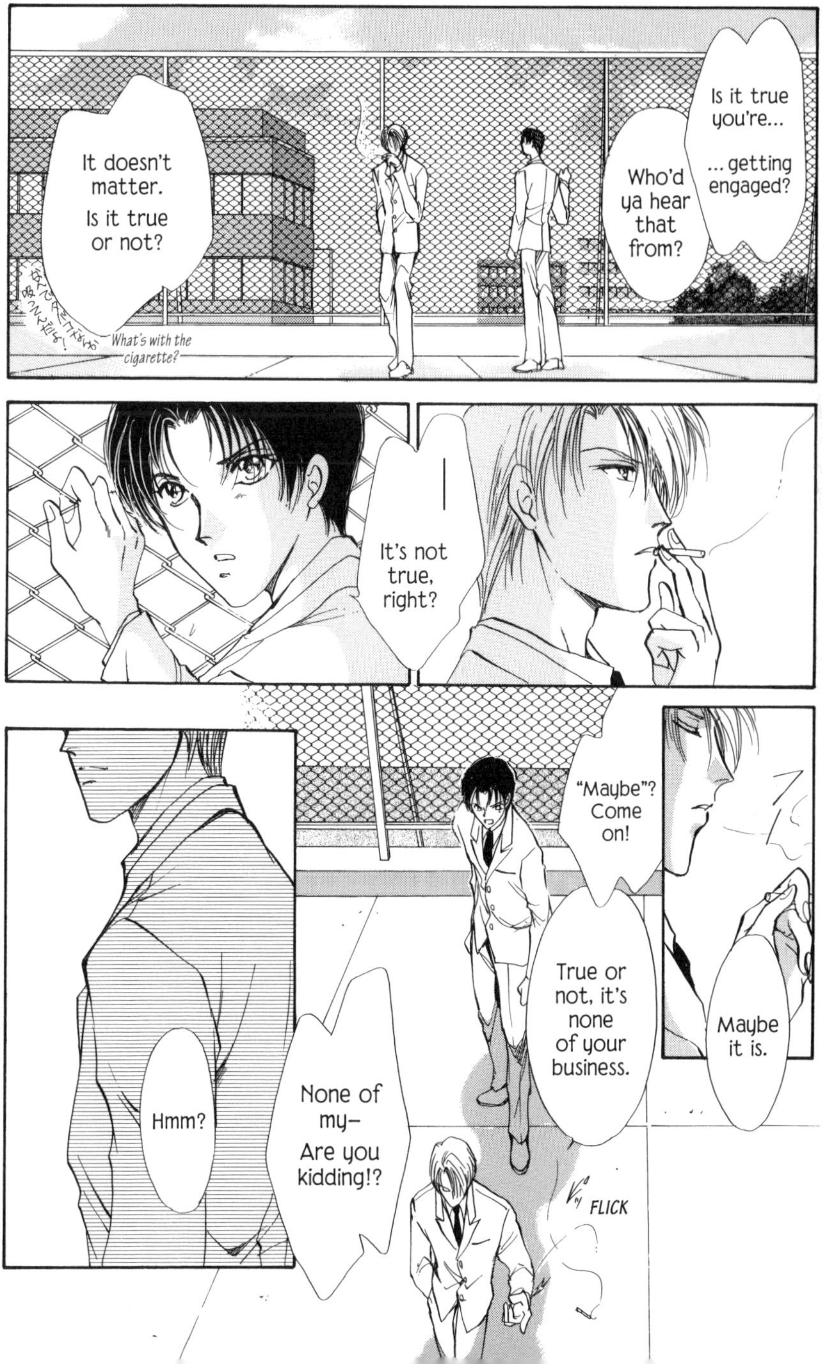
Is it true you're... ...getting engaged?
Who'd ya hear that from?
It doesn't matter. Is it true or not?
What's with the cigarette?
—
It's not true, right?
Maybe it is.
"Maybe"? Come on!
True or not, it's none of your business.
FLICK
None of my– Are you kidding!?
Hmm?

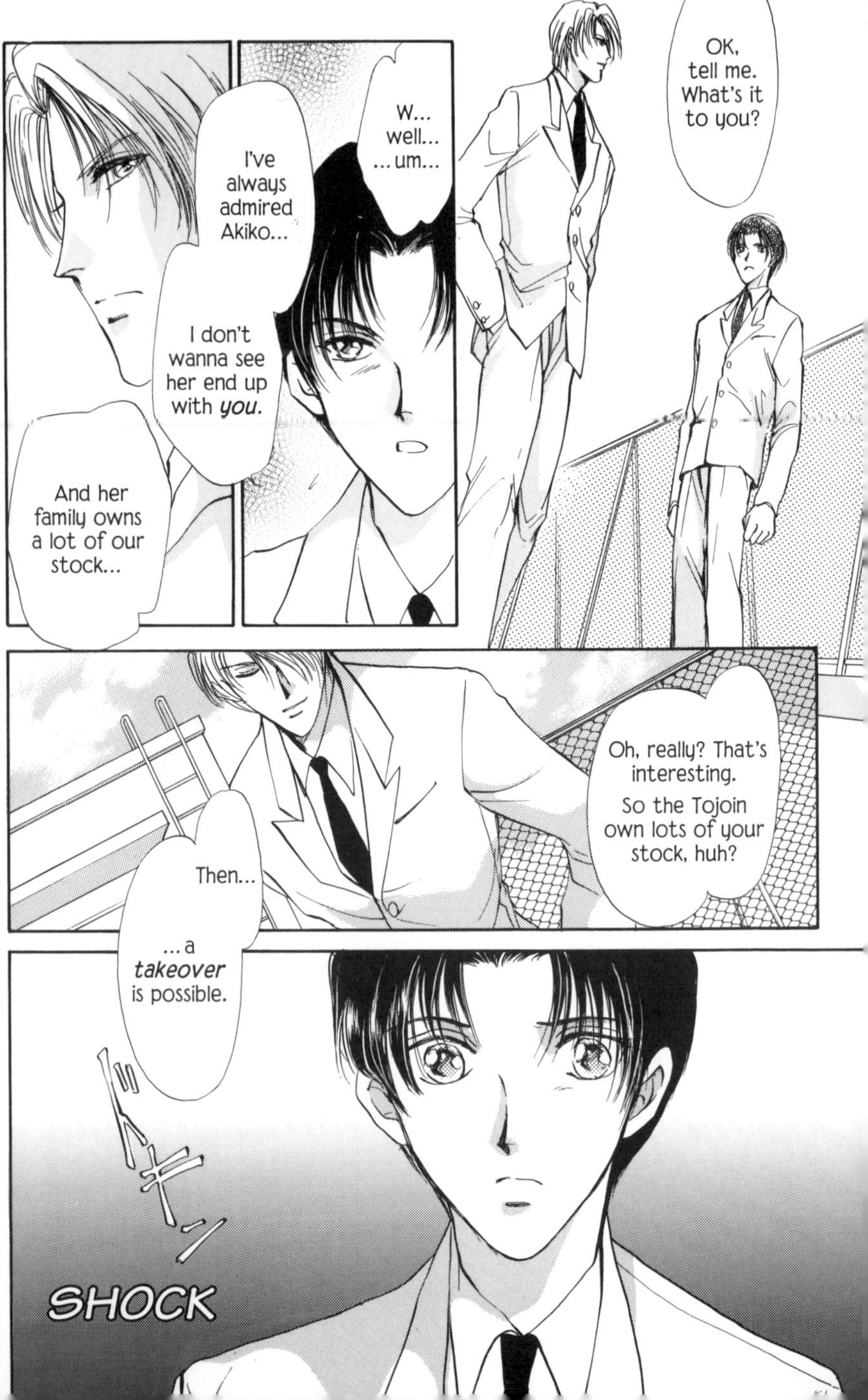
OK, tell me. What's it to you?
W... well... ...um...
I've always admired Akiko...
I don't wanna see her end up with *you.*
And her family owns a lot of our stock...
Oh, really? That's interesting.
So the Tojoin own lots of your stock, huh?
Then...
...a *takeover* is possible.
SHOCK

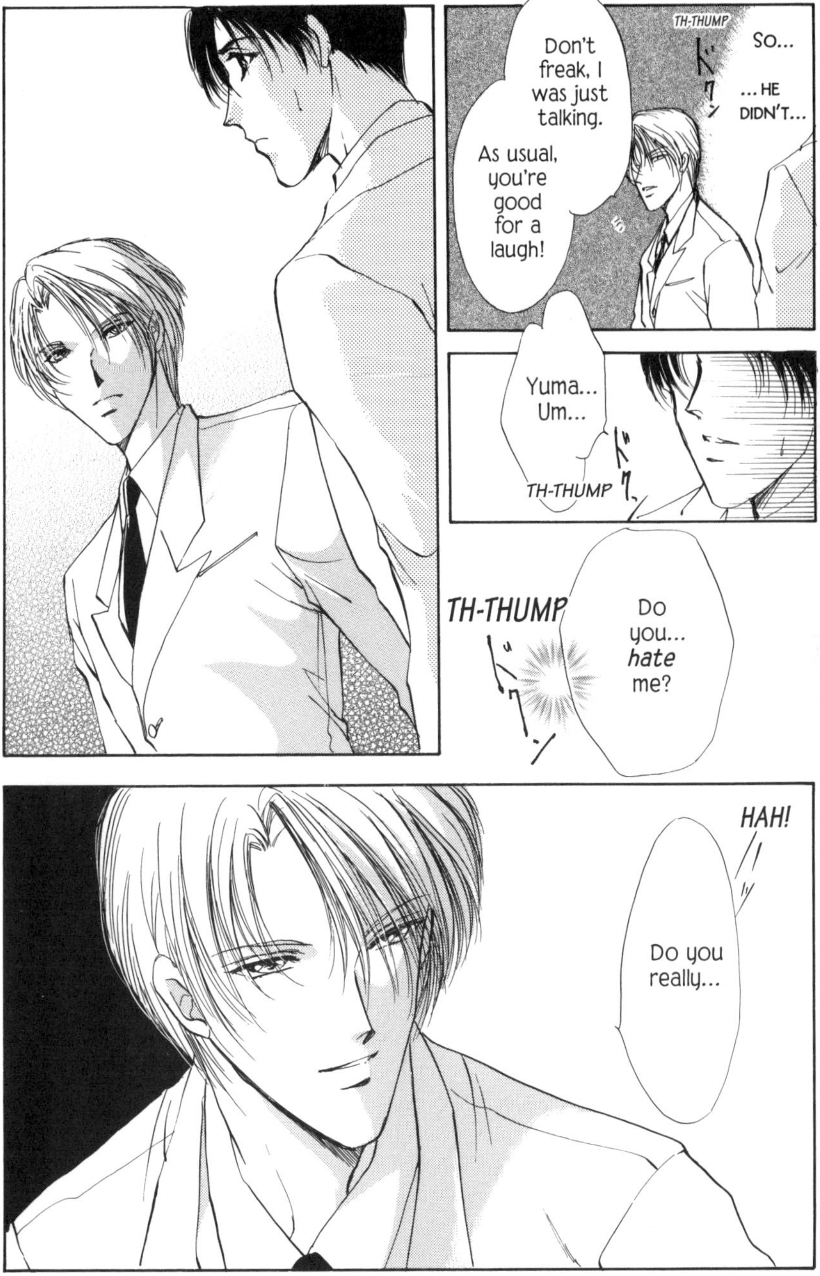
TH-THUMP
So...
...HE DIDN'T...
Don't freak, I was just talking.
As usual, you're good for a laugh!
Yuma... Um...
TH-THUMP
TH-THUMP
Do you... *hate* me?
HAH!
Do you really...

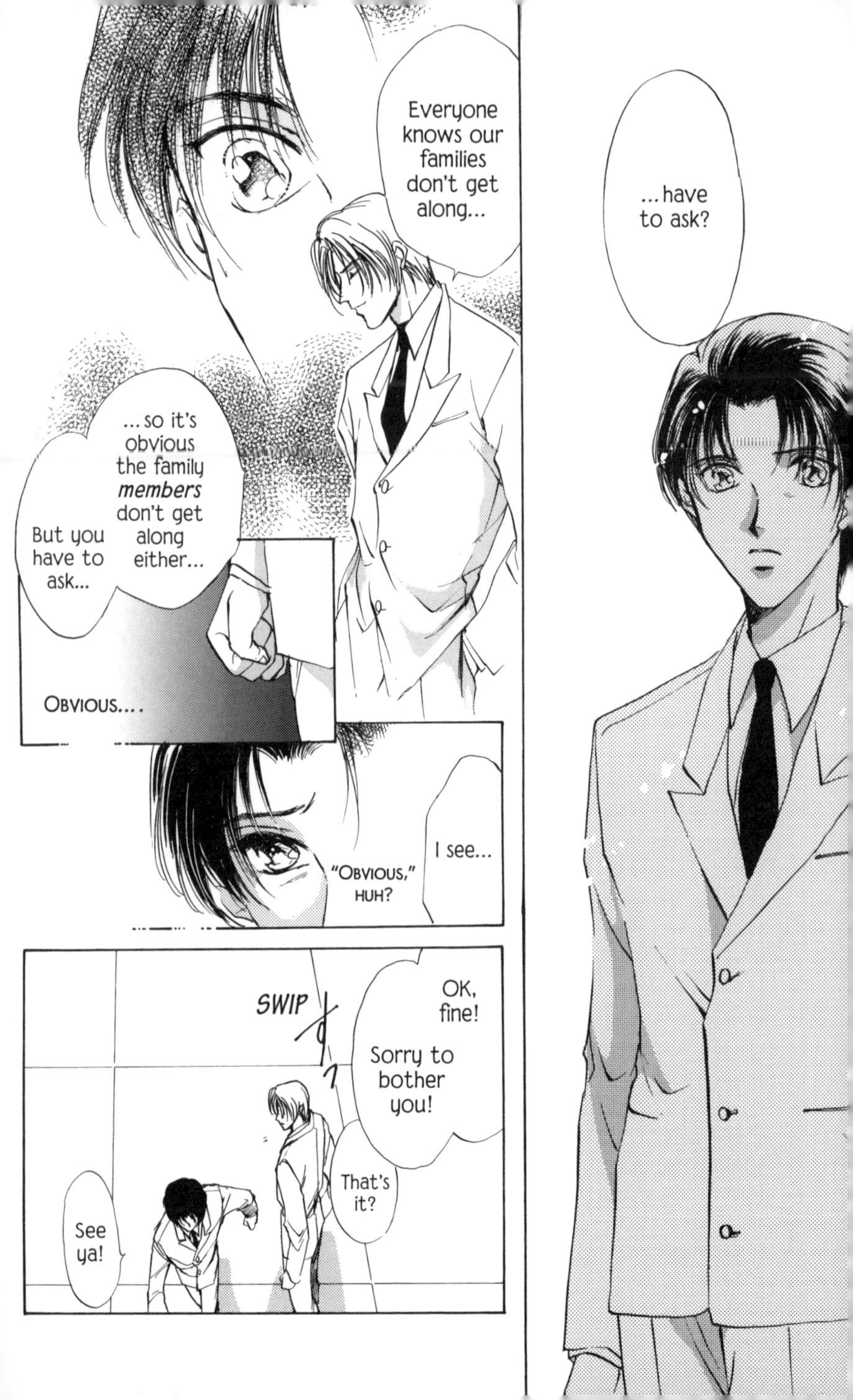
Everyone knows our families don't get along...
...so it's obvious the family *members* don't get along either...
But you have to ask...
OBVIOUS....
I see...
"OBVIOUS," HUH?
OK, fine!
Sorry to bother you!
SWIP
That's it?
See ya!
...have to ask?

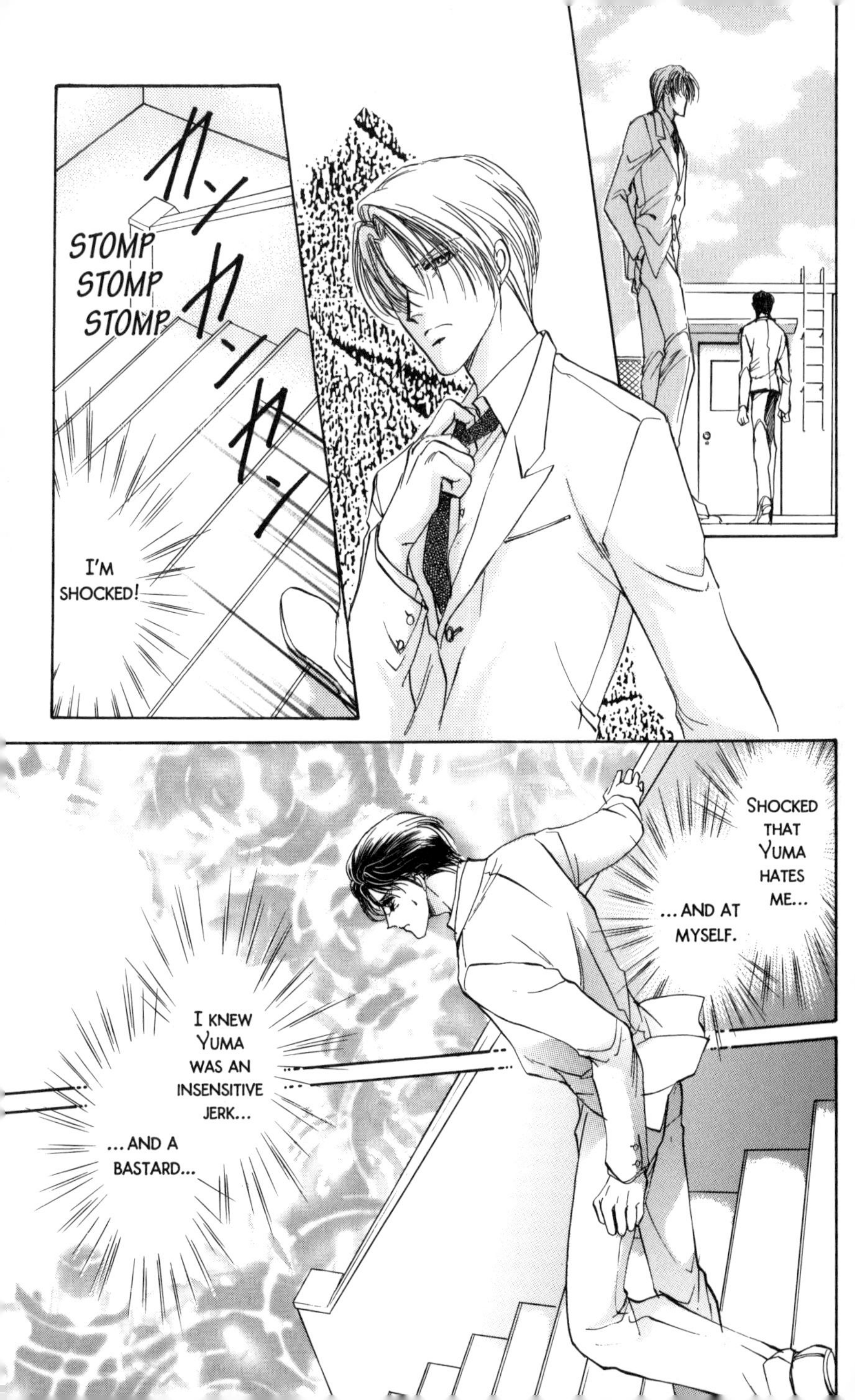
STOMP
STOMP
STOMP
I'M SHOCKED!
SHOCKED THAT YUMA HATES ME...
...AND AT MYSELF.
I KNEW YUMA WAS AN INSENSITIVE JERK...
...AND A BASTARD...

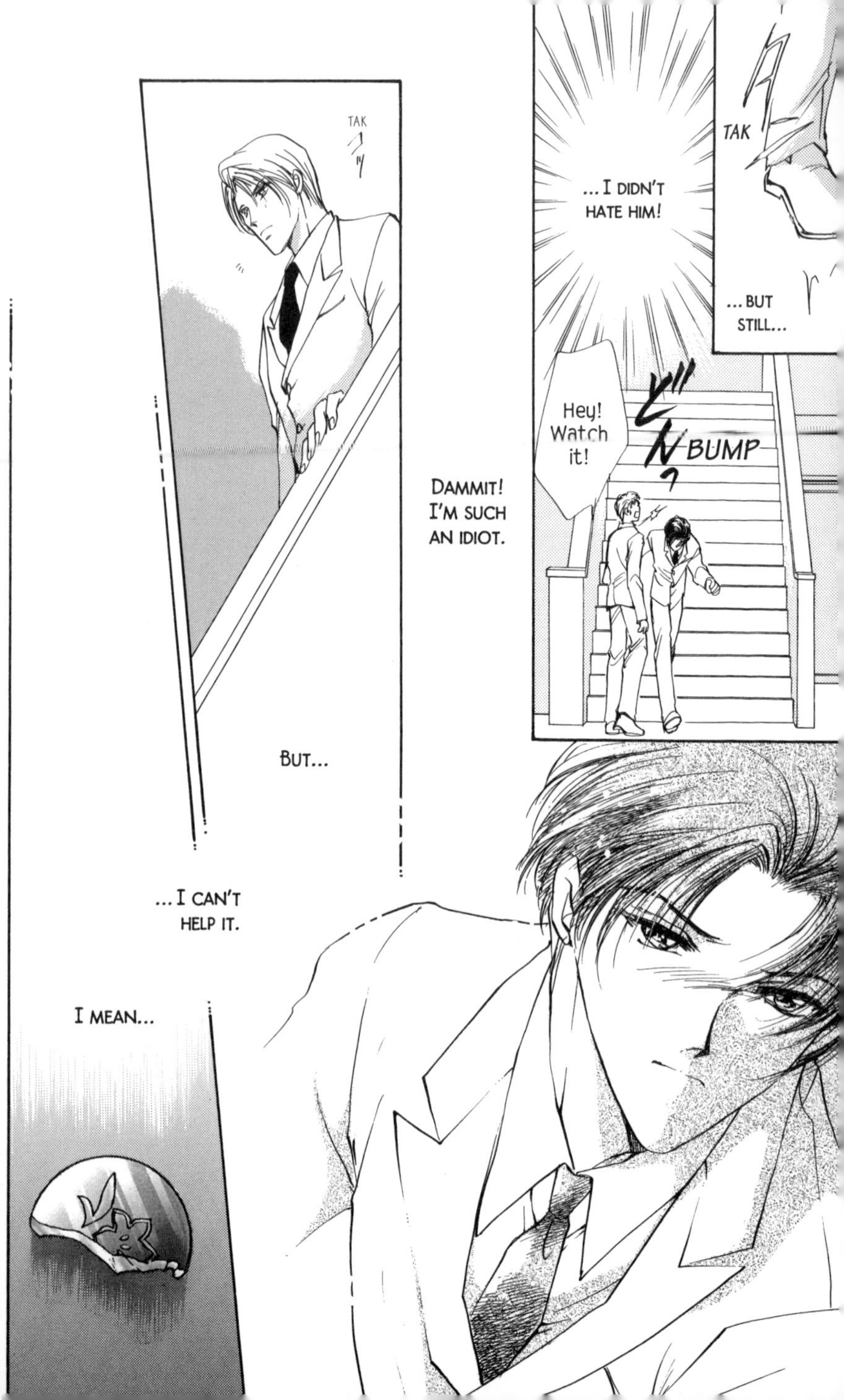
TAK
...BUT STILL...
...I DIDN'T HATE HIM!
Hey! Watch it!
BUMP
DAMMIT! I'M SUCH AN IDIOT.
TAK
BUT...
...I CAN'T HELP IT.
I MEAN...

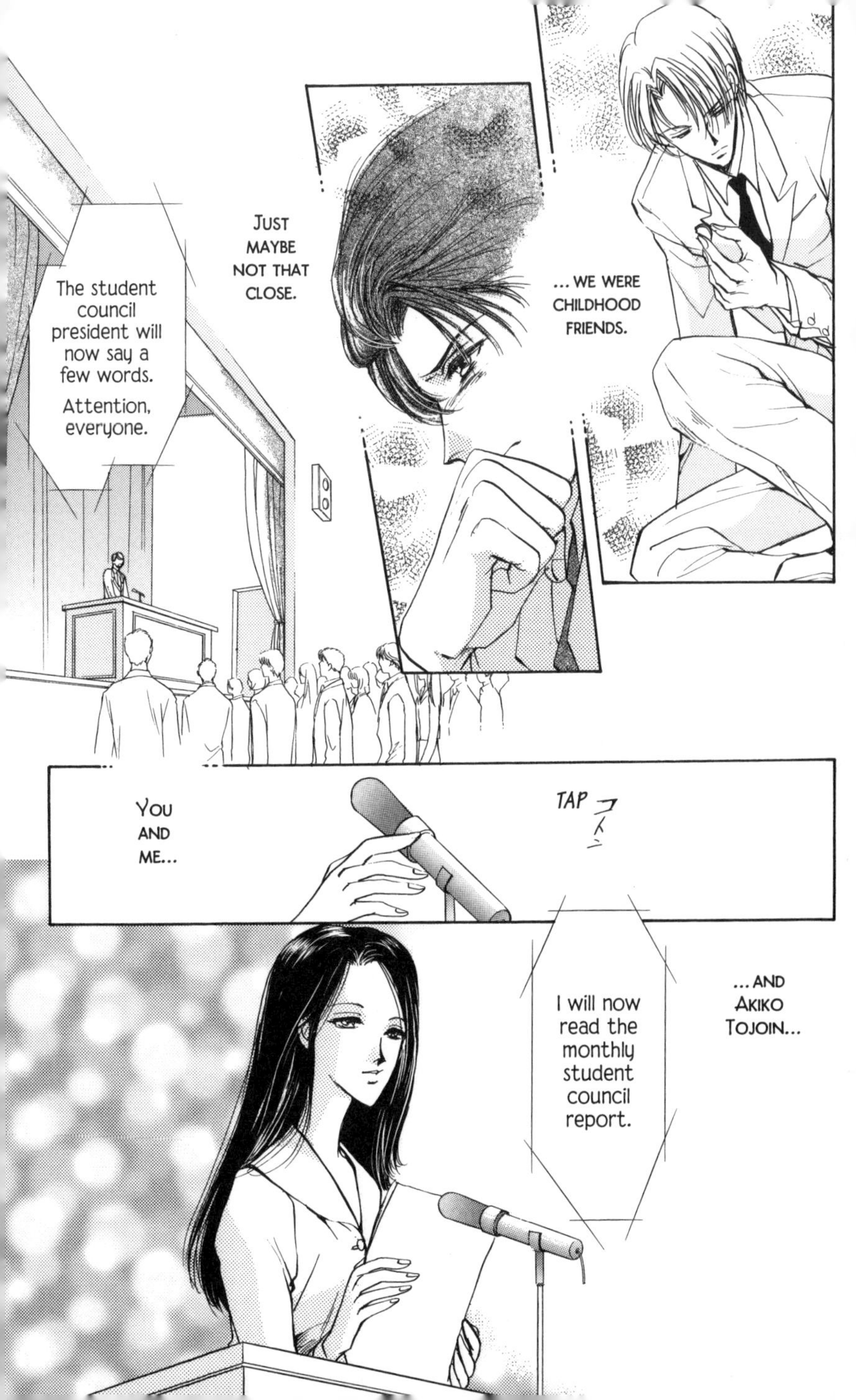
...WE WERE CHILDHOOD FRIENDS.
JUST MAYBE NOT THAT CLOSE.
The student council president will now say a few words.
Attention, everyone.
TAP コトン
YOU AND ME...
...AND AKIKO TOJOIN...
I will now read the monthly student council report.

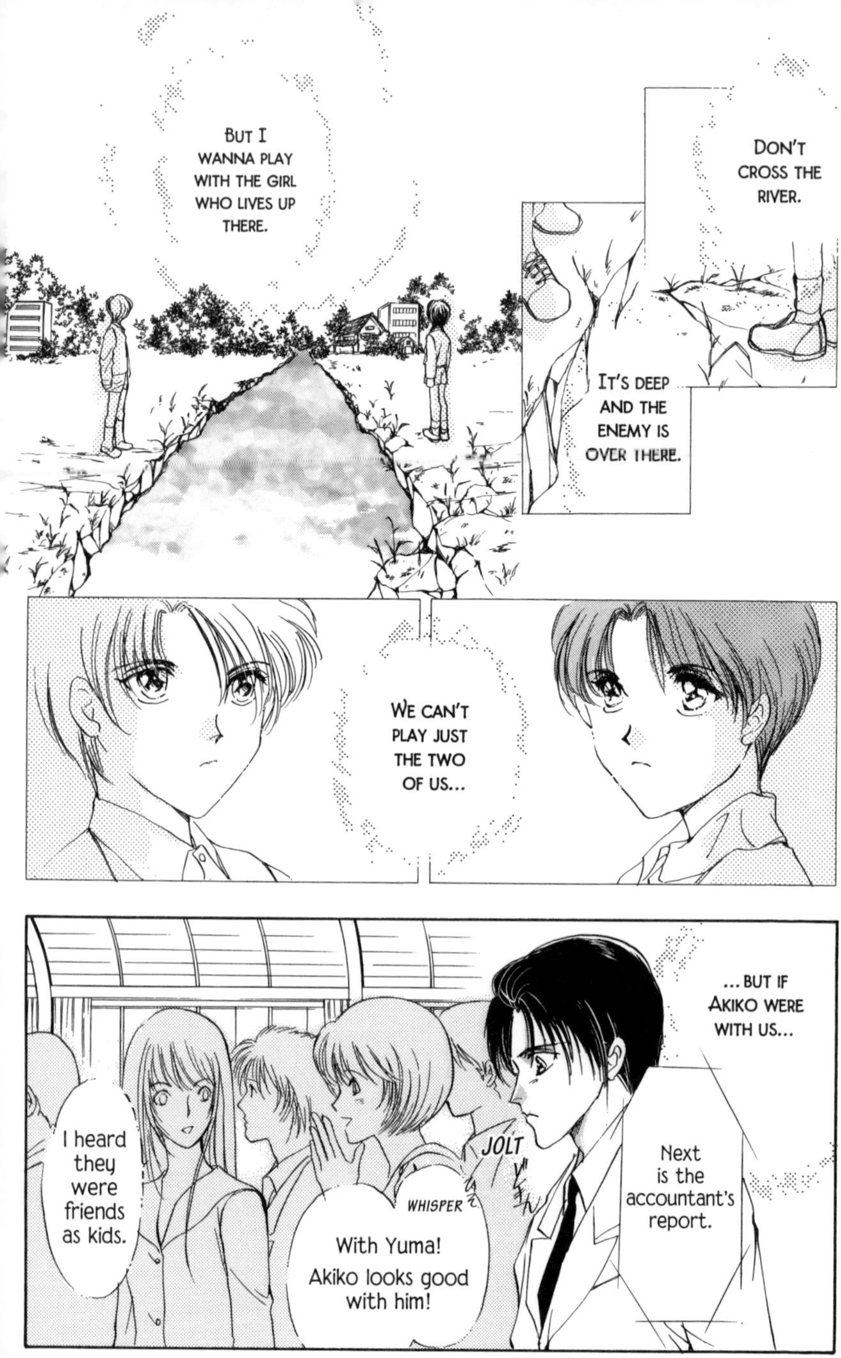
DON'T CROSS THE RIVER.
IT'S DEEP AND THE ENEMY IS OVER THERE.
BUT I WANNA PLAY WITH THE GIRL WHO LIVES UP THERE.
WE CAN'T PLAY JUST THE TWO OF US...
...BUT IF AKIKO WERE WITH US...
Next is the accountant's report.
JOLT
WHISPER
With Yuma! Akiko looks good with him!
I heard they were friends as kids.

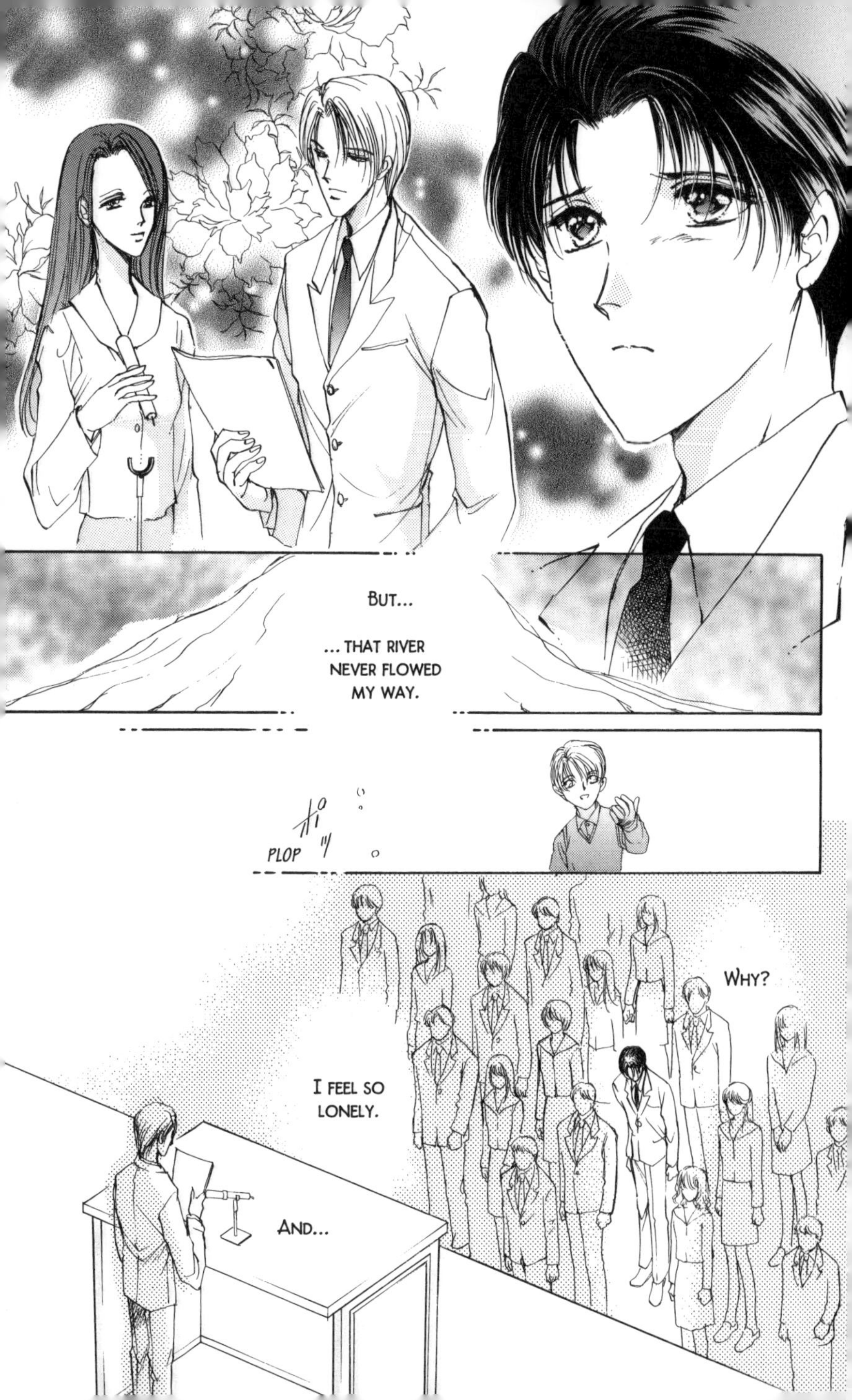
BUT...
...THAT RIVER NEVER FLOWED MY WAY.
PLOP
WHY?
I FEEL SO LONELY.
AND...

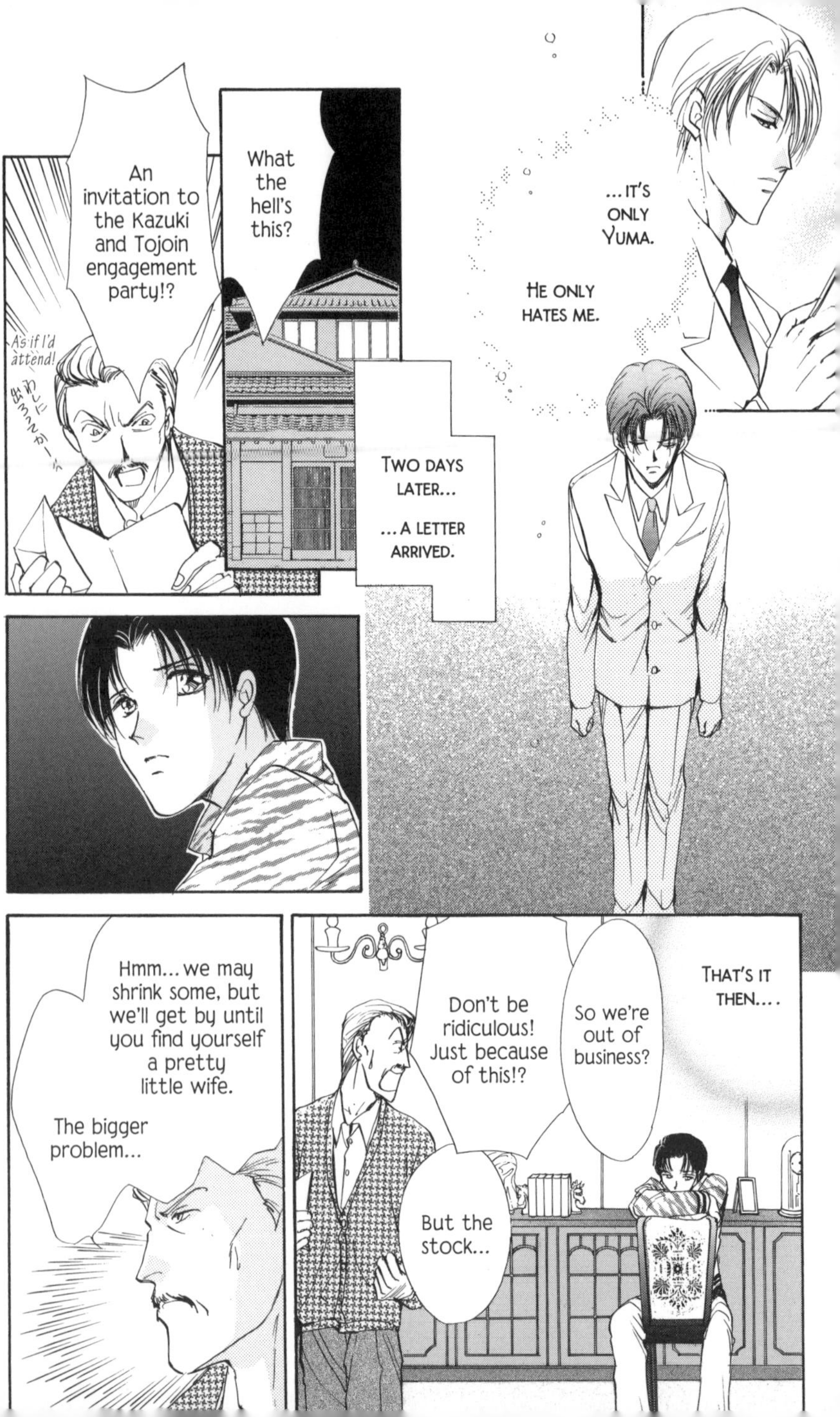
...IT'S ONLY YUMA.
HE ONLY HATES ME.
TWO DAYS LATER...
...A LETTER ARRIVED.
What the hell's this?
An invitation to the Kazuki and Tojoin engagement party!?
As if I'd attend!
わしに出ろってかー
THAT'S IT THEN....
So we're out of business?
Don't be ridiculous! Just because of this!?
But the stock...
Hmm... we may shrink some, but we'll get by until you find yourself a pretty little wife.
The bigger problem...

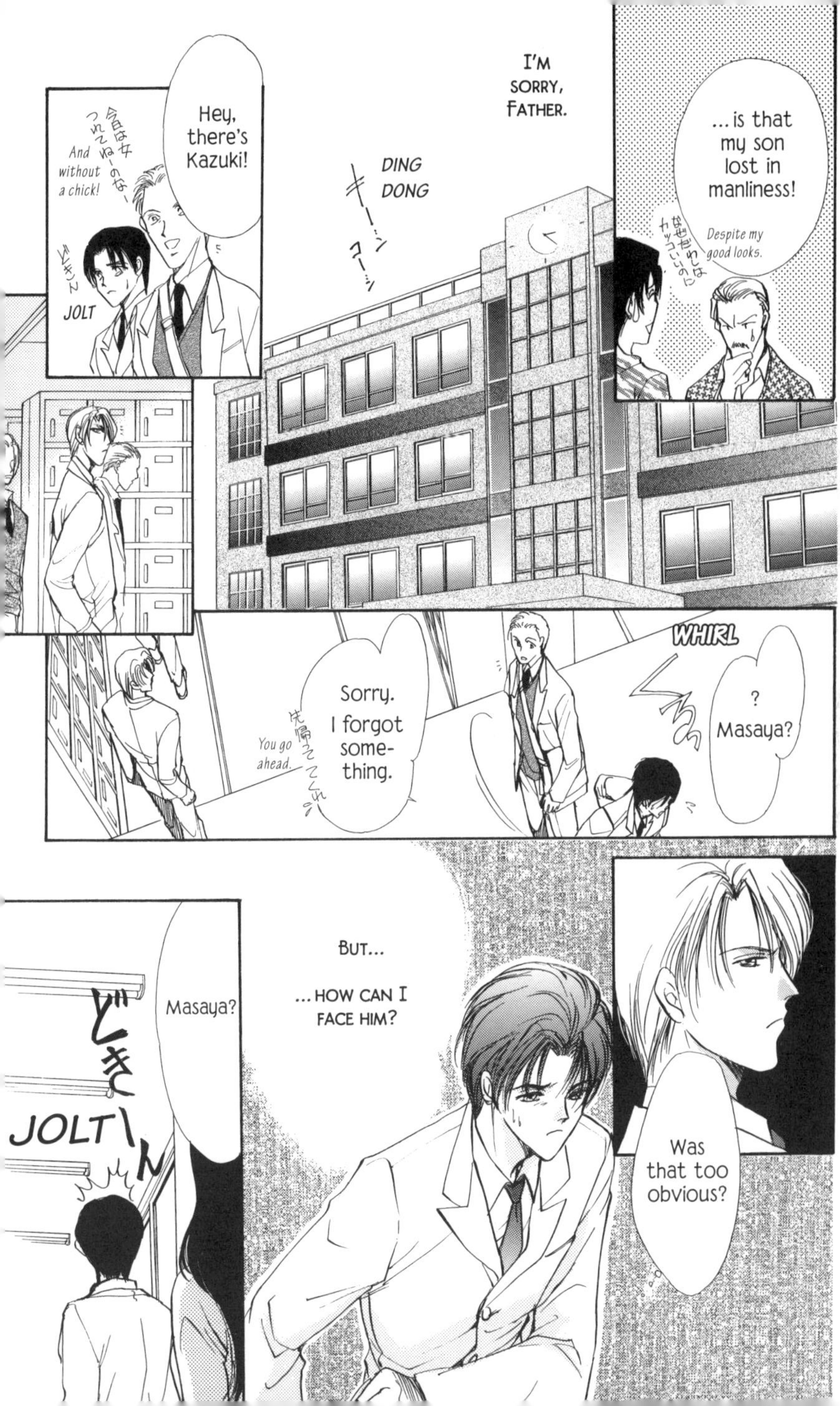

...is that my son lost in manliness!
なぜだわしはカッコいいのに
Despite my good looks.
I'M SORRY, FATHER.
キーンコーン
DING DONG
Hey, there's Kazuki!
今日は女つれてねーのな
And without a chick!
どきん
JOLT
くるっ
WHIRL
? Masaya?
Sorry. I forgot something.
先帰っててくれ
You go ahead.
Was that too obvious?
BUT...
...HOW CAN I FACE HIM?
Masaya?
どきん
JOLT

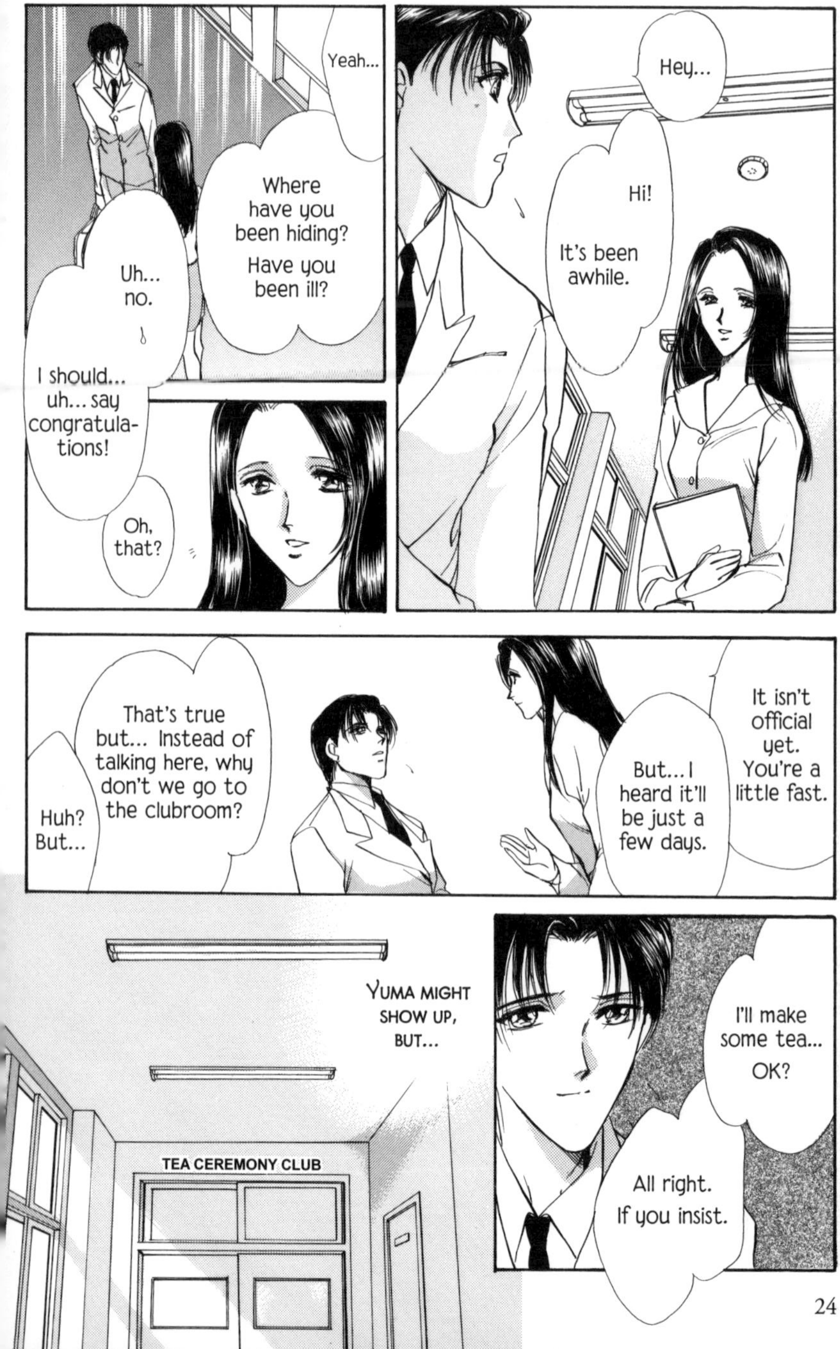
Hey...
Hi!
It's been awhile.
Yeah...
Where have you been hiding?
Have you been ill?
Uh... no.
I should... uh... say congratula-tions!
Oh, that?
It isn't official yet. You're a little fast.
But... I heard it'll be just a few days.
That's true but... Instead of talking here, why don't we go to the clubroom?
Huh? But...
I'll make some tea...
OK?
All right.
If you insist.
YUMA MIGHT SHOW UP, BUT...
TEA CEREMONY CLUB

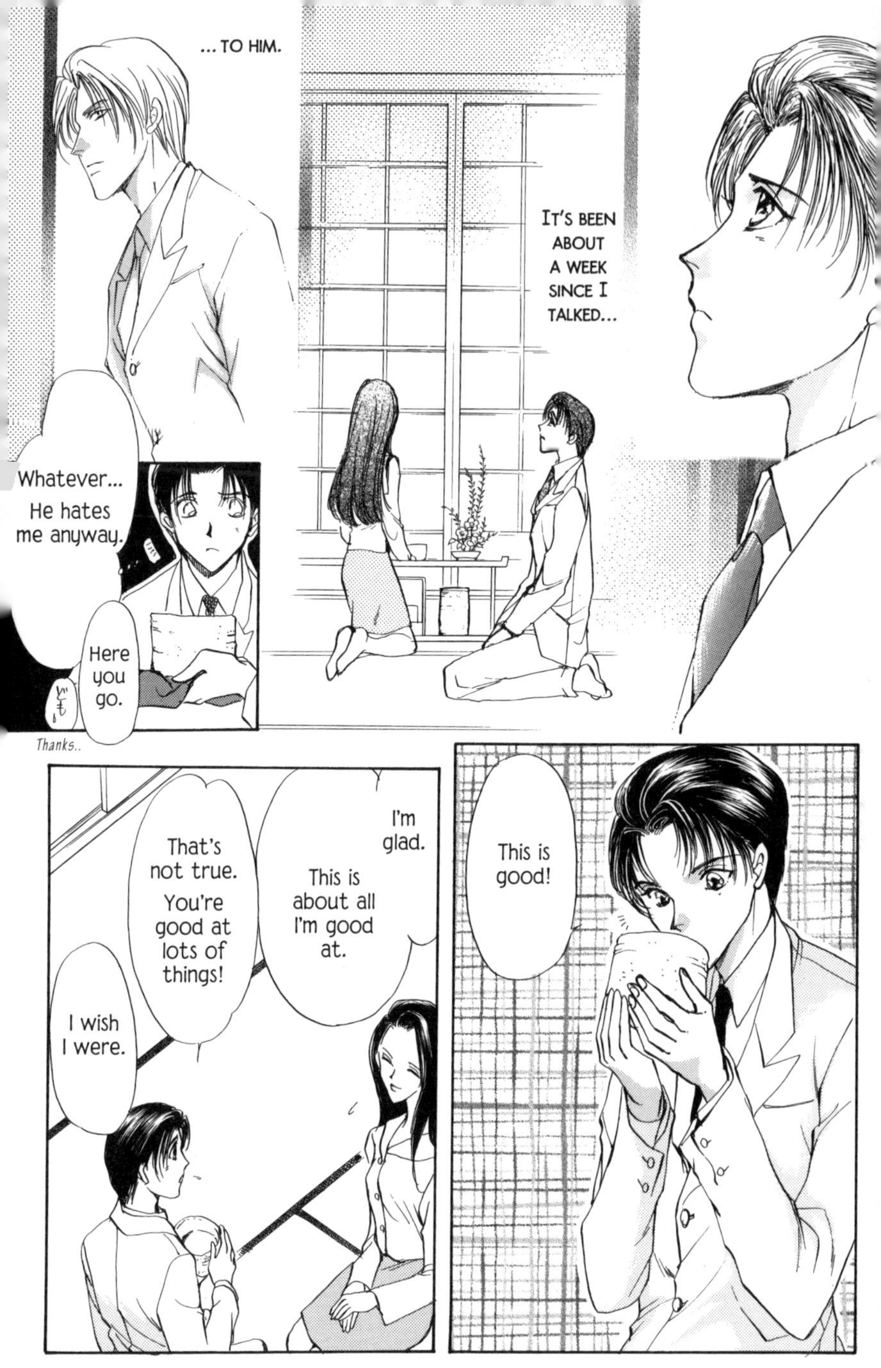

It's been about a week since I talked...
... to him.
Whatever... He hates me anyway.
Here you go.
Thanks..
This is good!
I'm glad.
This is about all I'm good at.
That's not true. You're good at lots of things!
I wish I were.

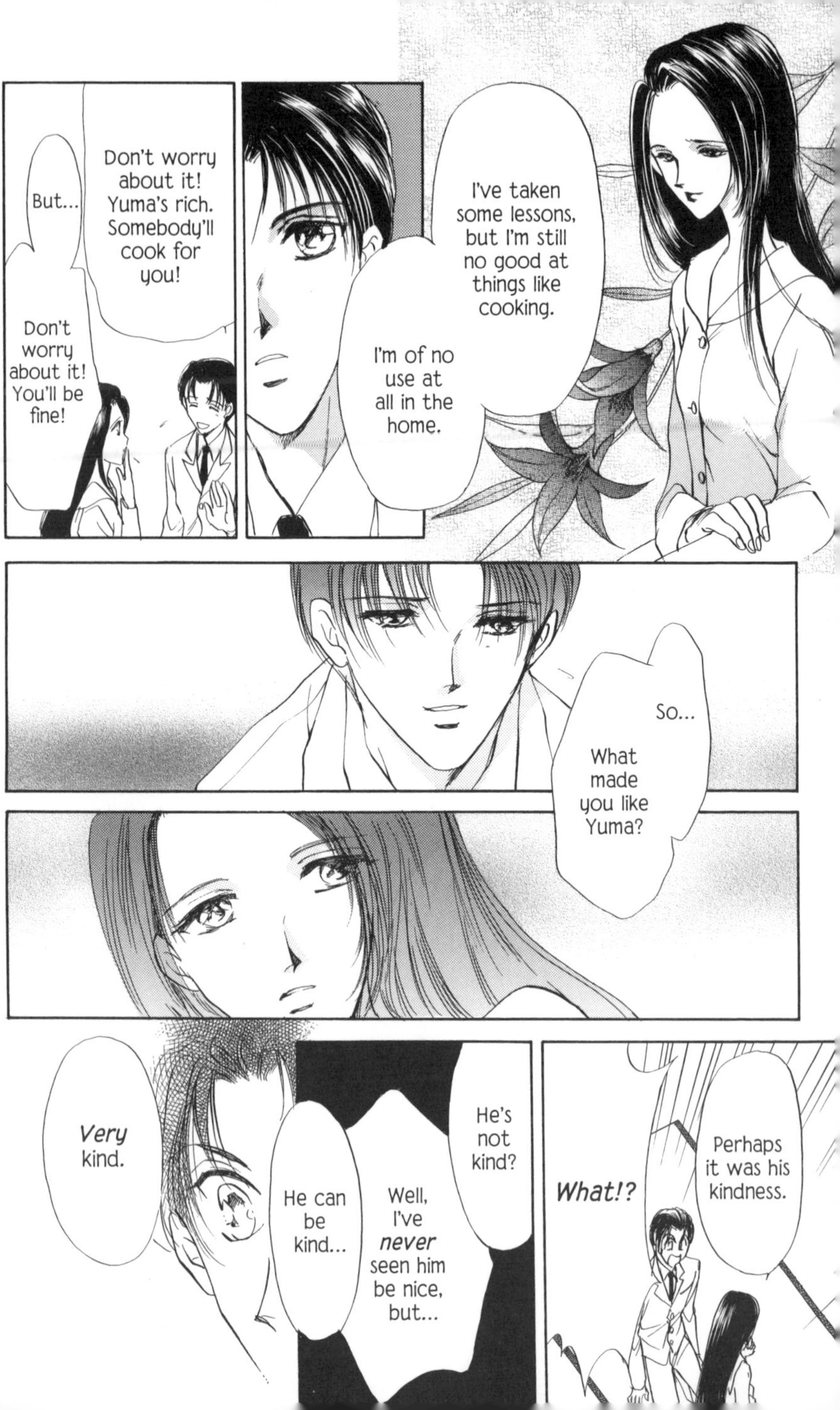
I've taken some lessons, but I'm still no good at things like cooking.
I'm of no use at all in the home.
Don't worry about it! Yuma's rich. Somebody'll cook for you!
But...
Don't worry about it! You'll be fine!
So...
What made you like Yuma?
Perhaps it was his kindness.
What!?
He's not kind?
Well, I've *never* seen him be nice, but...
He can be kind...
Very kind.

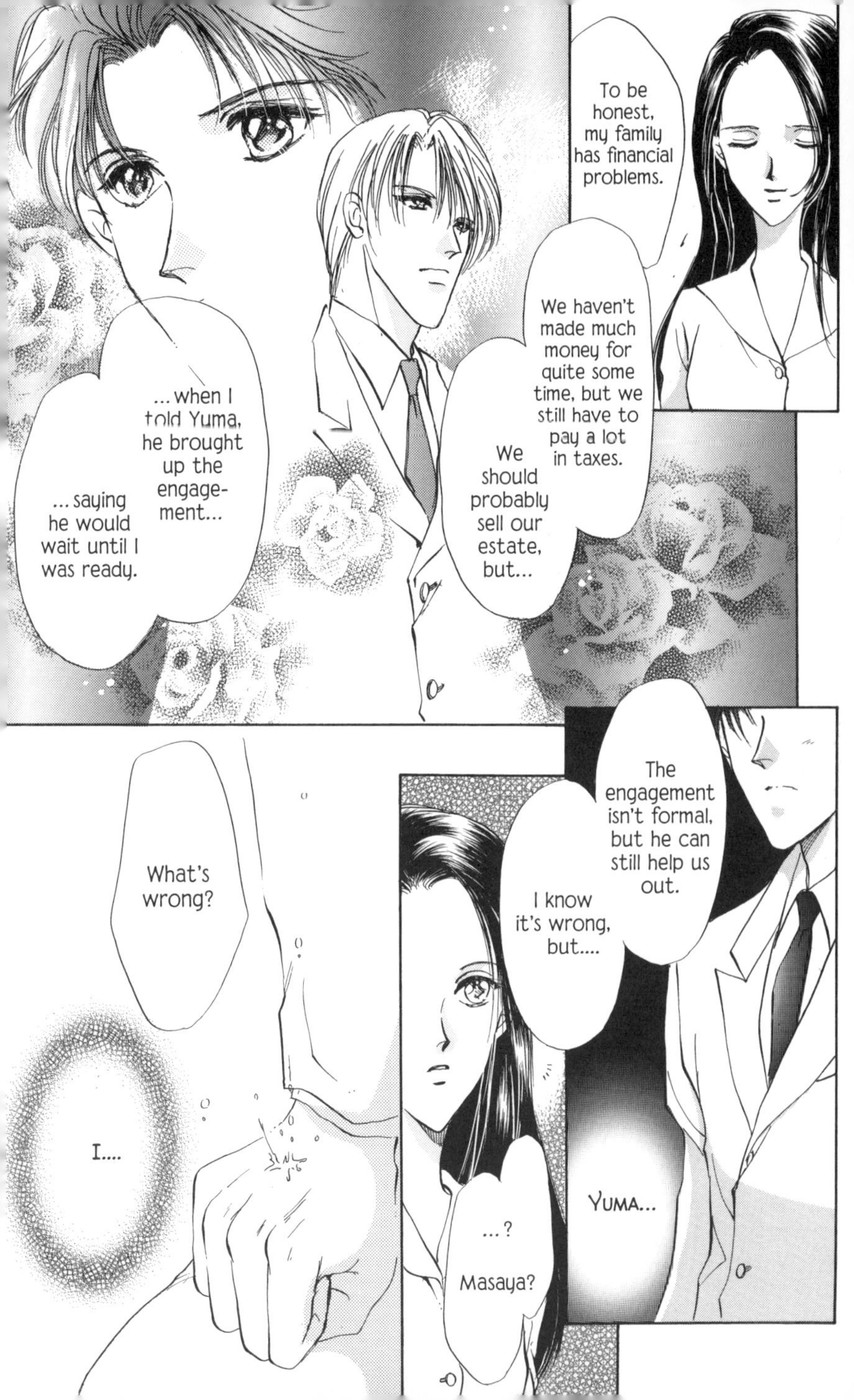
To be honest, my family has financial problems.
We haven't made much money for quite some time, but we still have to pay a lot in taxes.
We should probably sell our estate, but...
...when I told Yuma, he brought up the engagement...
...saying he would wait until I was ready.
The engagement isn't formal, but he can still help us out.
I know it's wrong, but....
YUMA...
...?
Masaya?
What's wrong?
I....

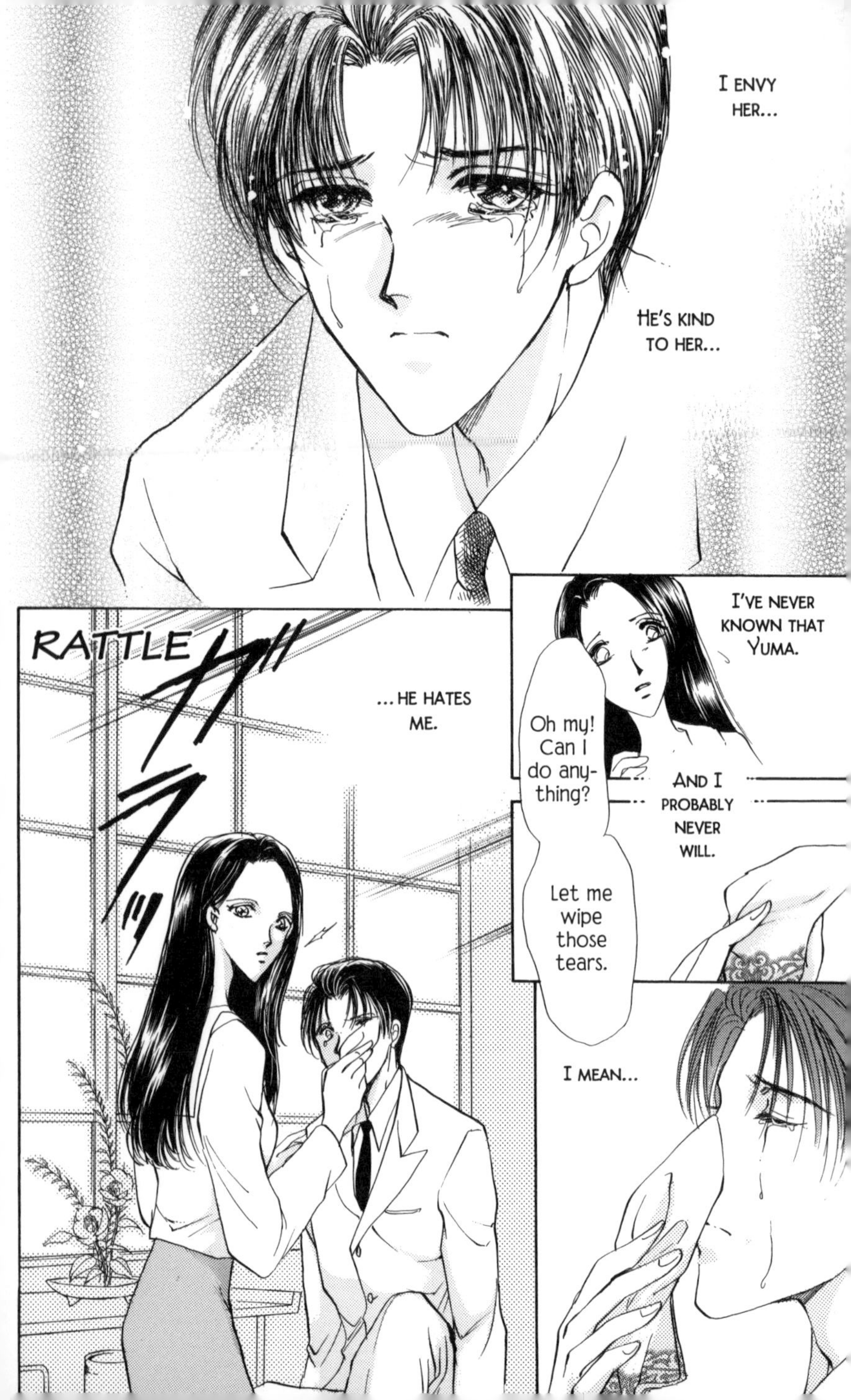
I ENVY HER...
HE'S KIND TO HER...
I'VE NEVER KNOWN THAT YUMA.
Oh my! Can I do any-thing?
AND I PROBABLY NEVER WILL.
Let me wipe those tears.
I MEAN...
...HE HATES ME.
RATTLE

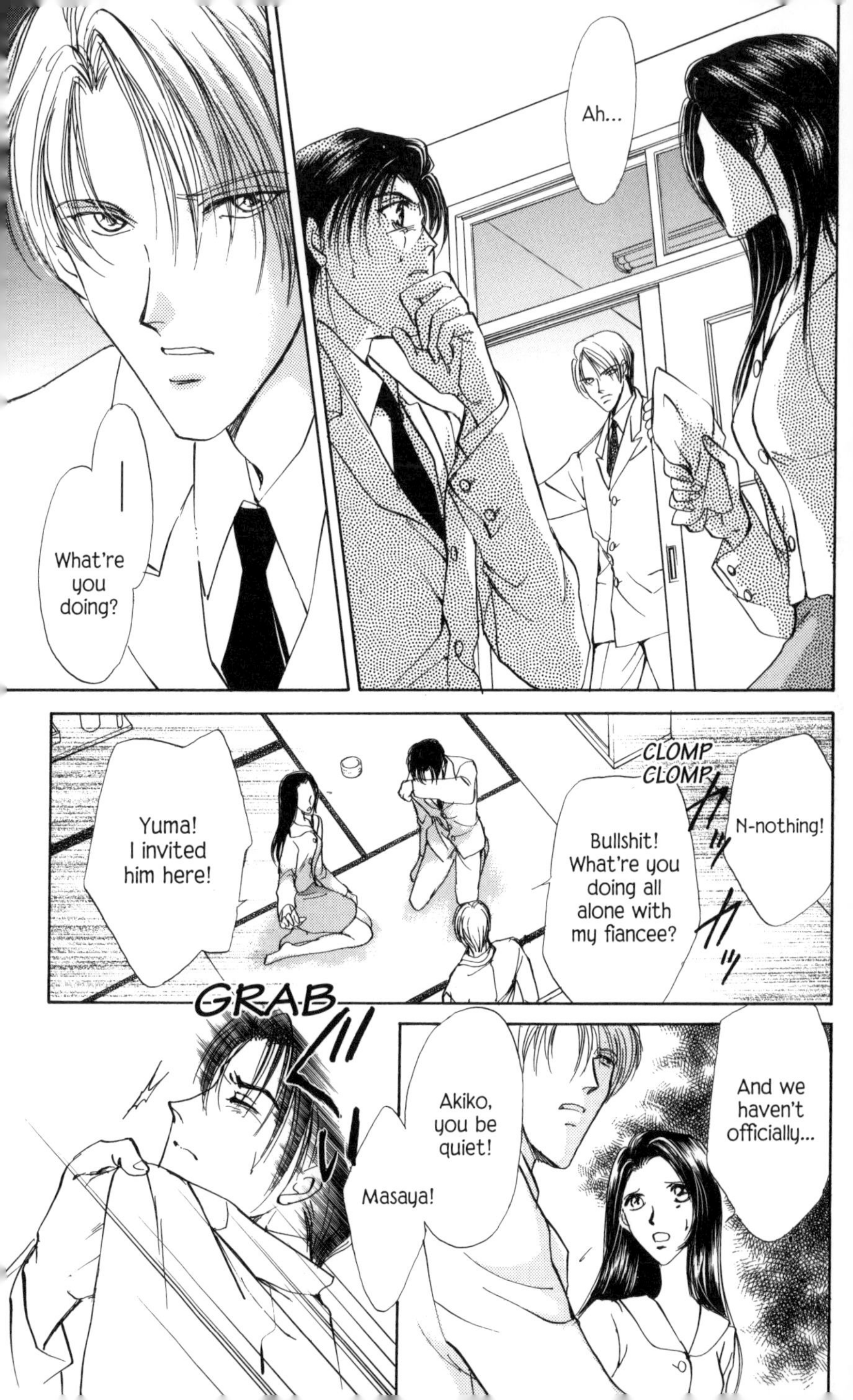
Ah...
What're you doing?
N-nothing!
CLOMP CLOMP
Bullshit! What're you doing all alone with my fiancee?
Yuma! I invited him here!
And we haven't officially...
Akiko, you be quiet!
Masaya!
GRAB

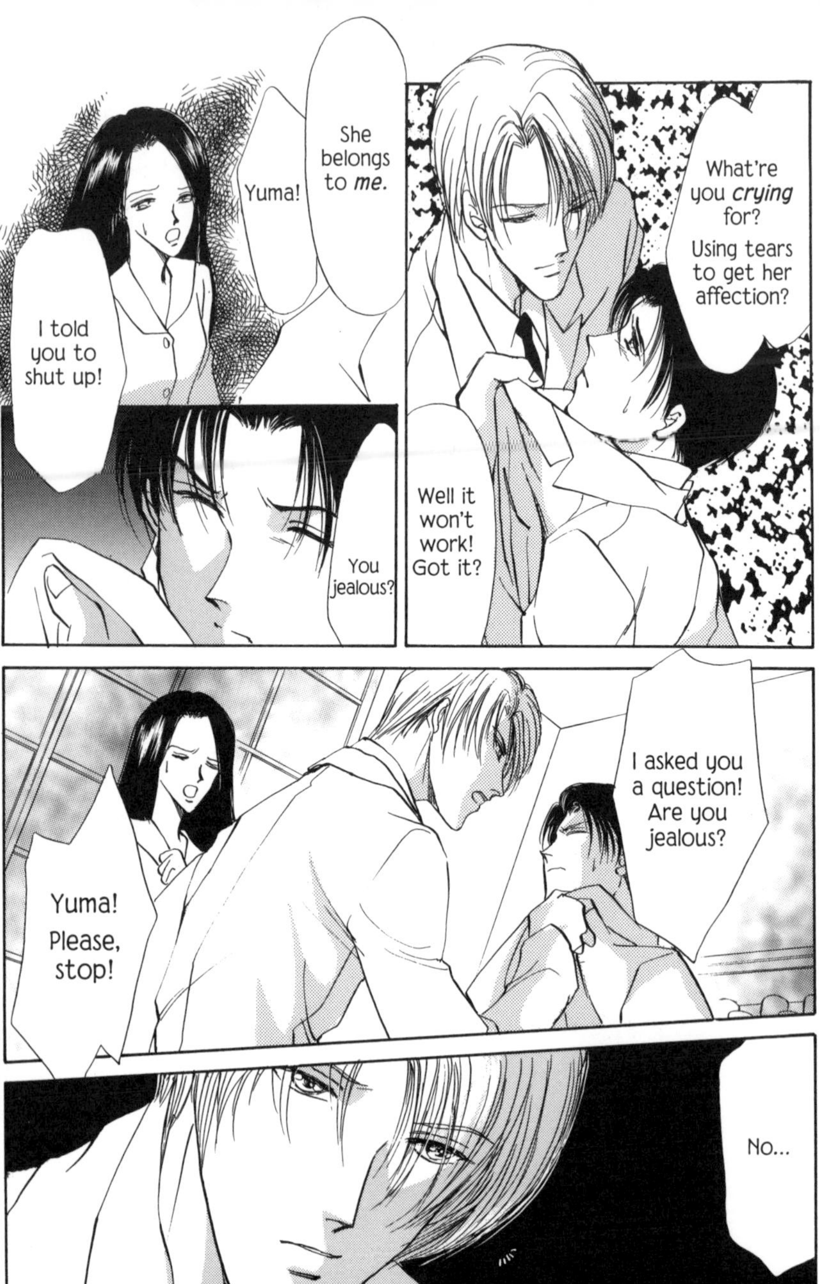
What're you *crying* for?
Using tears to get her affection?
Well it won't work! Got it?
She belongs to *me*.
Yuma!
I told you to shut up!
You jealous?
I asked you a question! Are you jealous?
Yuma! Please, stop!
No...

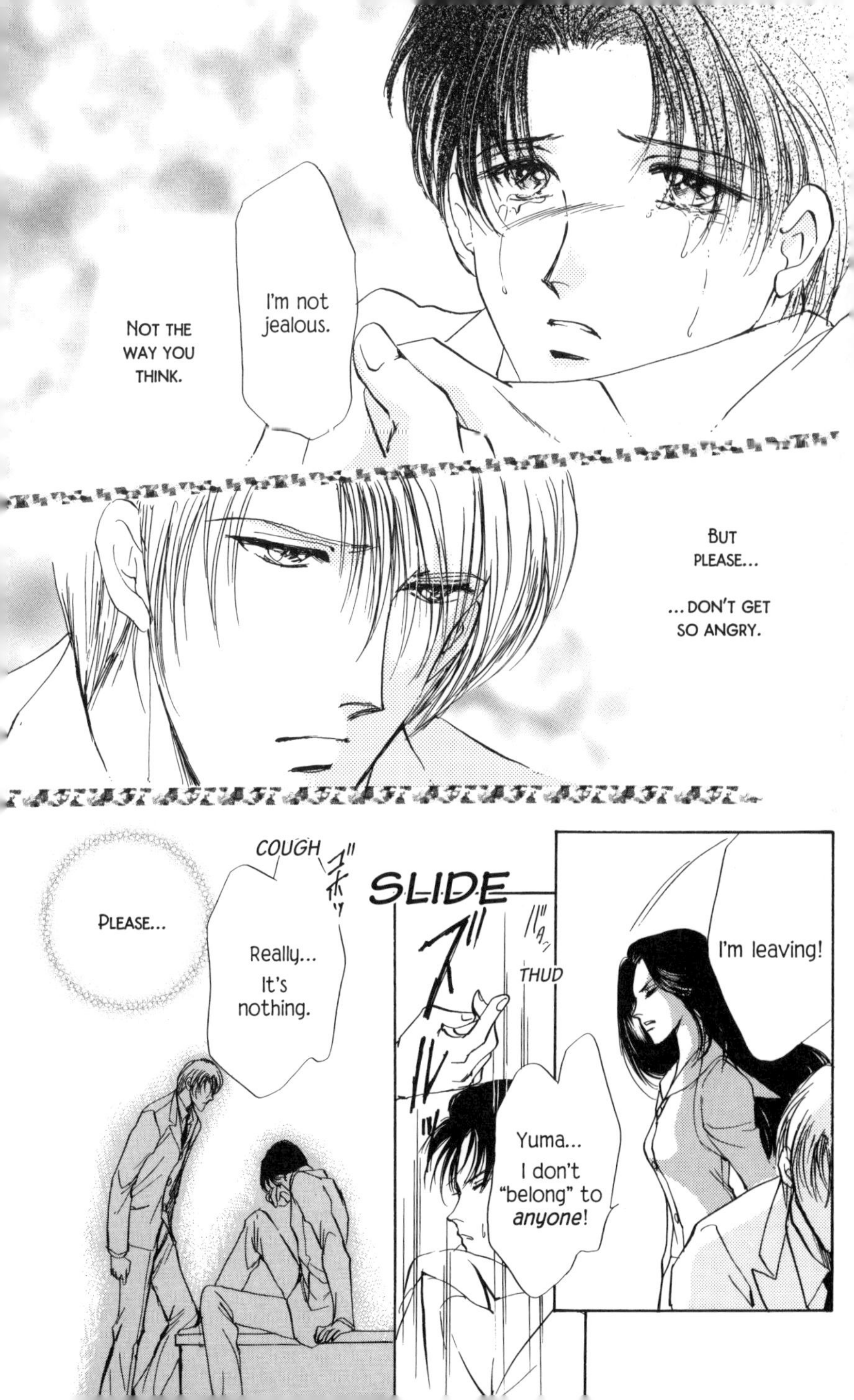

I'm not jealous.
Not the way you think.
But please...
...don't get so angry.
I'm leaving!
SLIDE
THUD
Yuma... I don't "belong" to *anyone*!
COUGH
Please...
Really... It's nothing.

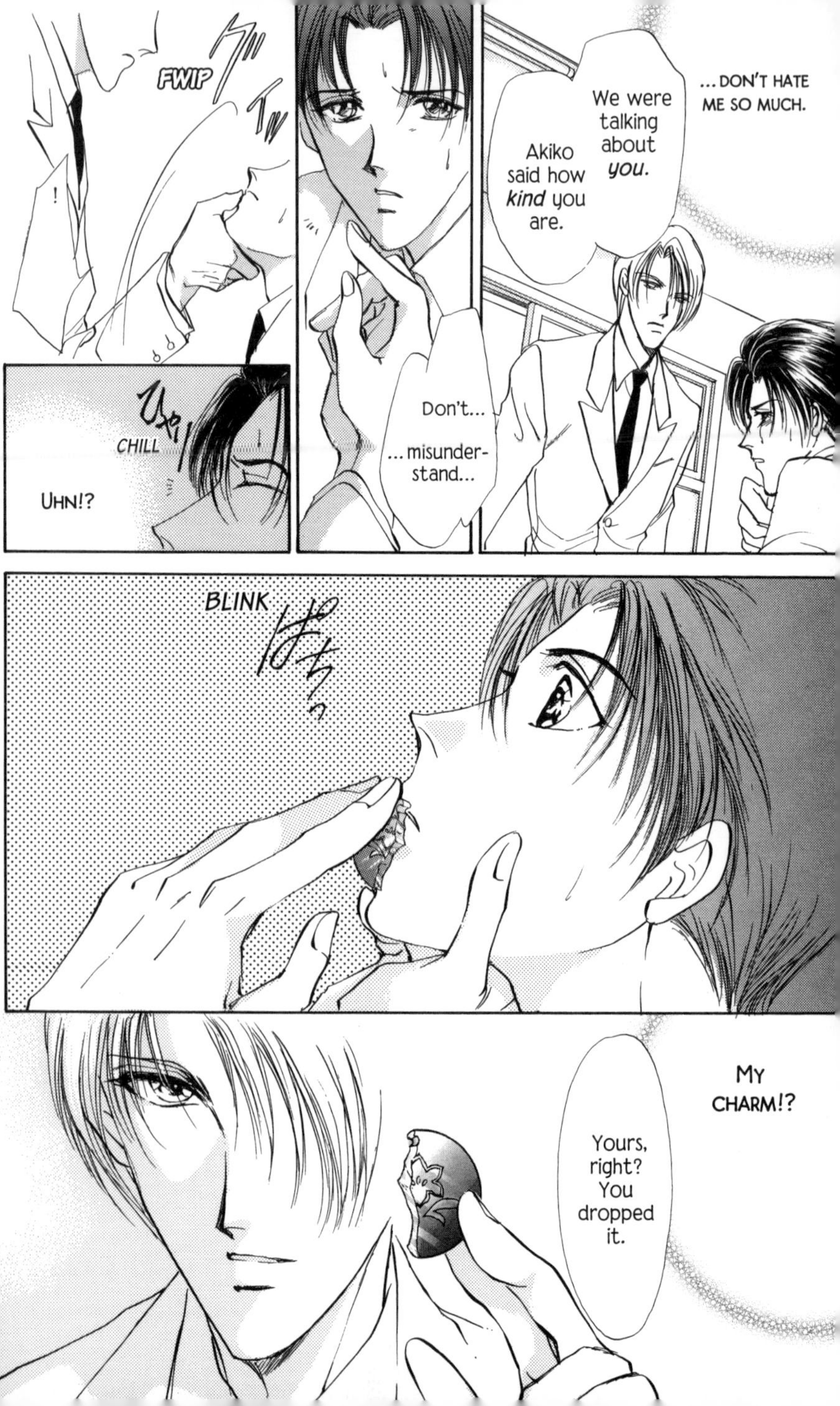

...DON'T HATE ME SO MUCH.
We were talking about *you*.
Akiko said how *kind* you are.
Don't...
...misunderstand...
FWIP
!
CHILL
UHN!?
BLINK
MY CHARM!?
Yours, right? You dropped it.

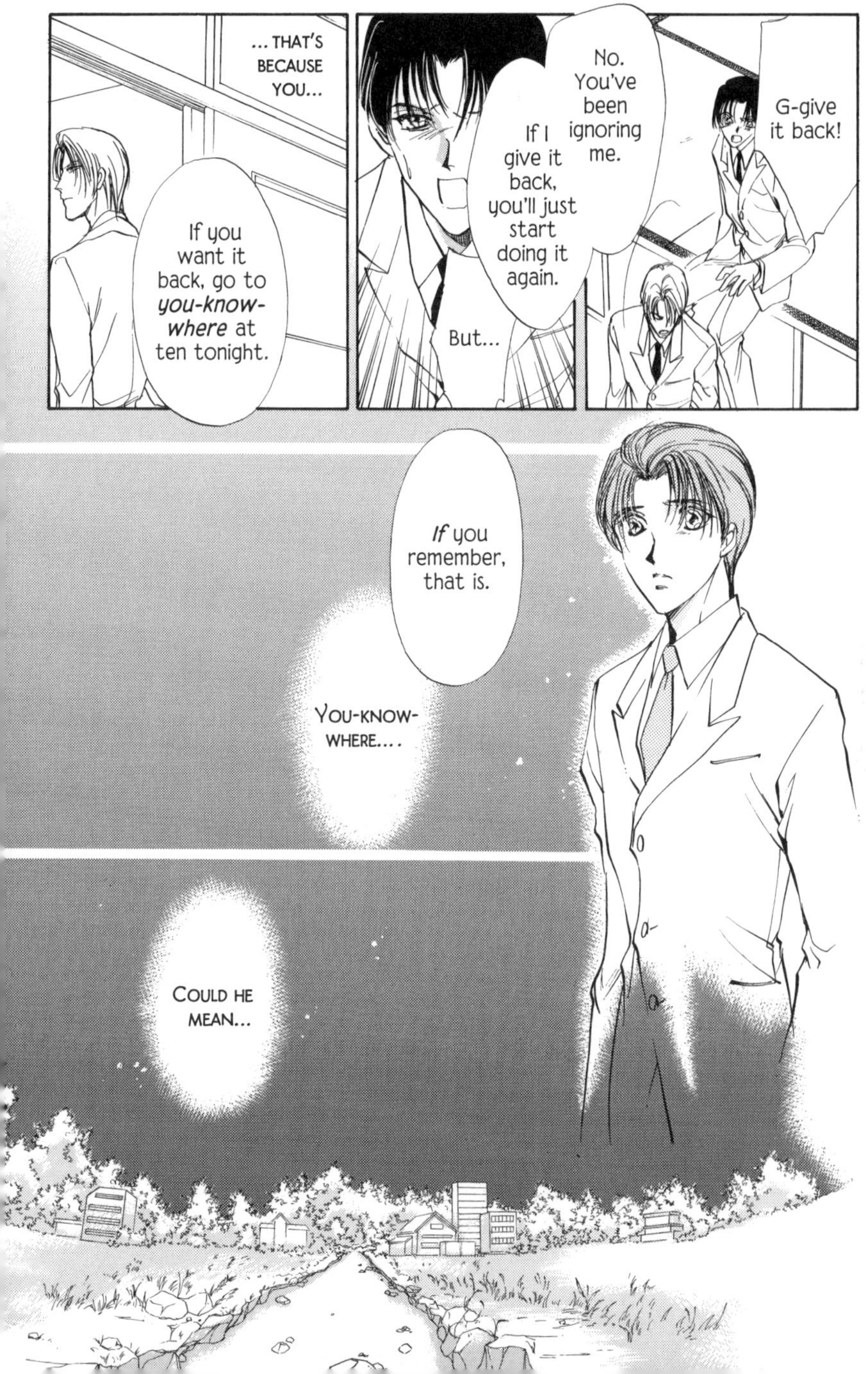
G-give it back!
No. You've been ignoring me.
If I give it back, you'll just start doing it again.
But...
...THAT'S BECAUSE YOU...
If you want it back, go to *you-know-where* at ten tonight.
If you remember, that is.
YOU-KNOW-WHERE....
COULD HE MEAN...

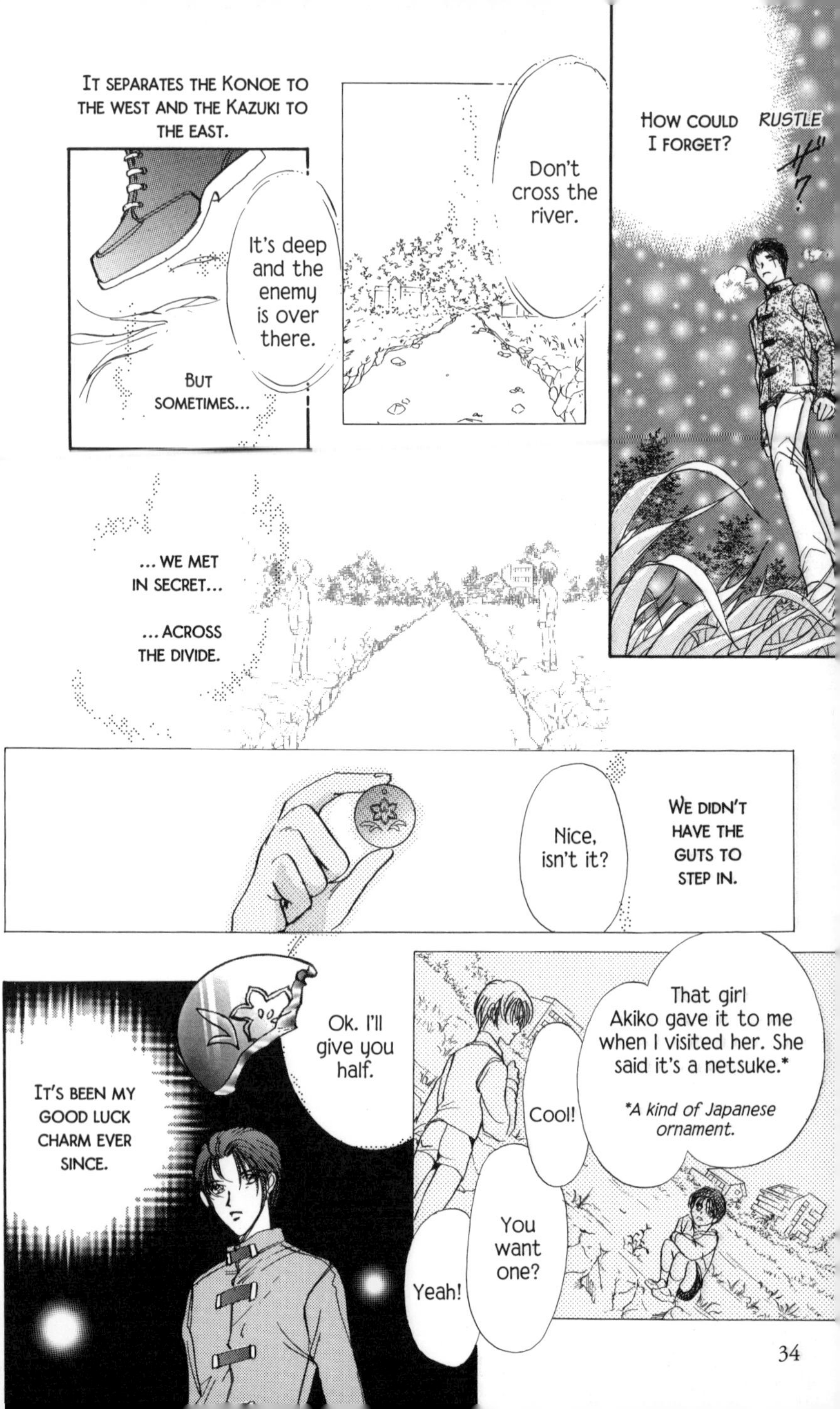

How could I forget?
RUSTLE
Don't cross the river.
It separates the Konoe to the west and the Kazuki to the east.
It's deep and the enemy is over there.
But sometimes...
...we met in secret...
...across the divide.
We didn't have the guts to step in.
Nice, isn't it?
That girl Akiko gave it to me when I visited her. She said it's a netsuke.*
*A kind of Japanese ornament.
Cool!
You want one?
Yeah!
Ok. I'll give you half.
It's been my good luck charm ever since.

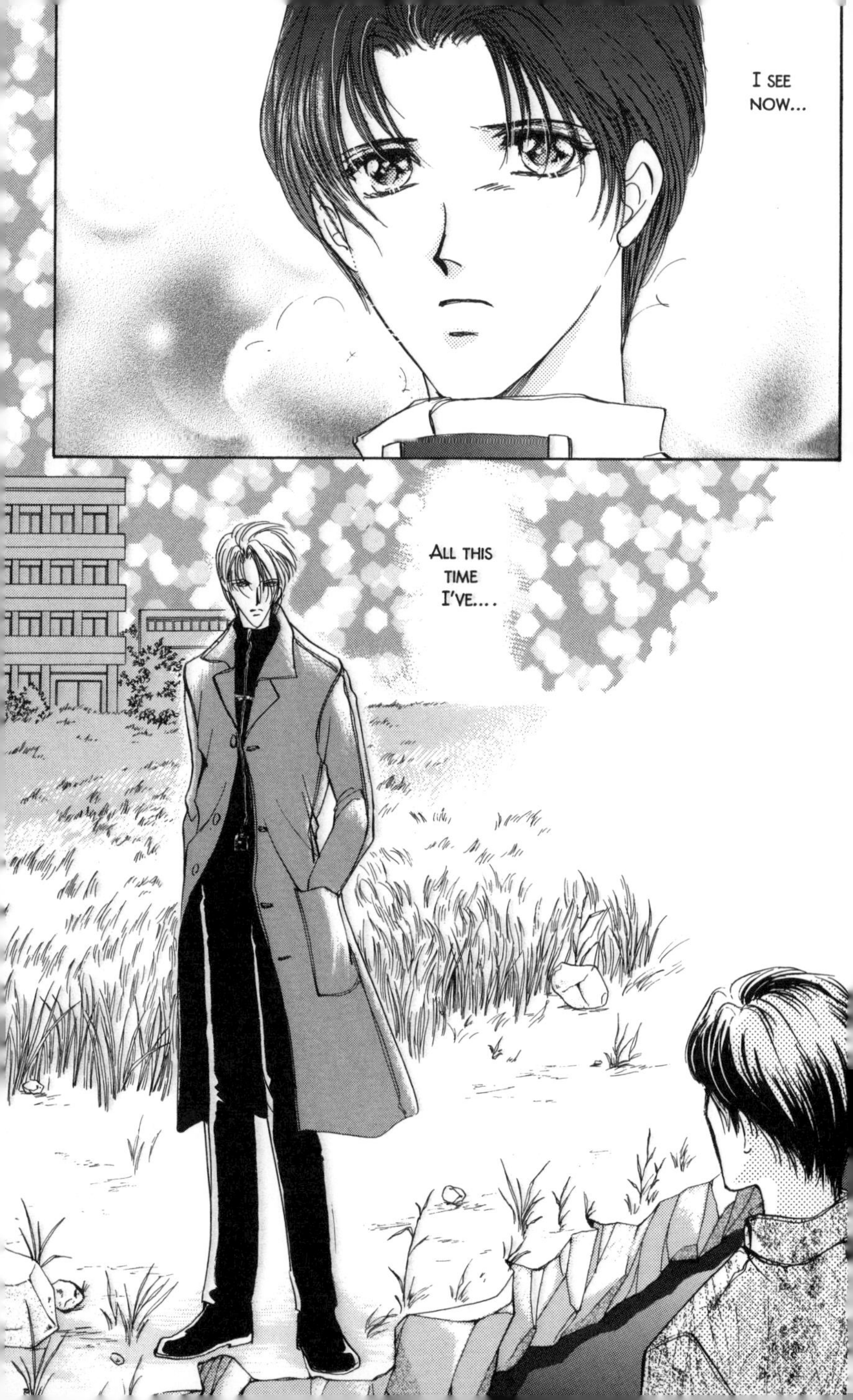
I SEE NOW...
ALL THIS TIME I'VE....

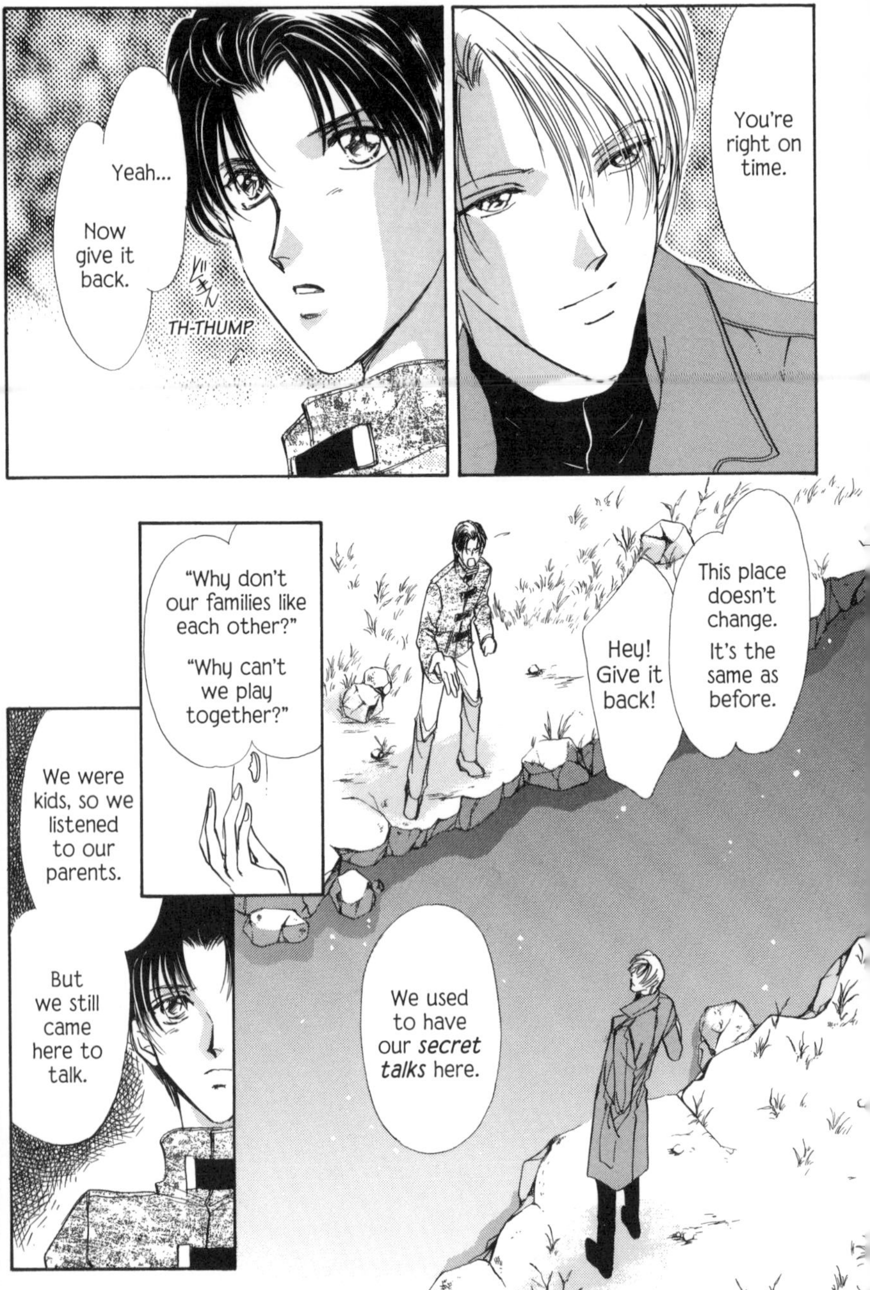

You're right on time.
Yeah...
Now give it back.
TH-THUMP
This place doesn't change.
It's the same as before.
Hey! Give it back!
"Why don't our families like each other?"
"Why can't we play together?"
We used to have our *secret talks* here.
We were kids, so we listened to our parents.
But we still came here to talk.

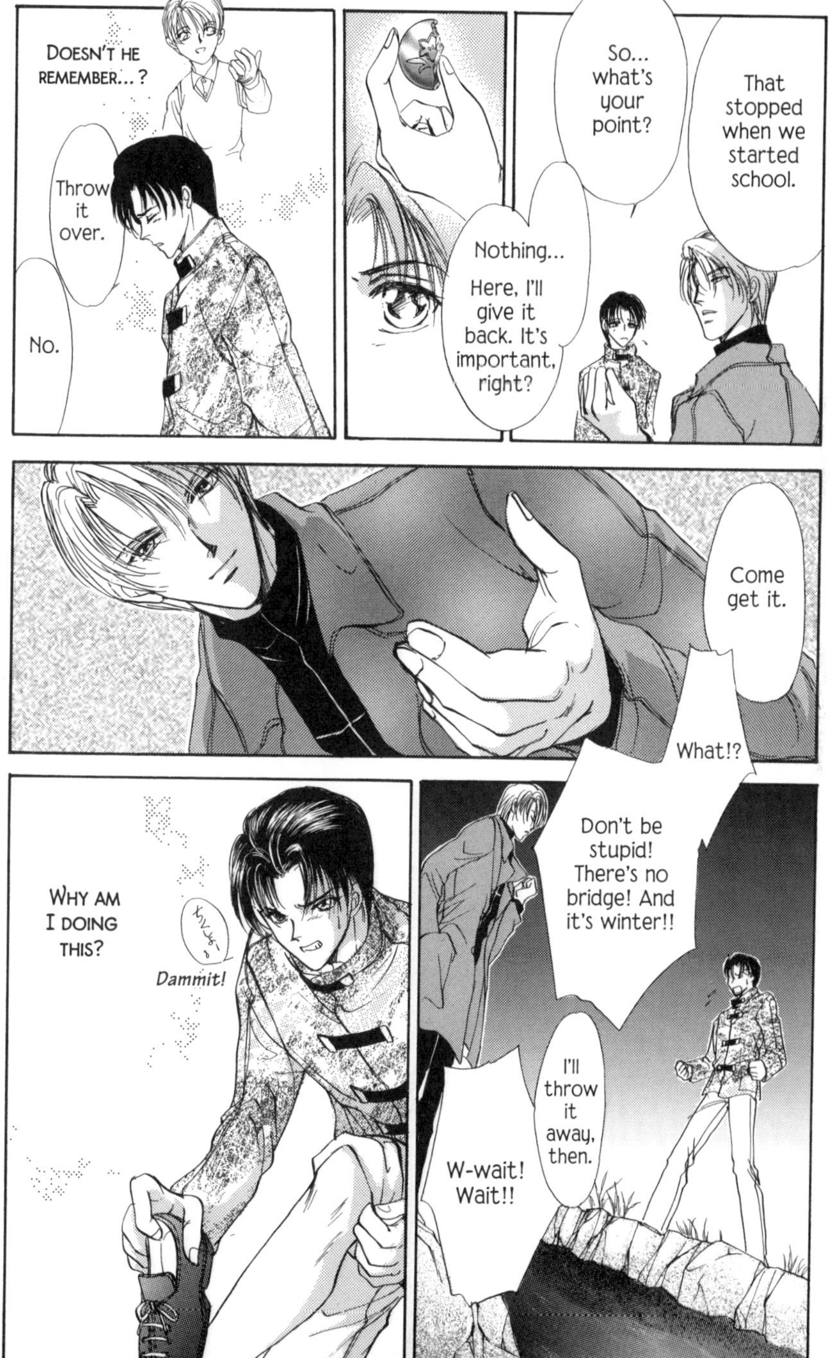
That stopped when we started school.
So... what's your point?
Nothing...
Here, I'll give it back. It's important, right?
DOESN'T HE REMEMBER...?
Throw it over.
No.
Come get it.
What!?
Don't be stupid! There's no bridge! And it's winter!!
I'll throw it away, then.
W-wait! Wait!!
WHY AM I DOING THIS?
Dammit!

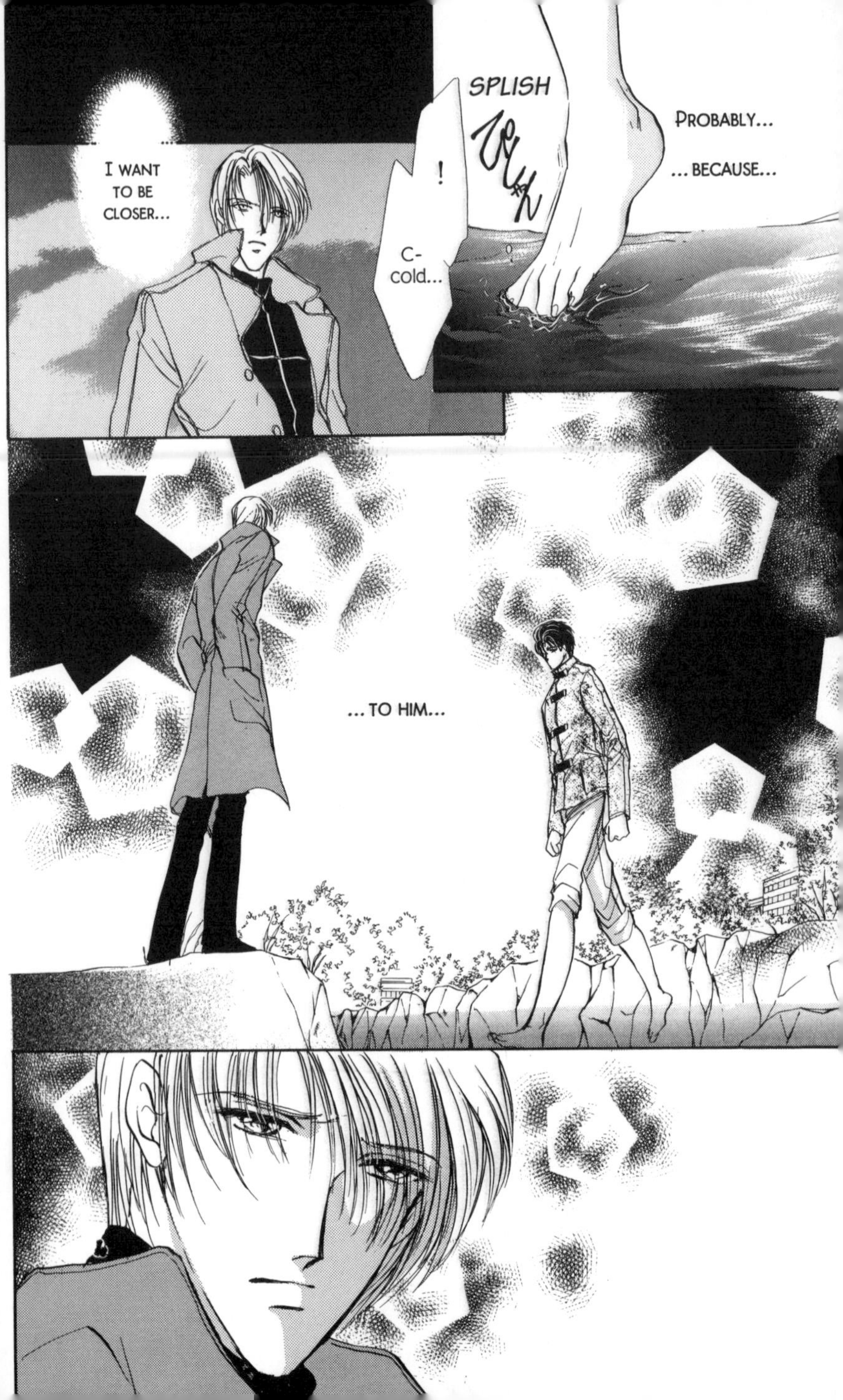
PROBABLY...
...BECAUSE...
SPLISH
!
C-cold...
I WANT TO BE CLOSER...
...TO HIM...

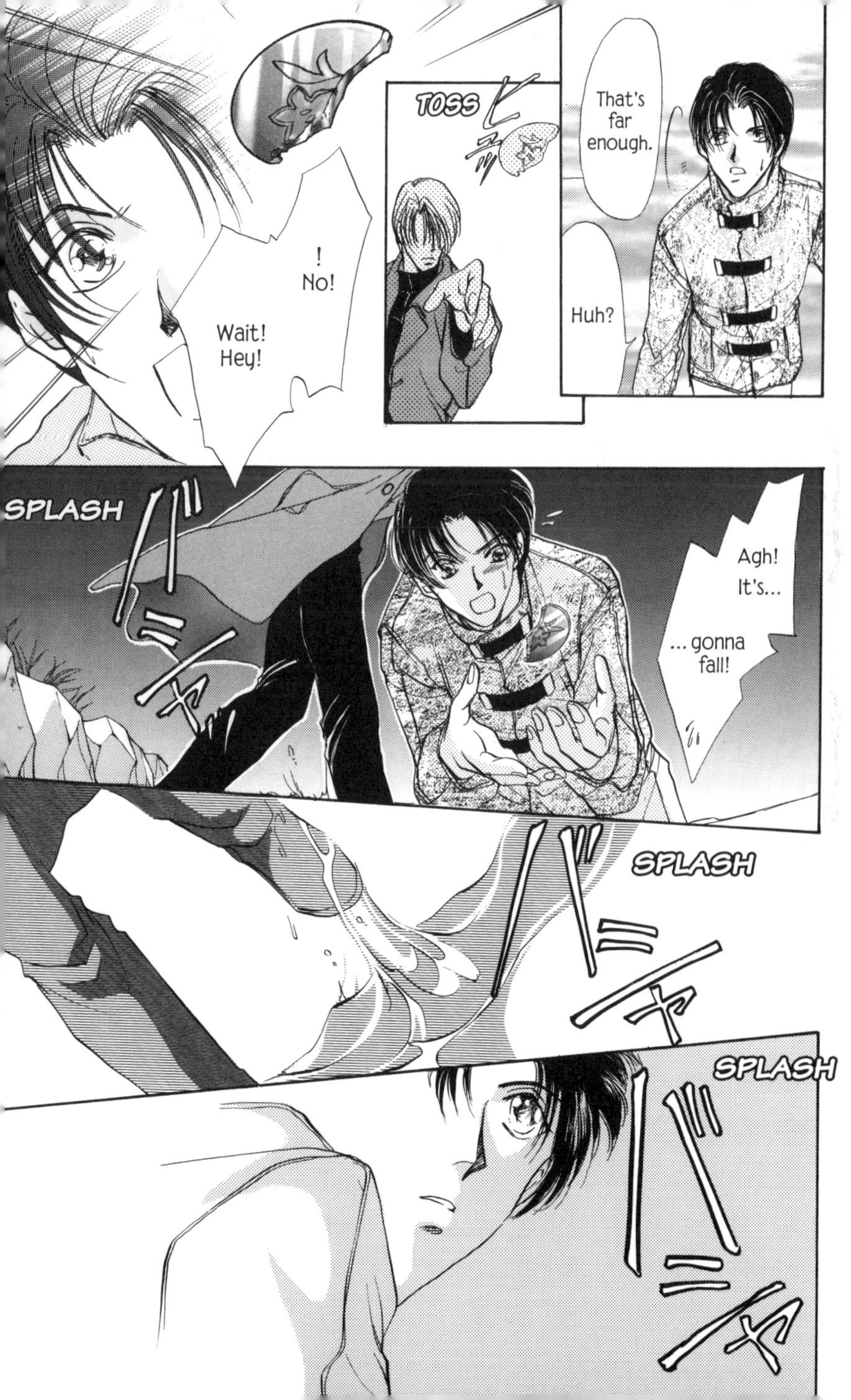
That's far enough.
Huh?
TOSS
! No!
Wait! Hey!
Agh! It's...
... gonna fall!
SPLASH
SPLASH
SPLASH

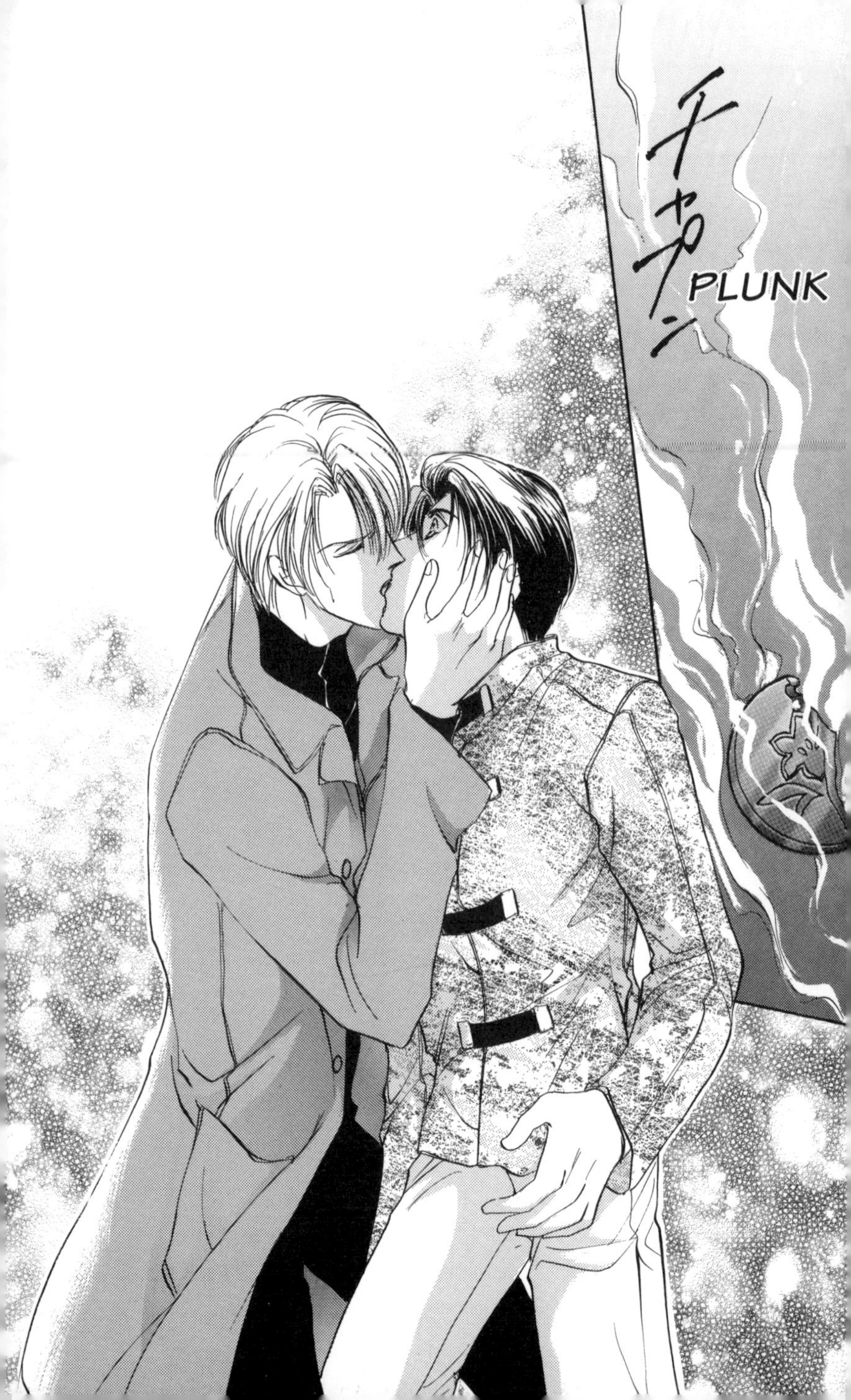
チャプン
PLUNK

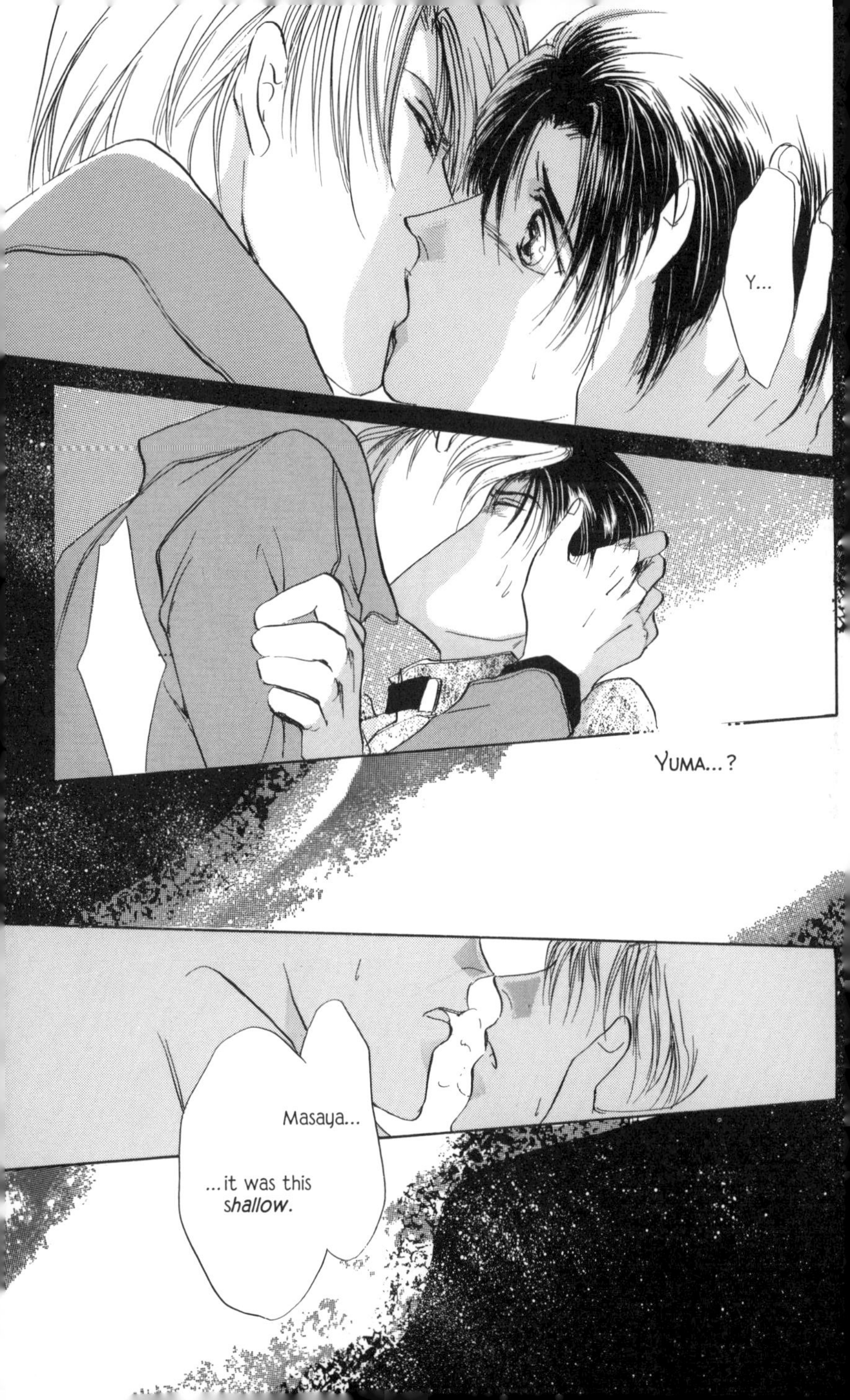
Y...
YUMA...?
Masaya...
...it was this *shallow.*

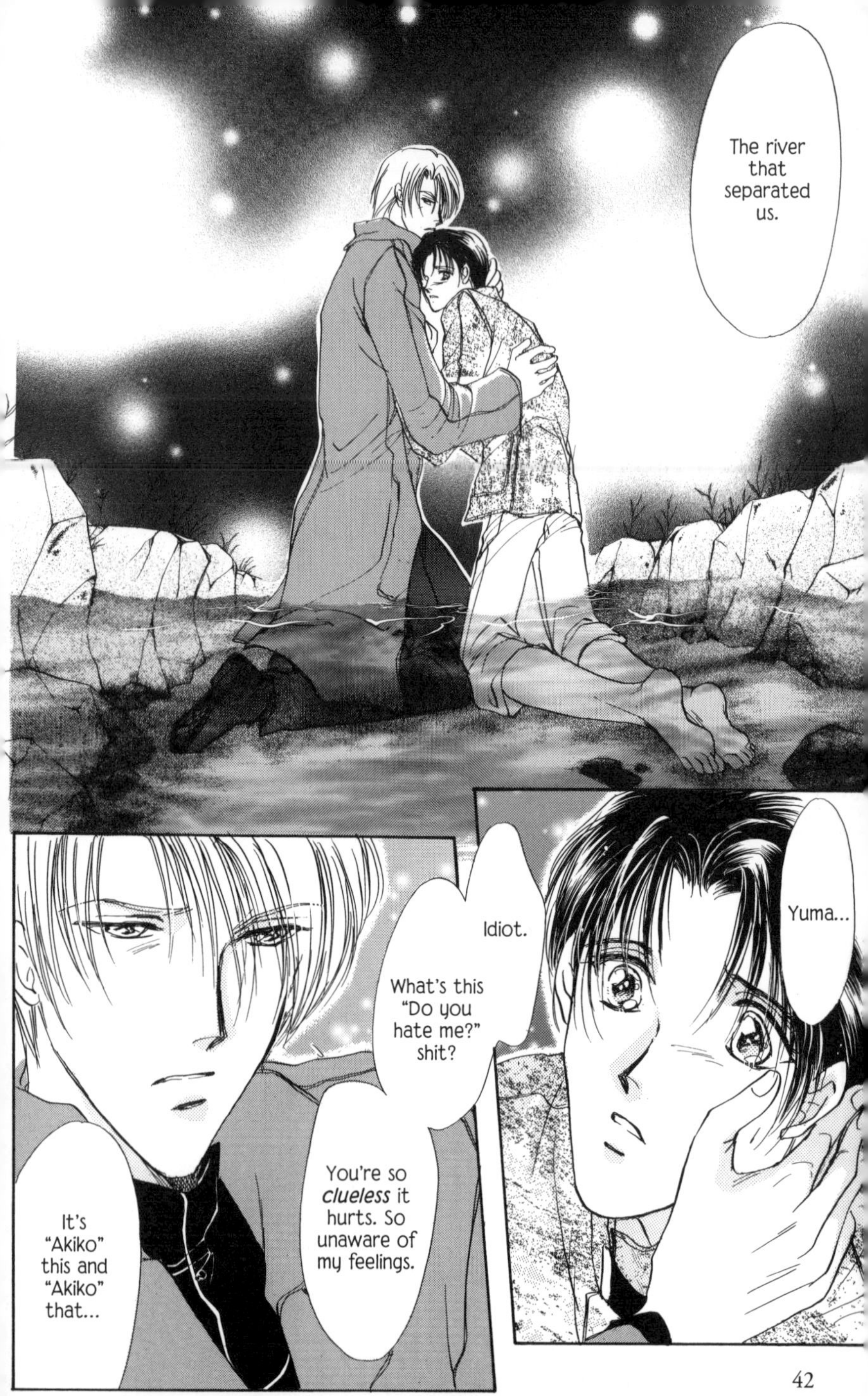

The river that separated us.
Yuma...
Idiot.
What's this "Do you hate me?" shit?
You're so *clueless* it hurts. So unaware of my feelings.
It's "Akiko" this and "Akiko" that...

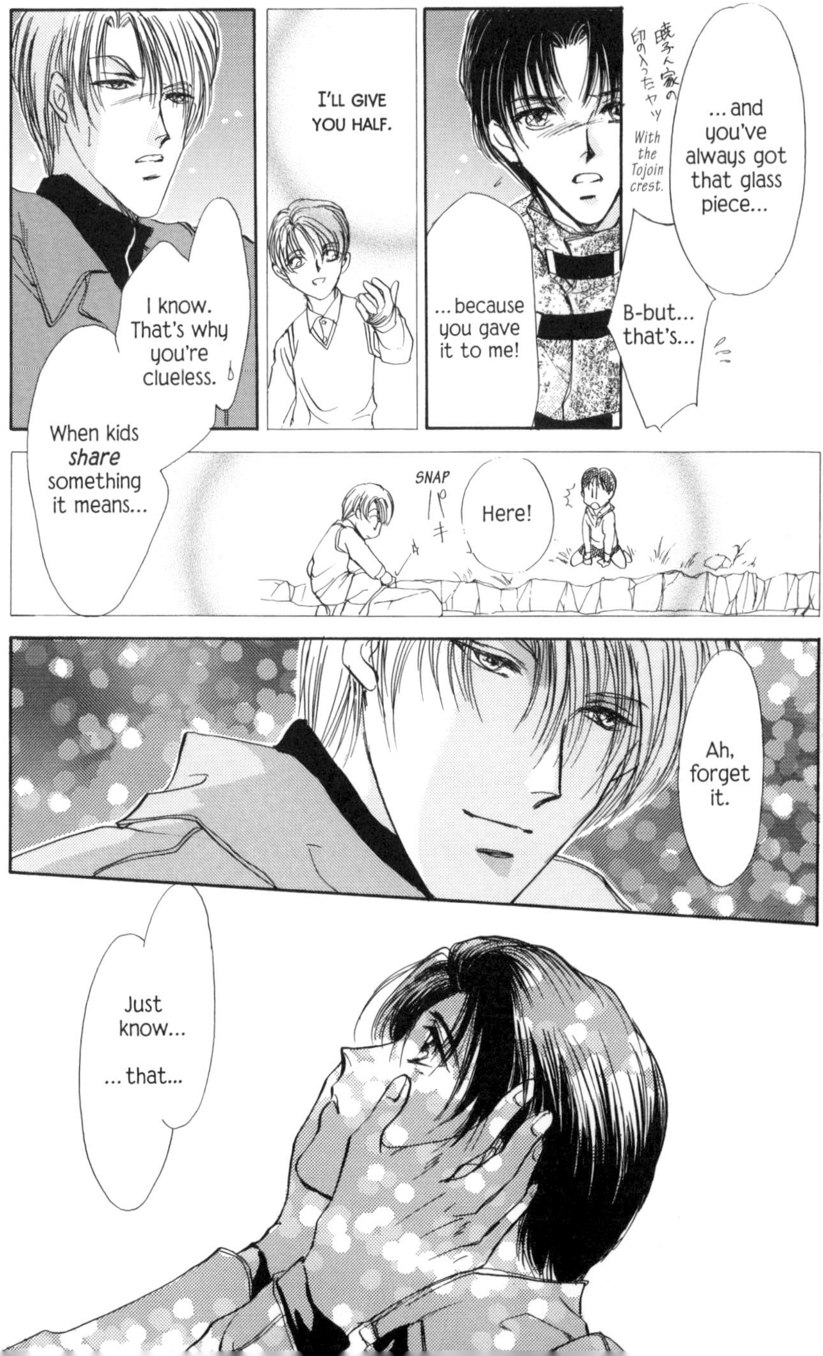
...and you've always got that glass piece...
暁子ん家の印の入ったヤツ
With the Tojoin crest.
B-but... that's...
...because you gave it to me!
I'LL GIVE YOU HALF.
I know. That's why you're clueless.
Here!
SNAP
パキ
When kids *share* something it means...
Ah, forget it.
Just know...
...that...

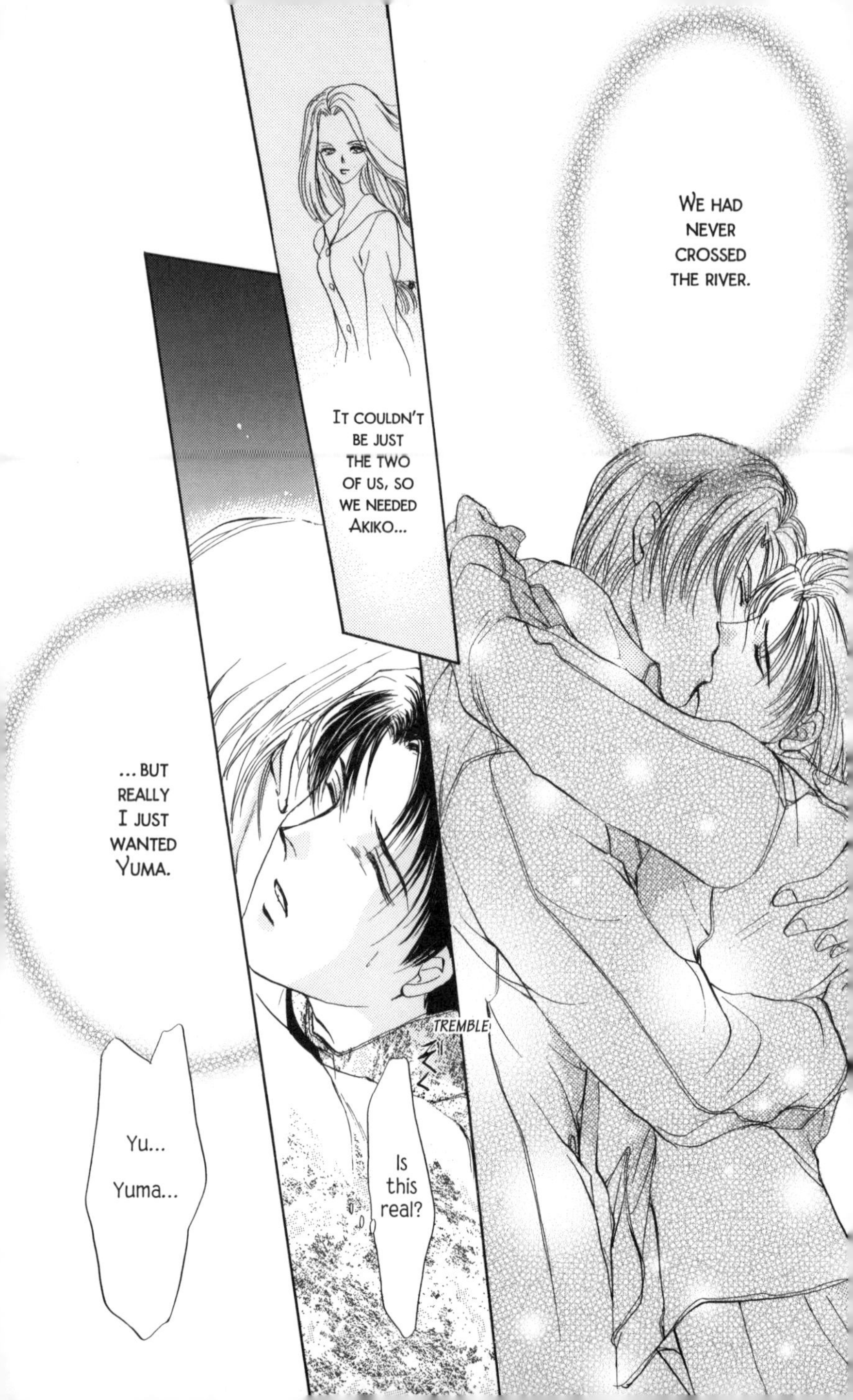
We had never crossed the river.
It couldn't be just the two of us, so we needed Akiko...
...but really I just wanted Yuma.
TREMBLE
Is this real?
Yu...
Yuma...

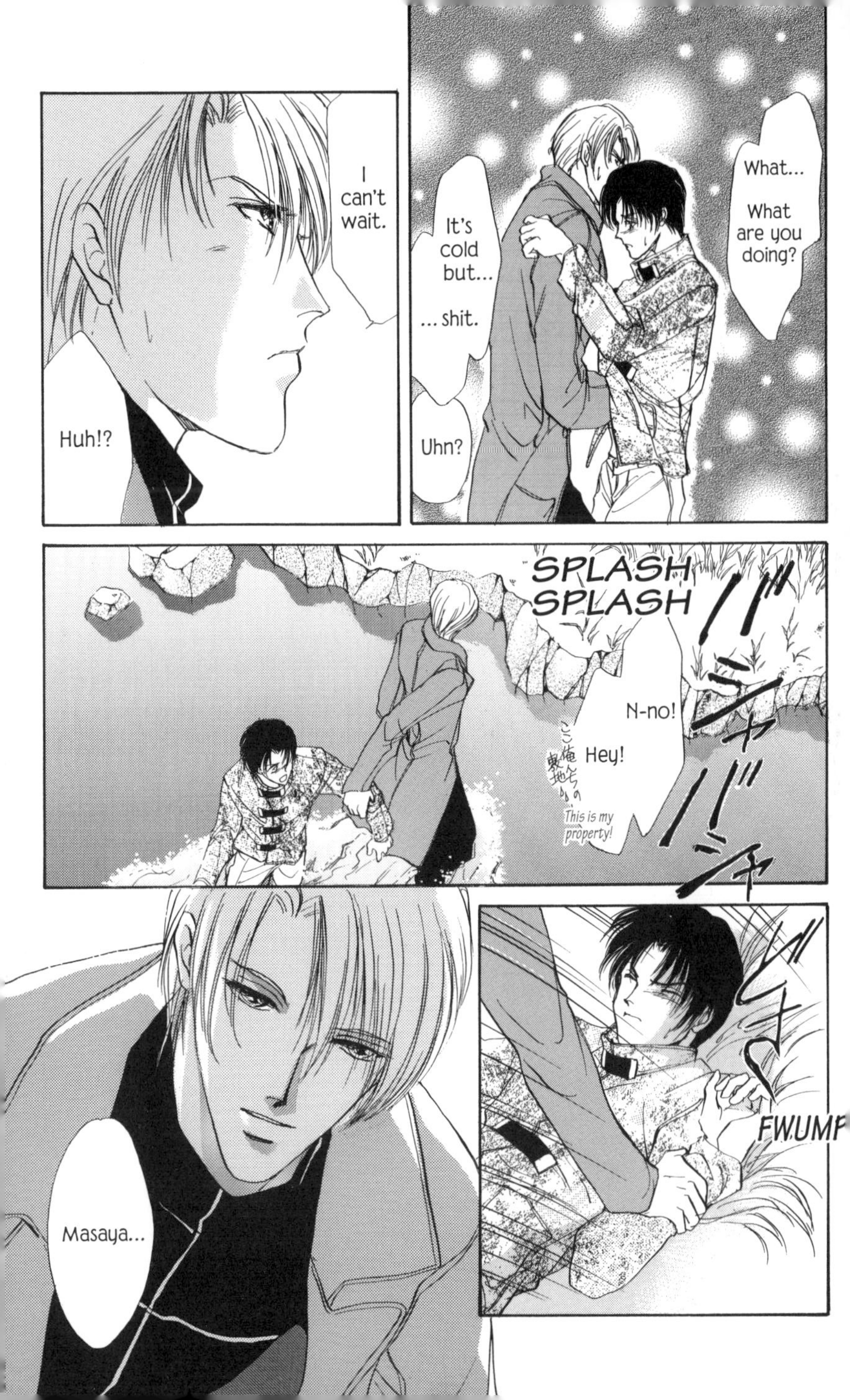
What...
What are you doing?
It's cold but...
...shit.
Uhn?
I can't wait.
Huh!?
SPLASH SPLASH
N-no!
Hey!
This is my property!
FWUMP
Masaya...

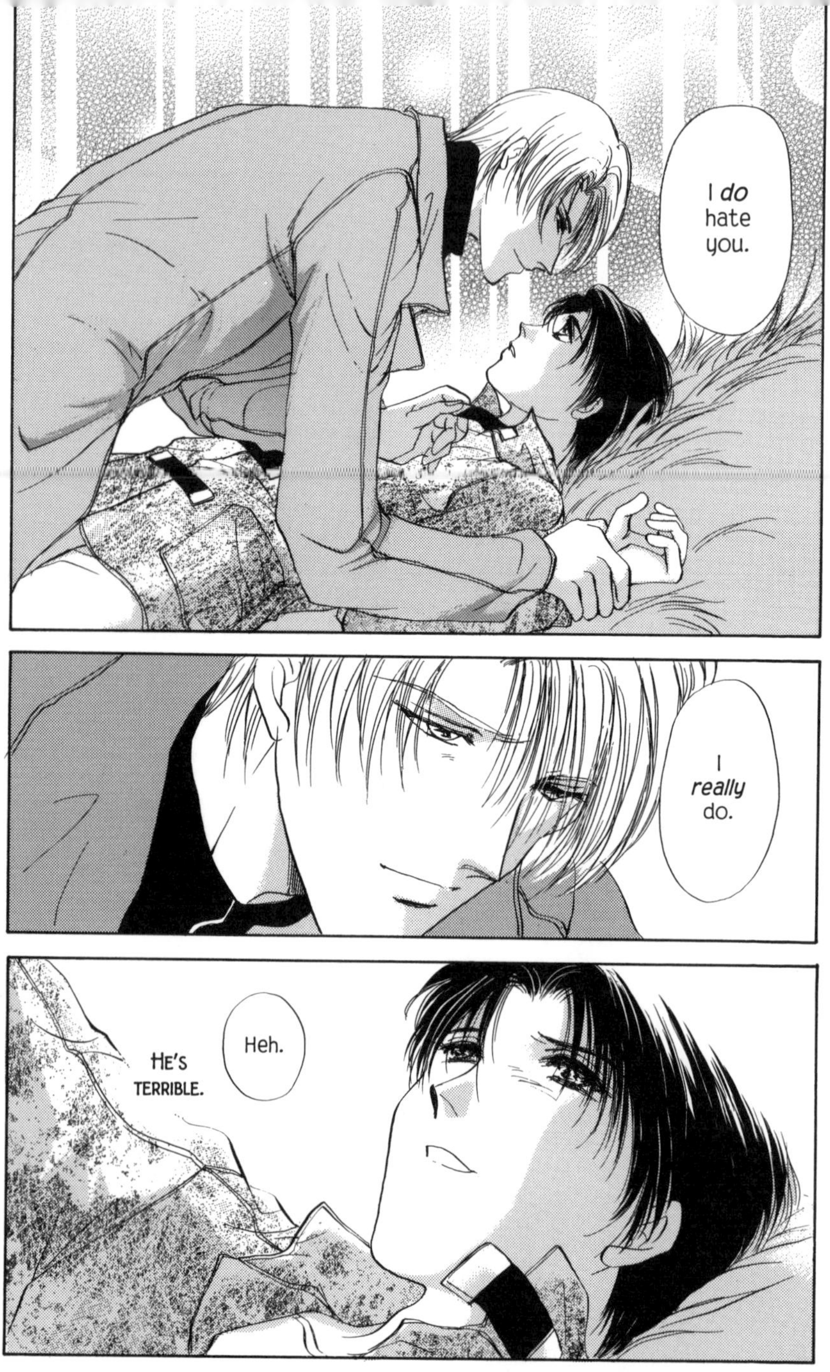
I *do* hate you.
I *really* do.
Heh.
HE'S TERRIBLE.

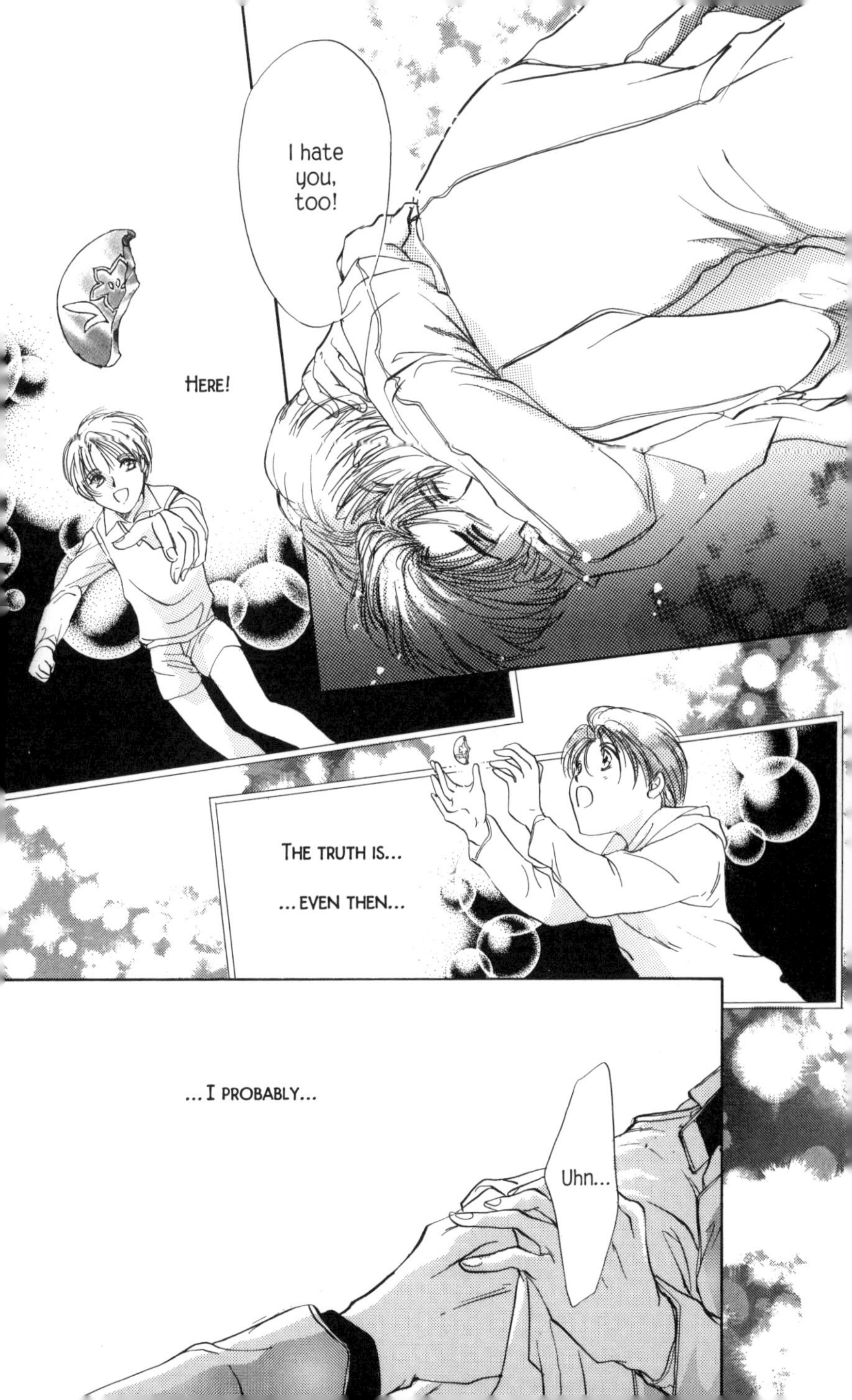
I hate you, too!
Here!
The truth is...
...even then...
...I probably...
Uhn...

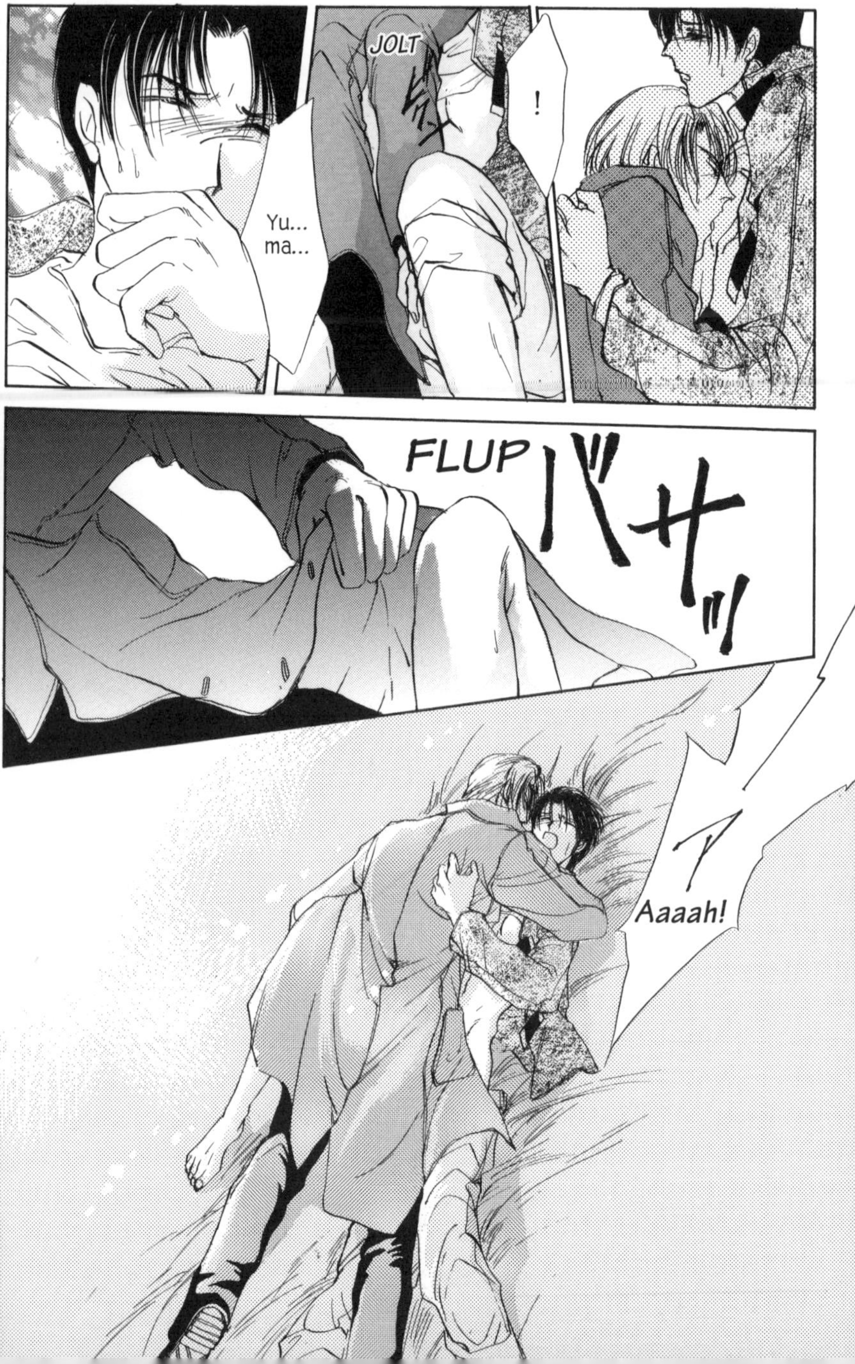
!
JOLT
Yu... ma...
FLUP
バサッ
Aaaah!

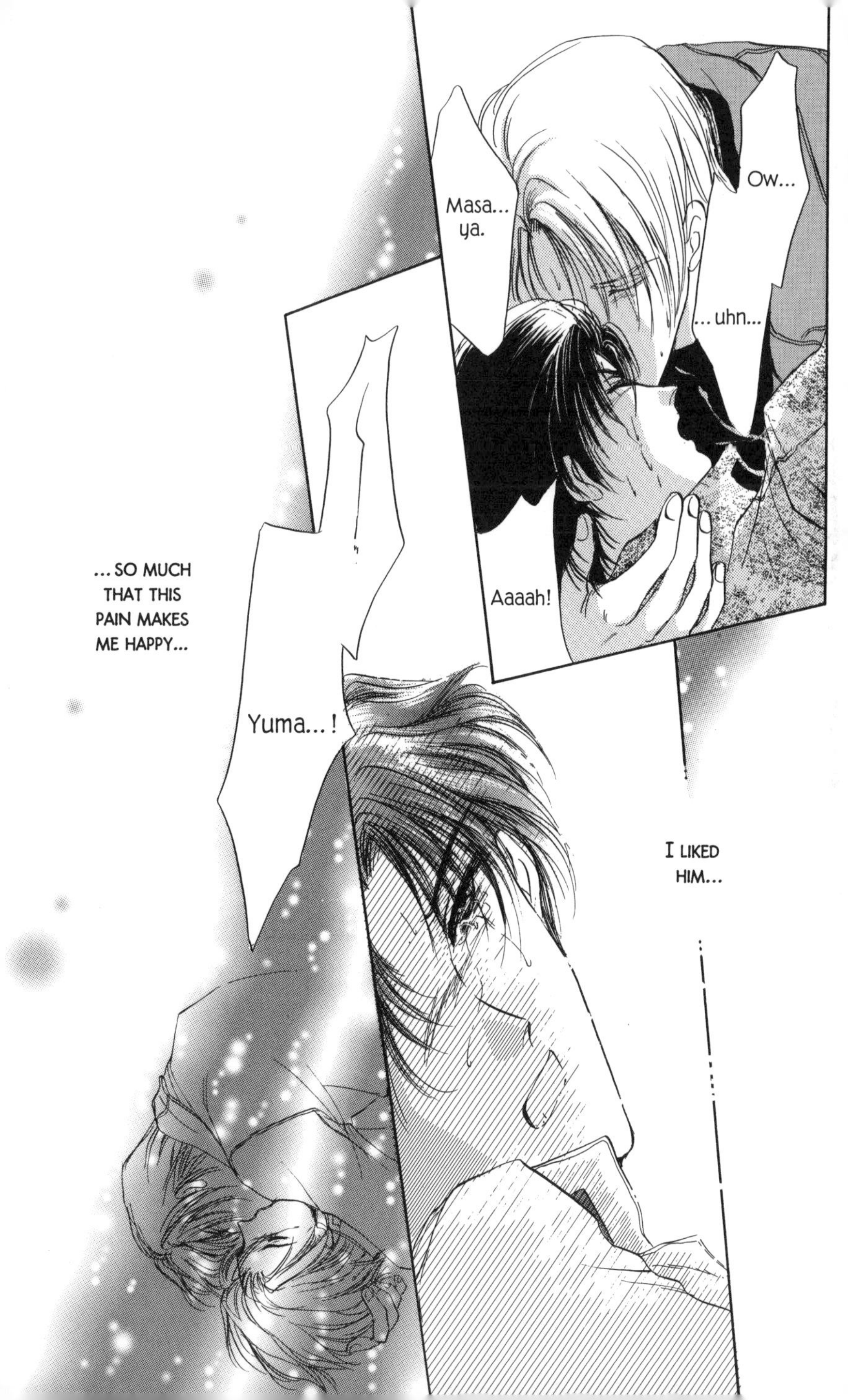
Ow...
Masa... ya.
...uhn...
Aaaah!
I LIKED HIM...
Yuma...!
...SO MUCH THAT THIS PAIN MAKES ME HAPPY...

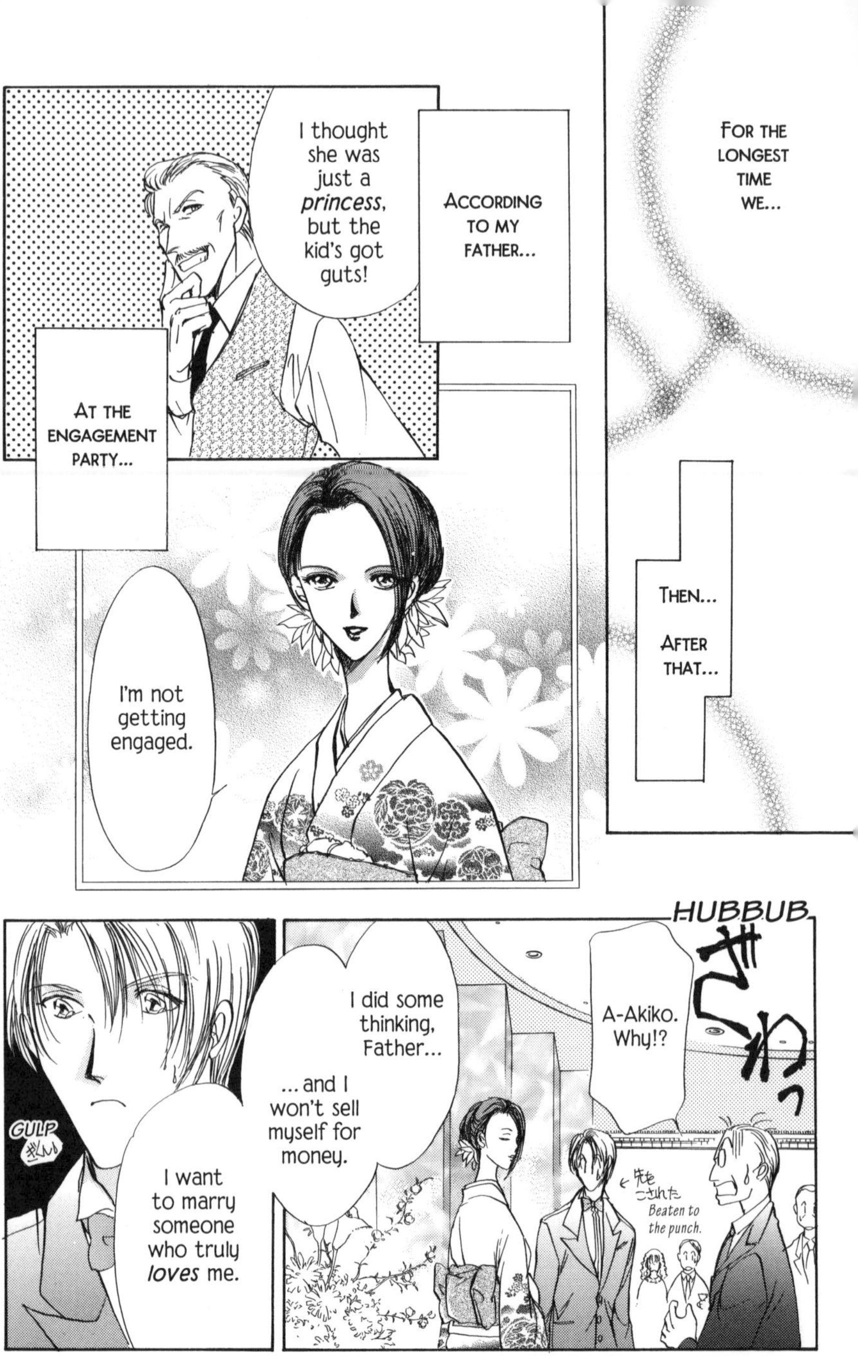
For the longest time we...
Then...
After that...
According to my father...
I thought she was just a *princess*, but the kid's got guts!
At the engagement party...
I'm not getting engaged.
HUBBUB
ざわっ
A-Akiko. Why!?
I did some thinking, Father...
...and I won't sell myself for money.
← 先をこされた
Beaten to the punch.
GULP
I want to marry someone who truly *loves* me.

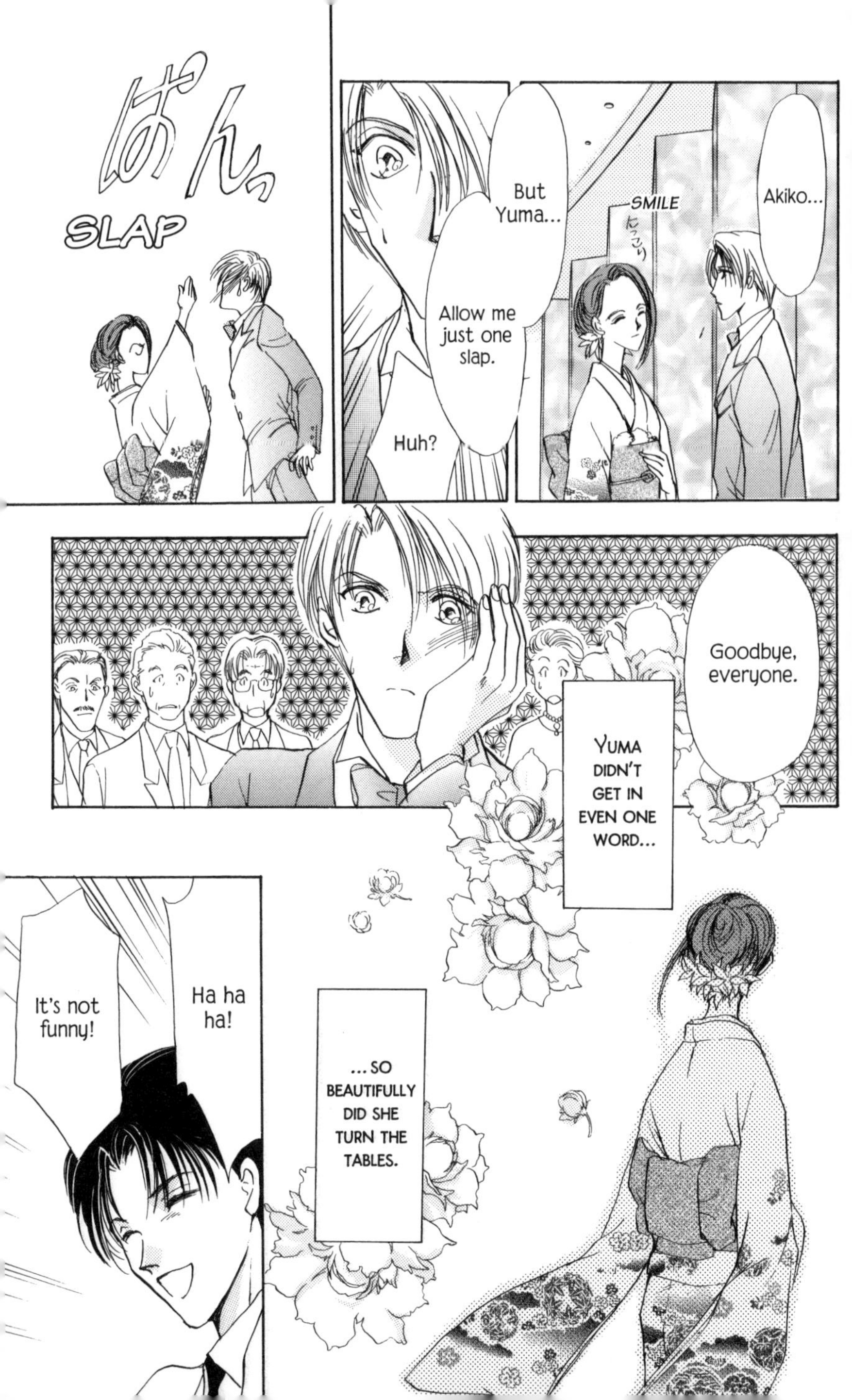
Akiko...
SMILE
にっこり
But Yuma...
Allow me just one slap.
Huh?
ぱんっ
SLAP
Goodbye, everyone.
YUMA DIDN'T GET IN EVEN ONE WORD...
...SO BEAUTIFULLY DID SHE TURN THE TABLES.
Ha ha ha!
It's not funny!

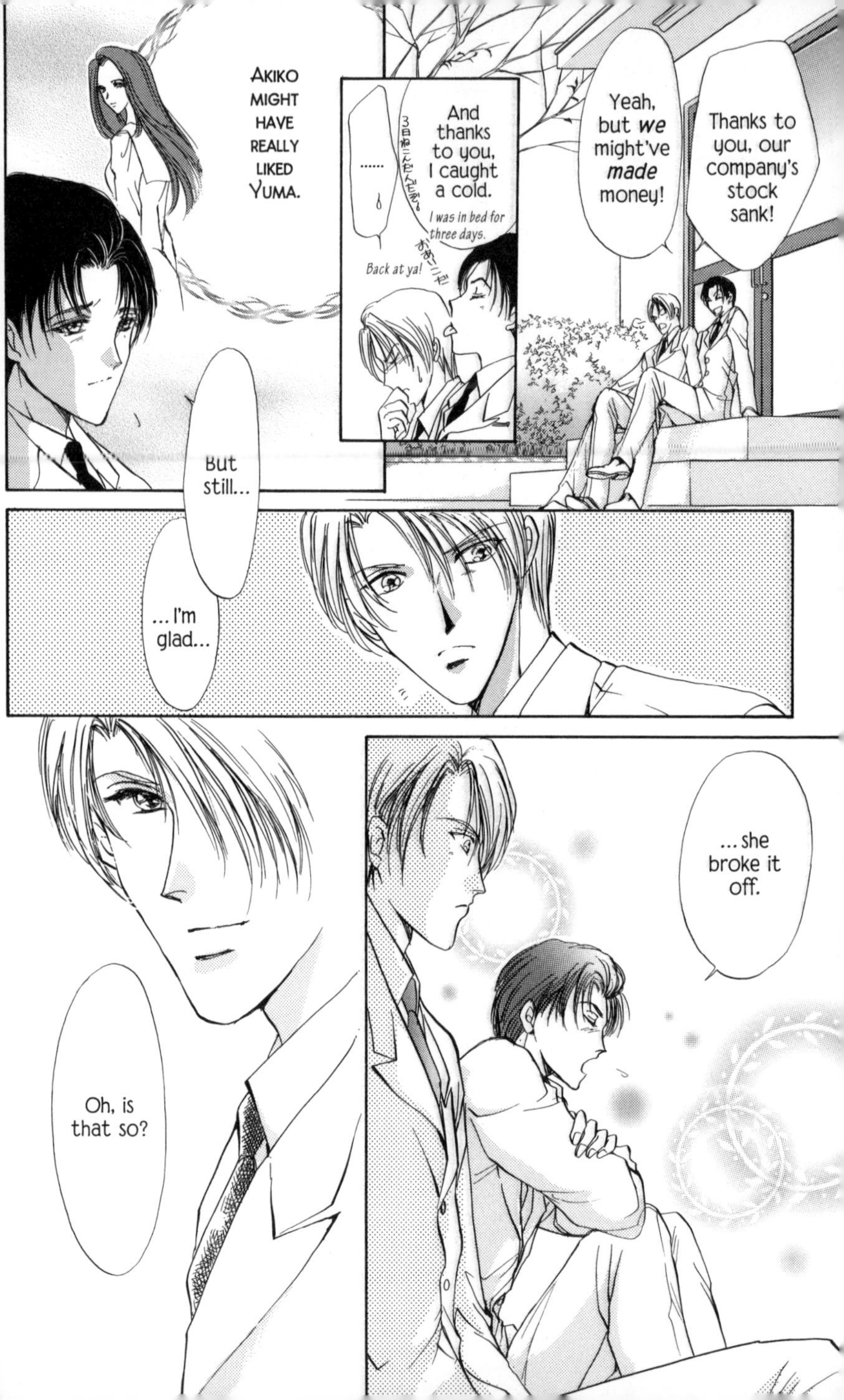
Thanks to you, our company's stock sank!
Yeah, but **we** might've ***made*** money!
And thanks to you, I caught a cold.
3日ねこんだんだぞ。
I was in bed for three days.
......
おあいこだ
Back at ya!
AKIKO MIGHT HAVE REALLY LIKED YUMA.
But still...
...I'm glad...
...she broke it off.
Oh, is that so?

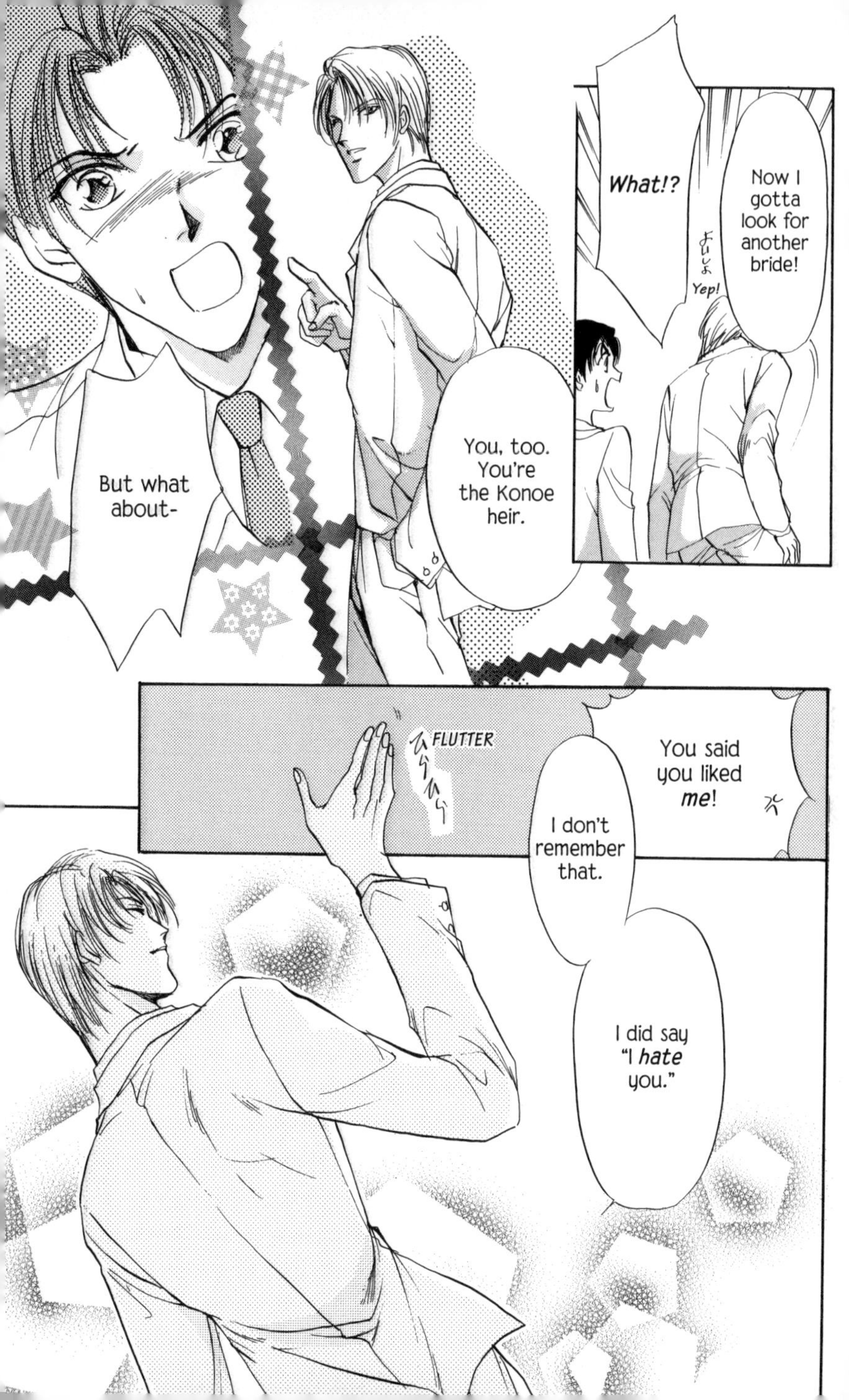
Now I gotta look for another bride!
Yep!
What!?
You, too. You're the Konoe heir.
But what about-
You said you liked *me*!
FLUTTER
I don't remember that.
I did say "I *hate* you."

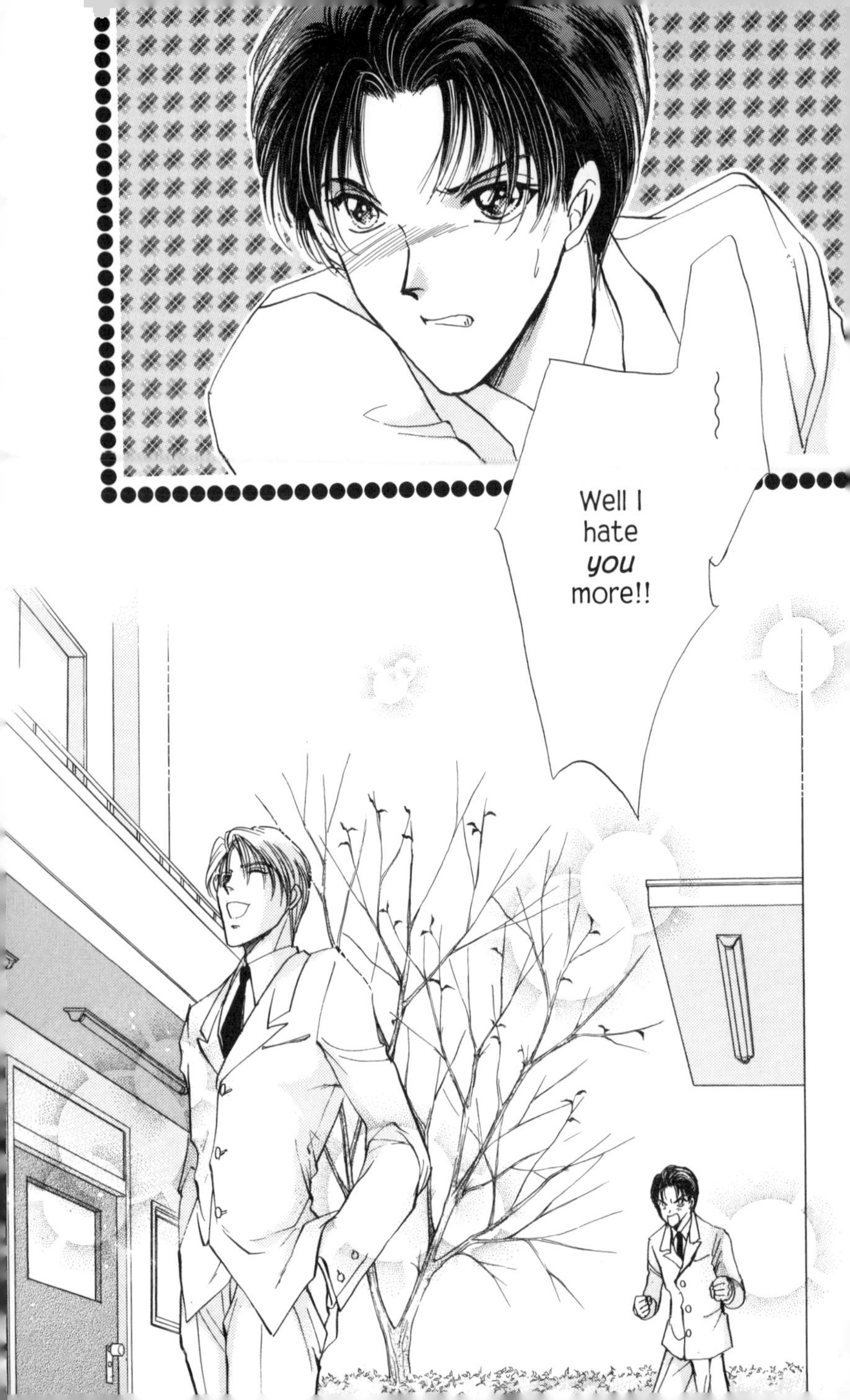
Well I hate *you* more!!

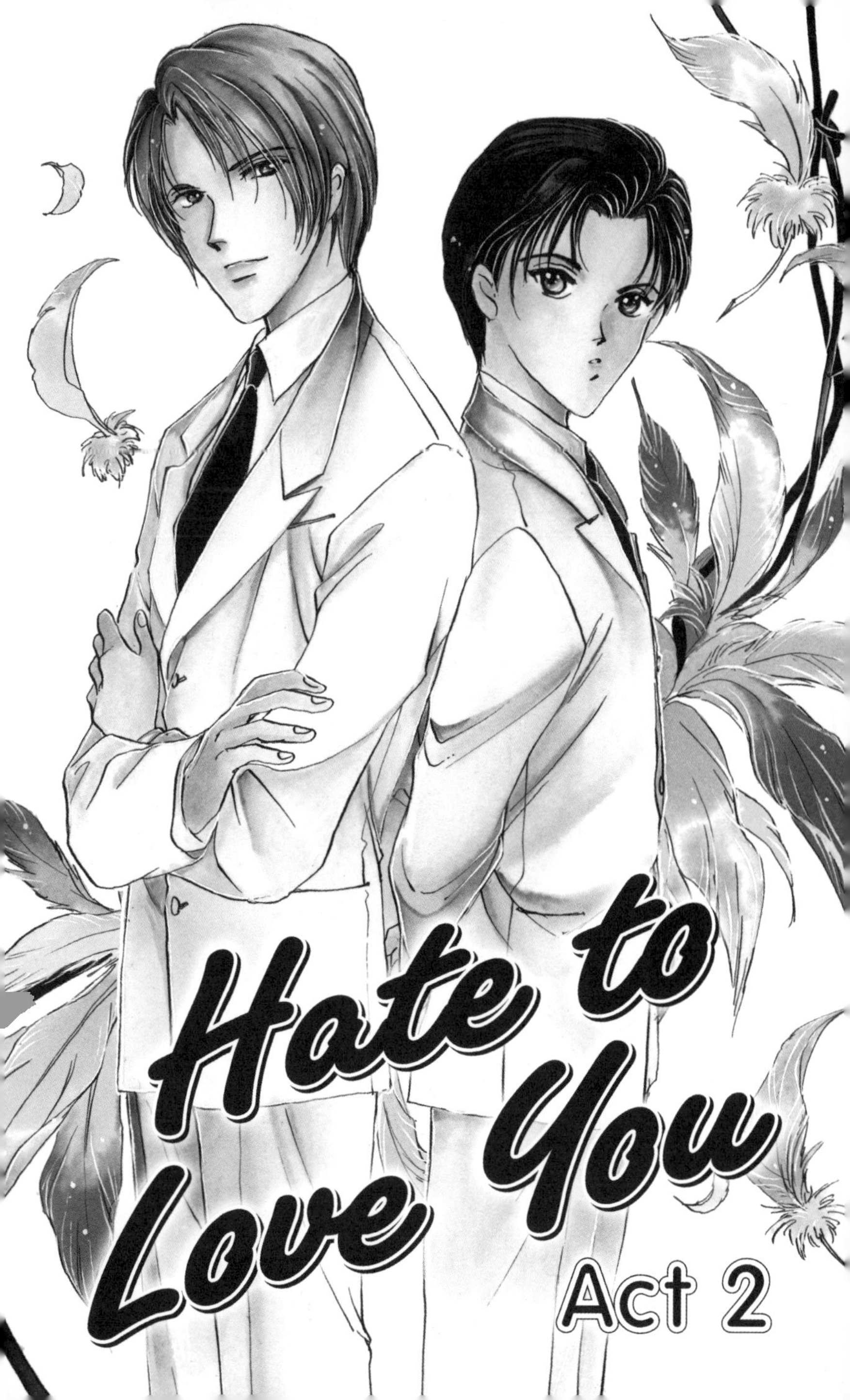
Hate to Love You
Act 2

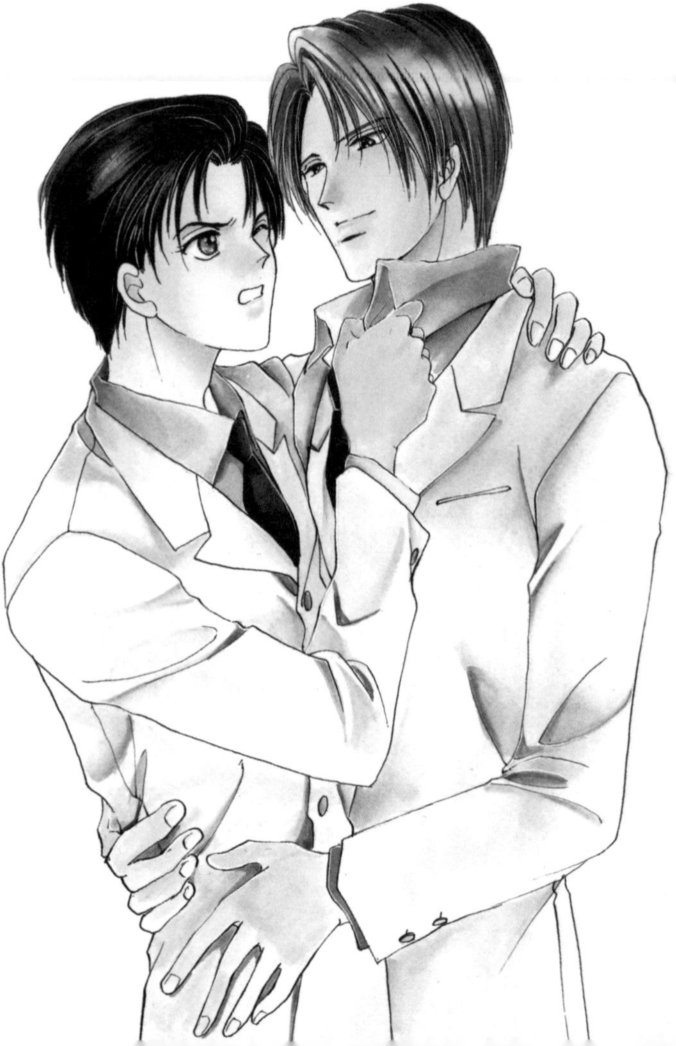

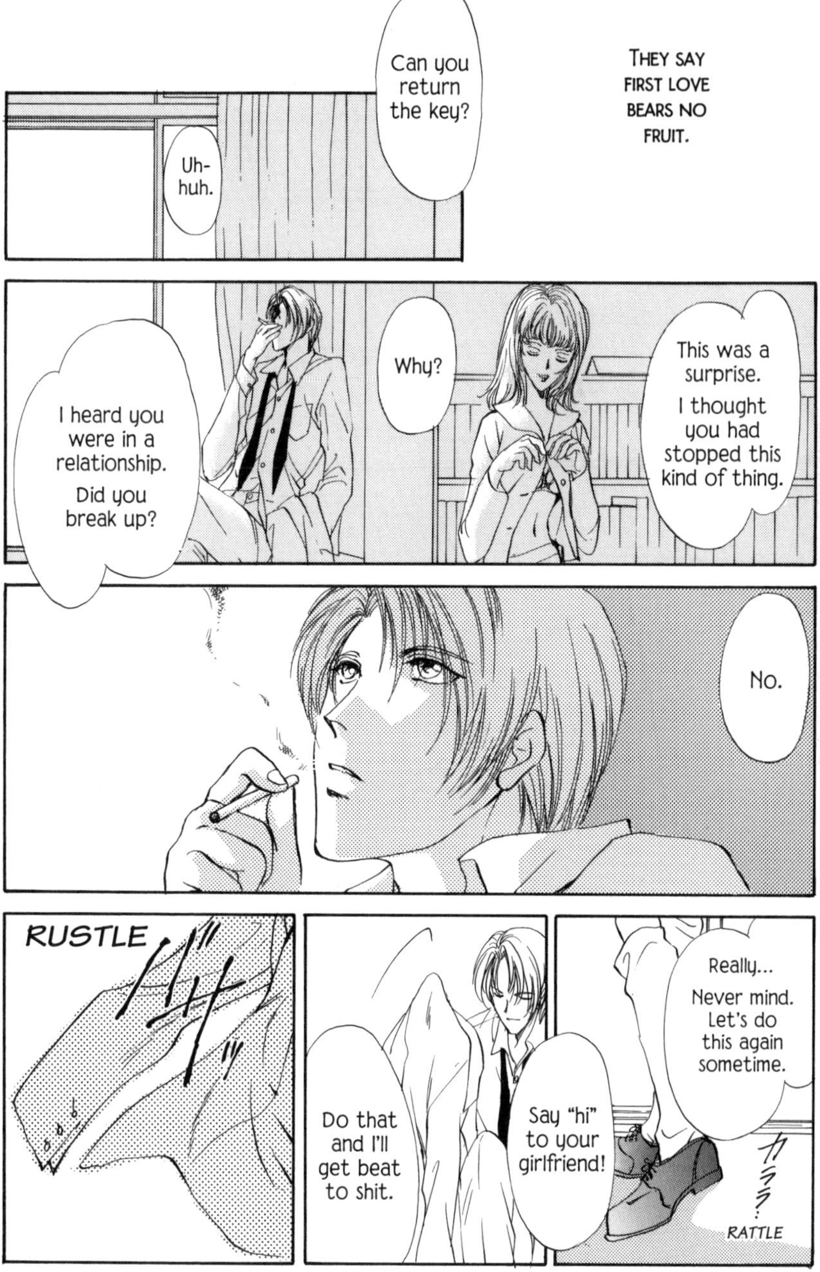
THEY SAY FIRST LOVE BEARS NO FRUIT.
Can you return the key?
Uh-huh.
This was a surprise.
I thought you had stopped this kind of thing.
Why?
I heard you were in a relationship.
Did you break up?
No.
Really...
Never mind. Let's do this again sometime.
カララ
RATTLE
Say "hi" to your girlfriend!
Do that and I'll get beat to shit.
RUSTLE

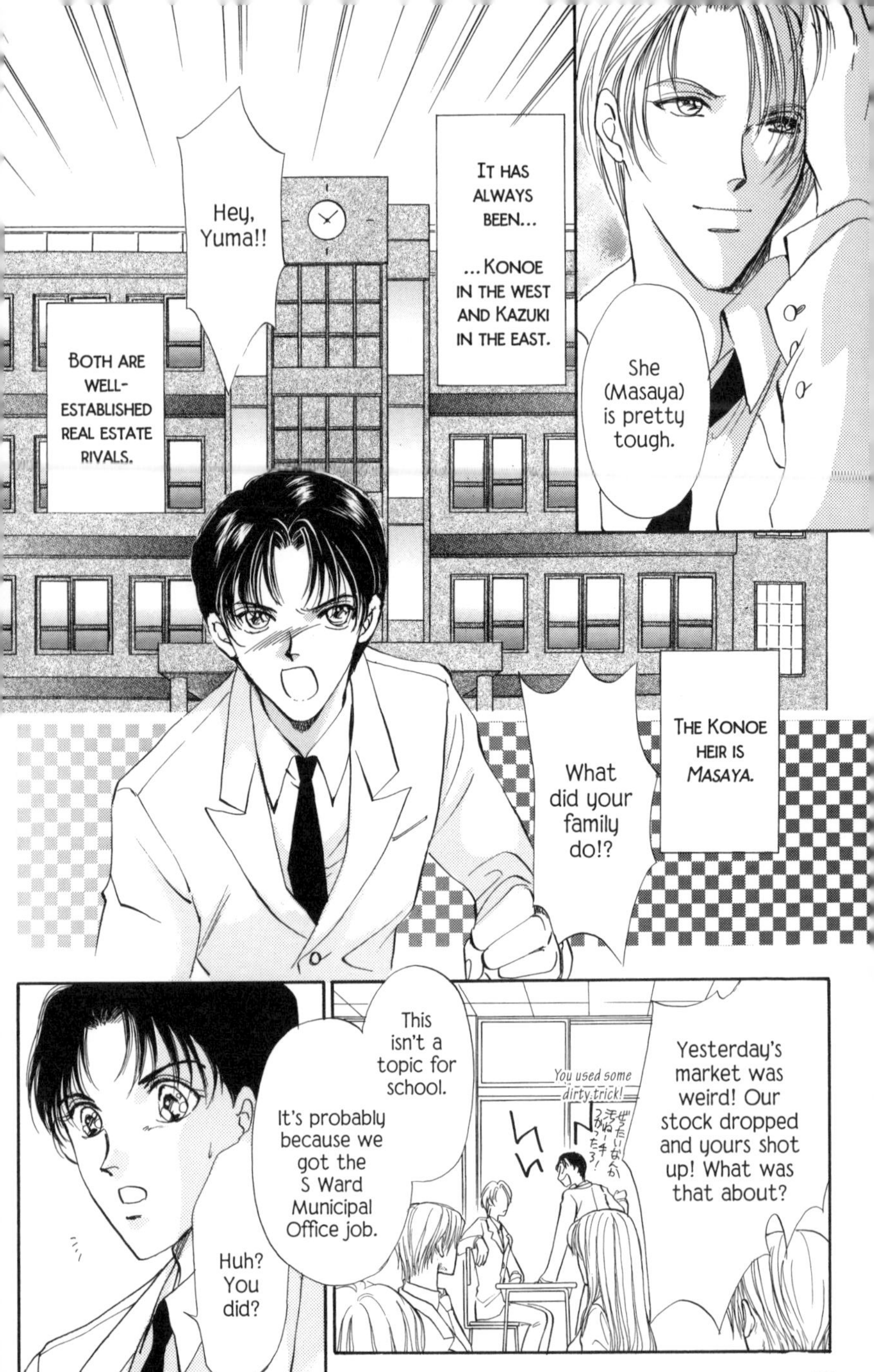
She (Masaya) is pretty tough.
It has always been...
...Konoe in the west and Kazuki in the east.
Hey, Yuma!!
Both are well-established real estate rivals.
The Konoe heir is Masaya.
What did your family do!?
Yesterday's market was weird! Our stock dropped and yours shot up! What was that about?
You used some dirty trick!
This isn't a topic for school.
It's probably because we got the S Ward Municipal Office job.
Huh? You did?

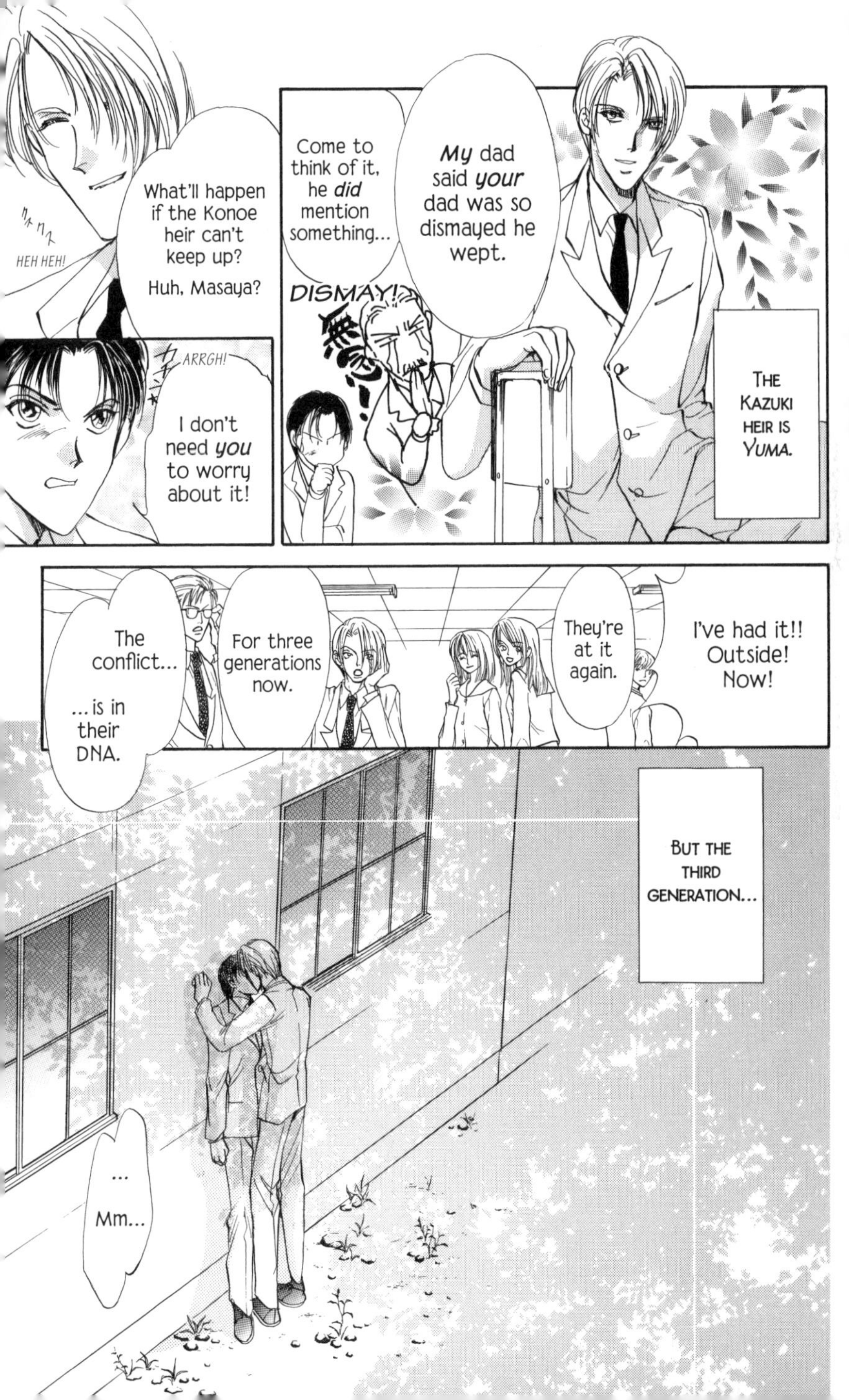
THE KAZUKI HEIR IS YUMA.
My dad said *your* dad was so dismayed he wept.
Come to think of it, he *did* mention something...
DISMAY!
What'll happen if the Konoe heir can't keep up? Huh, Masaya?
HEH HEH!
ARRGH!
I don't need *you* to worry about it!
I've had it!! Outside! Now!
They're at it again.
For three generations now.
The conflict... ...is in their DNA.
BUT THE THIRD GENERATION...
... Mm...

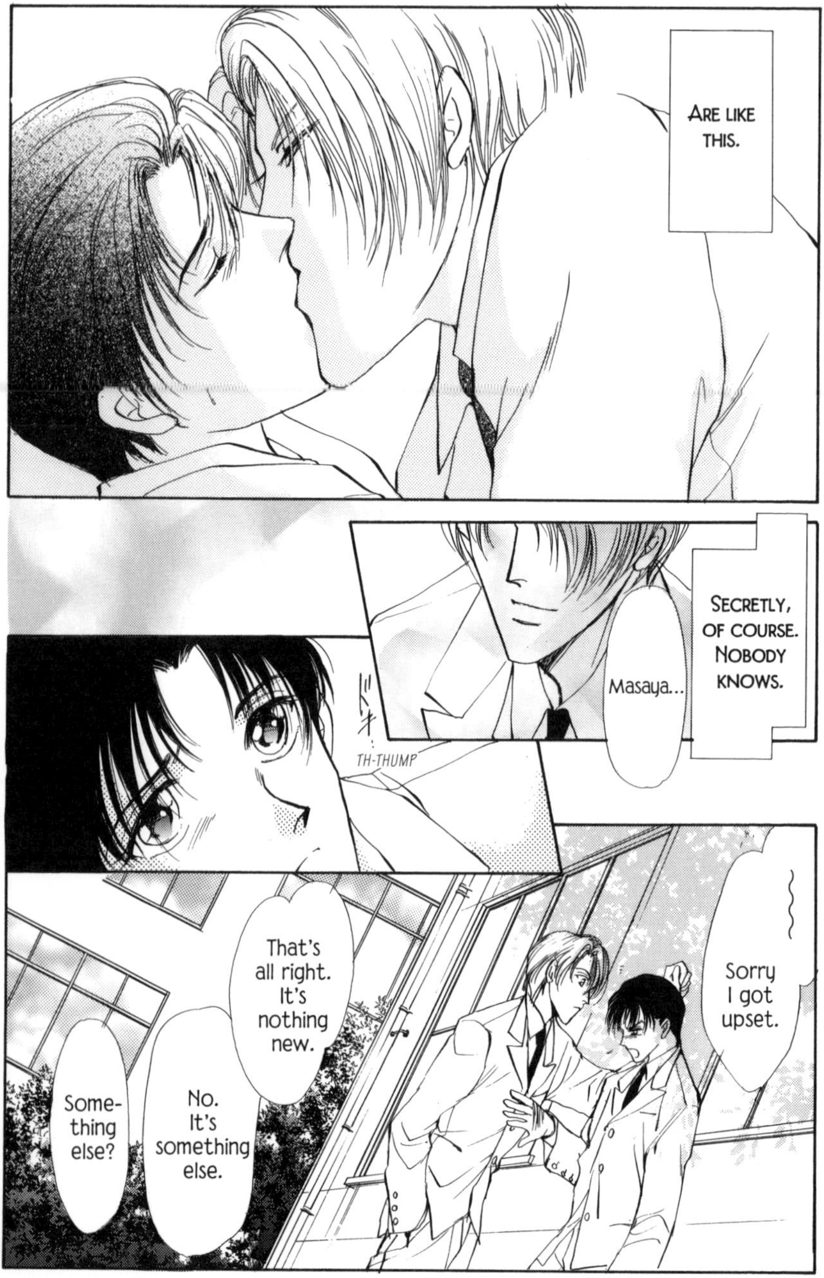
Are like this.
Secretly, of course. Nobody knows.
Masaya...
TH-THUMP
Sorry I got upset.
That's all right. It's nothing new.
No. It's something else.
Something else?

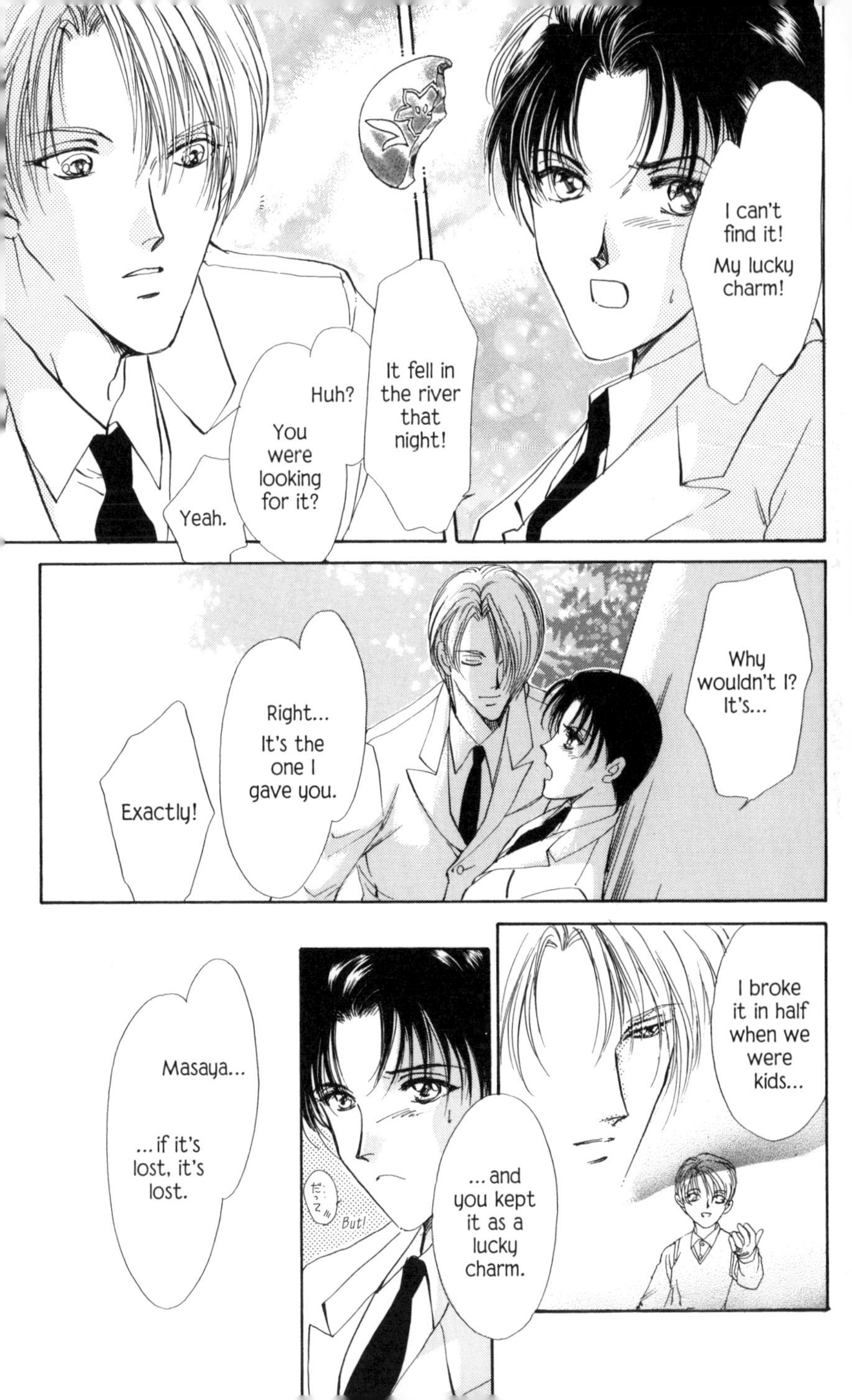
I can't find it! My lucky charm!
It fell in the river that night!
Huh? You were looking for it?
Yeah.
Why wouldn't I? It's...
Right... It's the one I gave you.
Exactly!
I broke it in half when we were kids...
...and you kept it as a lucky charm.
But!
Masaya...
...if it's lost, it's lost.

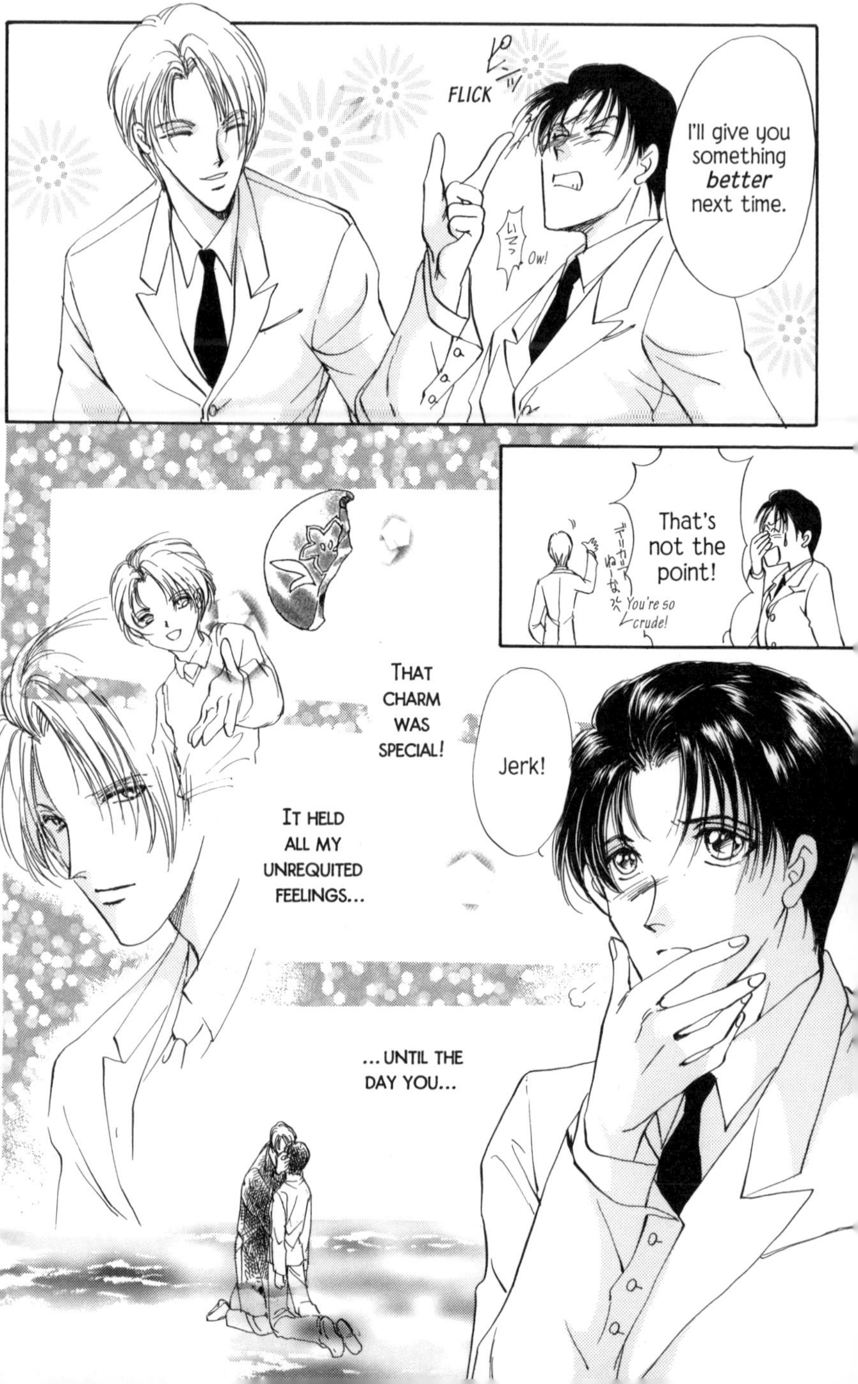
I'll give you something better next time.
FLICK
いてっ
Ow!
That's not the point!
You're so crude!
Jerk!
THAT CHARM WAS SPECIAL!
IT HELD ALL MY UNREQUITED FEELINGS...
...UNTIL THE DAY YOU...

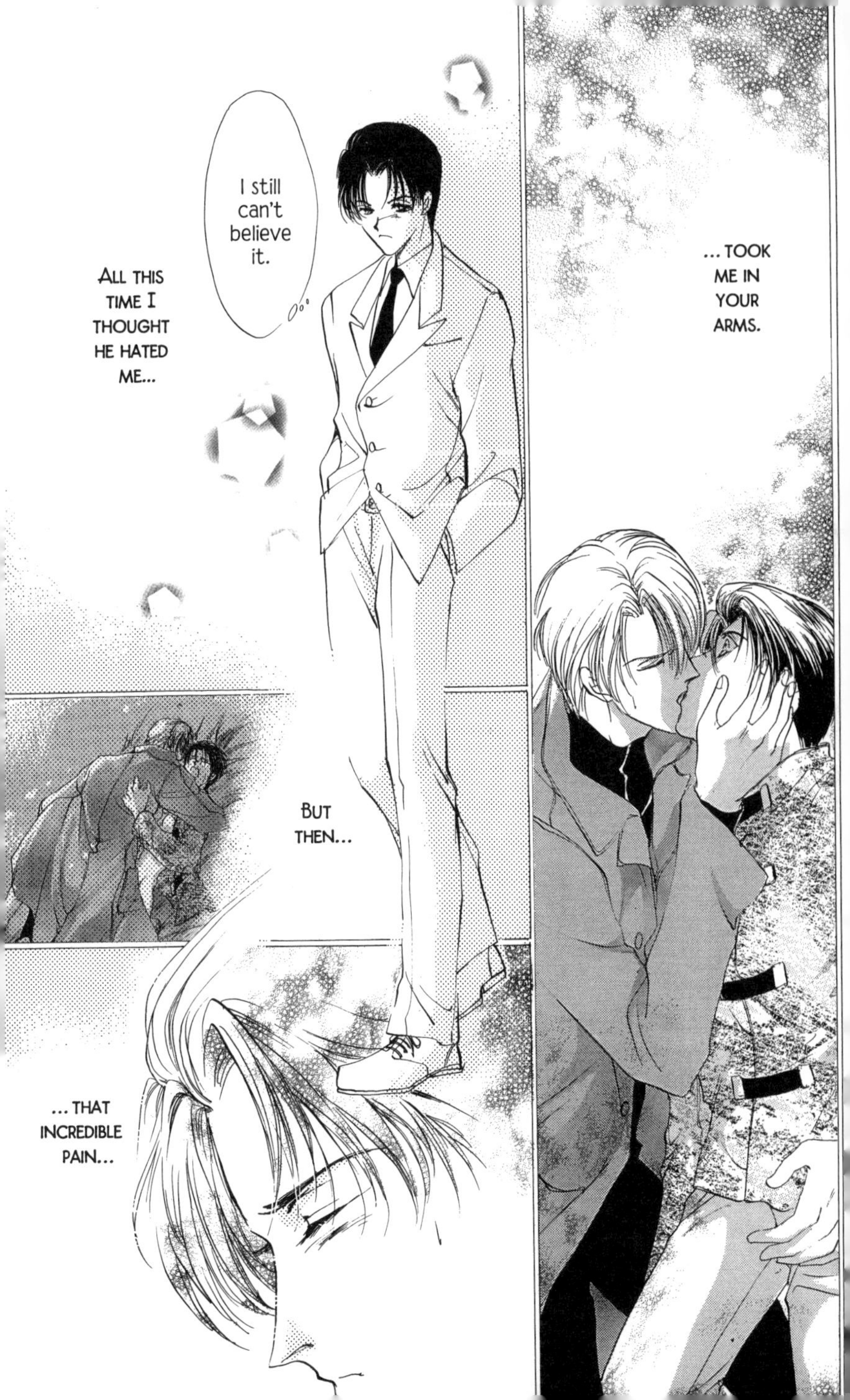
I still can't believe it.
ALL THIS TIME I THOUGHT HE HATED ME...
BUT THEN...
...THAT INCREDIBLE PAIN...
...TOOK ME IN YOUR ARMS.

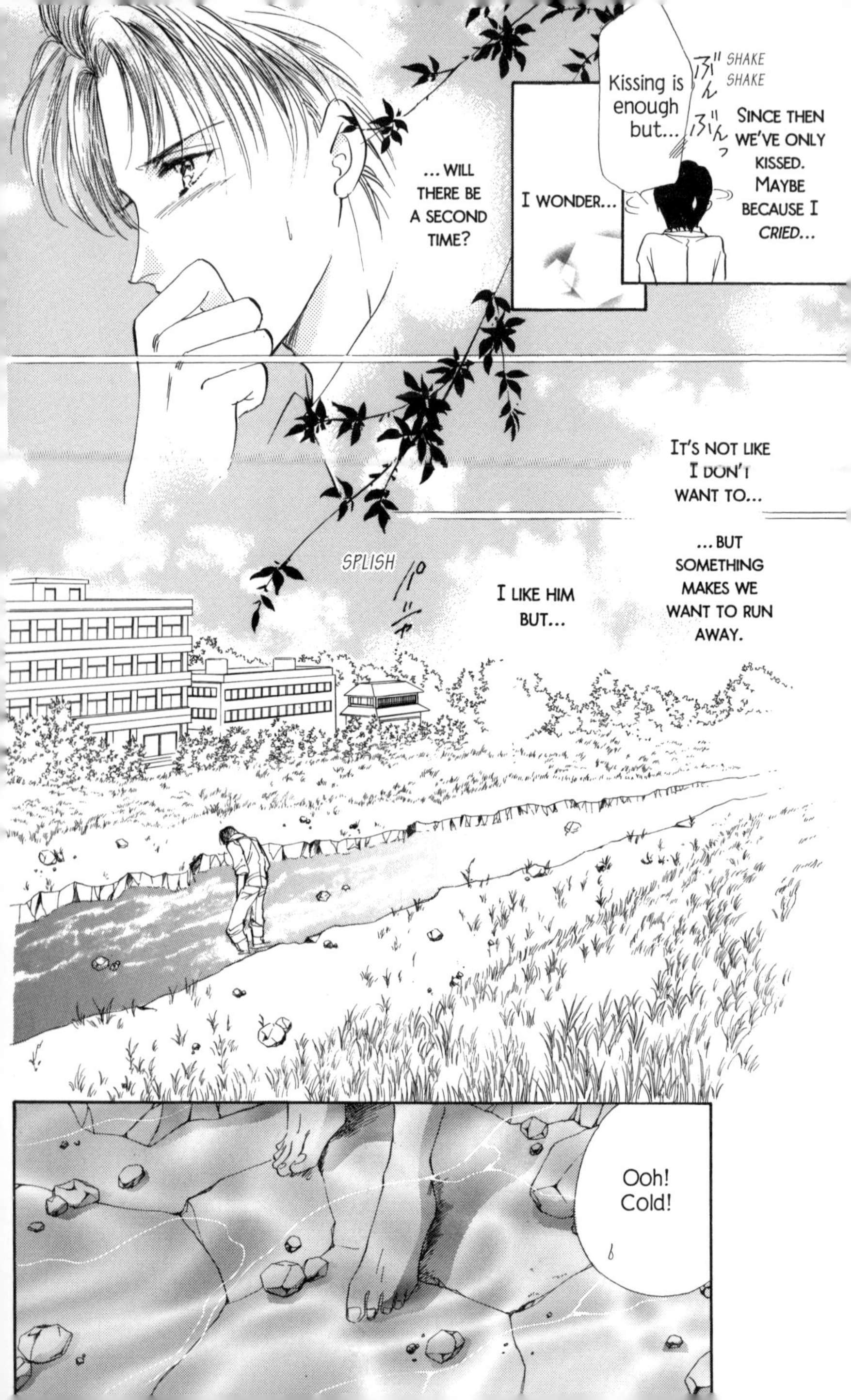
ぶんぶんっ
SHAKE SHAKE
Since then we've only kissed. Maybe because I *cried*...
Kissing is enough but...
I wonder...
...will there be a second time?
It's not like I don't want to...
...but something makes we want to run away.
I like him but...
パシャ
SPLISH
Ooh! Cold!

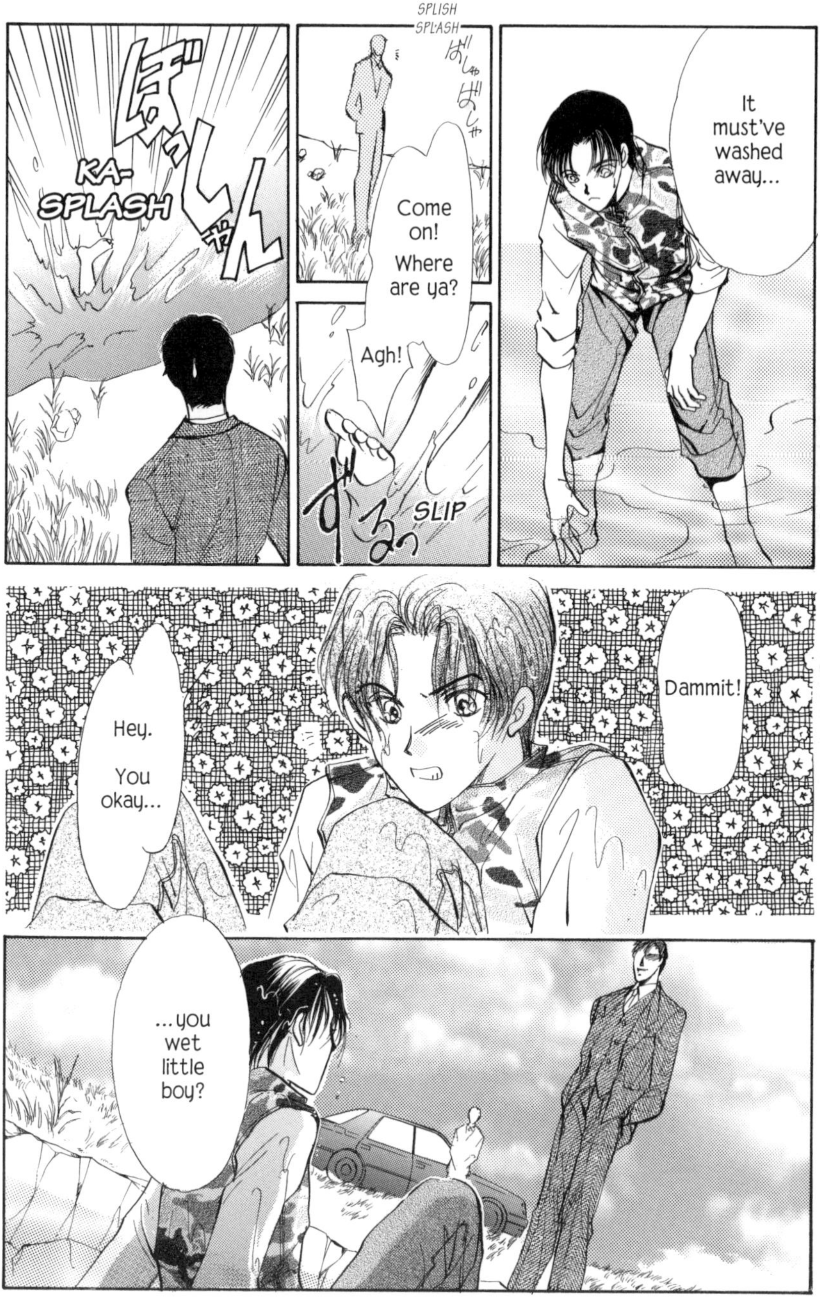
It must've washed away...
SPLISH SPLASH
ばしゃばしゃ
Come on! Where are ya?
Agh!
SLIP
ずるっ
KA-SPLASH
ぼっしゃん
Dammit!
Hey. You okay...
...you wet little boy?

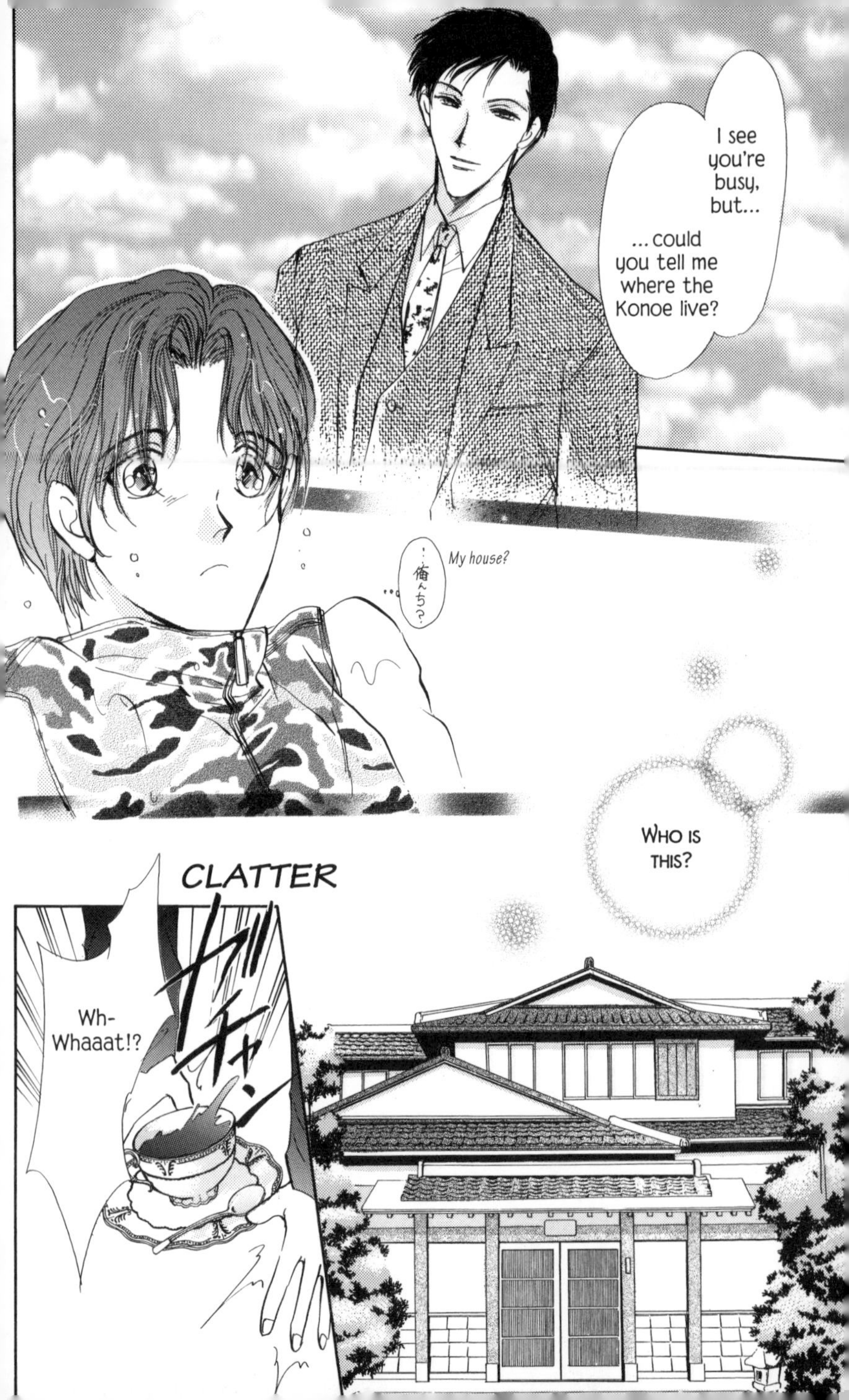
I see you're busy, but...
... could you tell me where the Konoe live?
…俺んち？
My house?
WHO IS THIS?
CLATTER
Wh- Whaaat!?

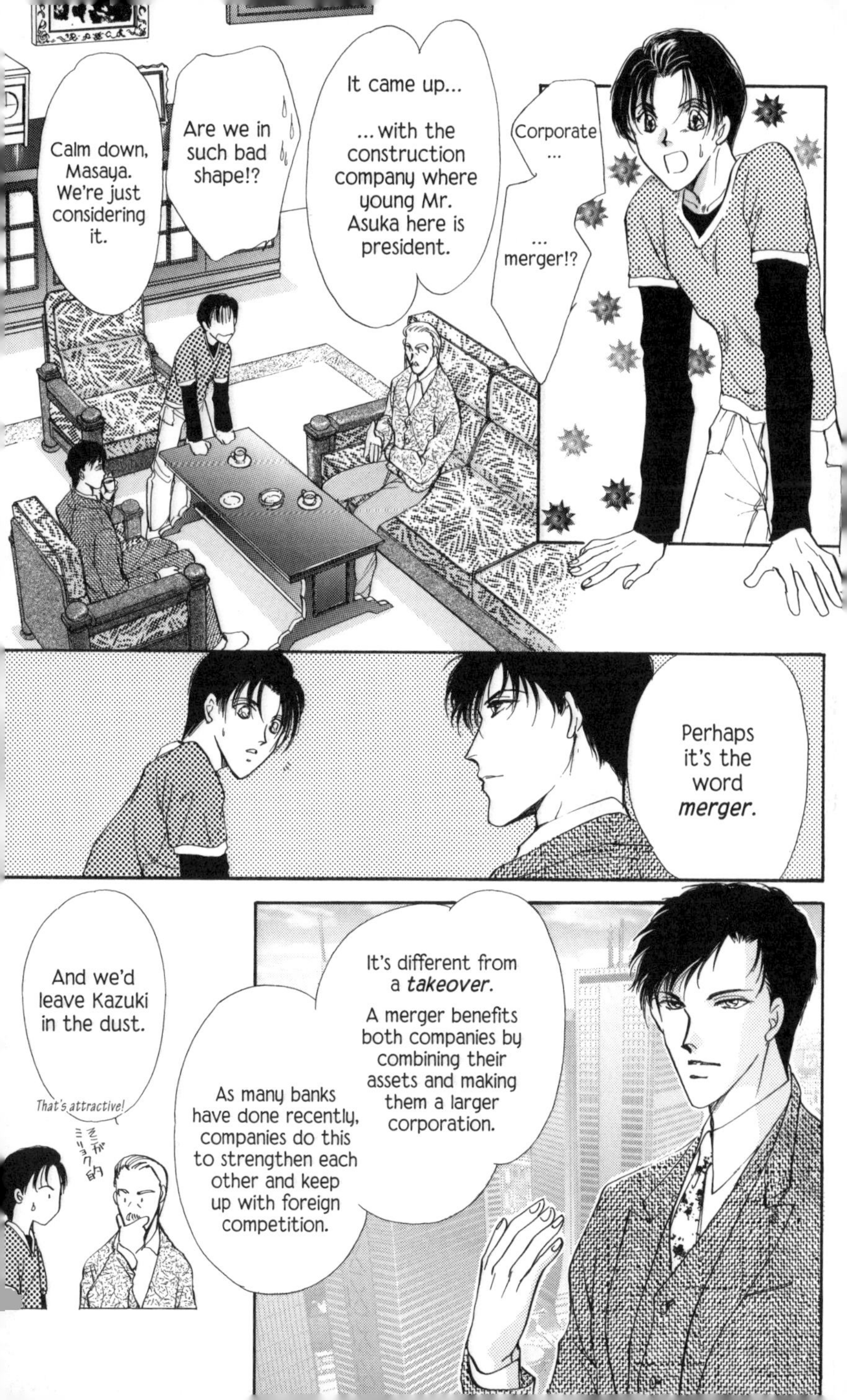
Corporate ... ... merger!?
It came up... ...with the construction company where young Mr. Asuka here is president.
Are we in such bad shape!?
Calm down, Masaya. We're just considering it.
Perhaps it's the word *merger*.
It's different from a *takeover*. A merger benefits both companies by combining their assets and making them a larger corporation.
As many banks have done recently, companies do this to strengthen each other and keep up with foreign competition.
And we'd leave Kazuki in the dust.
That's attractive!

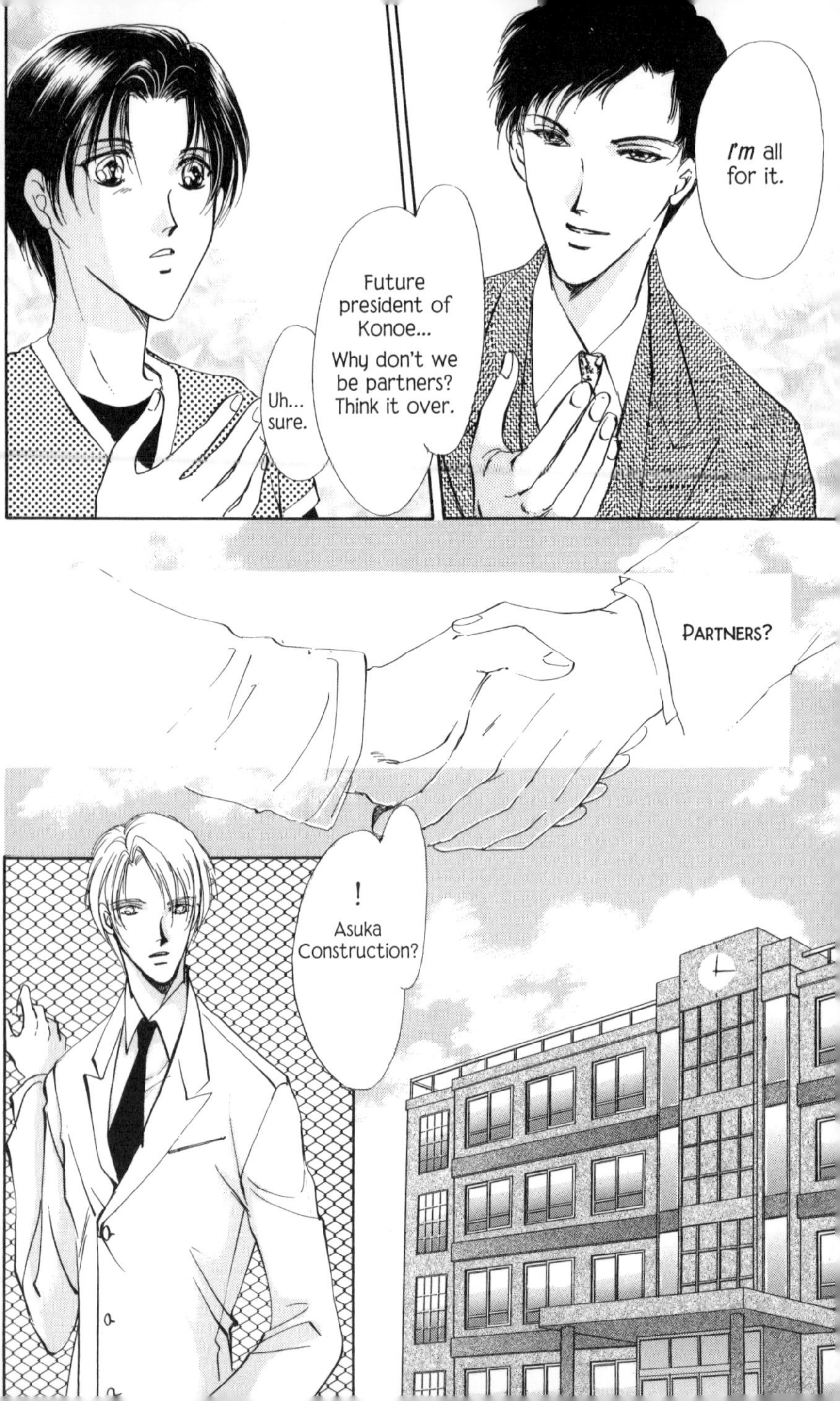
I'm all for it.
Future president of Konoe... Why don't we be partners? Think it over.
Uh... sure.
Partners?
! Asuka Construction?

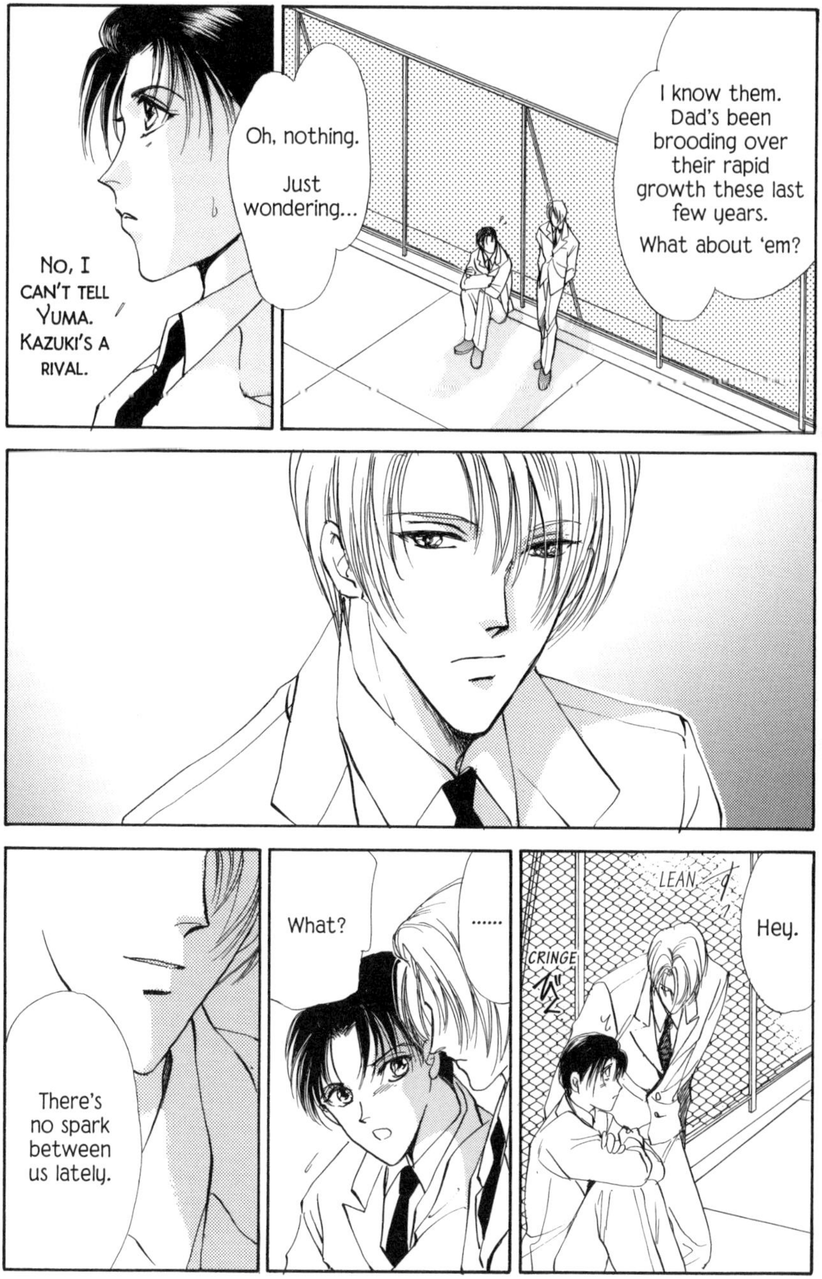
I know them. Dad's been brooding over their rapid growth these last few years.
What about 'em?
Oh, nothing.
Just wondering...
No, I can't tell Yuma. Kazuki's a rival.
LEAN
Hey.
CRINGE
......
What?
There's no spark between us lately.

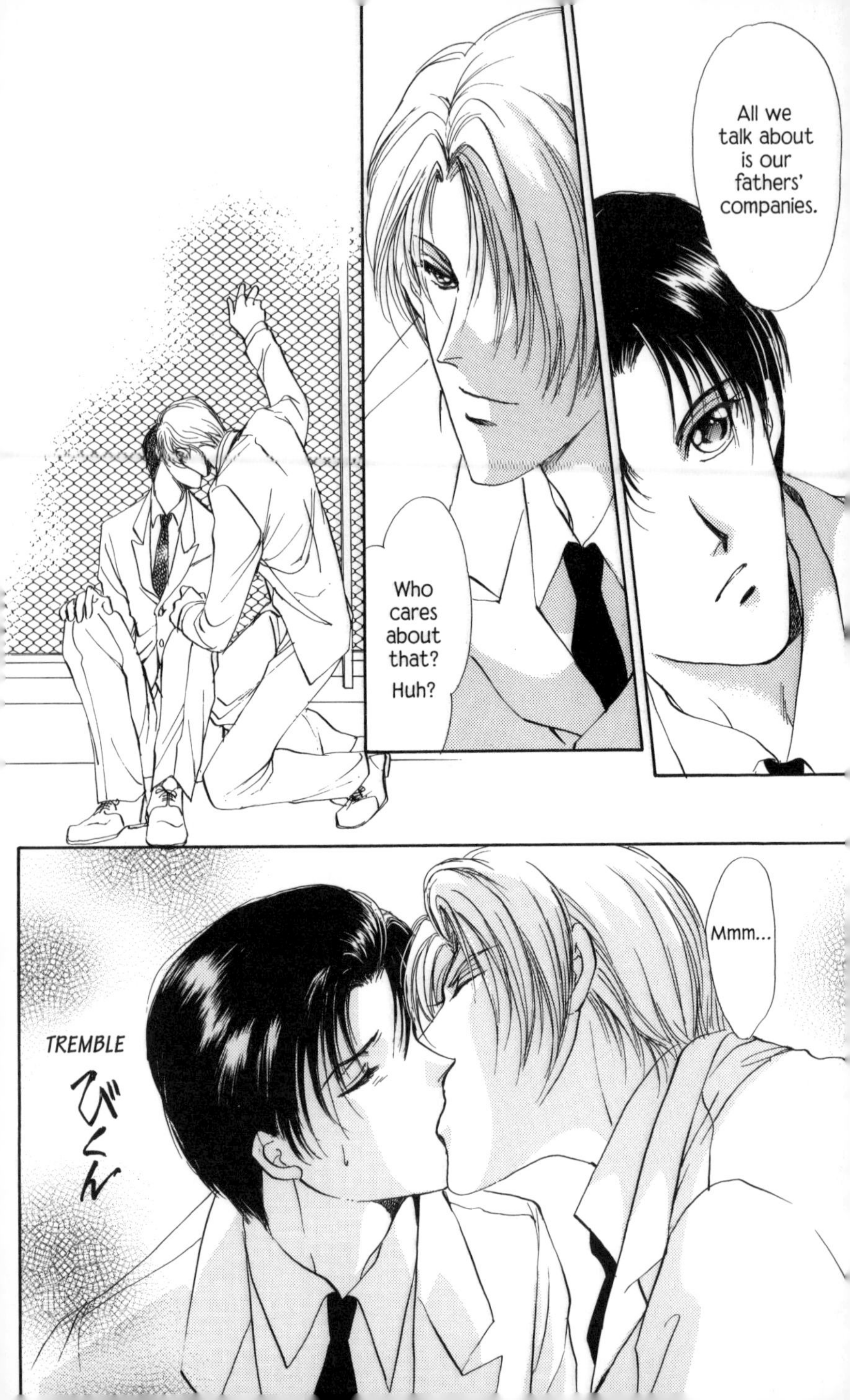

All we talk about is our fathers' companies.
Who cares about that?
Huh?
Mmm...
TREMBLE
びくん

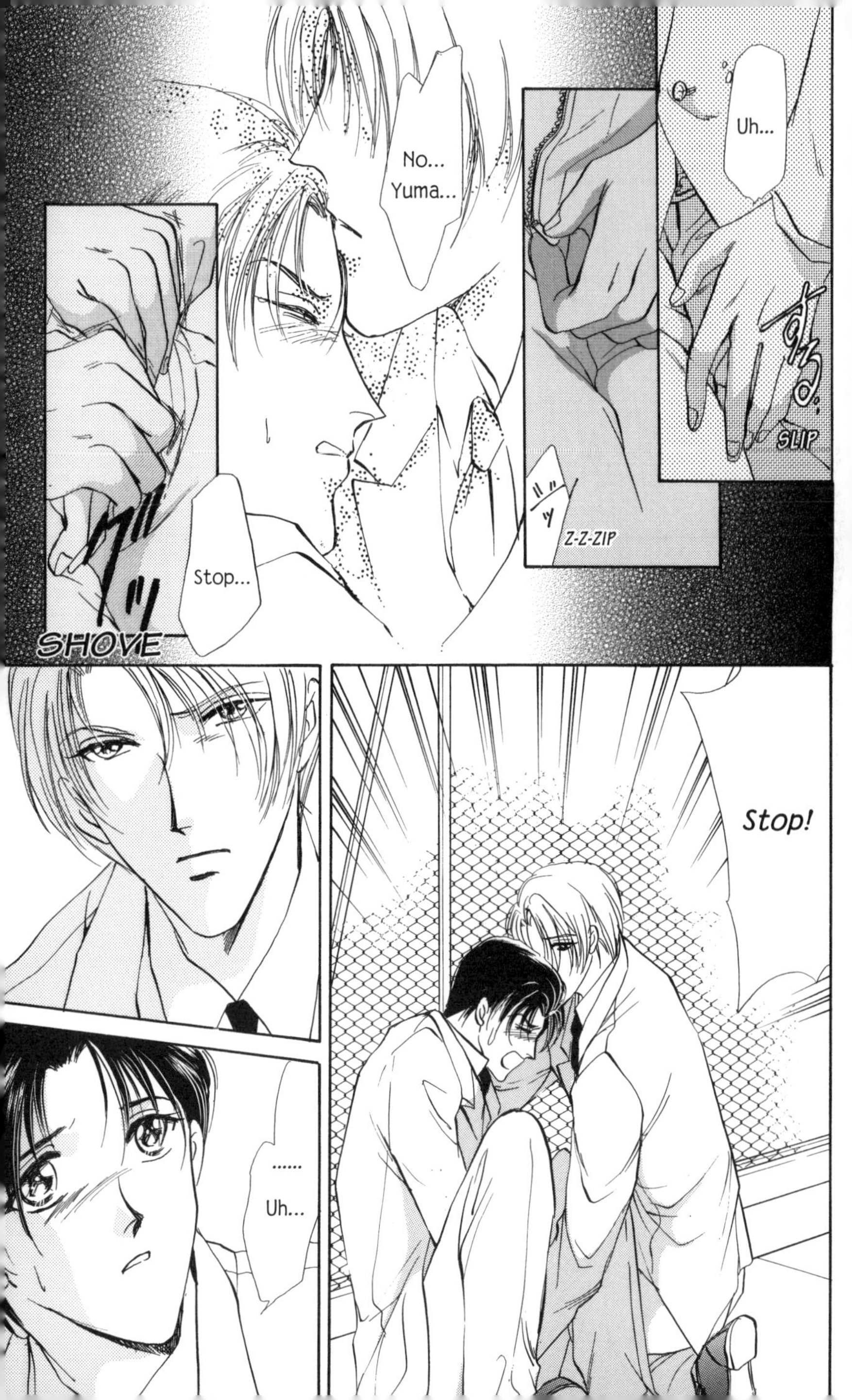

Uh...
SLIP
Z-Z-ZIP
No... Yuma...
Stop...
SHOVE
Stop!
......
Uh...

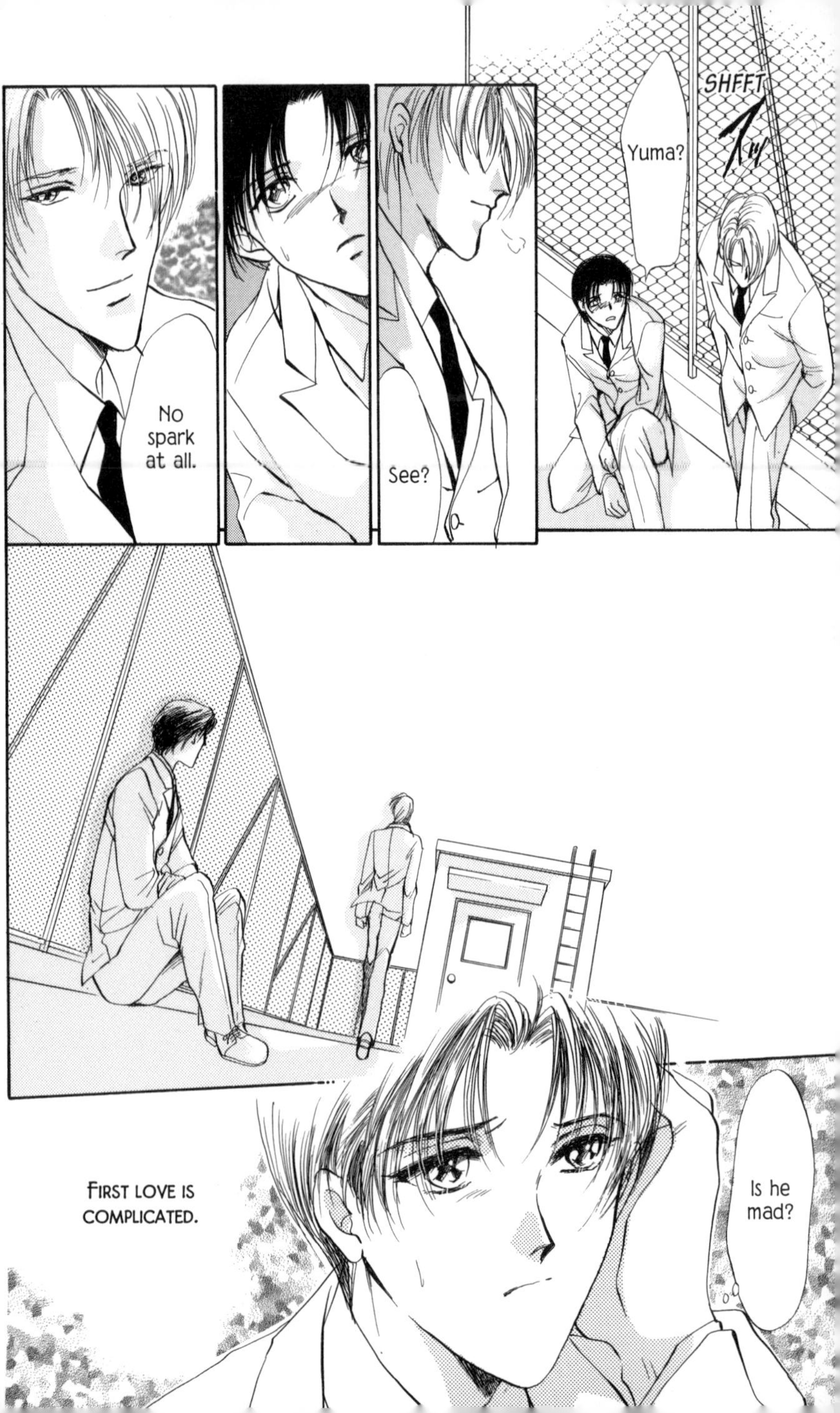
SHFFT
Yuma?
See?
No spark at all.
Is he mad?
First love is complicated.

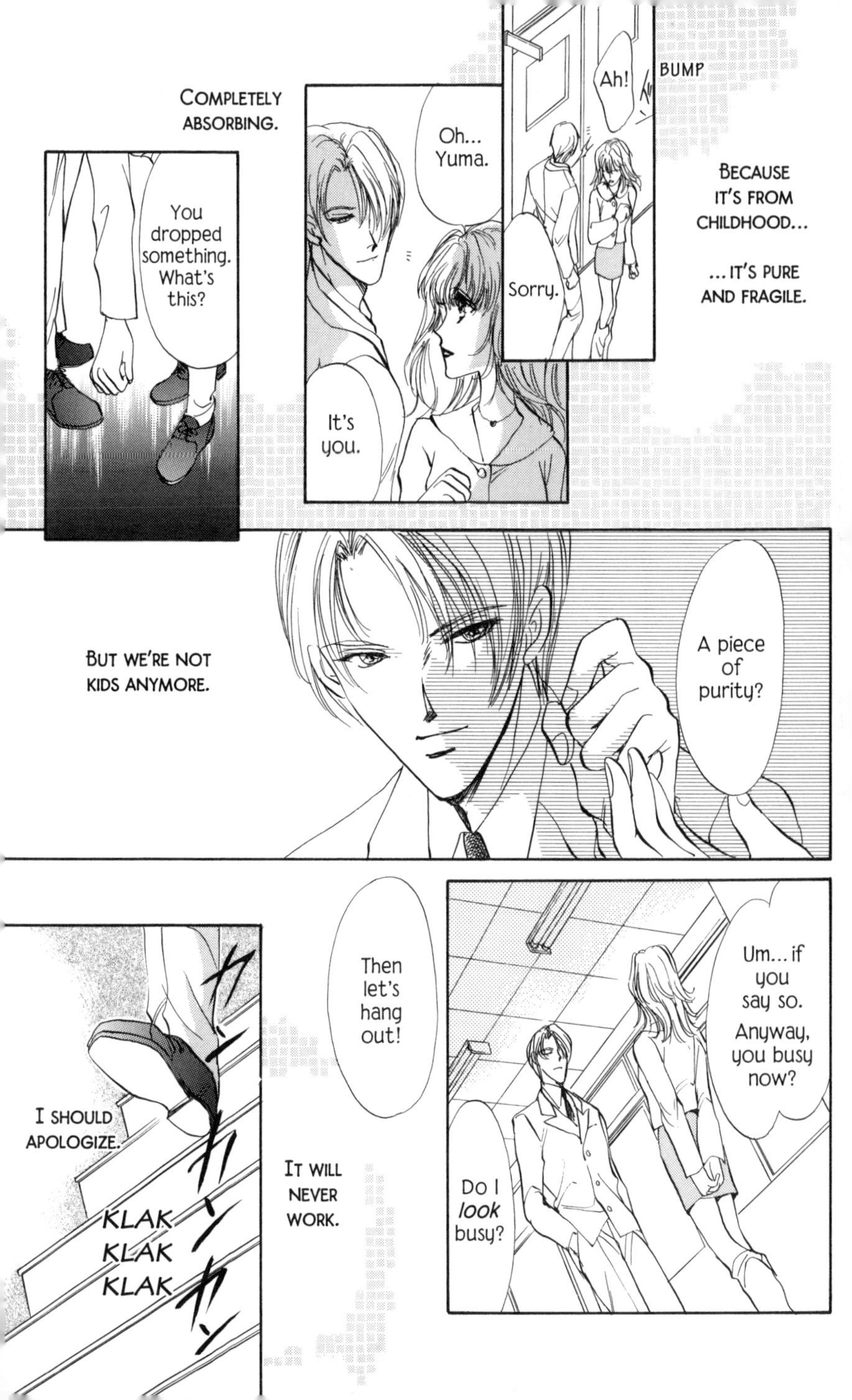

BECAUSE IT'S FROM CHILDHOOD...
...IT'S PURE AND FRAGILE.
BUMP
Ah!
Sorry.
Oh... Yuma.
It's you.
COMPLETELY ABSORBING.
You dropped something. What's this?
A piece of purity?
BUT WE'RE NOT KIDS ANYMORE.
Um... if you say so. Anyway, you busy now?
Do I *look* busy?
Then let's hang out!
IT WILL NEVER WORK.
I SHOULD APOLOGIZE.
KLAK
KLAK
KLAK

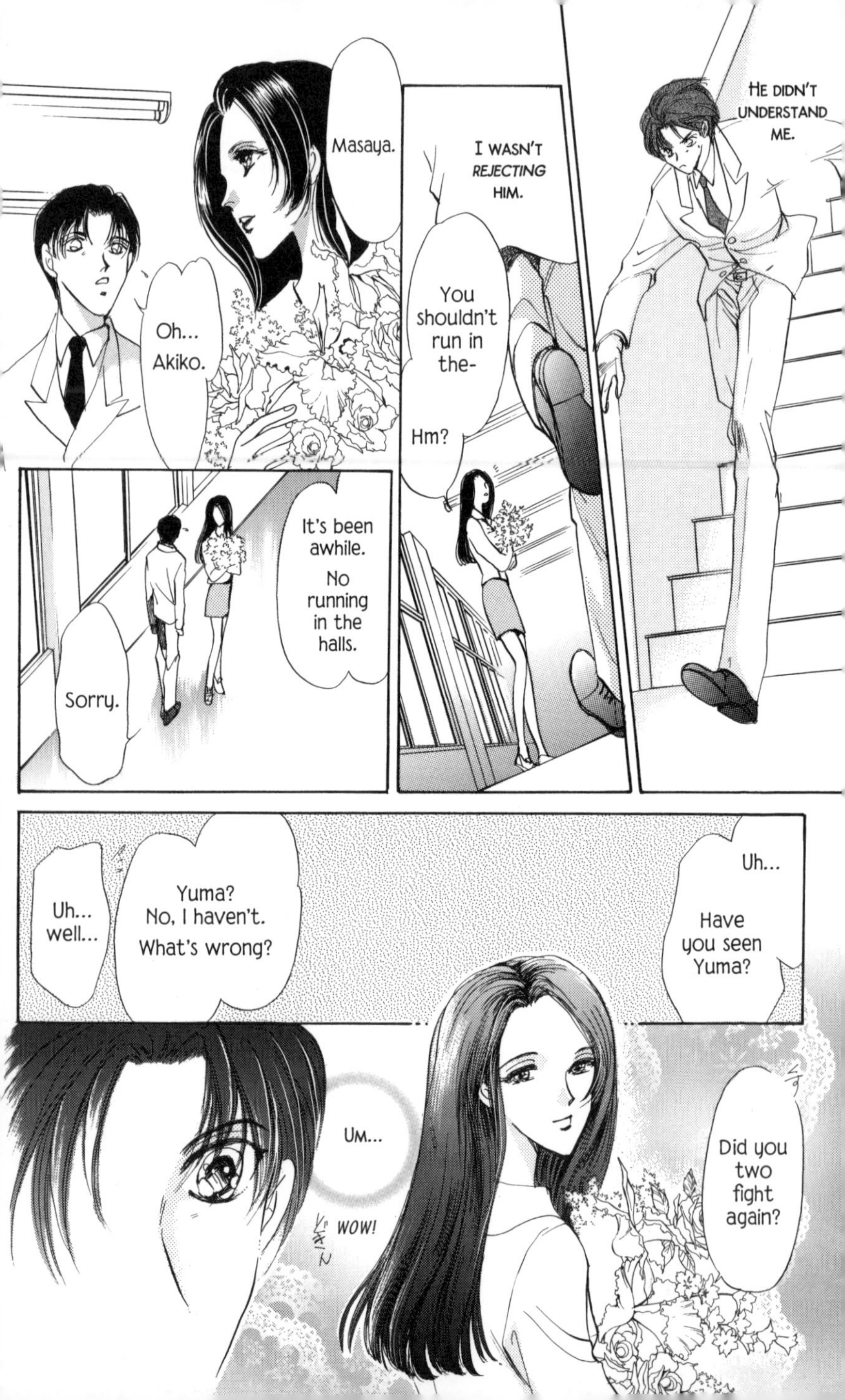
HE DIDN'T UNDERSTAND ME.
I WASN'T *REJECTING* HIM.
You shouldn't run in the-
Hm?
Masaya.
Oh... Akiko.
It's been awhile.
No running in the halls.
Sorry.
Uh...
Have you seen Yuma?
Yuma? No, I haven't. What's wrong?
Uh... well...
Did you two fight again?
UM...
WOW!

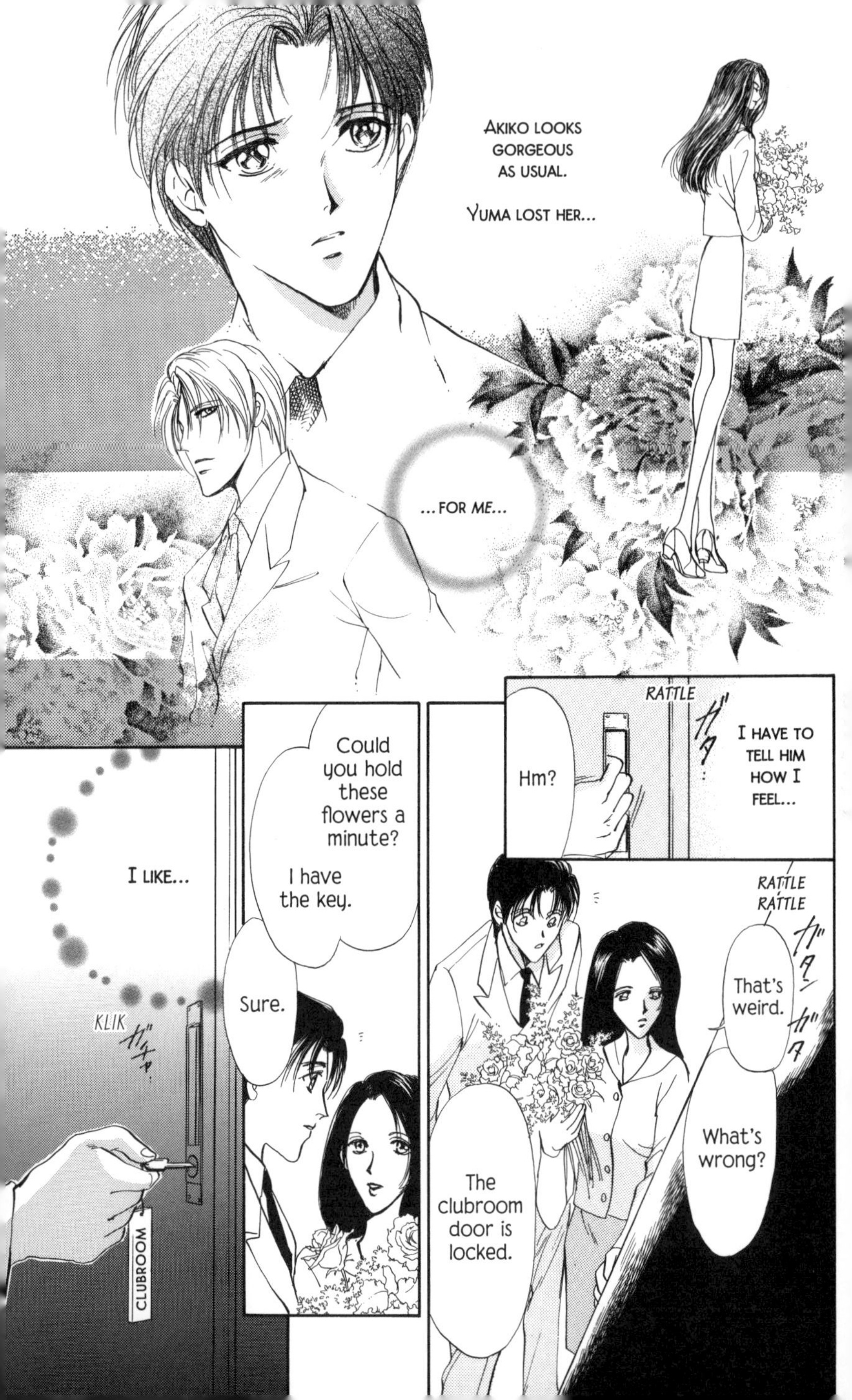

Akiko looks gorgeous as usual.
Yuma lost her...
...for me...
RATTLE
ガタ
I have to tell him how I feel...
Hm?
RATTLE RATTLE
ガタンガタ
That's weird.
What's wrong?
The clubroom door is locked.
Could you hold these flowers a minute?
I have the key.
Sure.
I like...
KLIK
ガチャ
CLUBROOM

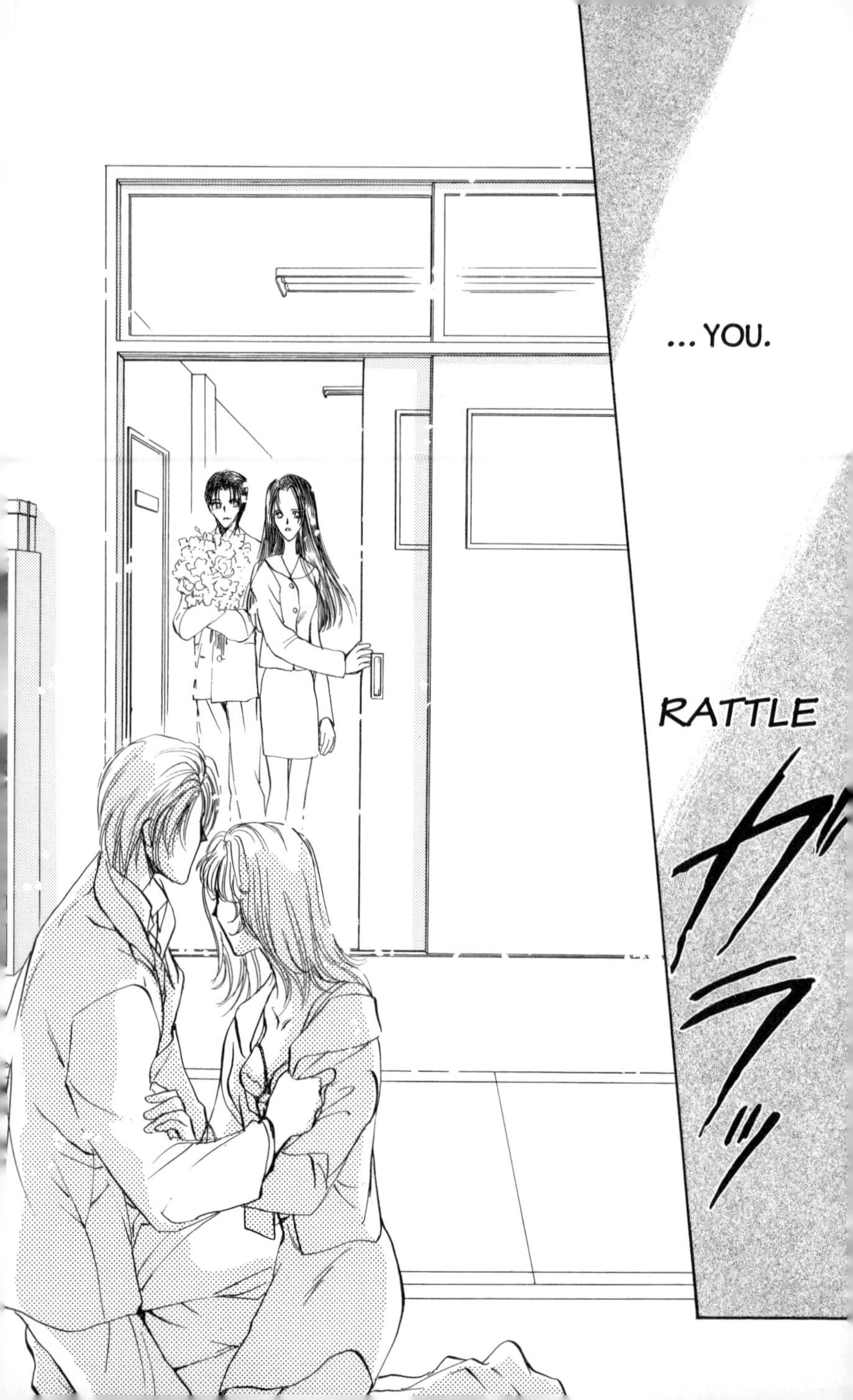
...YOU.
RATTLE
ガラッ

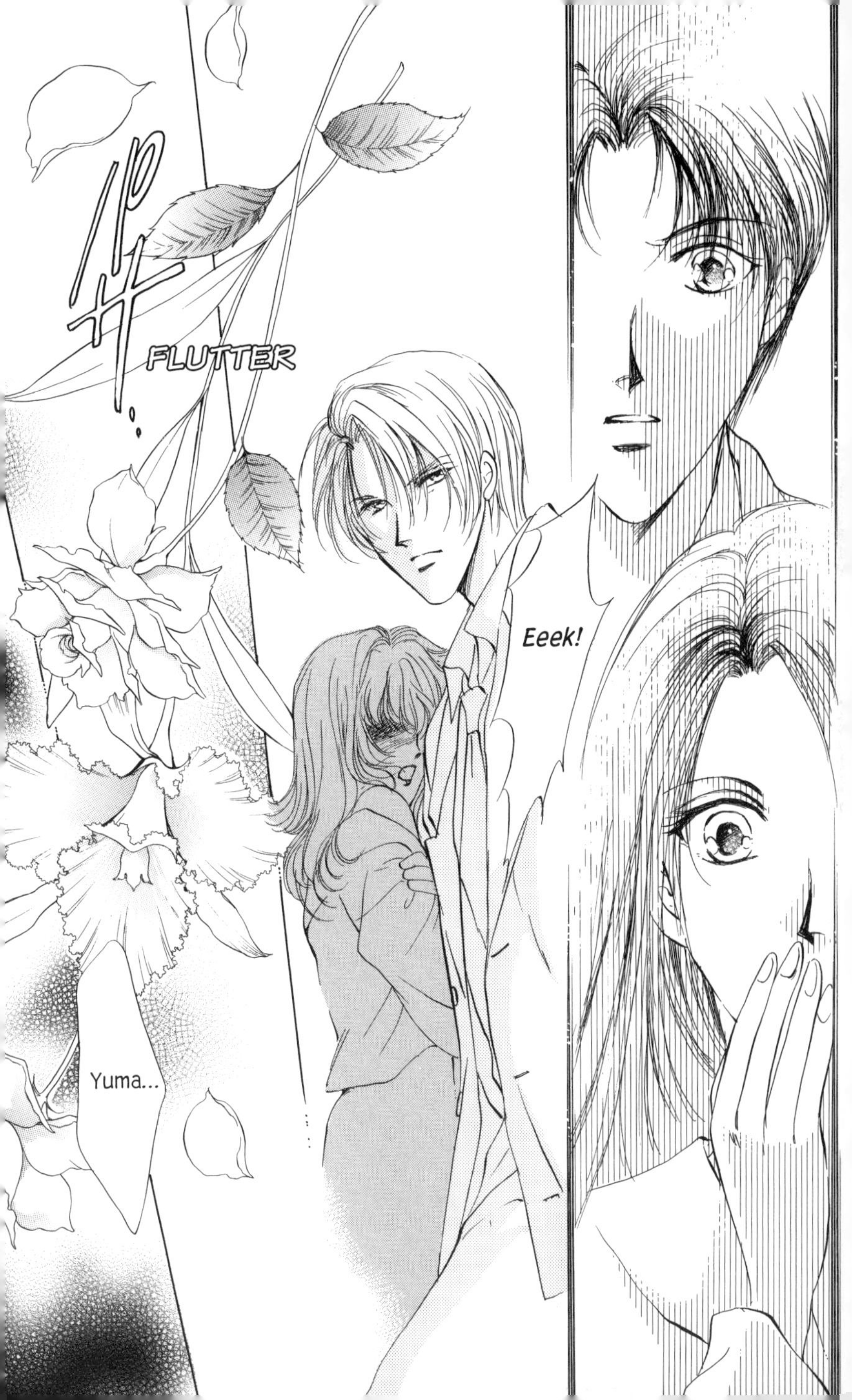
FLUTTER
Eeek!
Yuma...

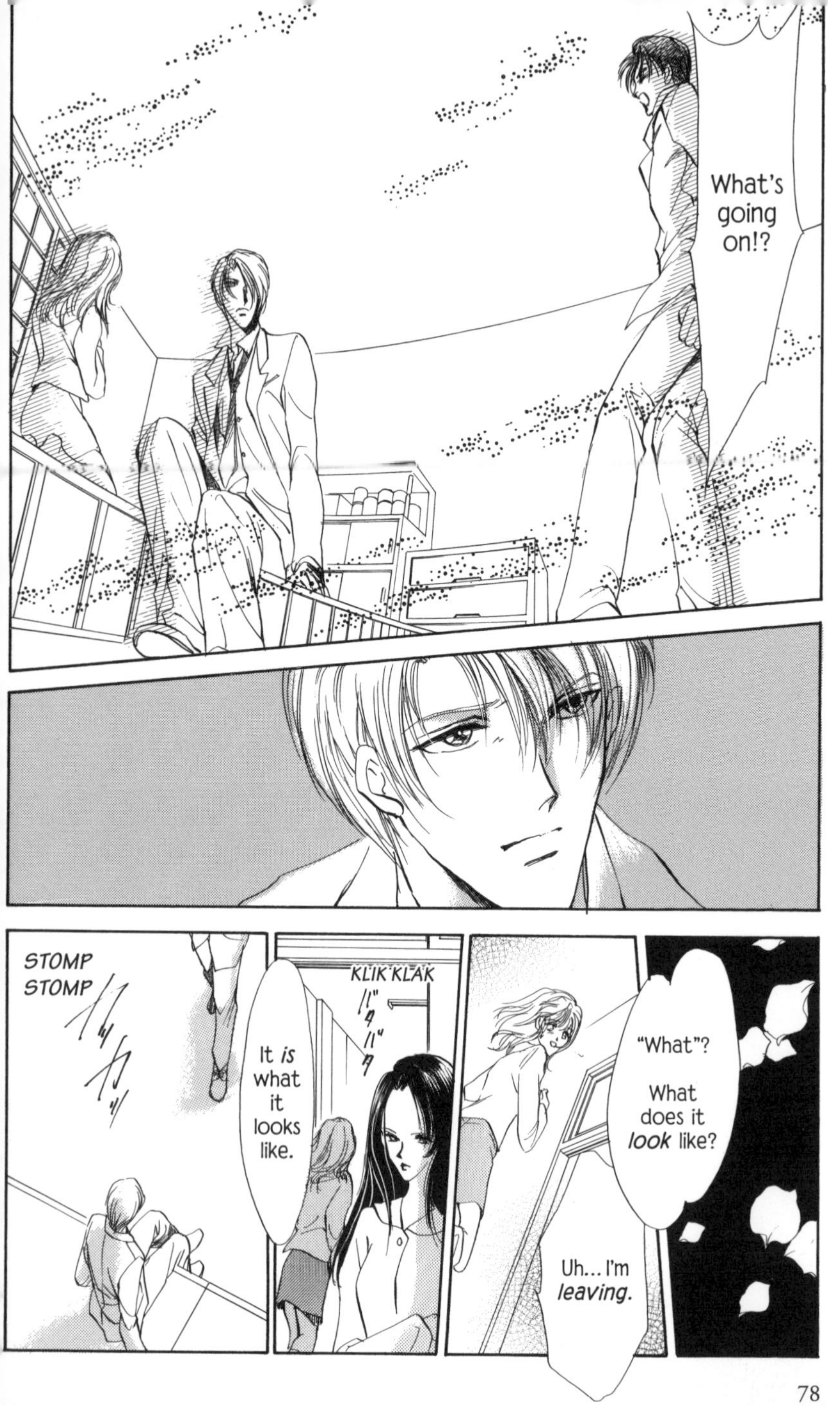
What's going on!?
"What"? What does it *look* like?
Uh... I'm *leaving.*
KLIK KLAK
It *is* what it looks like.
STOMP STOMP

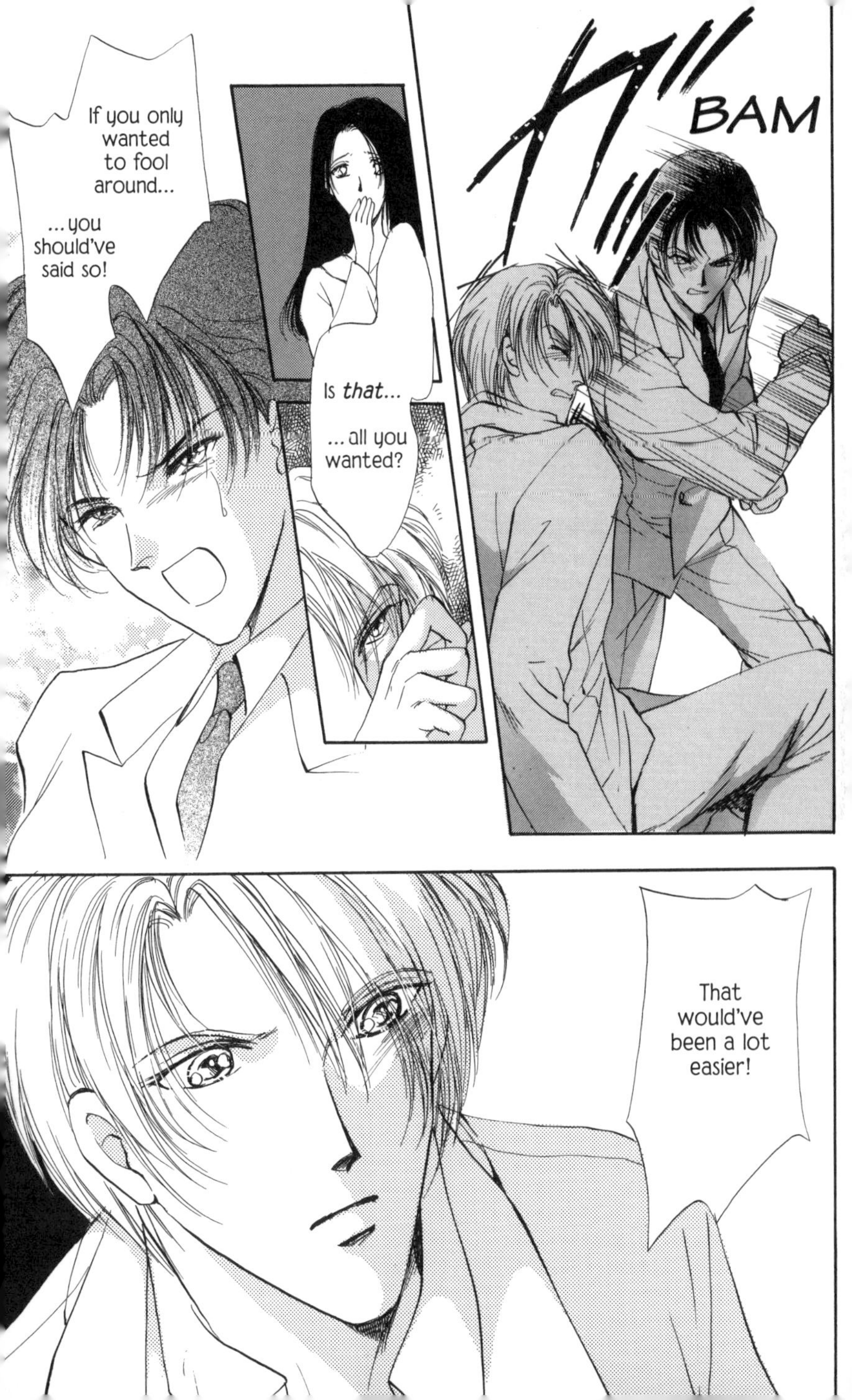
BAM
Is *that*...
...all you wanted?
If you only wanted to fool around...
...you should've said so!
That would've been a lot easier!

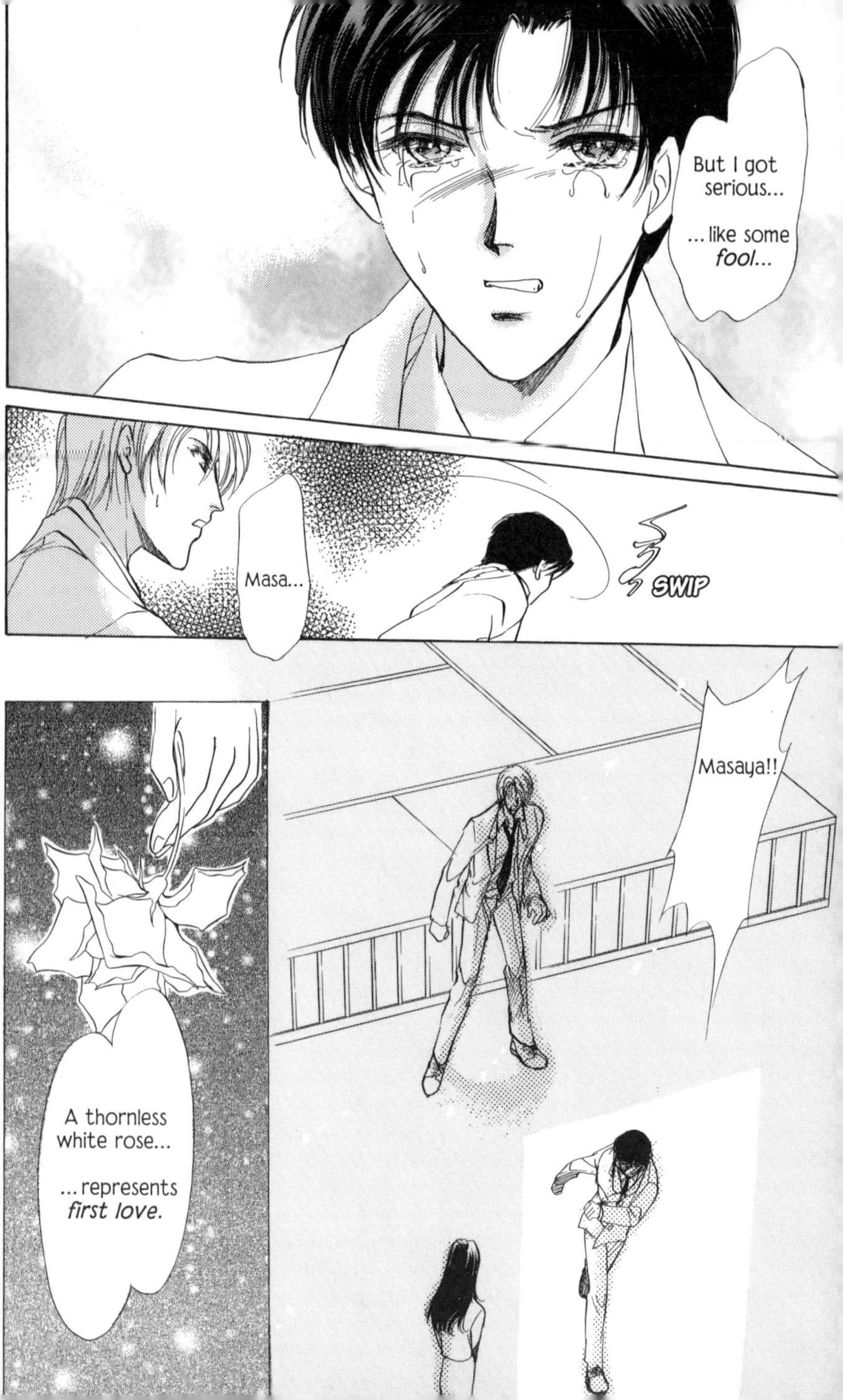
But I got serious...
...like some fool...
SWIP
Masa...
Masaya!!
A thornless white rose...
...represents first love.

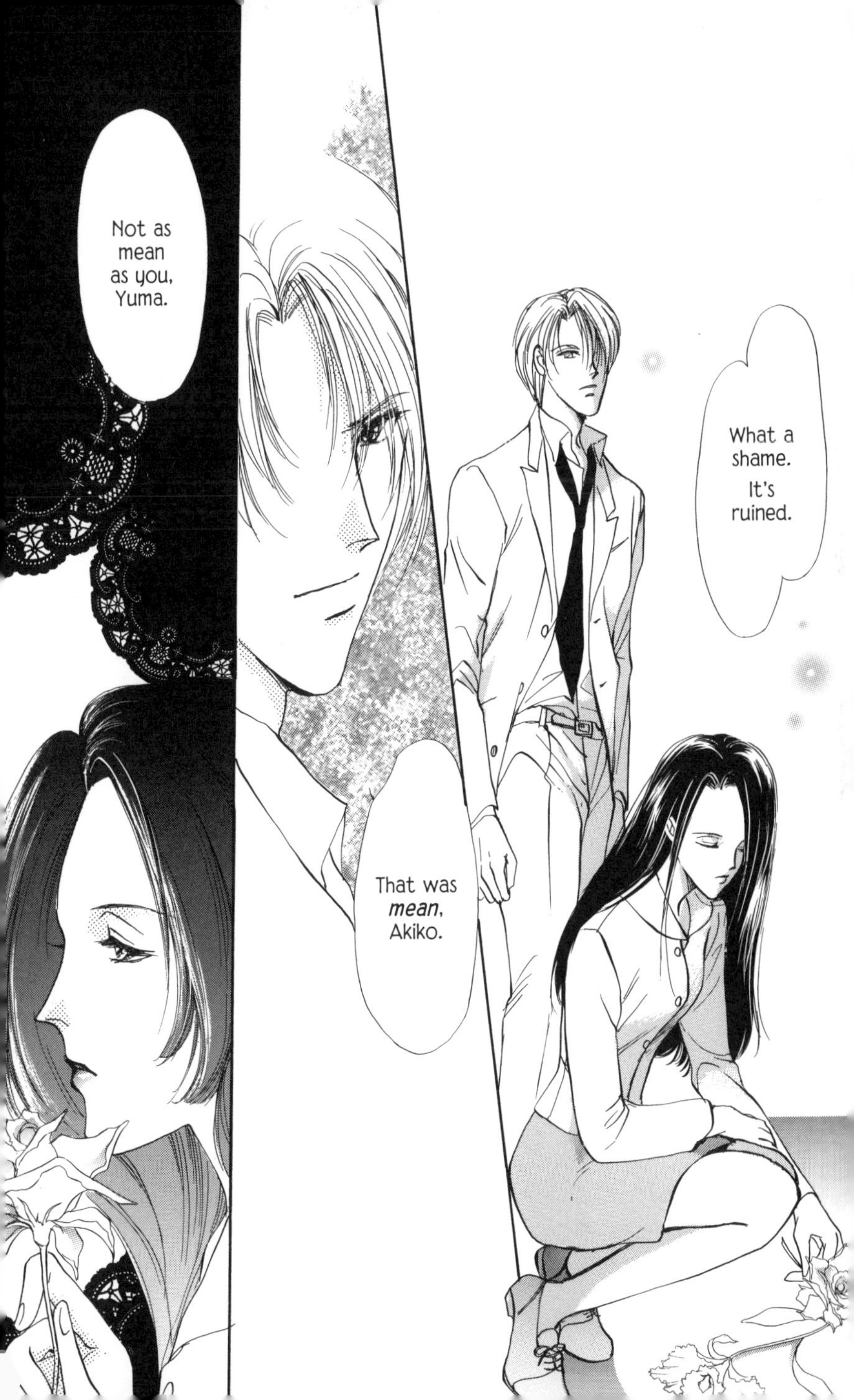

What a shame. It's ruined.
That was *mean*, Akiko.
Not as mean as you, Yuma.

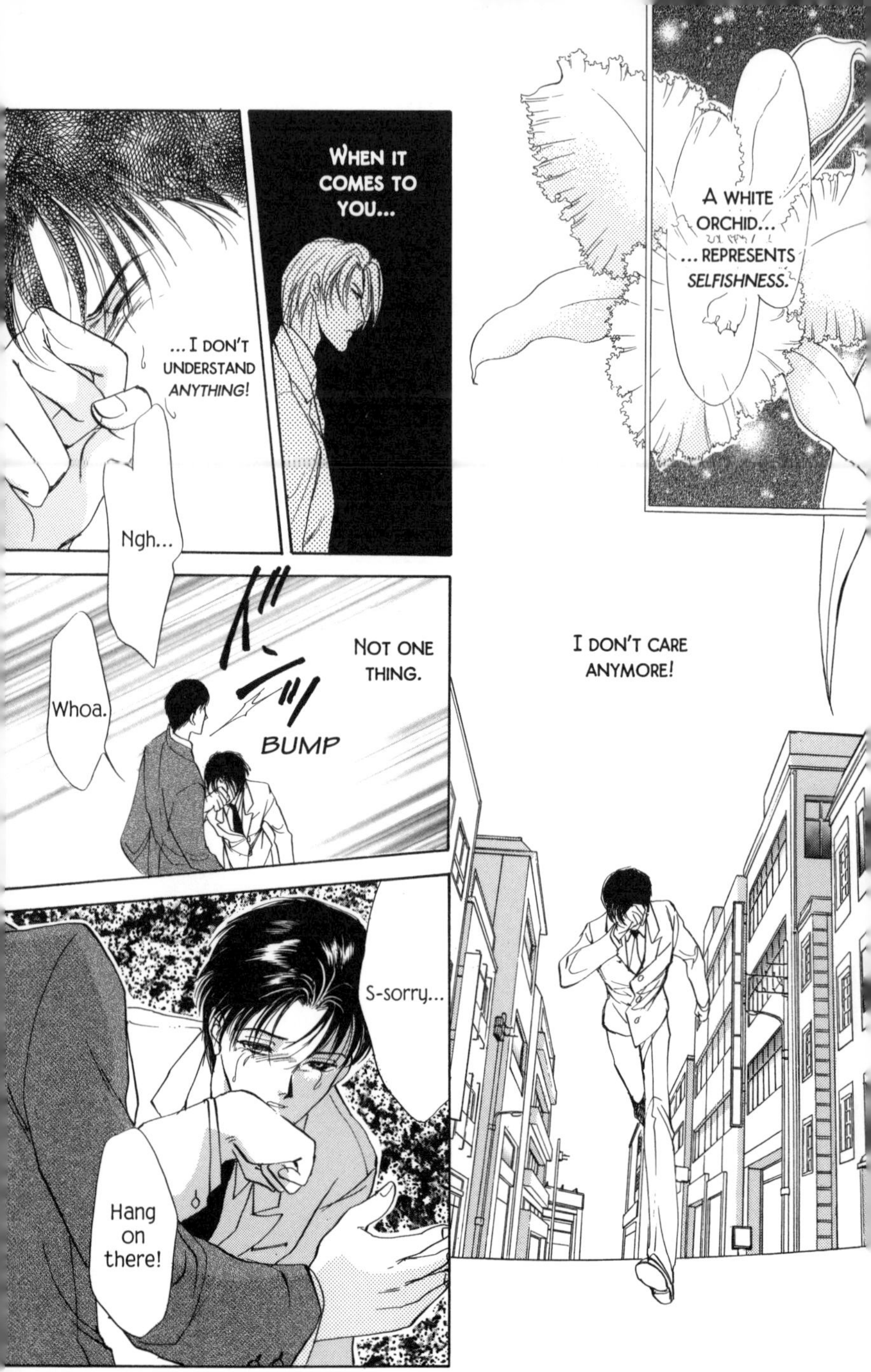
A WHITE ORCHID...
... REPRESENTS SELFISHNESS.
I DON'T CARE ANYMORE!
WHEN IT COMES TO YOU...
...I DON'T UNDERSTAND ANYTHING!
Ngh...
NOT ONE THING.
BUMP
Whoa.
S-sorry...
Hang on there!

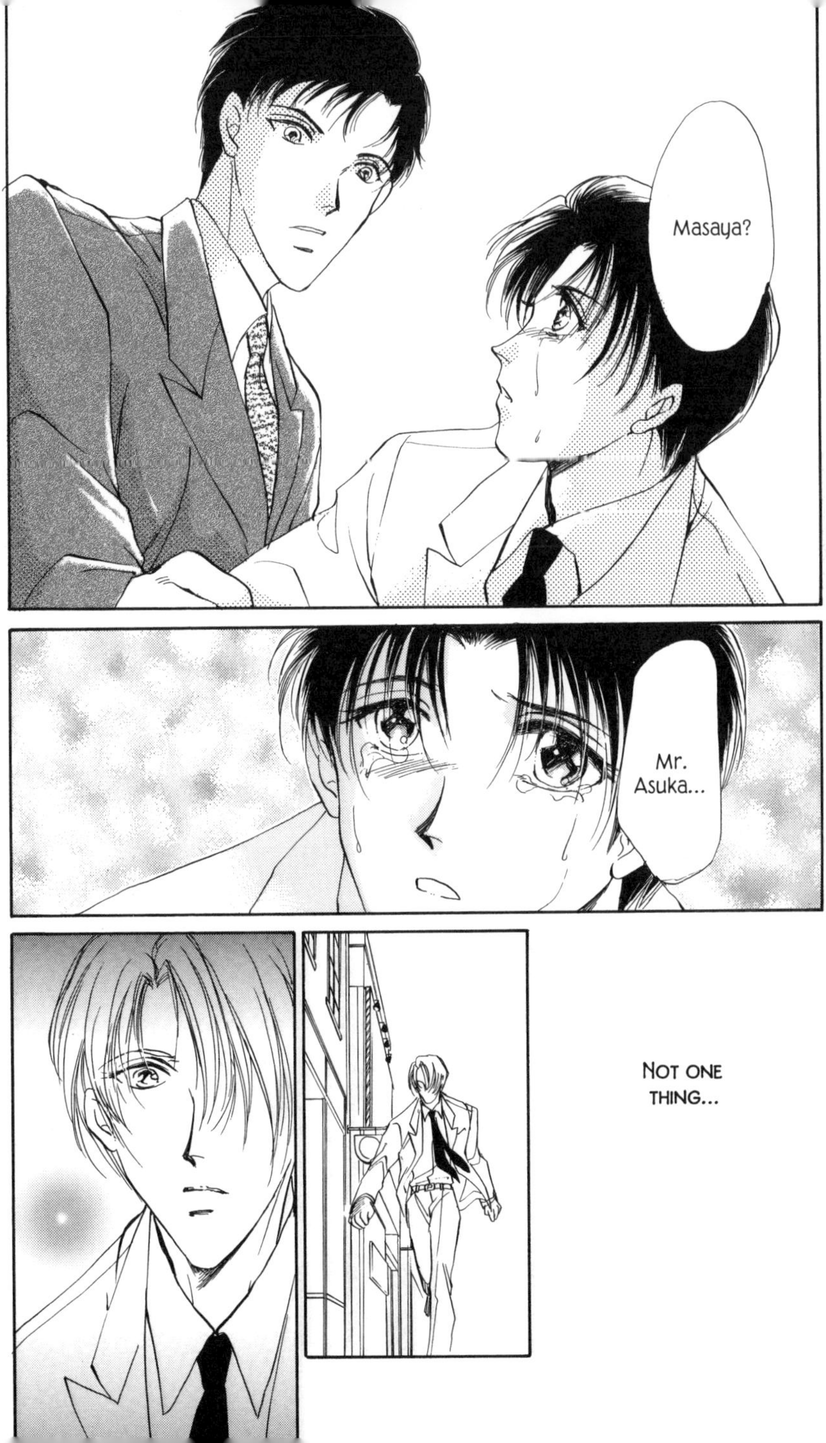
Masaya?
Mr. Asuka...
NOT ONE THING...

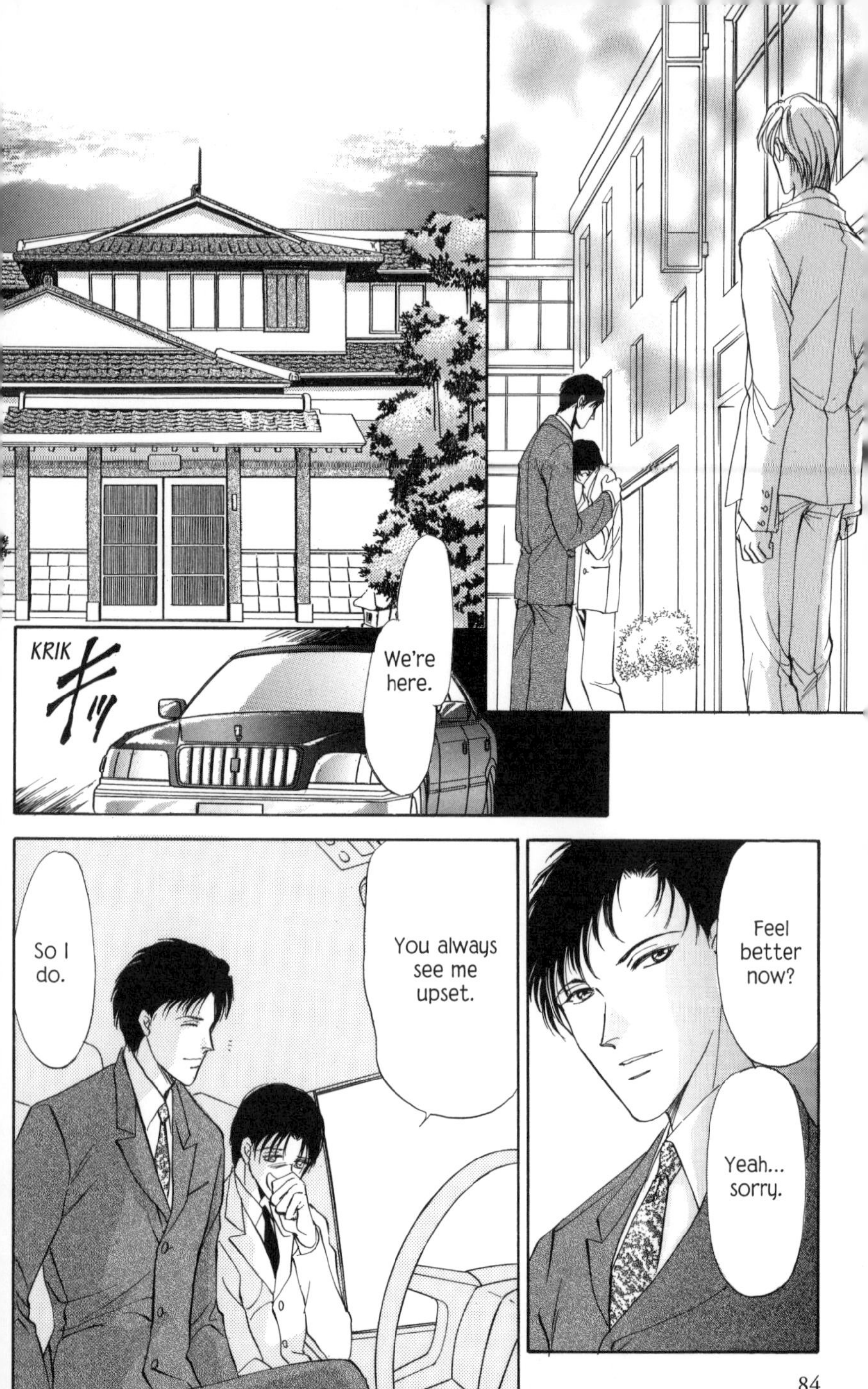
KRIK
ギッ
We're here.
Feel better now?
Yeah... sorry.
You always see me upset.
So I do.

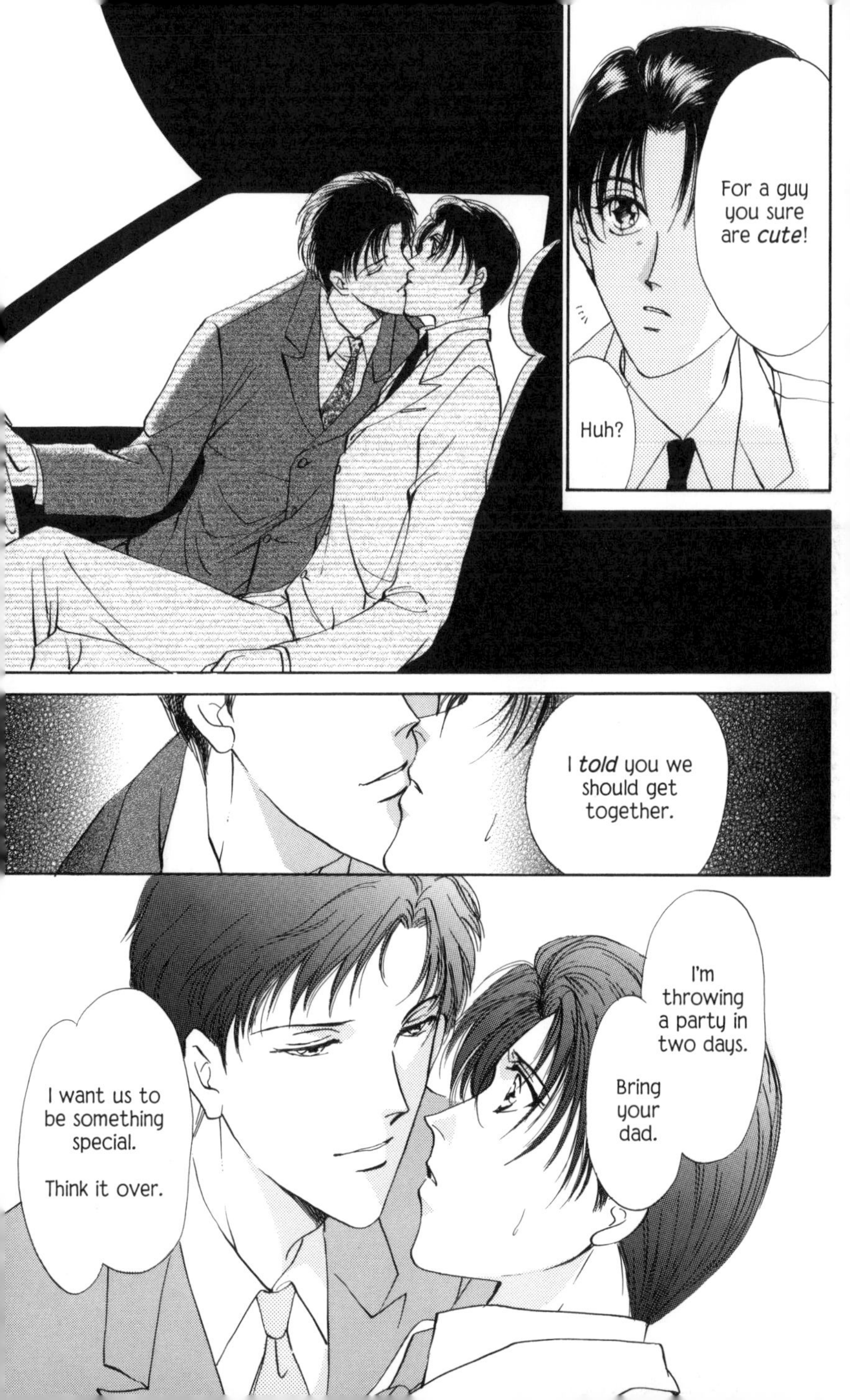
For a guy you sure are *cute*!
Huh?
I *told* you we should get together.
I'm throwing a party in two days.
Bring your dad.
I want us to be something special.
Think it over.

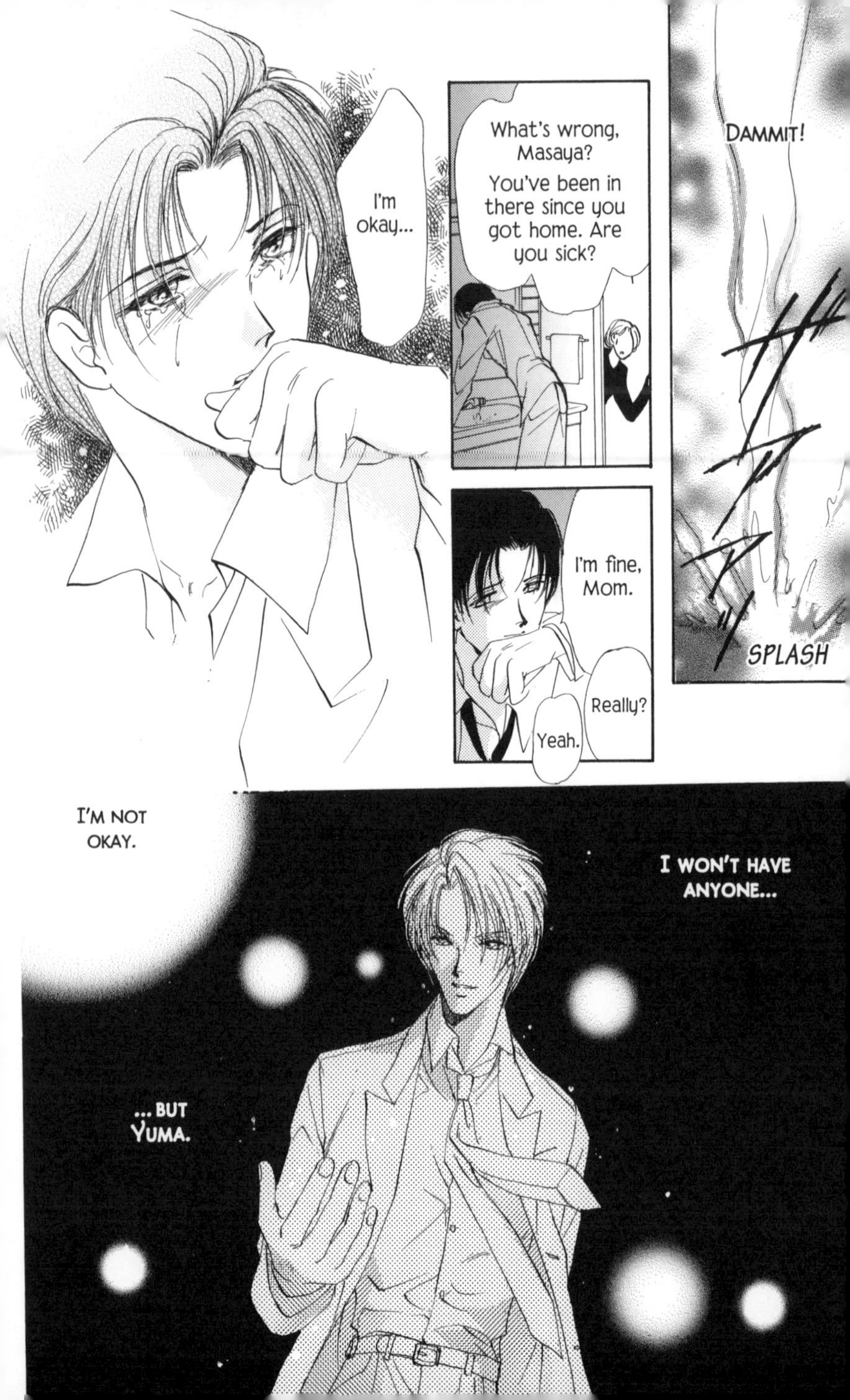
DAMMIT!
SPLASH
What's wrong, Masaya?
You've been in there since you got home. Are you sick?
I'm fine, Mom.
Really?
Yeah.
I'm okay...
I'M NOT OKAY.
I WON'T HAVE ANYONE...
...BUT YUMA.

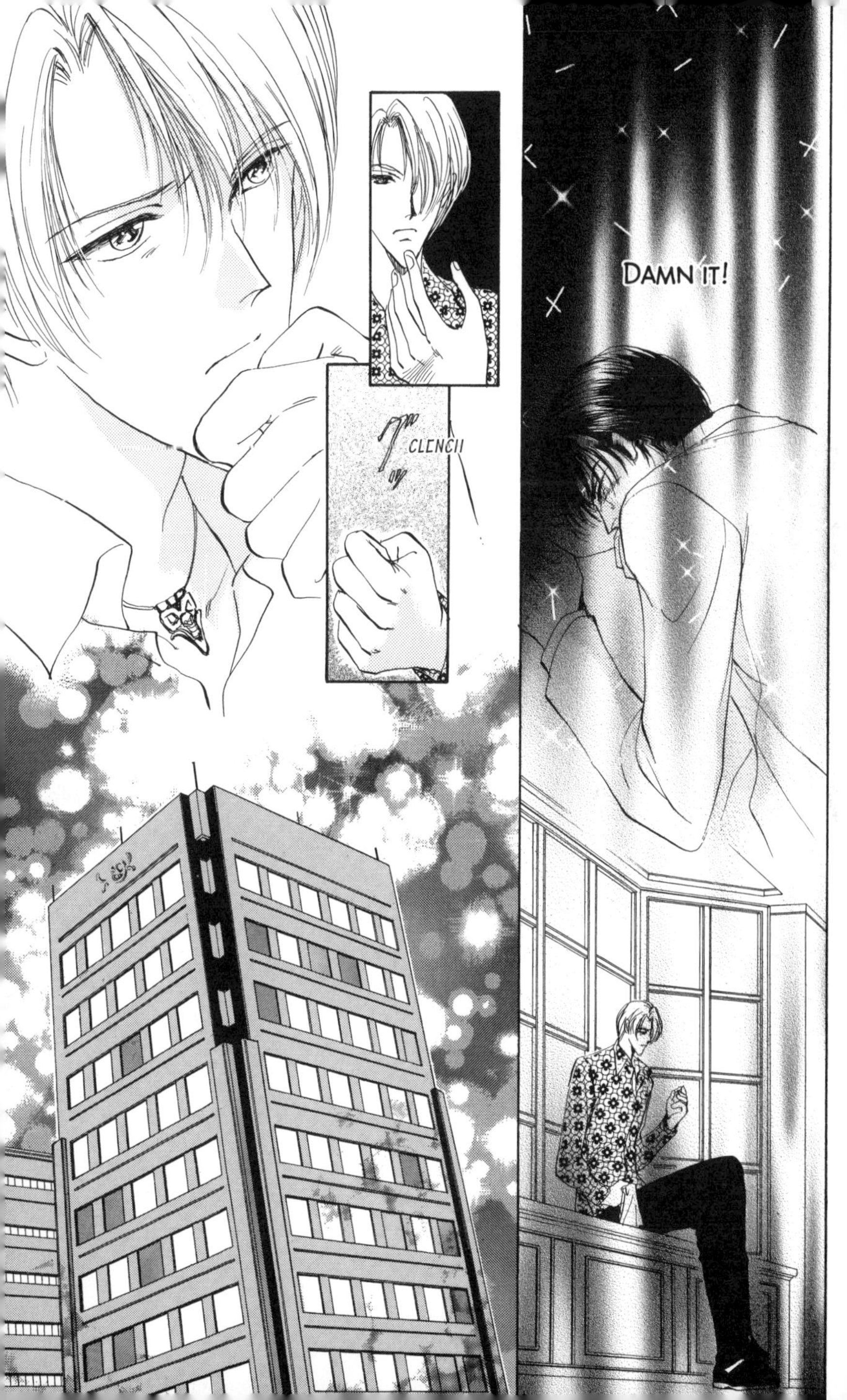
DAMN IT!
CLENCH

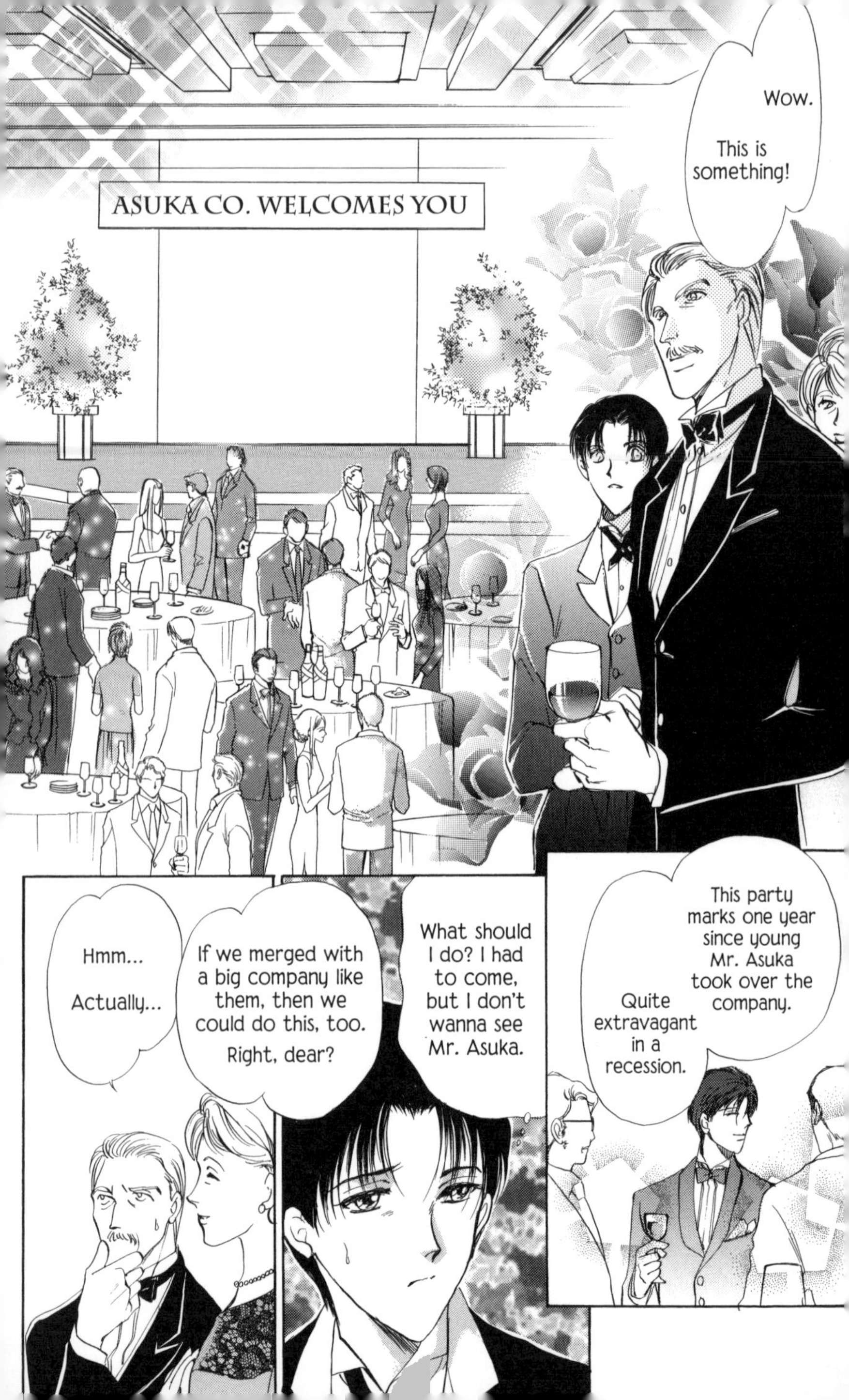
Wow. This is something!
ASUKA CO. WELCOMES YOU
This party marks one year since young Mr. Asuka took over the company.
Quite extravagant in a recession.
What should I do? I had to come, but I don't wanna see Mr. Asuka.
If we merged with a big company like them, then we could do this, too. Right, dear?
Hmm... Actually...

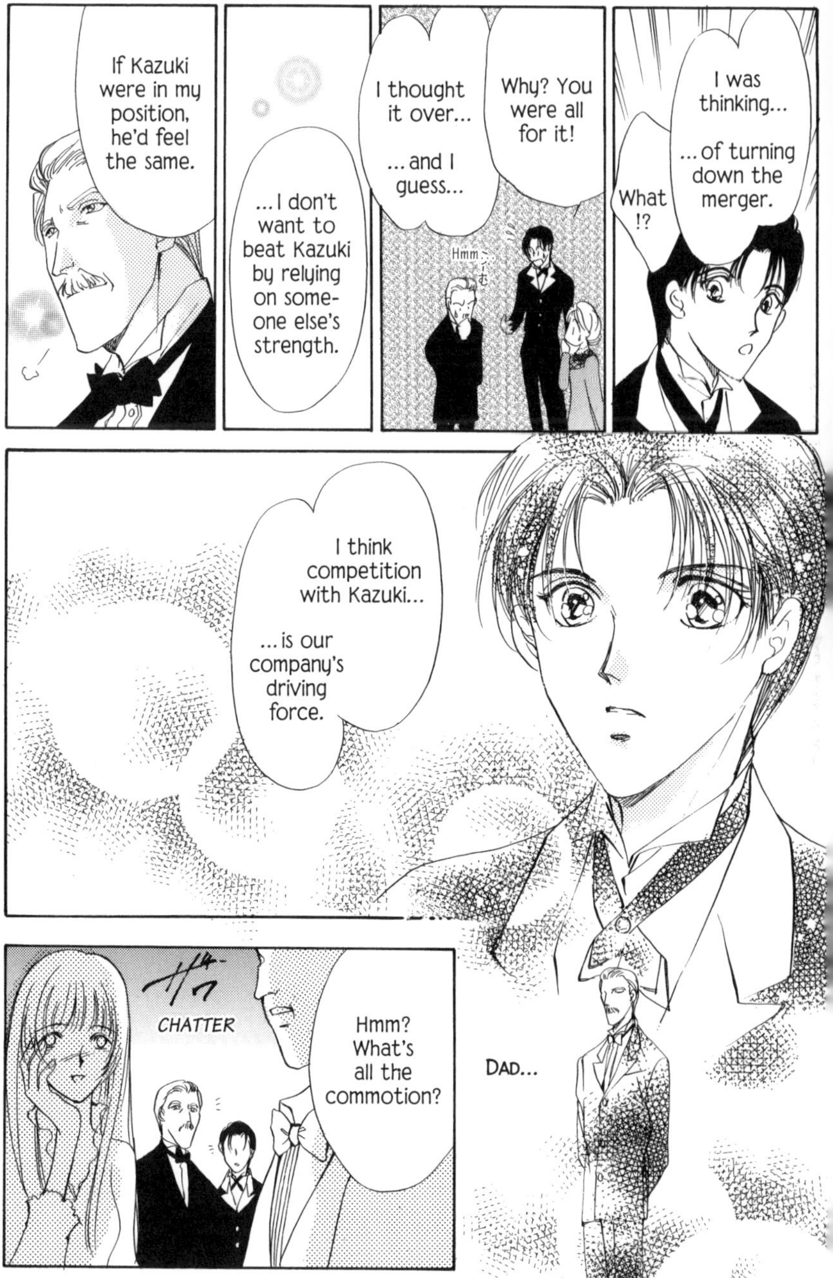
I was thinking... ...of turning down the merger.
What!?
Why? You were all for it!
I thought it over... ...and I guess...
Hmm
...I don't want to beat Kazuki by relying on some-one else's strength.
If Kazuki were in my position, he'd feel the same.
I think competition with Kazuki... ...is our company's driving force.
DAD...
Hmm? What's all the commotion?
CHATTER

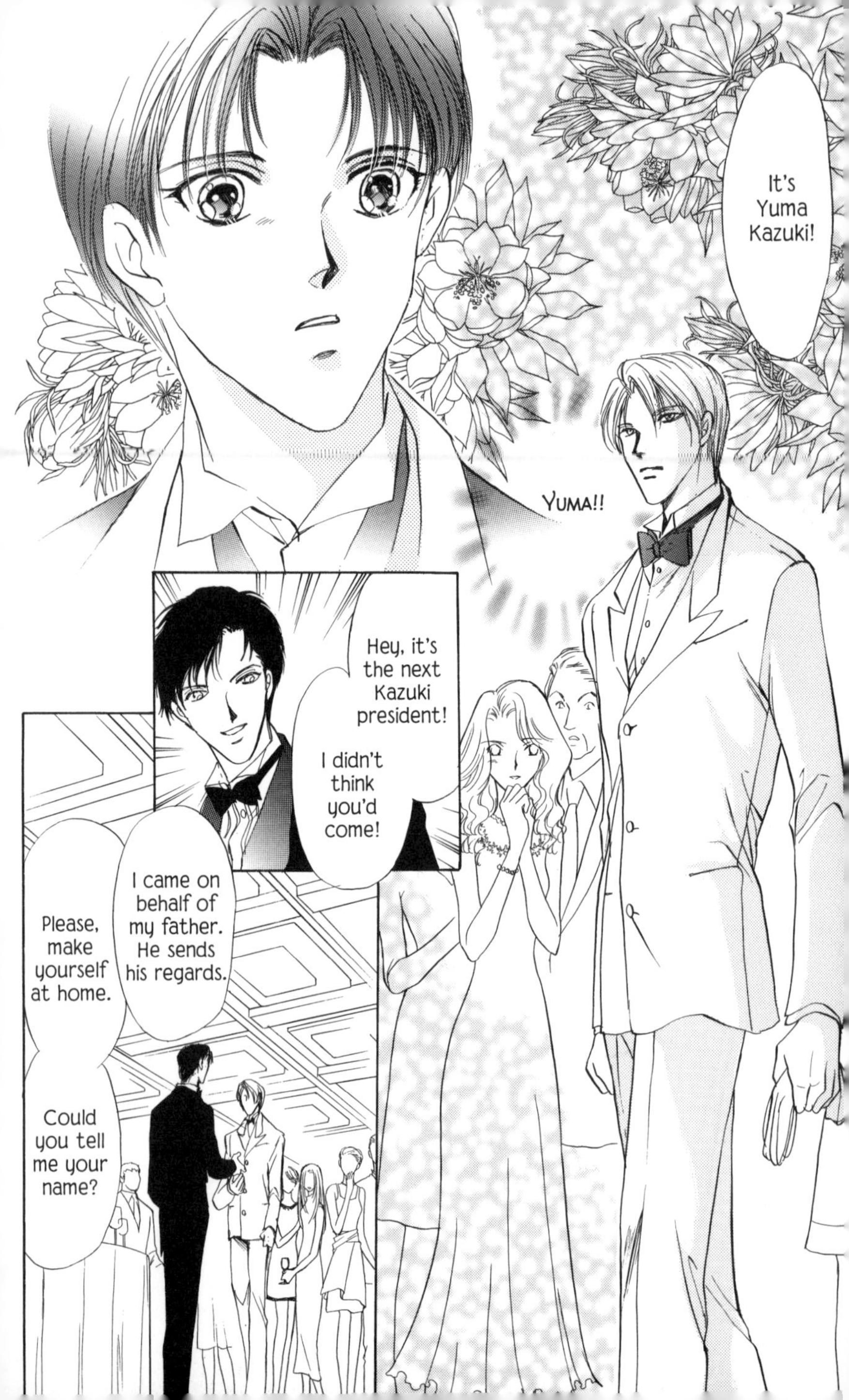

It's Yuma Kazuki!
YUMA!!
Hey, it's the next Kazuki president!
I didn't think you'd come!
I came on behalf of my father. He sends his regards.
Please, make yourself at home.
Could you tell me your name?

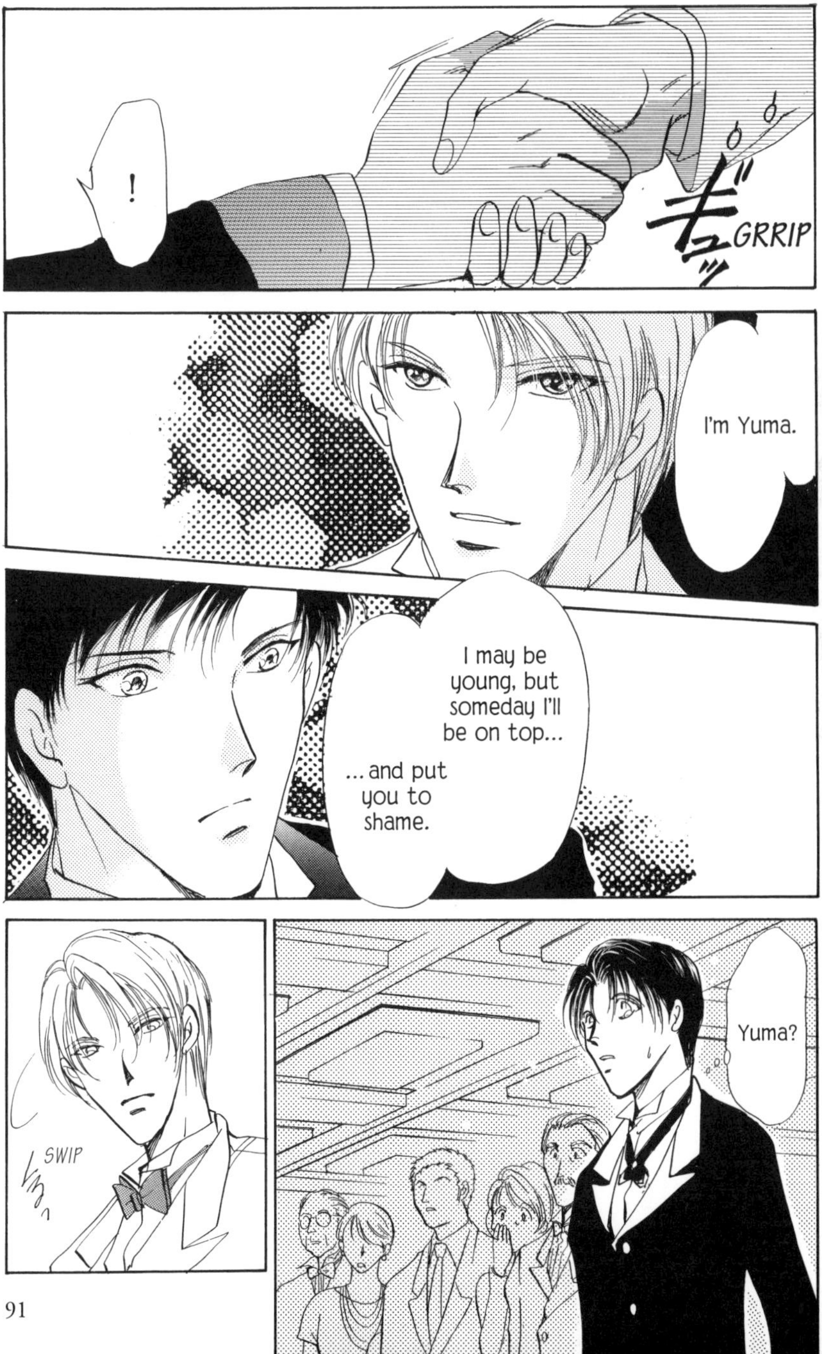
GRRIP
!
I'm Yuma.
I may be young, but someday I'll be on top...
...and put you to shame.
Yuma?
SWIP

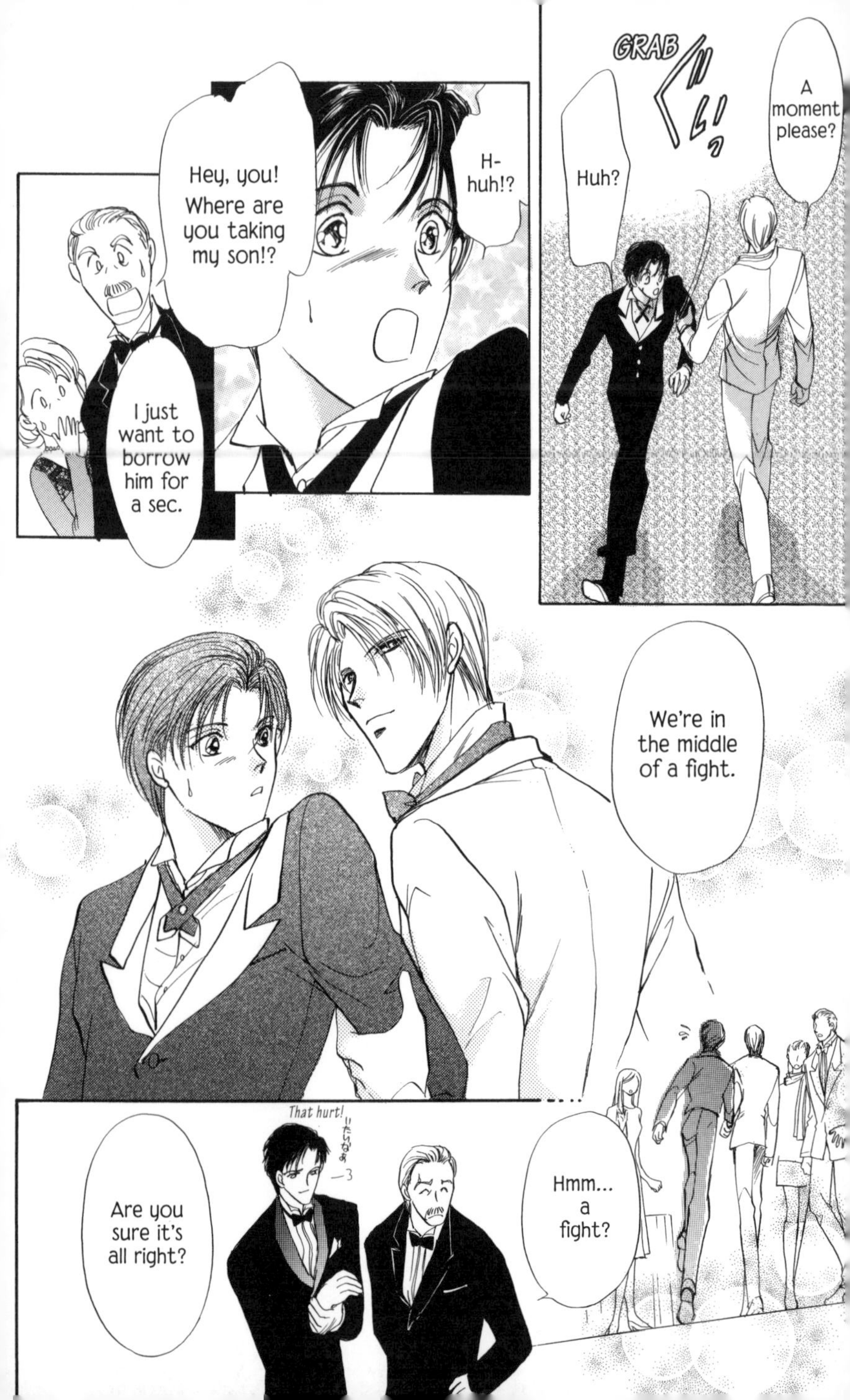
GRAB
A moment please?
Huh?
H-huh!?
Hey, you! Where are you taking my son!?
I just want to borrow him for a sec.
We're in the middle of a fight.
Hmm... a fight?
That hurt!
Are you sure it's all right?

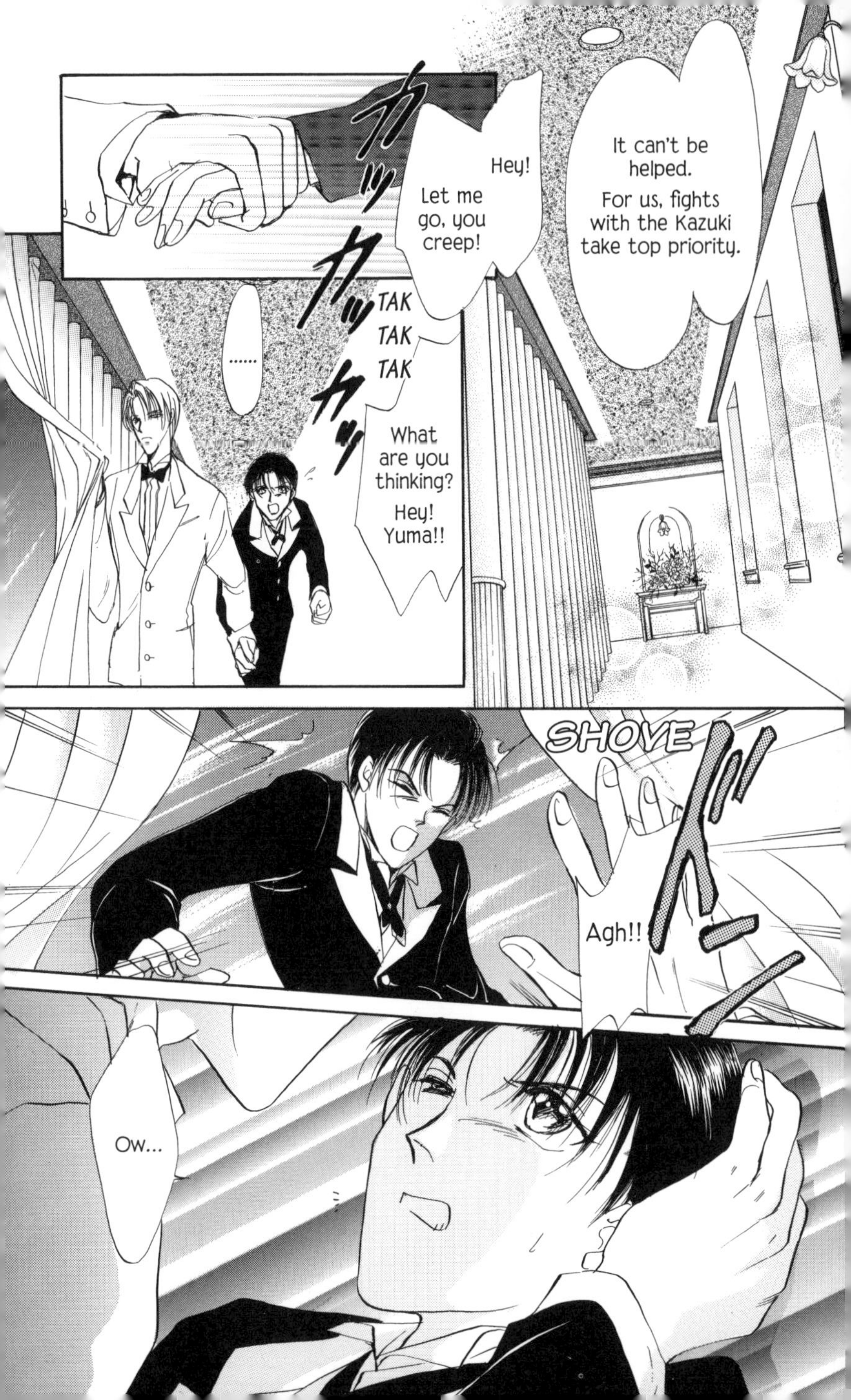
It can't be helped.
For us, fights with the Kazuki take top priority.
Hey!
Let me go, you creep!
TAK
TAK
TAK
What are you thinking?
Hey! Yuma!!
......
SHOVE
Agh!!
Ow...

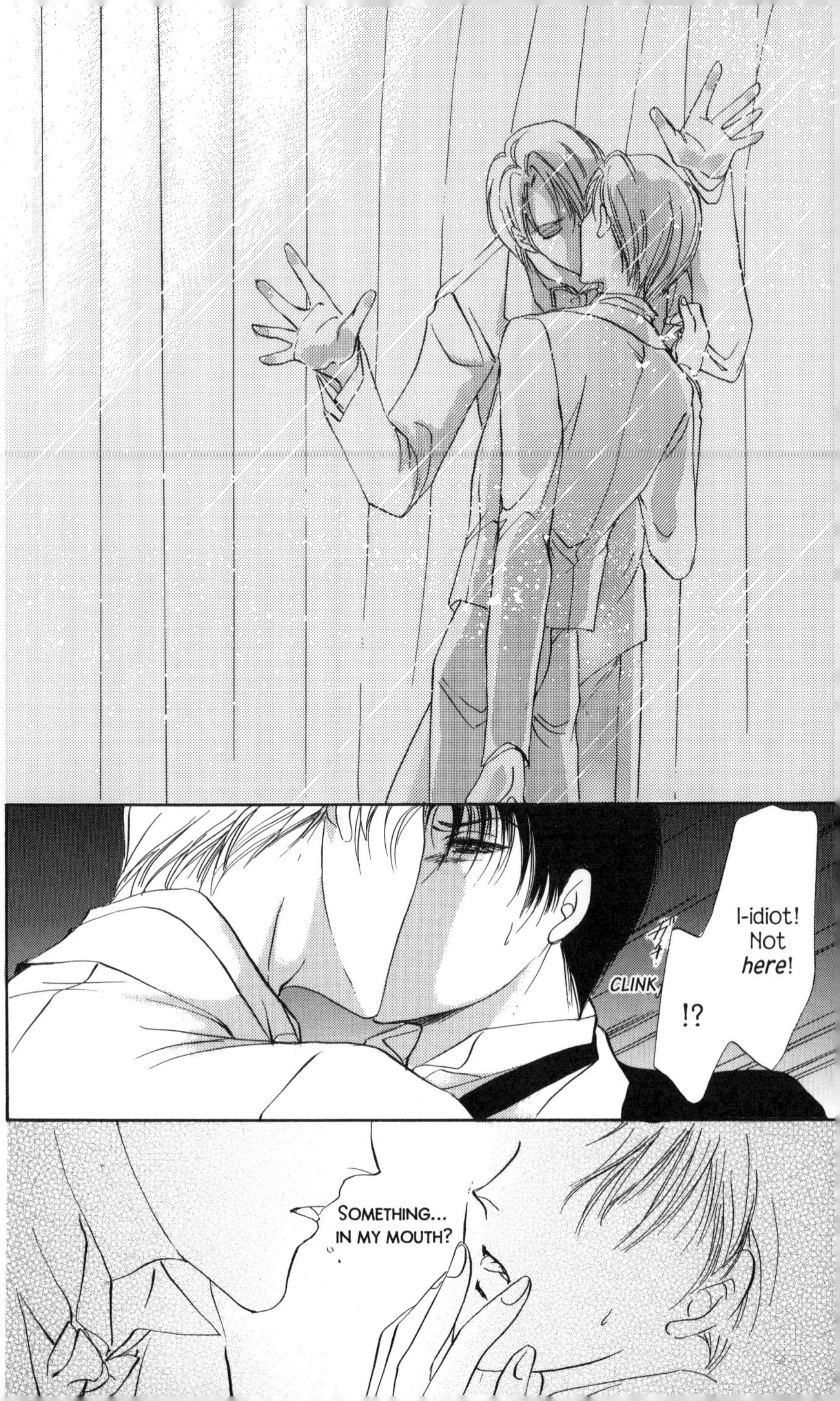
I-idiot! Not *here*!
!?
CLINK
SOMETHING... IN MY MOUTH?

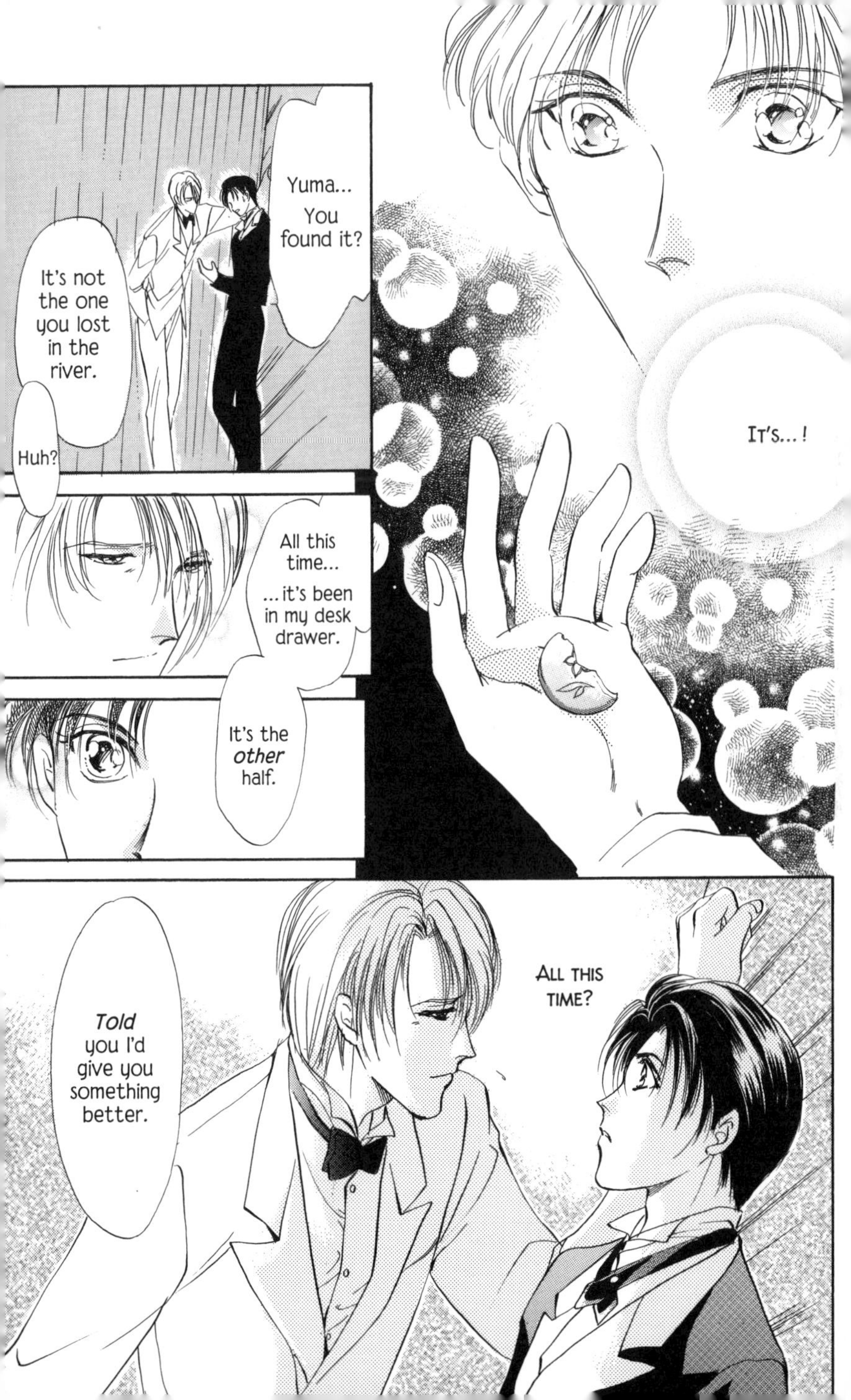

It's...!
Yuma... You found it?
It's not the one you lost in the river.
Huh?
All this time...
...it's been in my desk drawer.
It's the *other* half.
All this time?
Told you I'd give you something better.

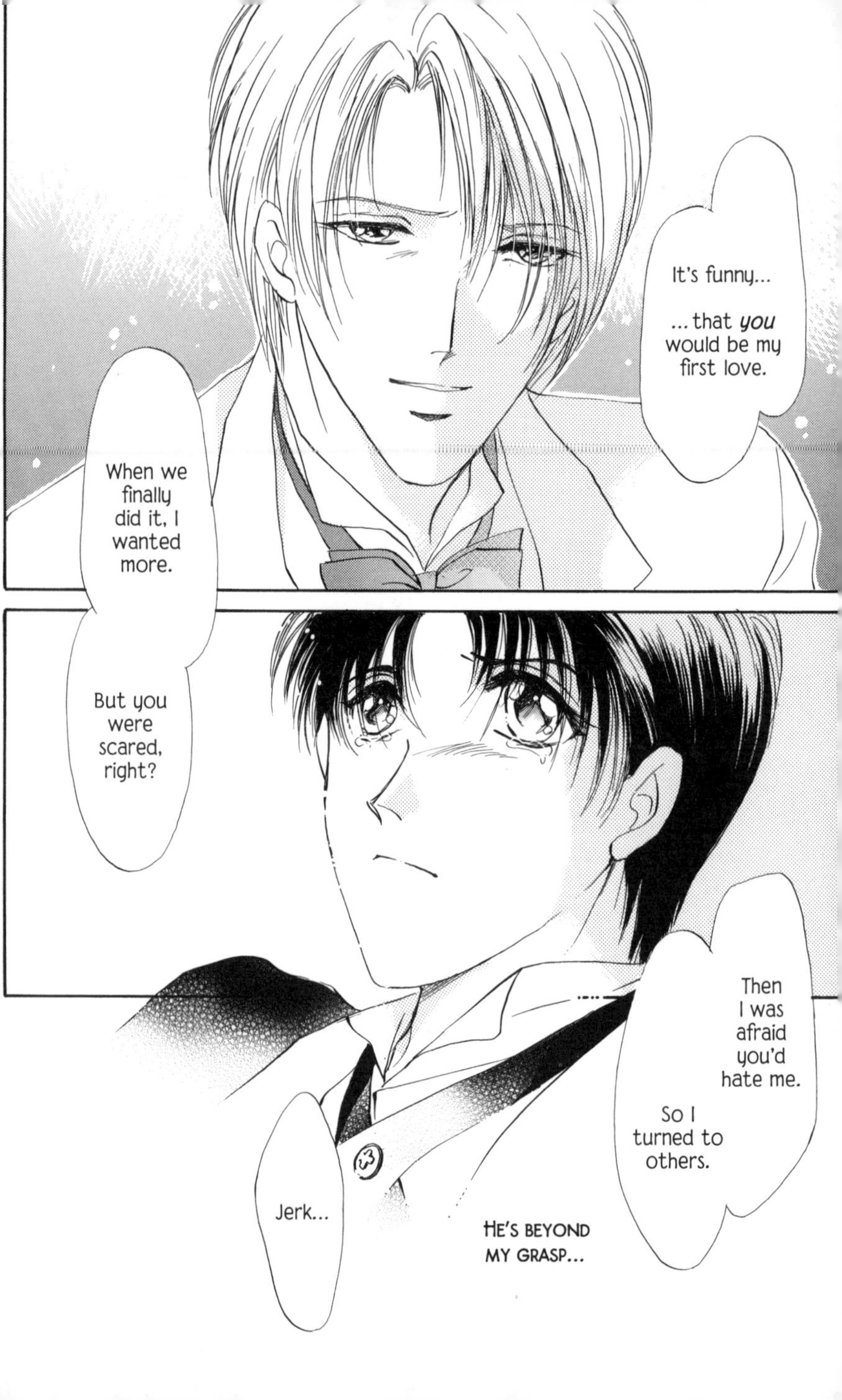
It's funny...
...that *you* would be my first love.
When we finally did it, I wanted more.
But you were scared, right?
Then I was afraid you'd hate me.
So I turned to others.
HE'S BEYOND MY GRASP...
Jerk...

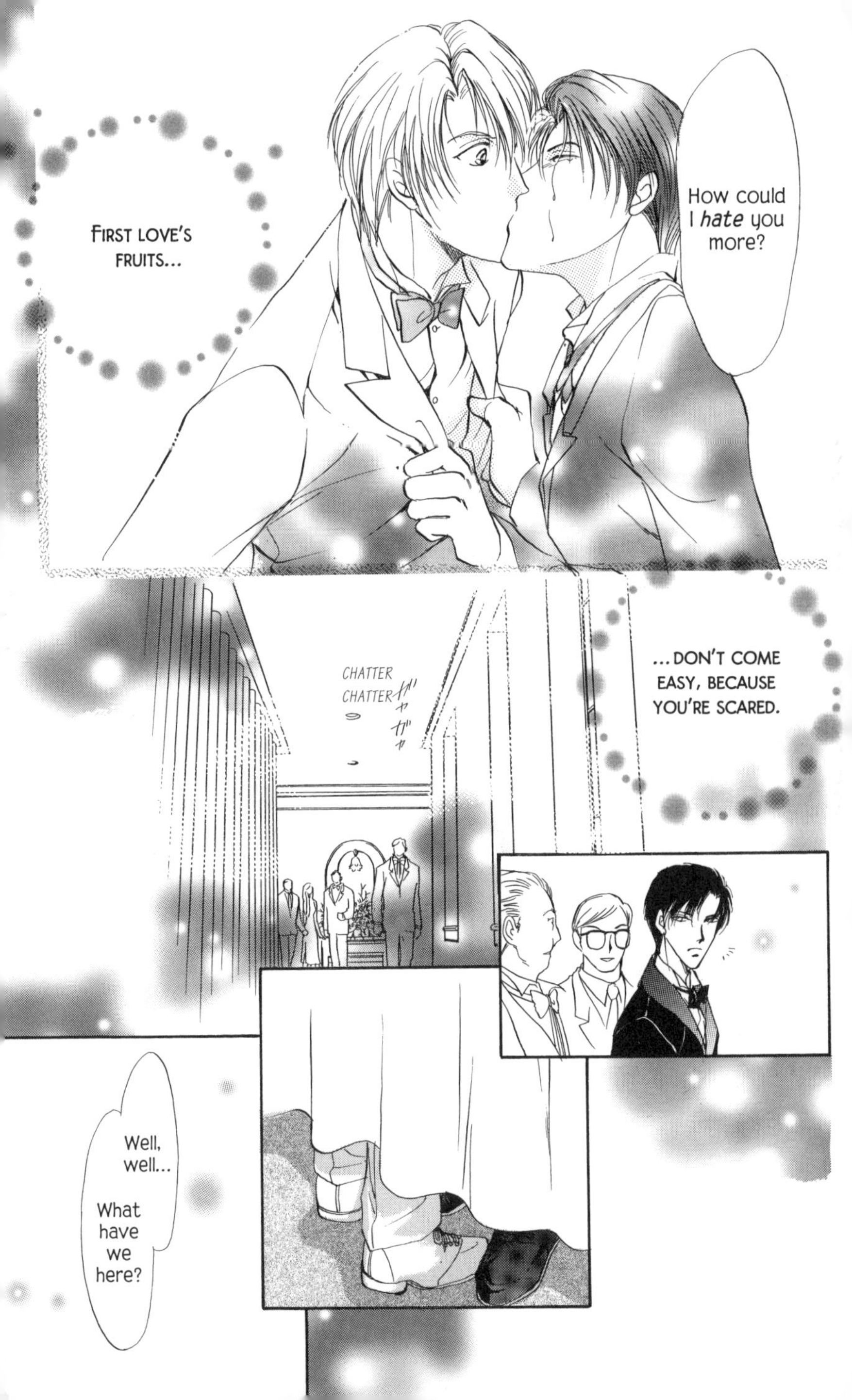
How could I *hate* you more?
FIRST LOVE'S FRUITS...
...DON'T COME EASY, BECAUSE YOU'RE SCARED.
CHATTER CHATTER
Well, well... What have we here?

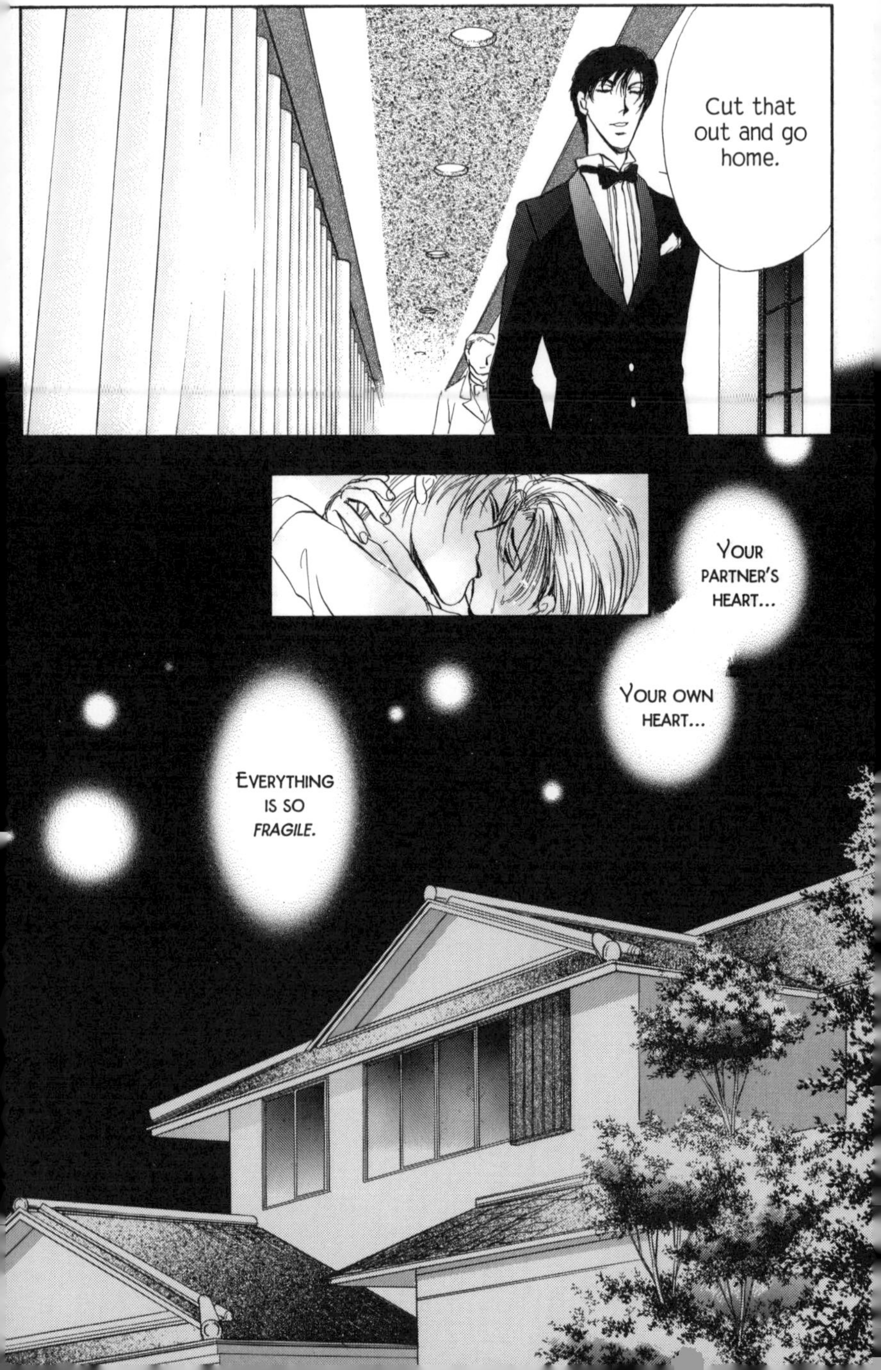
Cut that out and go home.
Your partner's heart...
Your own heart...
Everything is so *fragile.*

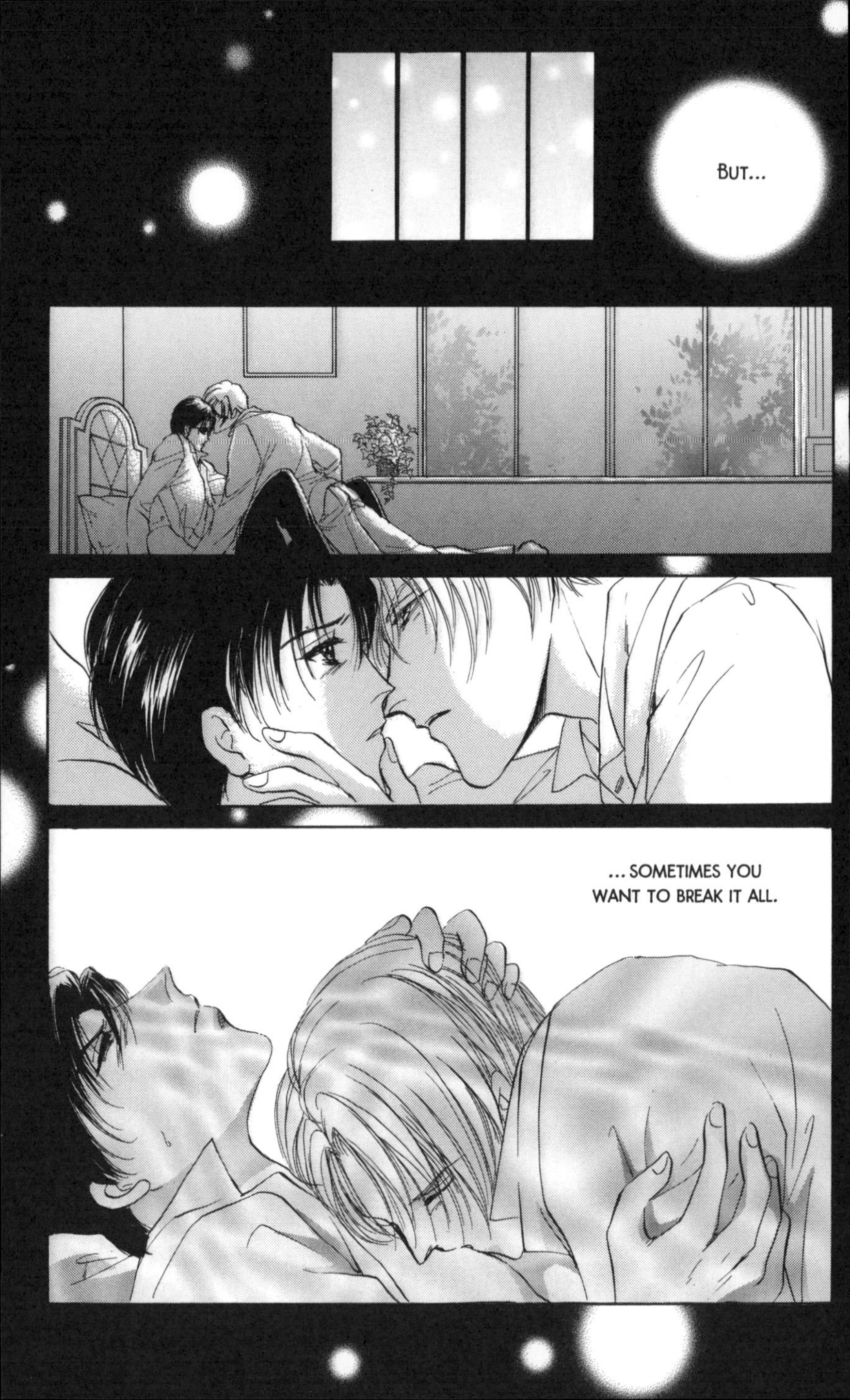
BUT...
...SOMETIMES YOU WANT TO BREAK IT ALL.

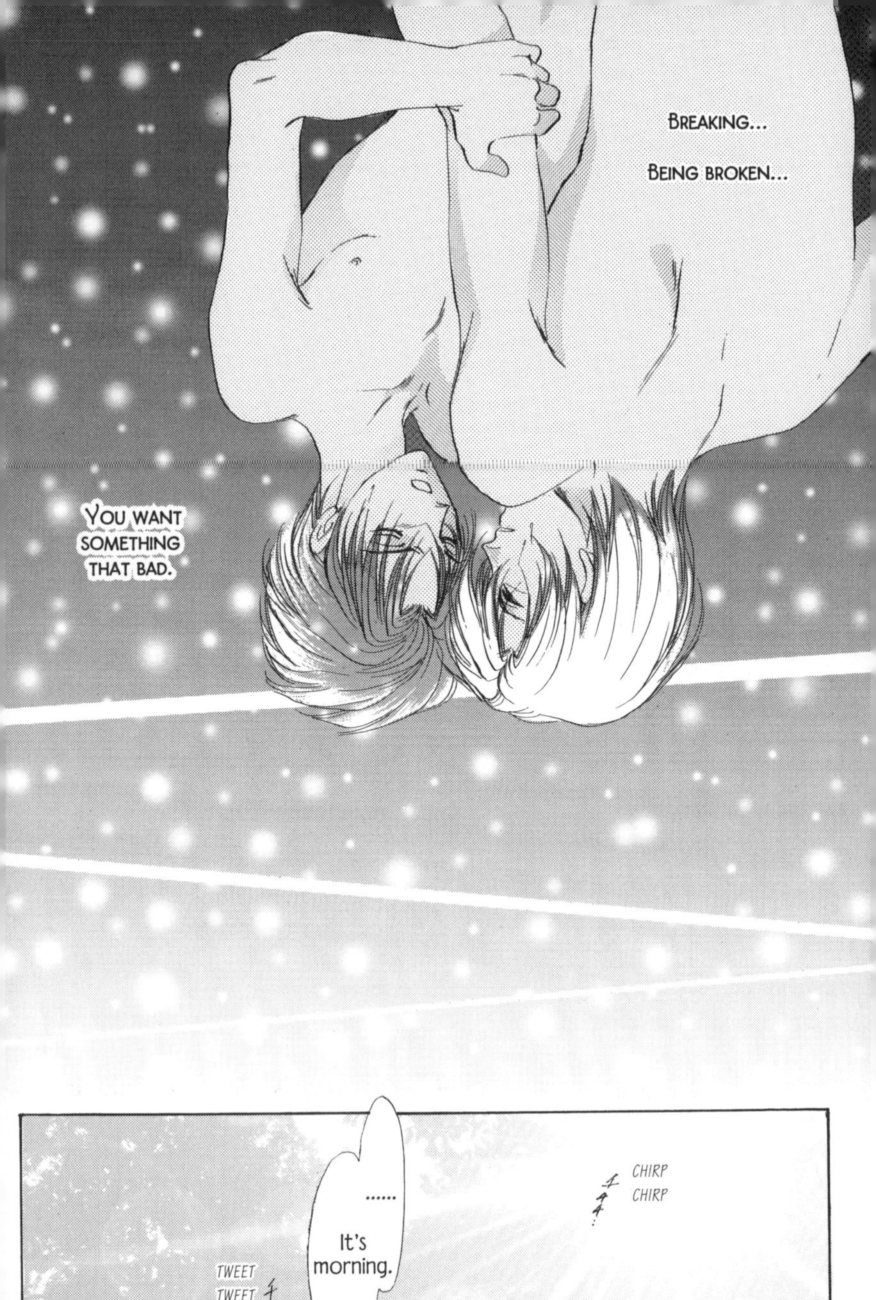
Breaking...
Being broken...
You want something that bad.
CHIRP CHIRP
......
It's morning.
TWEET TWEET

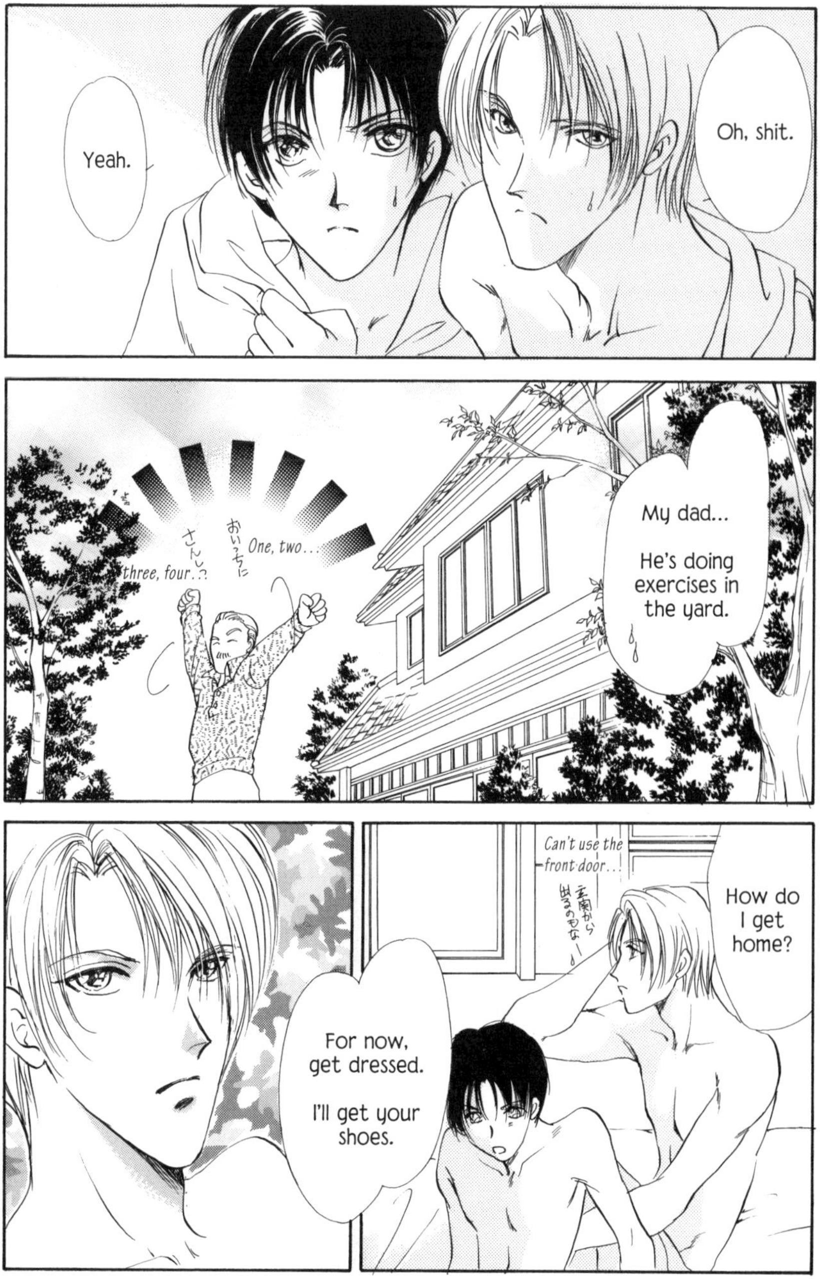
Oh, shit.
Yeah.
My dad...
He's doing exercises in the yard.
おいっちに
One, two...
さんし
three, four...
How do I get home?
Can't use the front door...
玄関から出るのもなー
For now, get dressed.
I'll get your shoes.

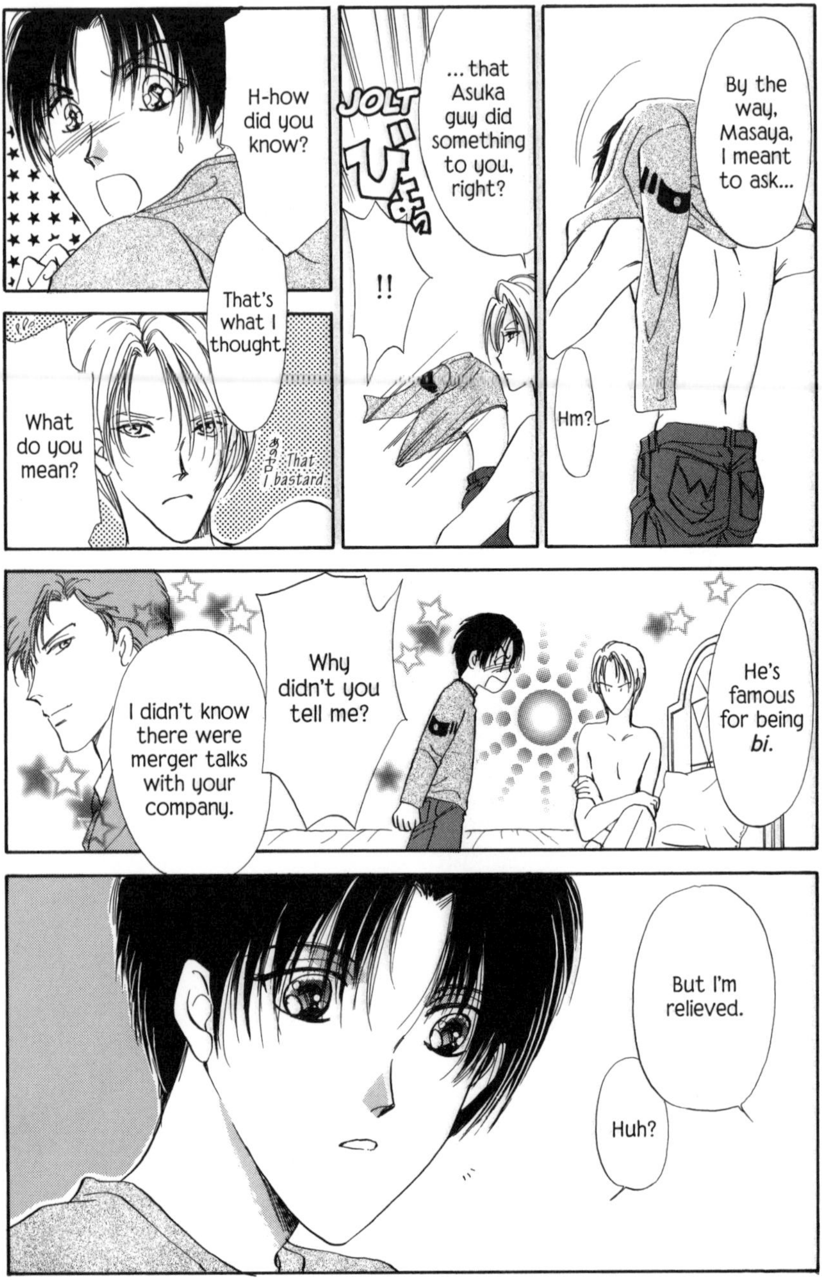
By the way, Masaya, I meant to ask...
Hm?
...that Asuka guy did something to you, right?
JOLT
!!
H-how did you know?
That's what I thought.
What do you mean?
That bastard.
He's famous for being *bi*.
Why didn't you tell me?
I didn't know there were merger talks with your company.
But I'm relieved.
Huh?

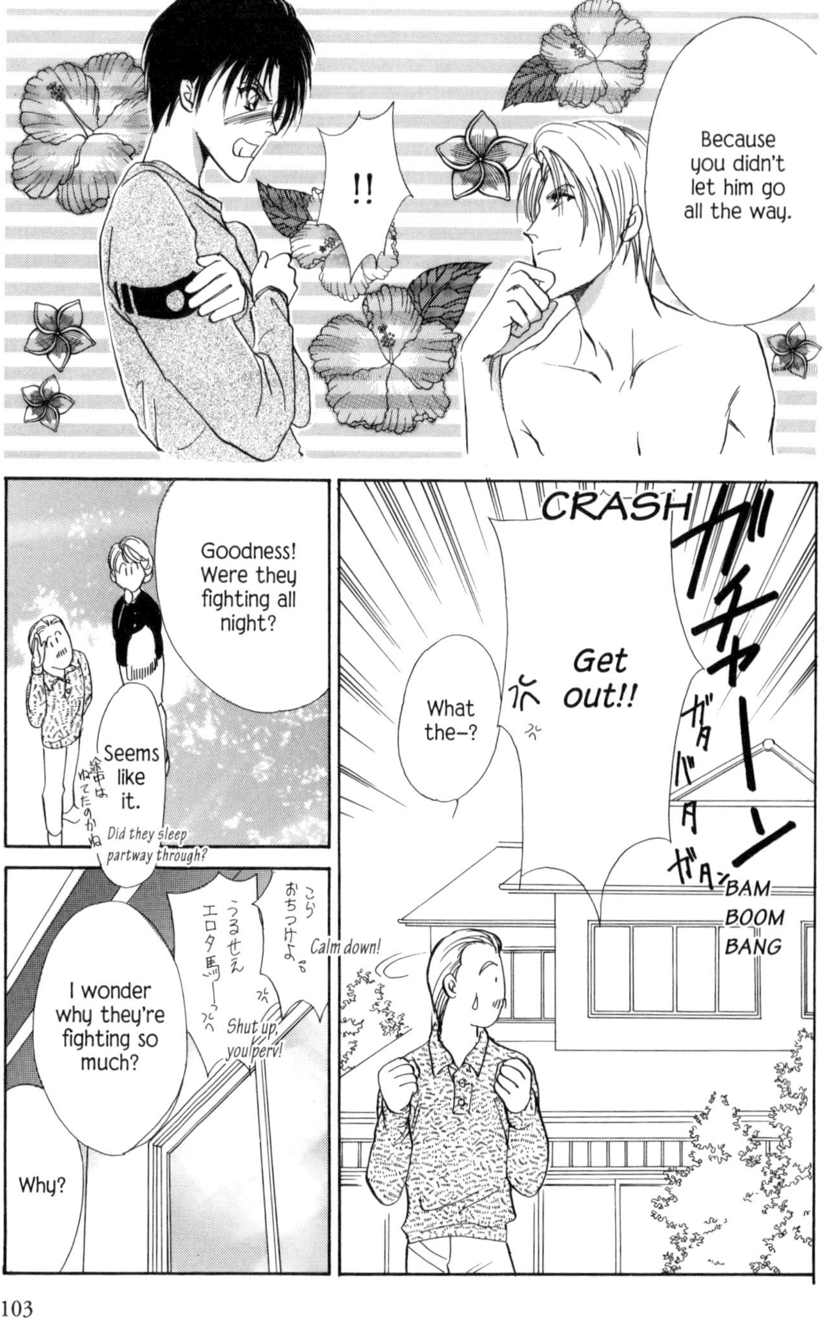
Because you didn't let him go all the way.
!!
CRASH
ガチャーン
Get out!!
What the-?
ガタバタガタン
BAM BOOM BANG
Goodness! Were they fighting all night?
Seems like it.
途中はねてたのかね
Did they sleep partway through?
こら おちつけよ
Calm down!
うるせぇエロタ馬ーっ
Shut up, you perv!
I wonder why they're fighting so much?
Why?

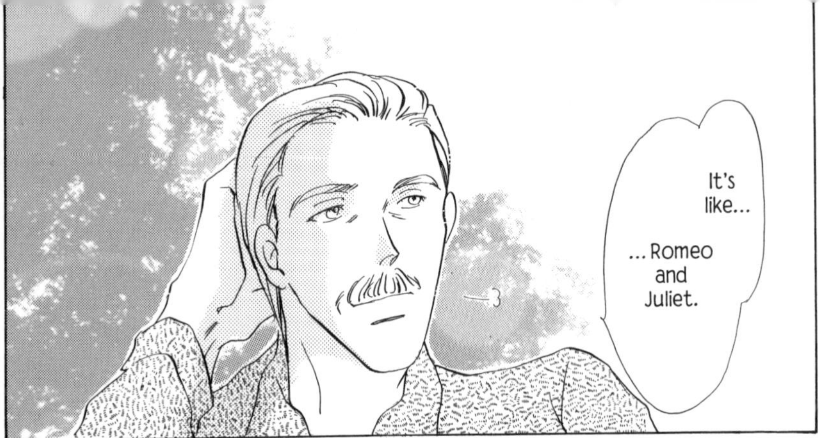
It's like...
...Romeo and Juliet.
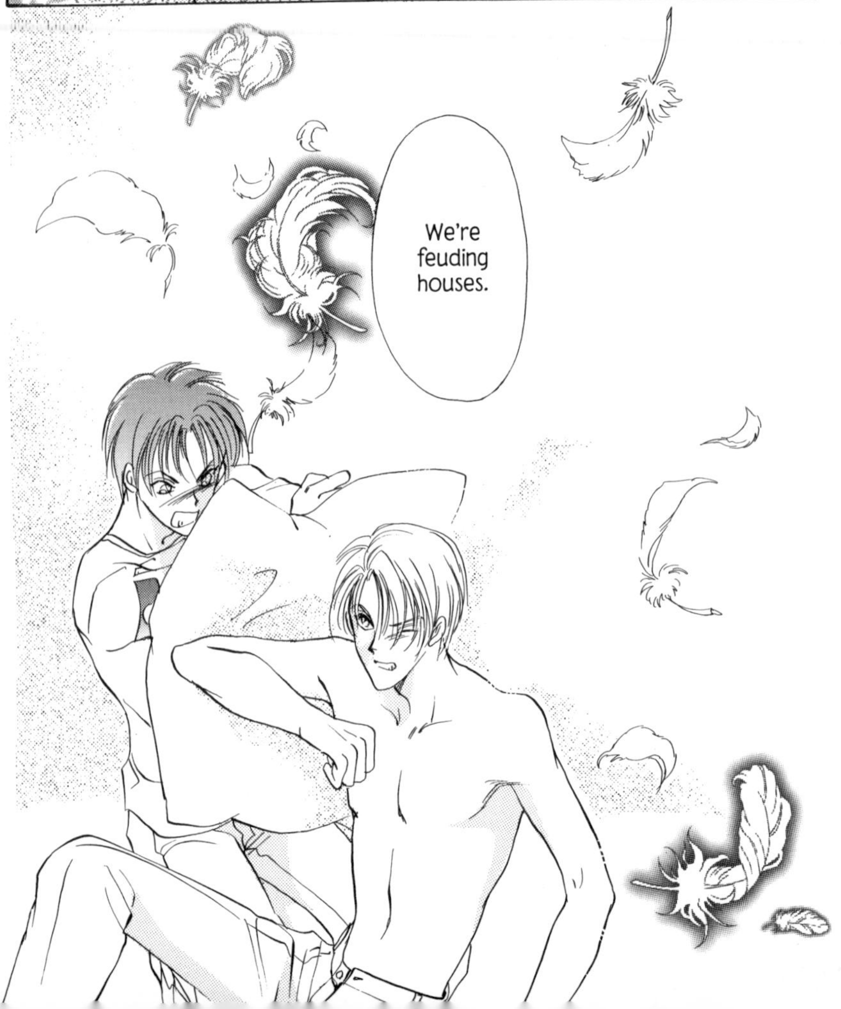
We're feuding houses.

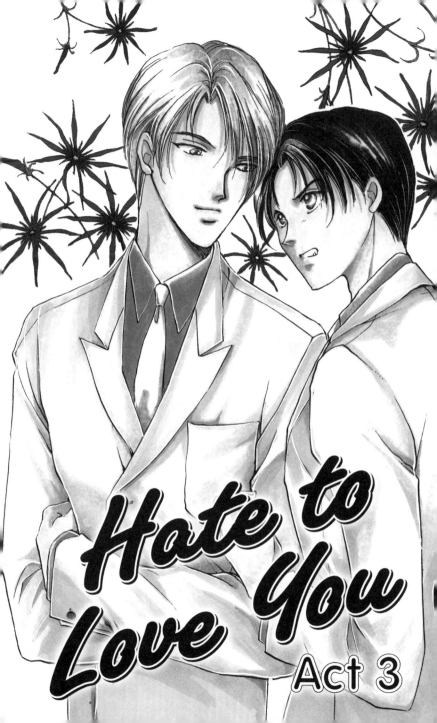

Hate to
Love You

Act 3

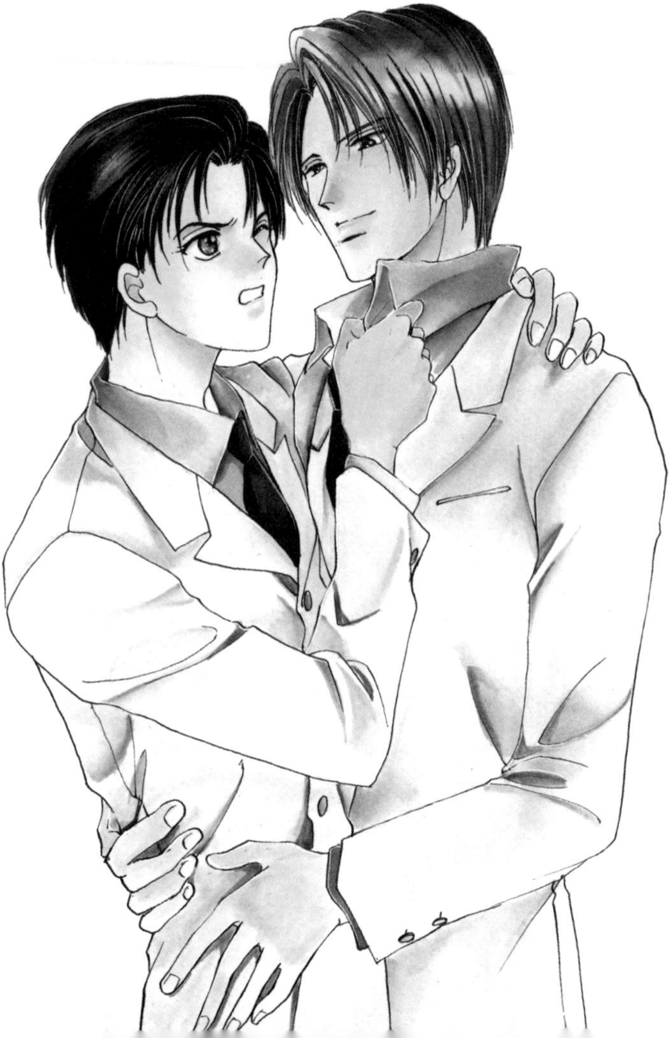

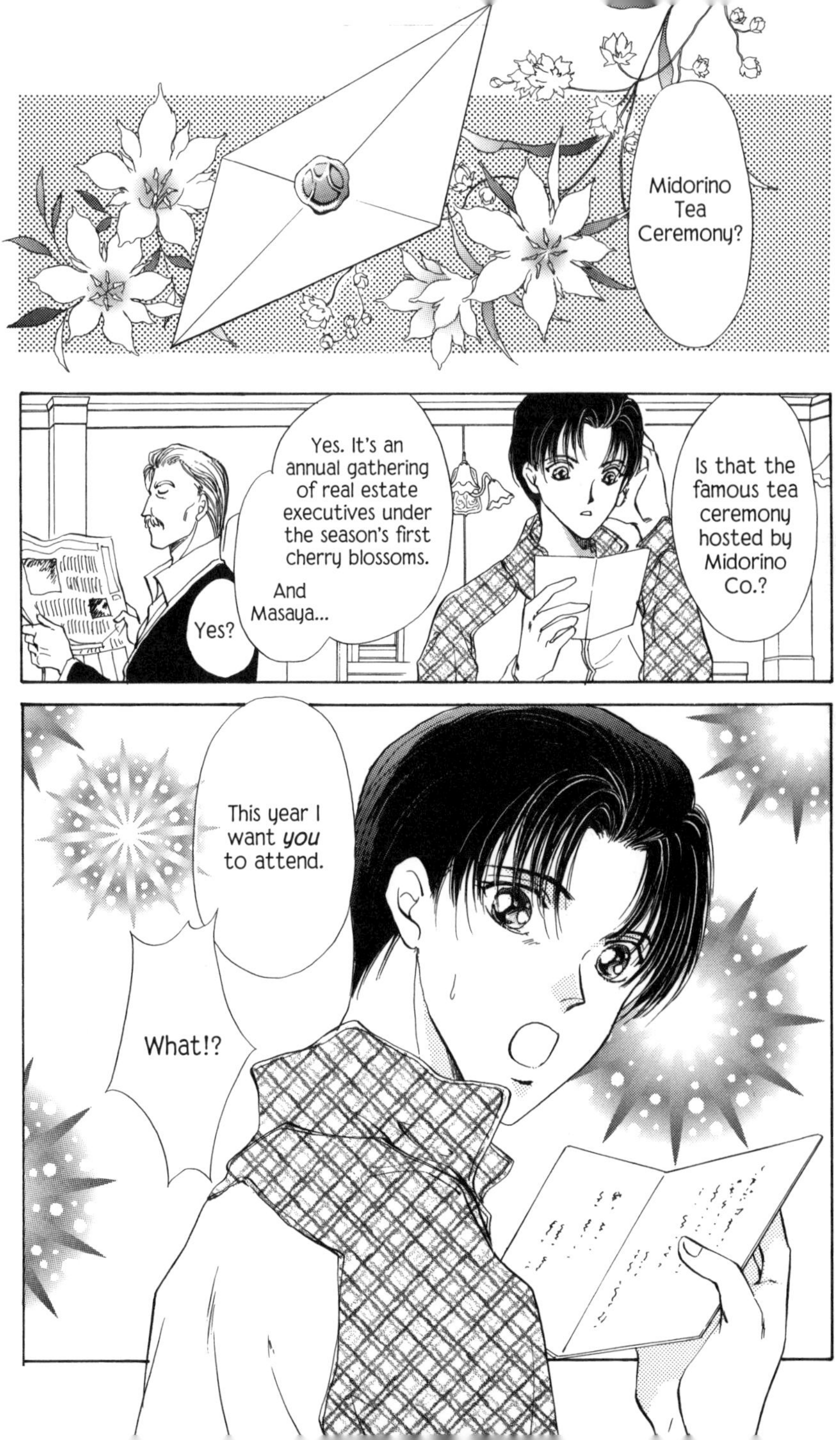
Midorino Tea Ceremony?
Is that the famous tea ceremony hosted by Midorino Co.?
Yes. It's an annual gathering of real estate executives under the season's first cherry blossoms.
And Masaya...
Yes?
This year I want *you* to attend.
What!?

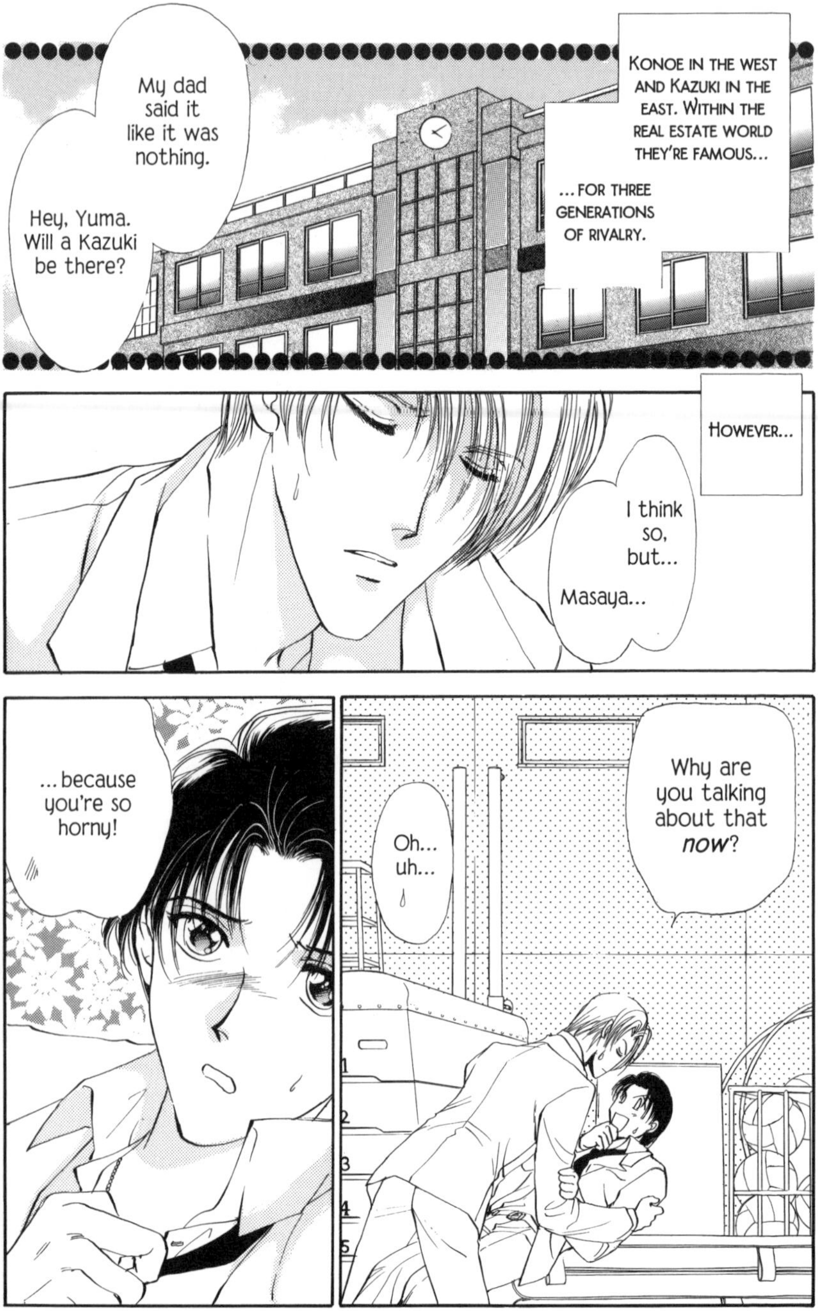

KONOE IN THE WEST AND KAZUKI IN THE EAST. WITHIN THE REAL ESTATE WORLD THEY'RE FAMOUS...
...FOR THREE GENERATIONS OF RIVALRY.
My dad said it like it was nothing.
Hey, Yuma. Will a Kazuki be there?
HOWEVER...
I think so, but...
Masaya...
Why are you talking about that *now*?
Oh... uh...
...because you're so horny!
1
2
3
4
5

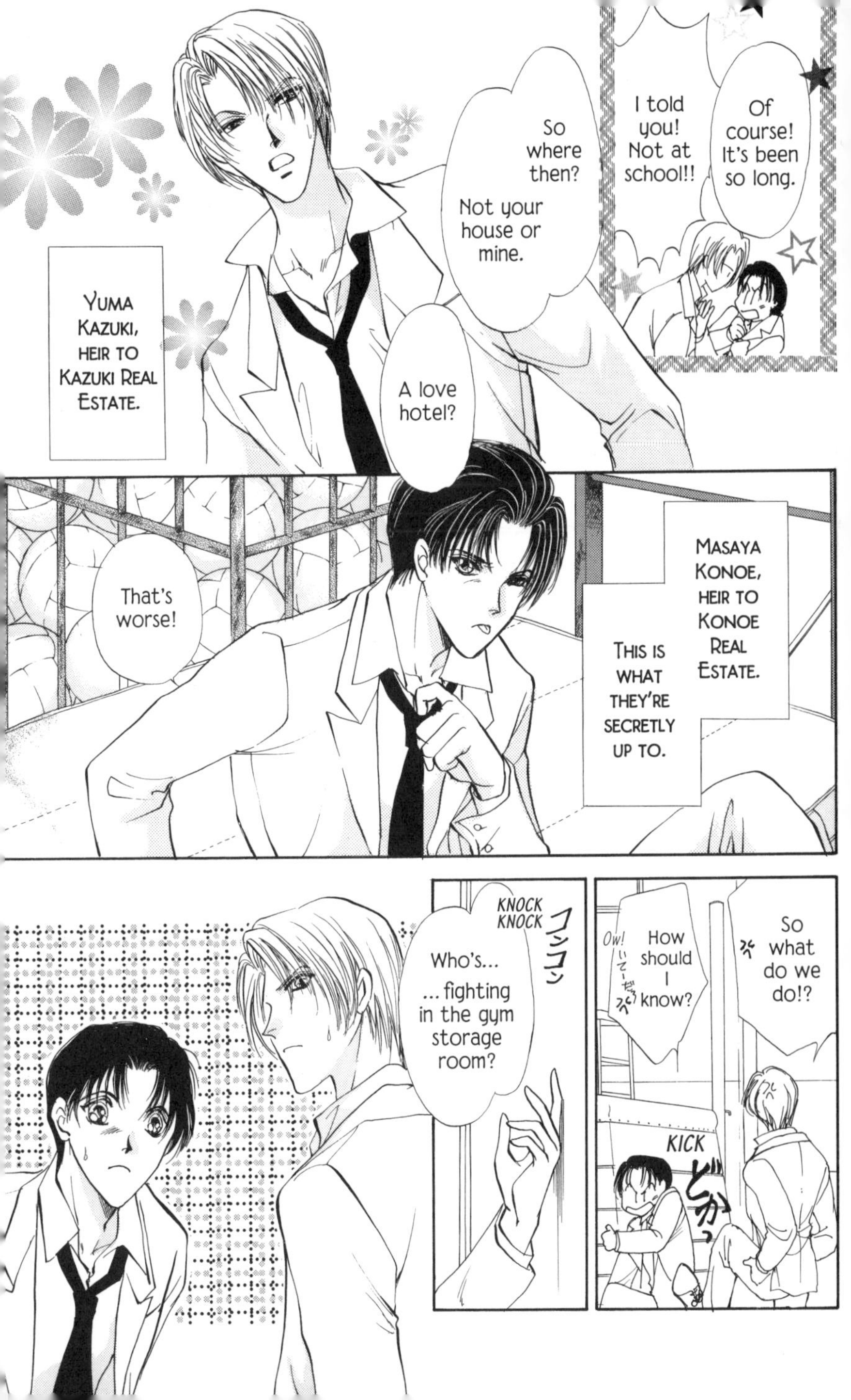
Of course! It's been so long.
I told you! Not at school!!
So where then?
Not your house or mine.
A love hotel?
YUMA KAZUKI, HEIR TO KAZUKI REAL ESTATE.
MASAYA KONOE, HEIR TO KONOE REAL ESTATE.
THIS IS WHAT THEY'RE SECRETLY UP TO.
That's worse!
So what do we do!?
How should I know?
Ow!
KICK
KNOCK KNOCK
Who's...
...fighting in the gym storage room?

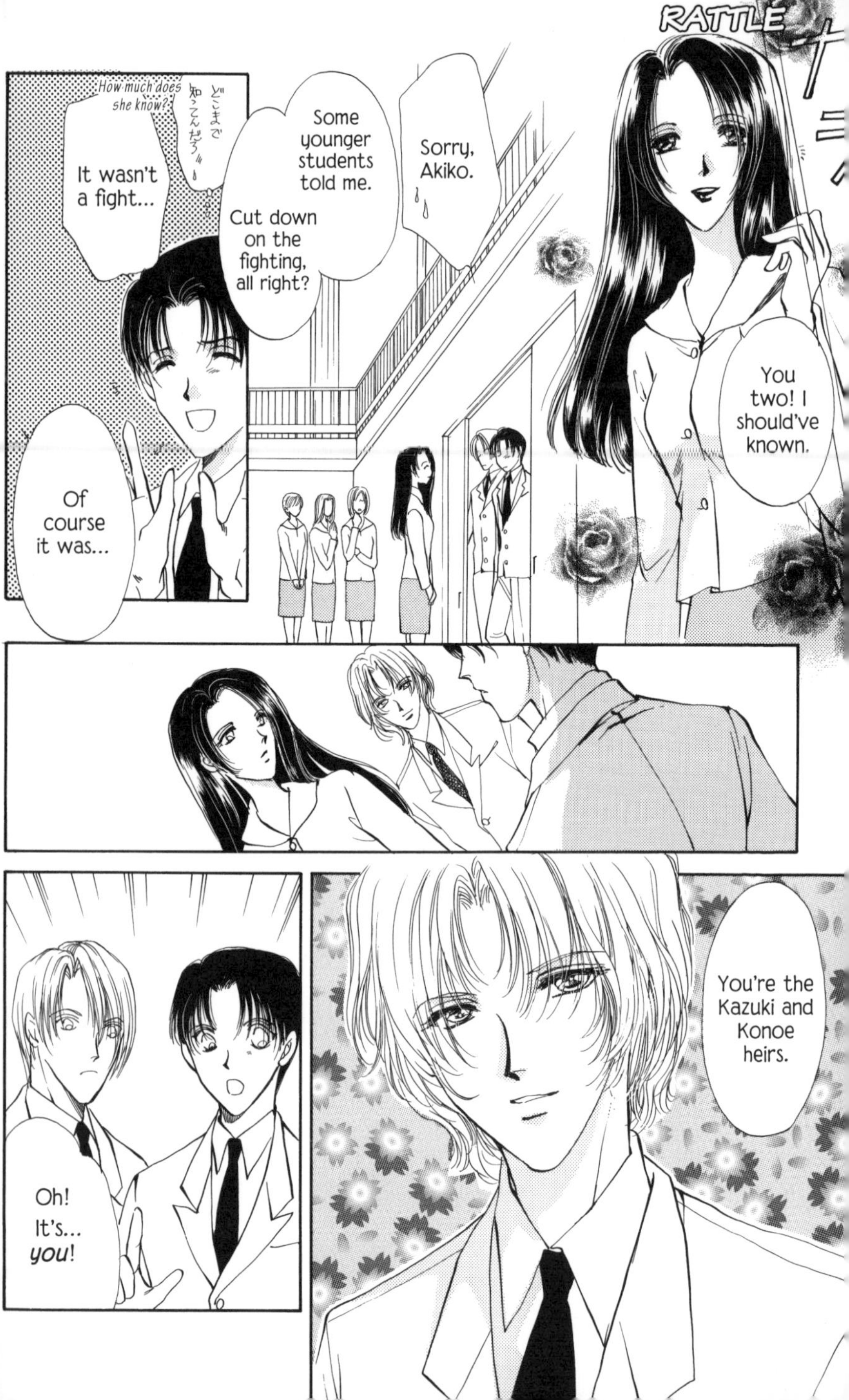
RATTLE
You two! I should've known.
Sorry, Akiko.
Some younger students told me.
Cut down on the fighting, all right?
どこまで知ってんだろ〃
How much does she know?
It wasn't a fight...
Of course it was...
You're the Kazuki and Konoe heirs.
Oh! It's... *you*!

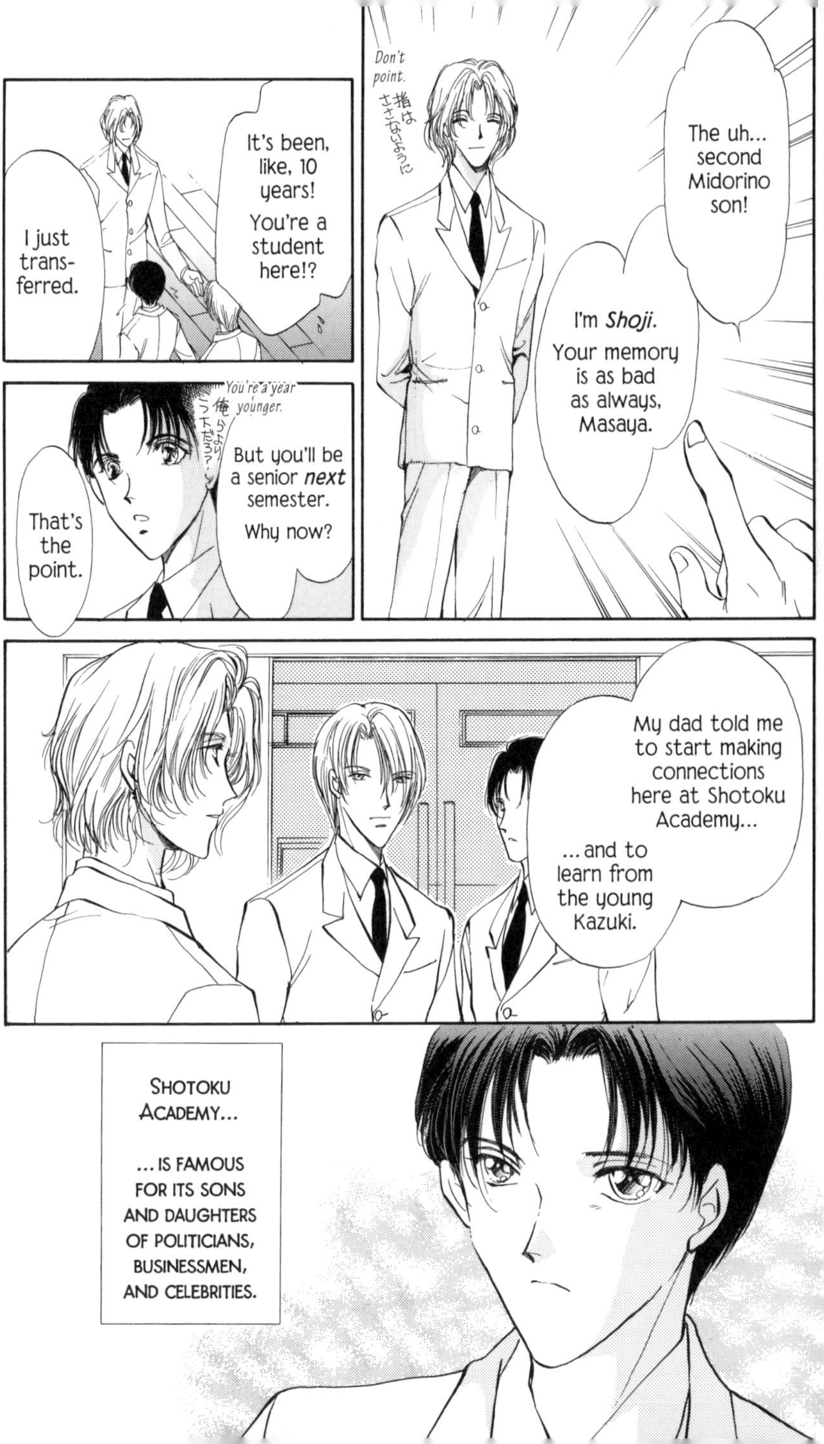
Don't point.
指はささないように
The uh... second Midorino son!
I'm *Shoji.* Your memory is as bad as always, Masaya.
It's been, like, 10 years! You're a student here!?
I just trans-ferred.
You're a year younger.
俺らより
コ下だろ?
But you'll be a senior *next* semester. Why now?
That's the point.
My dad told me to start making connections here at Shotoku Academy...
...and to learn from the young Kazuki.
SHOTOKU ACADEMY...
...IS FAMOUS FOR ITS SONS AND DAUGHTERS OF POLITICIANS, BUSINESSMEN, AND CELEBRITIES.

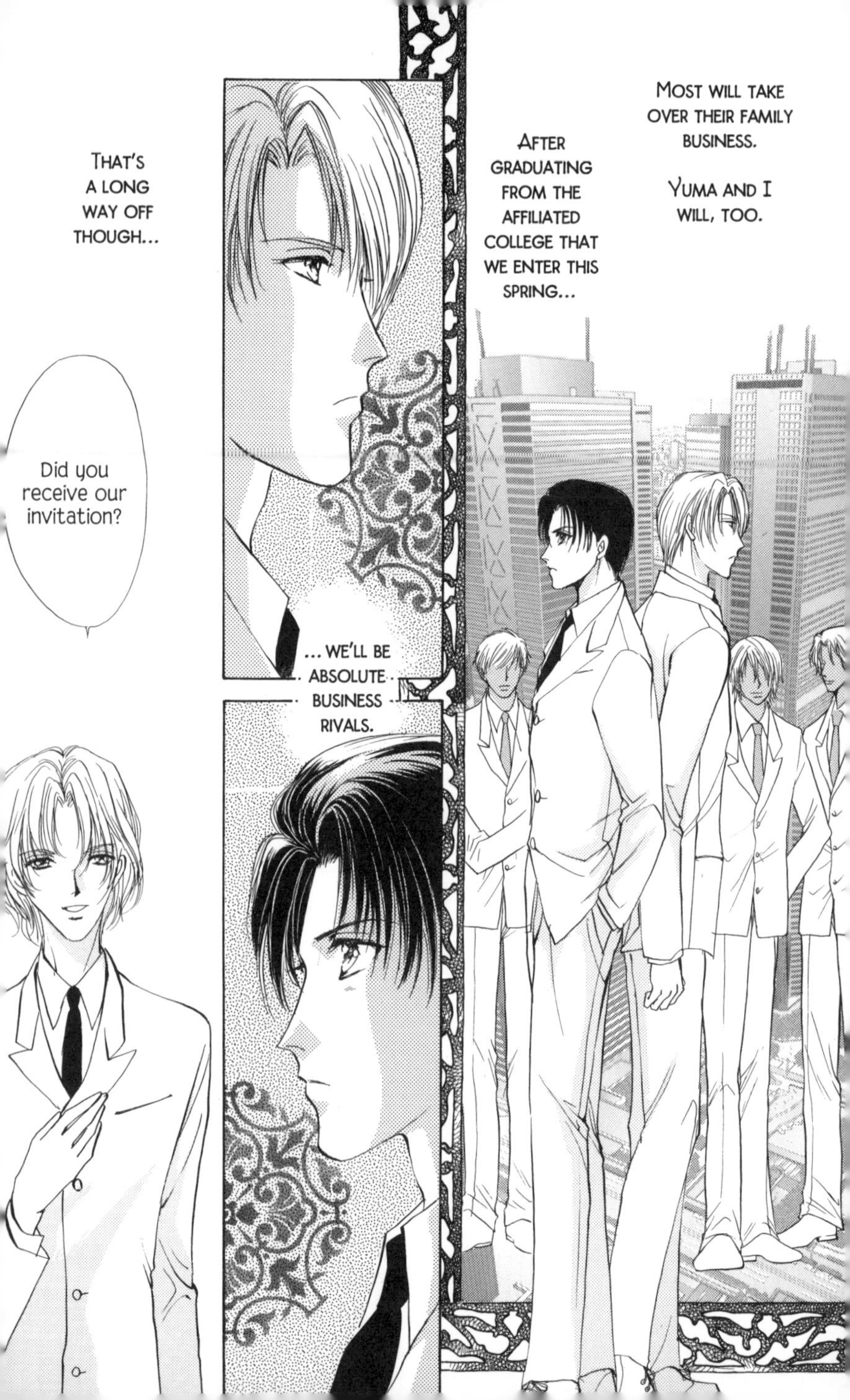
Most will take over their family business.
Yuma and I will, too.
After graduating from the affiliated college that we enter this spring...
...we'll be absolute business rivals.
That's a long way off though...
Did you receive our invitation?

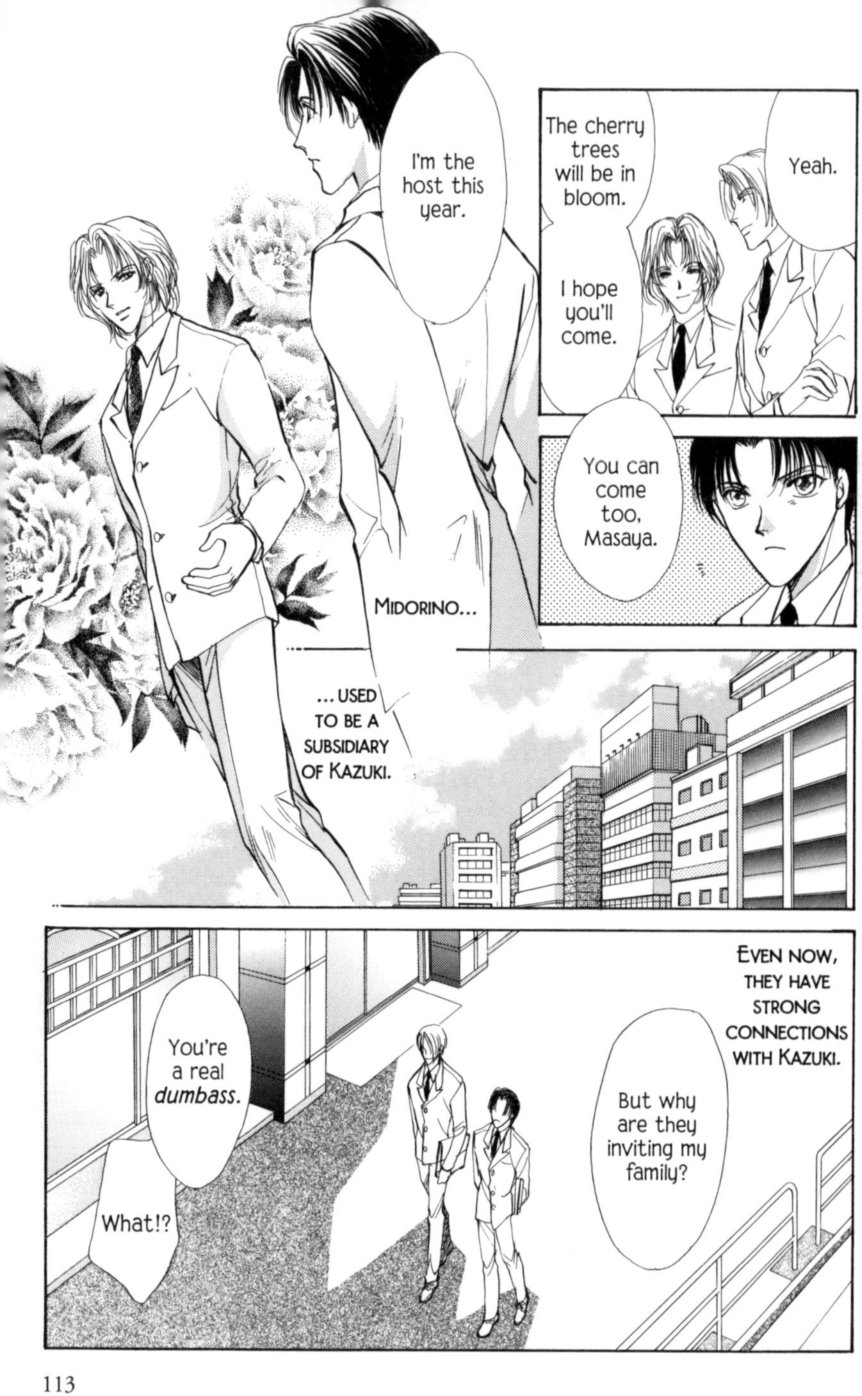
Yeah.
The cherry trees will be in bloom.
I hope you'll come.
You can come too, Masaya.
I'm the host this year.
MIDORINO...
...USED TO BE A SUBSIDIARY OF KAZUKI.
EVEN NOW, THEY HAVE STRONG CONNECTIONS WITH KAZUKI.
But why are they inviting my family?
You're a real *dumbass.*
What!?

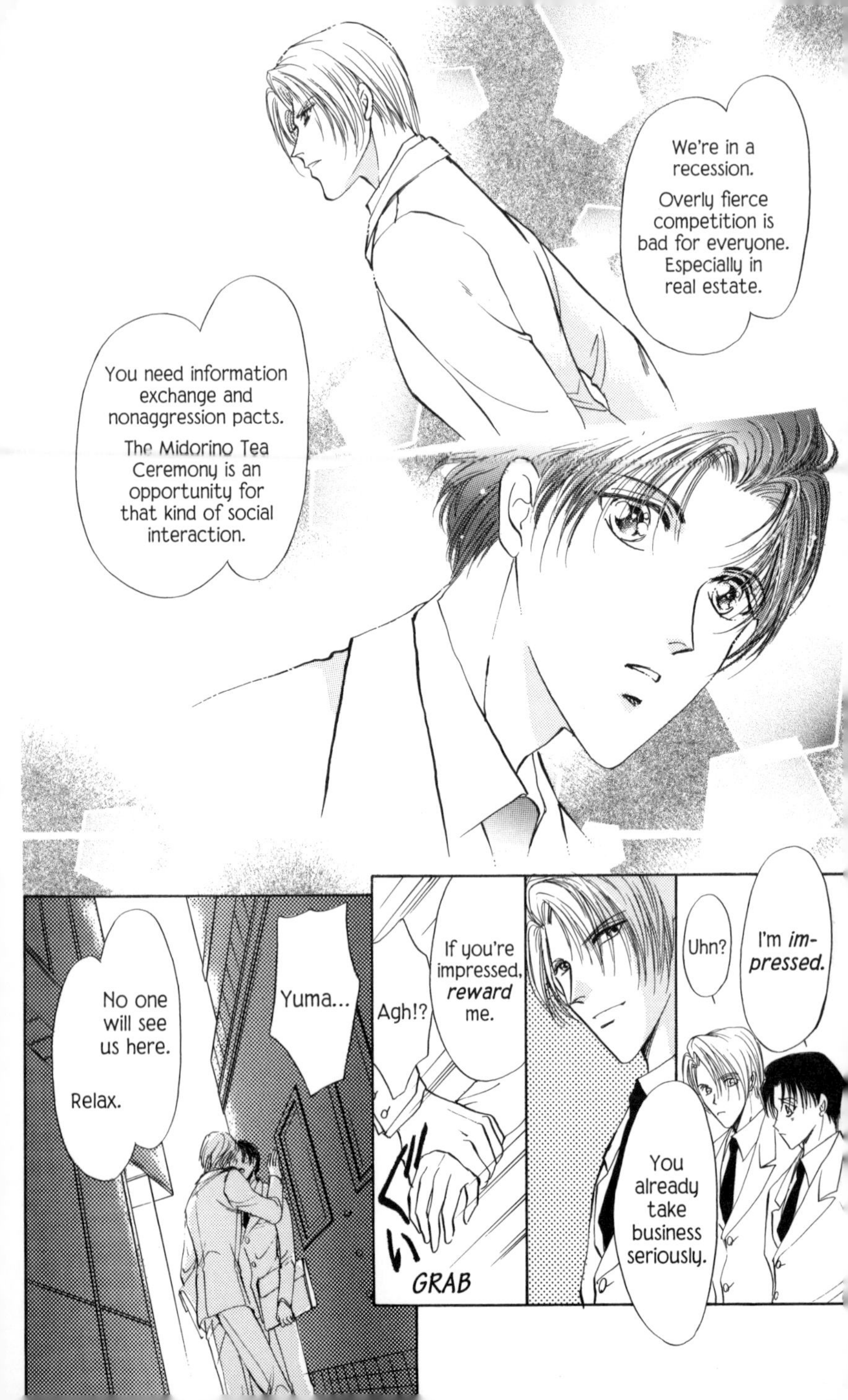
We're in a recession.
Overly fierce competition is bad for everyone. Especially in real estate.
You need information exchange and nonaggression pacts.
The Midorino Tea Ceremony is an opportunity for that kind of social interaction.
I'm *im-pressed.*
Uhn?
You already take business seriously.
If you're impressed, *reward* me.
Agh!?
GRAB
Yuma...
No one will see us here.
Relax.

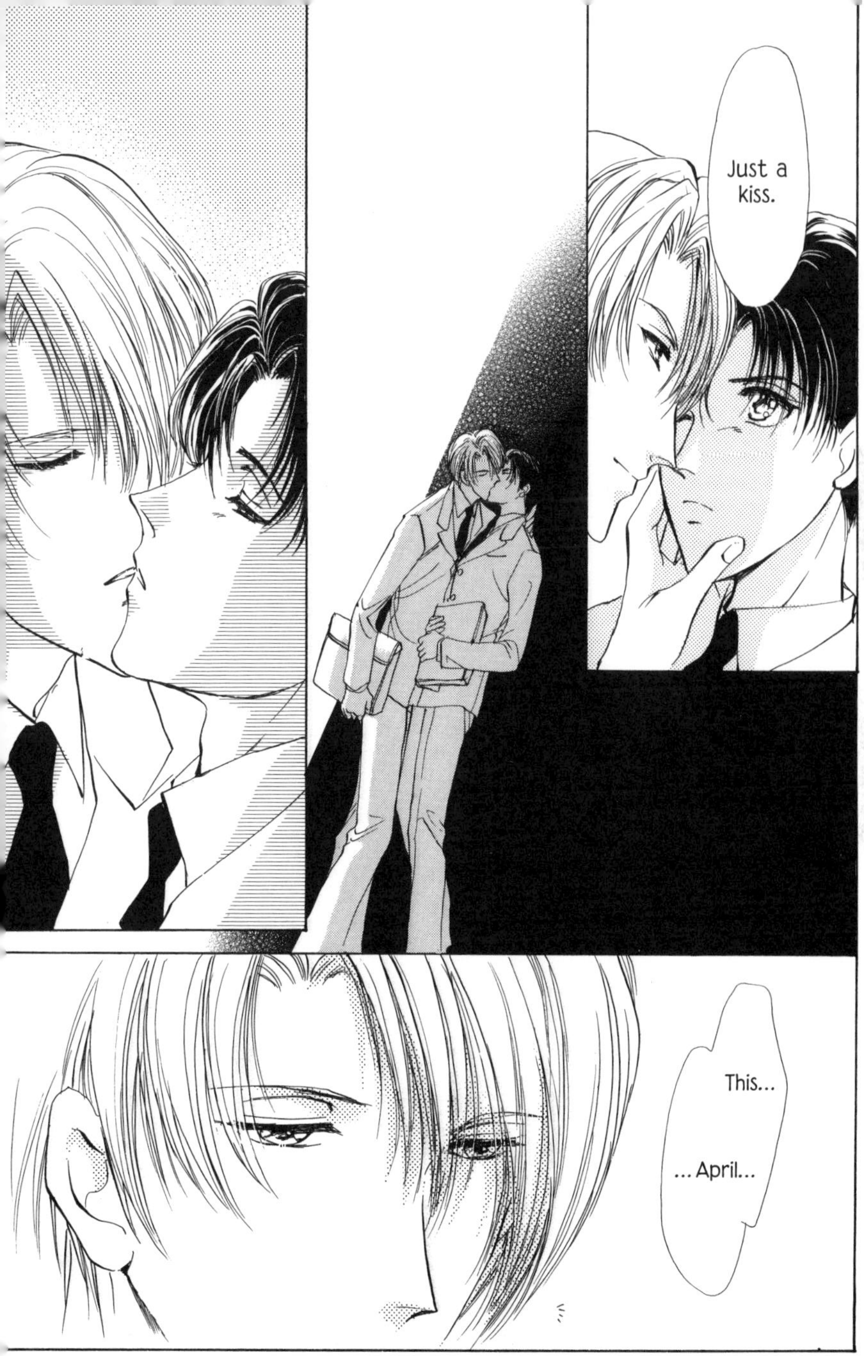
Just a kiss.
This...
...April...

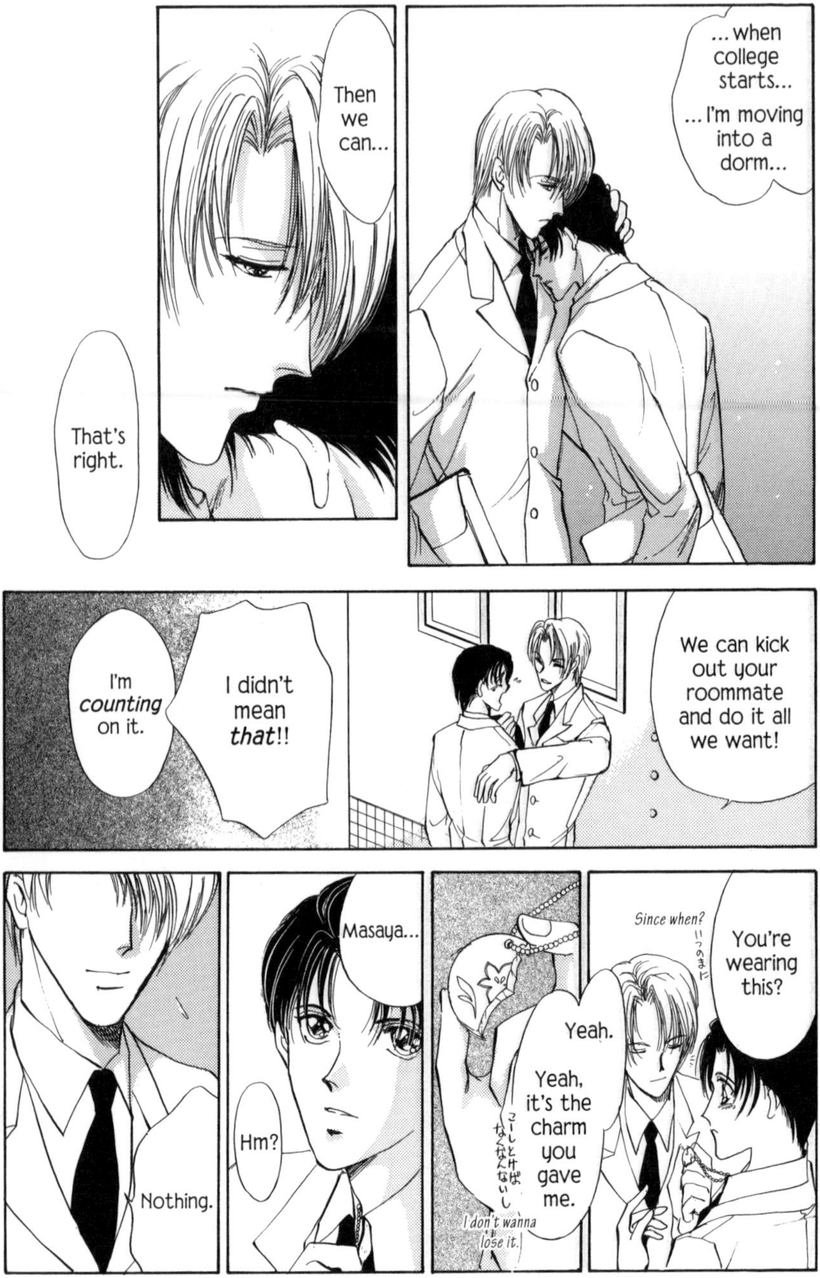
...when college starts...
...I'm moving into a dorm...
Then we can...
That's right.
We can kick out your roommate and do it all we want!
I didn't mean *that*!!
I'm *counting* on it.
You're wearing this?
Since when?
いつのまに
Yeah.
Yeah, it's the charm you gave me.
こーしとけばなくなんないし
I don't wanna lose it.
Masaya...
Hm?
Nothing.

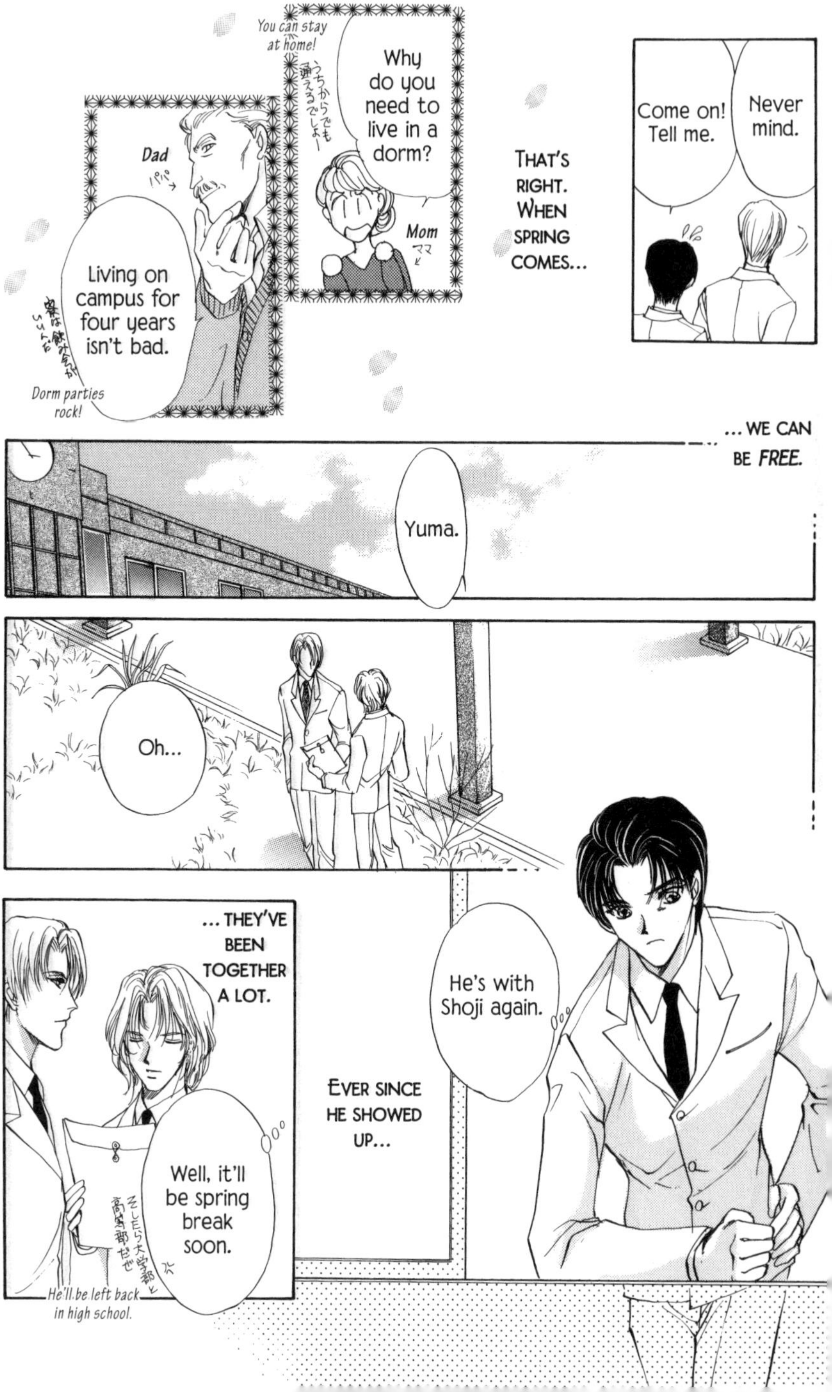
Never mind.
Come on! Tell me.
THAT'S RIGHT. WHEN SPRING COMES...
Why do you need to live in a dorm?
うちからでも通えるでしょー
You can stay at home!
ママ
Mom
パパ
Dad
Living on campus for four years isn't bad.
寮は飲み会がらしいぞ
Dorm parties rock!
...WE CAN BE FREE.
Yuma.
Oh...
He's with Shoji again.
EVER SINCE HE SHOWED UP...
...THEY'VE BEEN TOGETHER A LOT.
Well, it'll be spring break soon.
そしたら大学部と高等部だぜ
He'll be left back in high school.

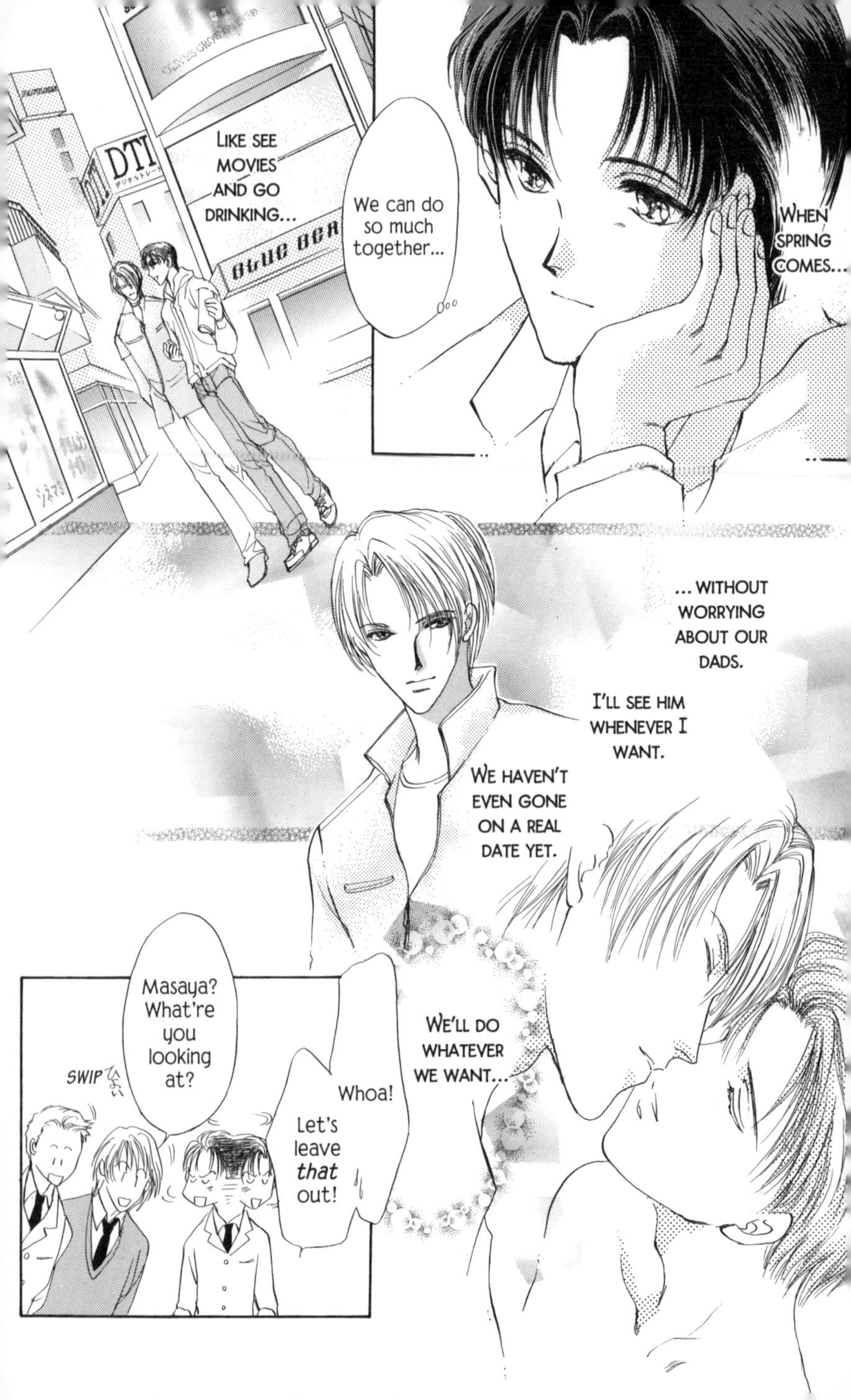
When spring comes...
We can do so much together...
Like see movies and go drinking...
...without worrying about our dads.
I'll see him whenever I want.
We haven't even gone on a real date yet.
We'll do whatever we want...
Masaya? What're you looking at?
SWIP
Whoa!
Let's leave *that* out!

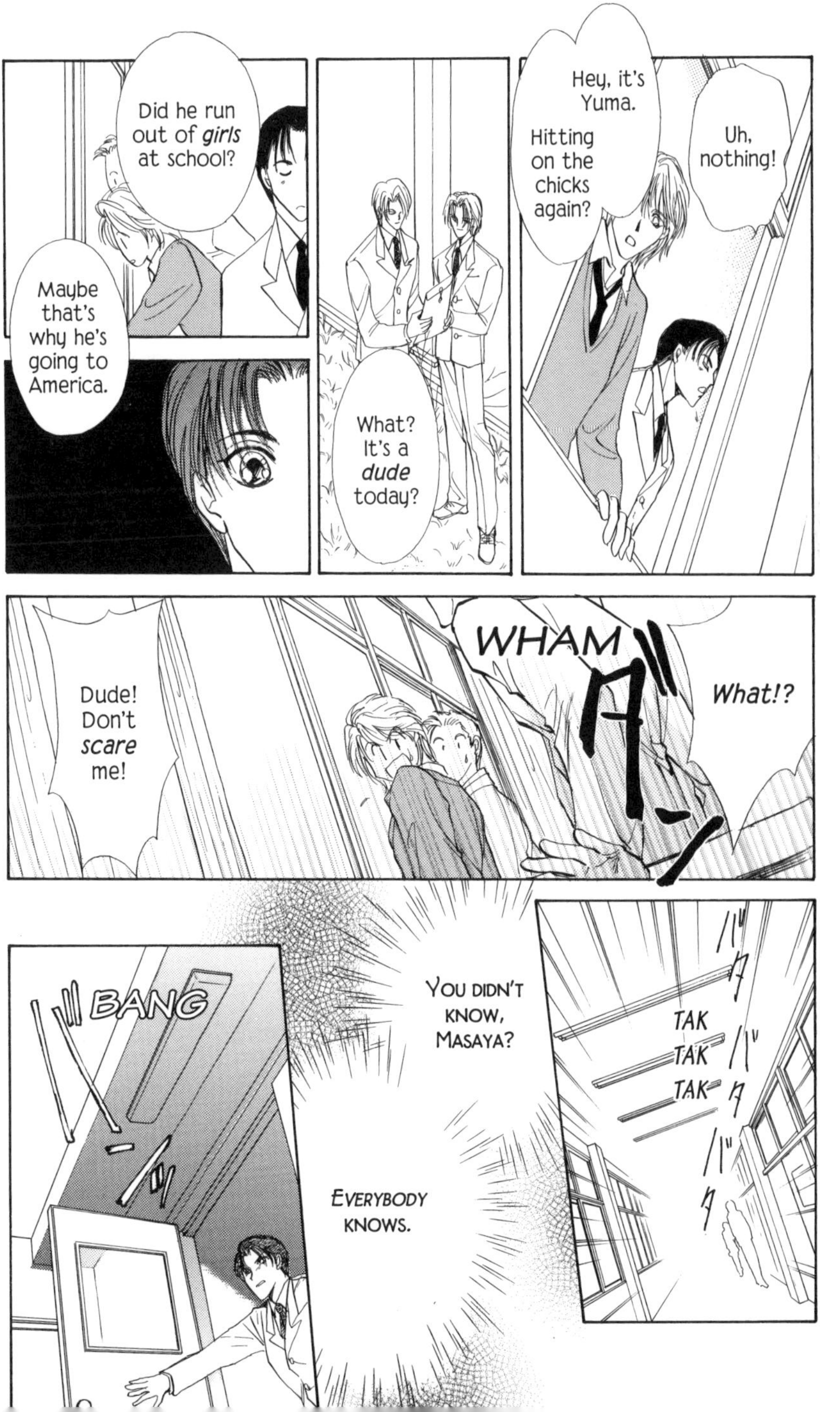
Hey, it's Yuma.
Hitting on the chicks again?
Uh, nothing!
What? It's a *dude* today?
Did he run out of *girls* at school?
Maybe that's why he's going to America.
What!?
WHAM
Dude! Don't *scare* me!
TAK TAK TAK
YOU DIDN'T KNOW, MASAYA?
EVERYBODY KNOWS.
BANG

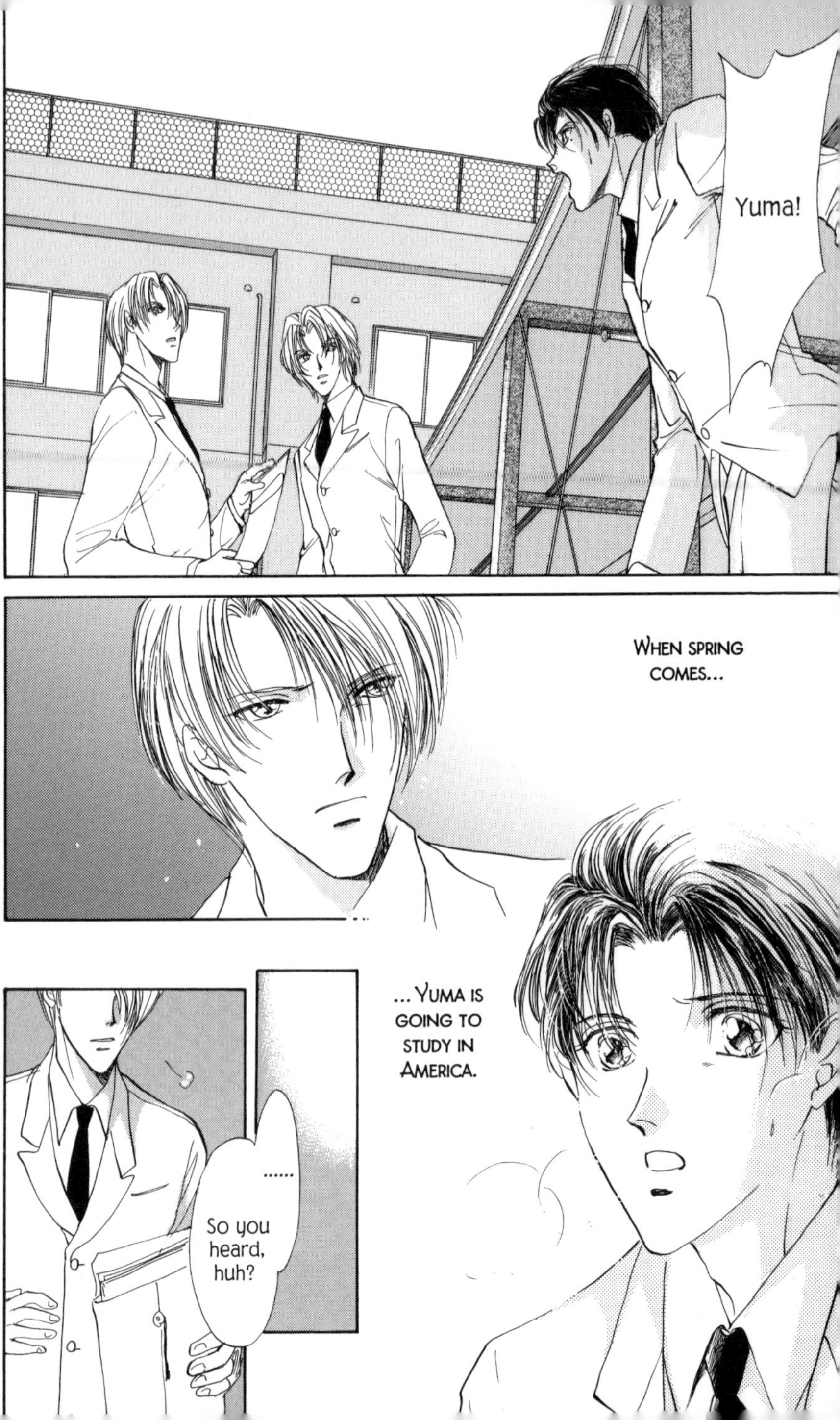
Yuma!
When spring comes...
...Yuma is going to study in America.
......
So you heard, huh?

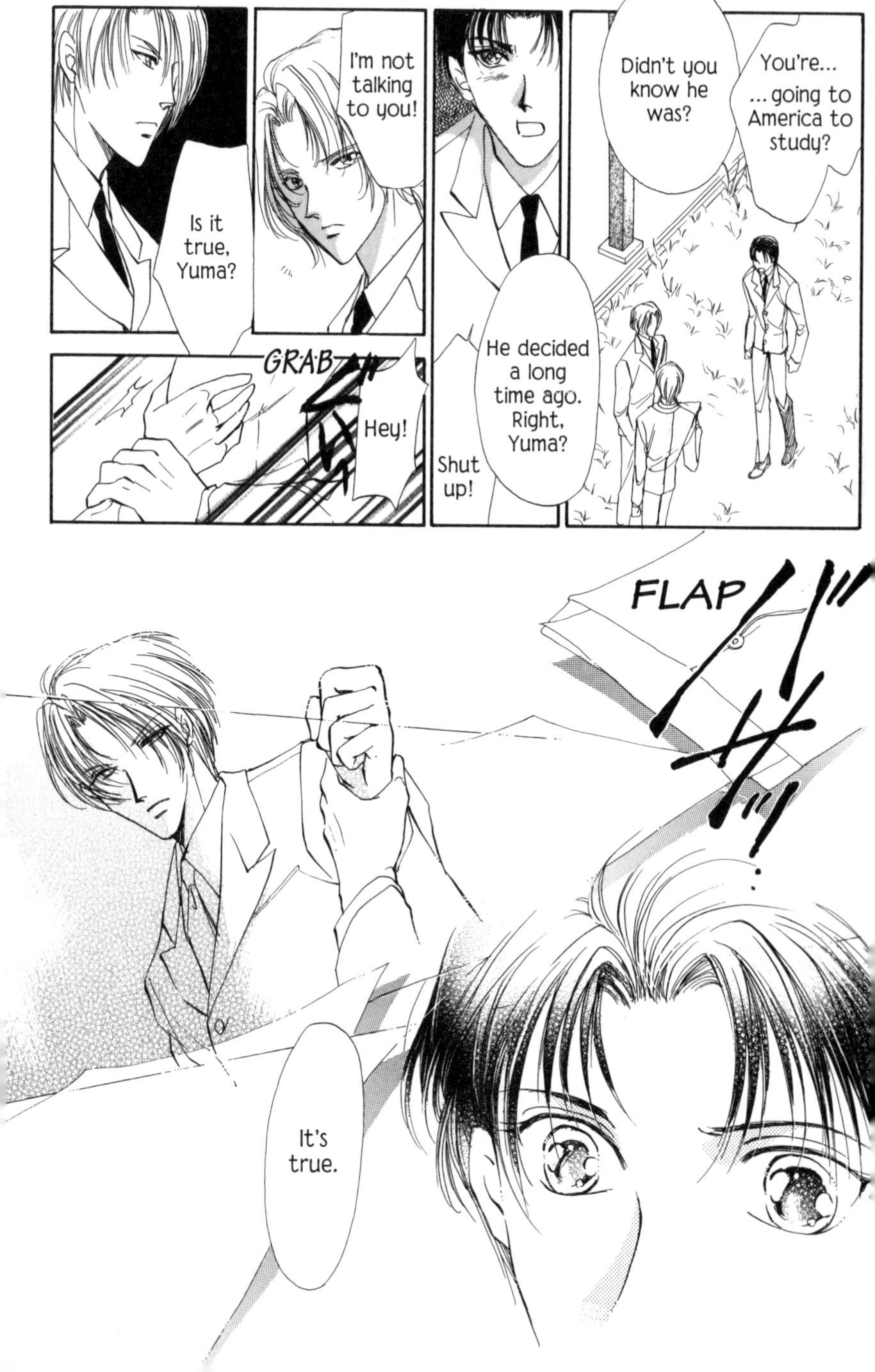
You're...
...going to America to study?
Didn't you know he was?
He decided a long time ago. Right, Yuma?
Shut up!
I'm not talking to you!
Is it true, Yuma?
GRAB
Hey!
FLAP
It's true.

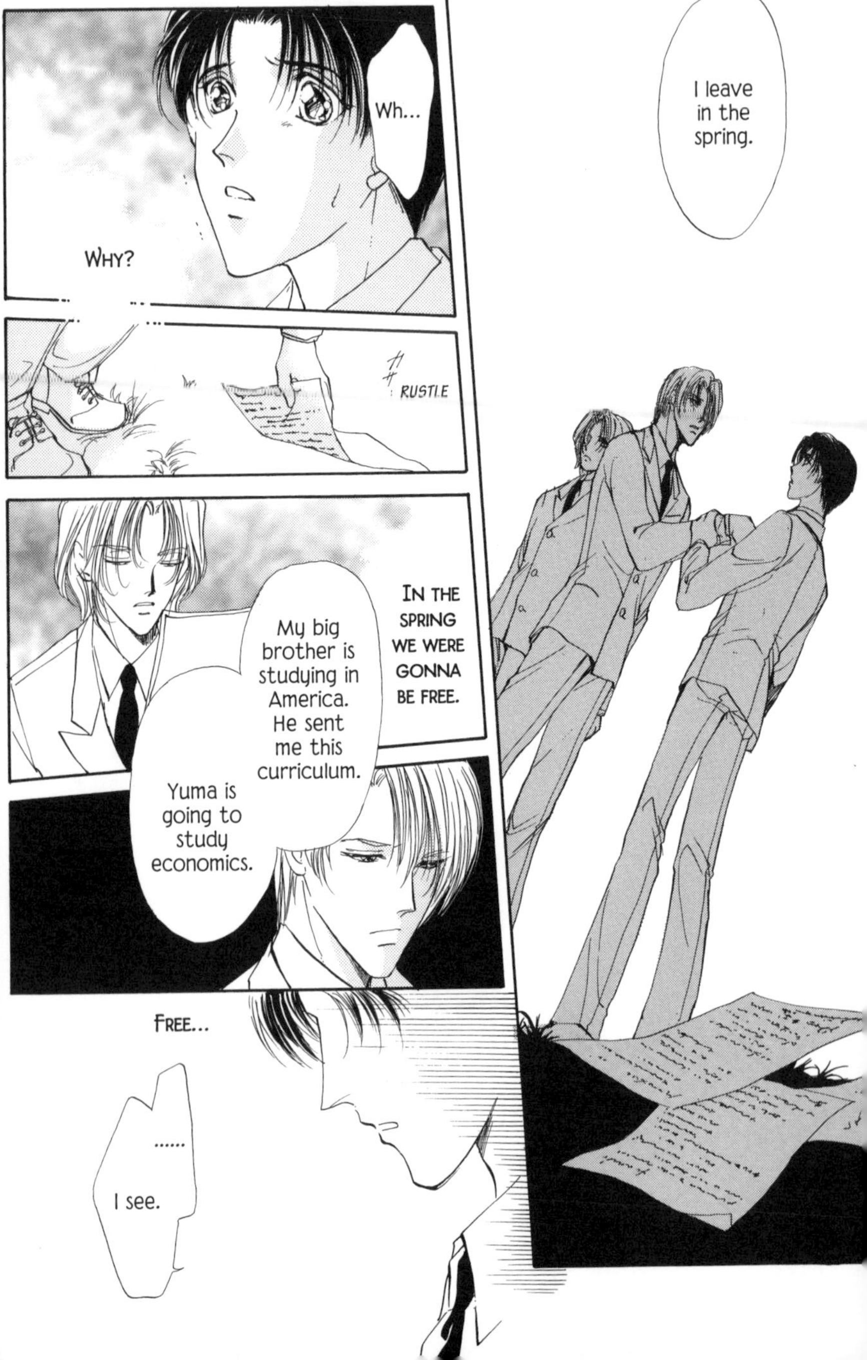
I leave in the spring.
Wh...
WHY?
RUSTLE
IN THE SPRING WE WERE GONNA BE FREE.
My big brother is studying in America. He sent me this curriculum.
Yuma is going to study economics.
FREE...
......
I see.

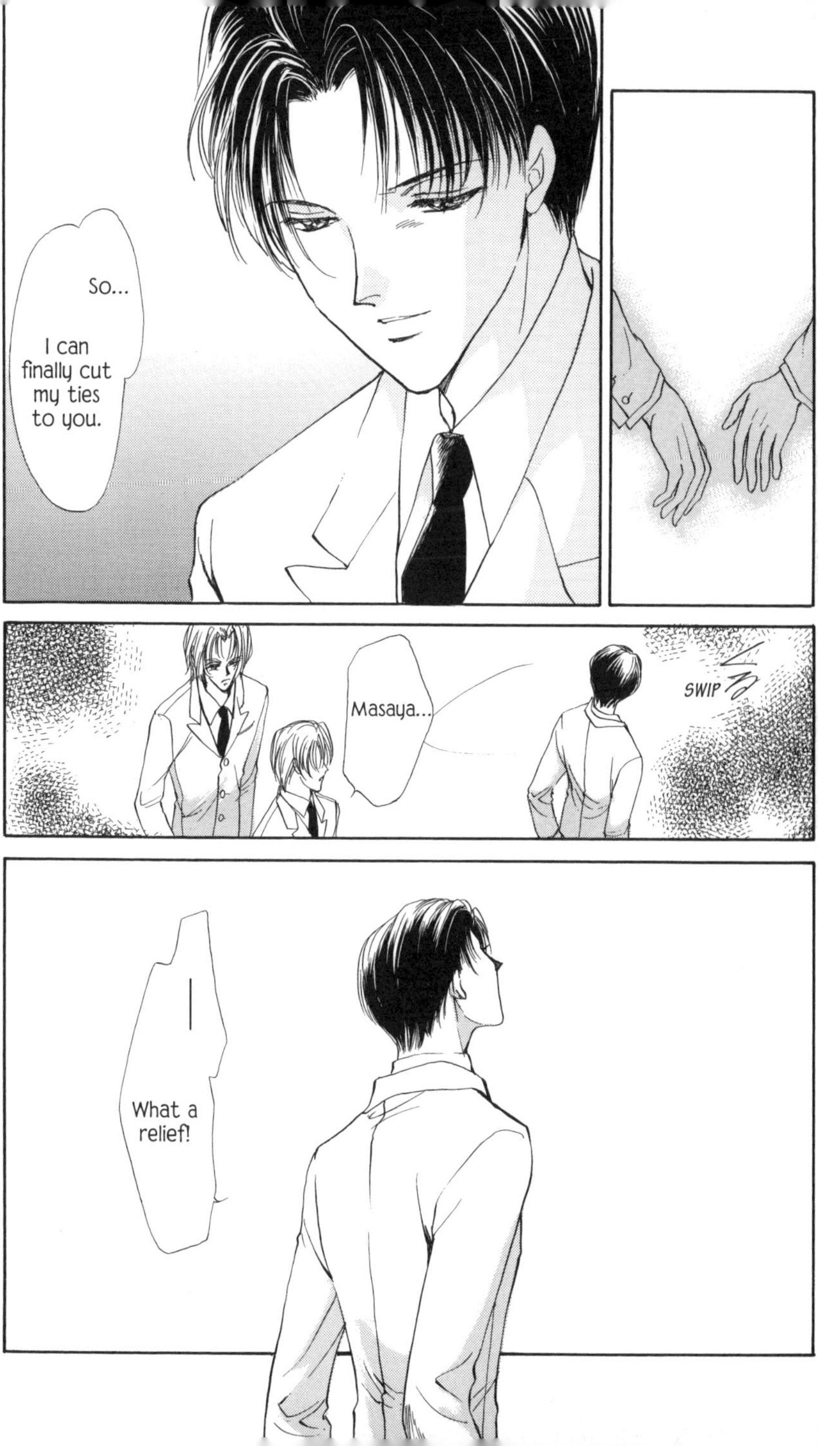
So... I can finally cut my ties to you.
SWIP
Masaya...
I
What a relief!

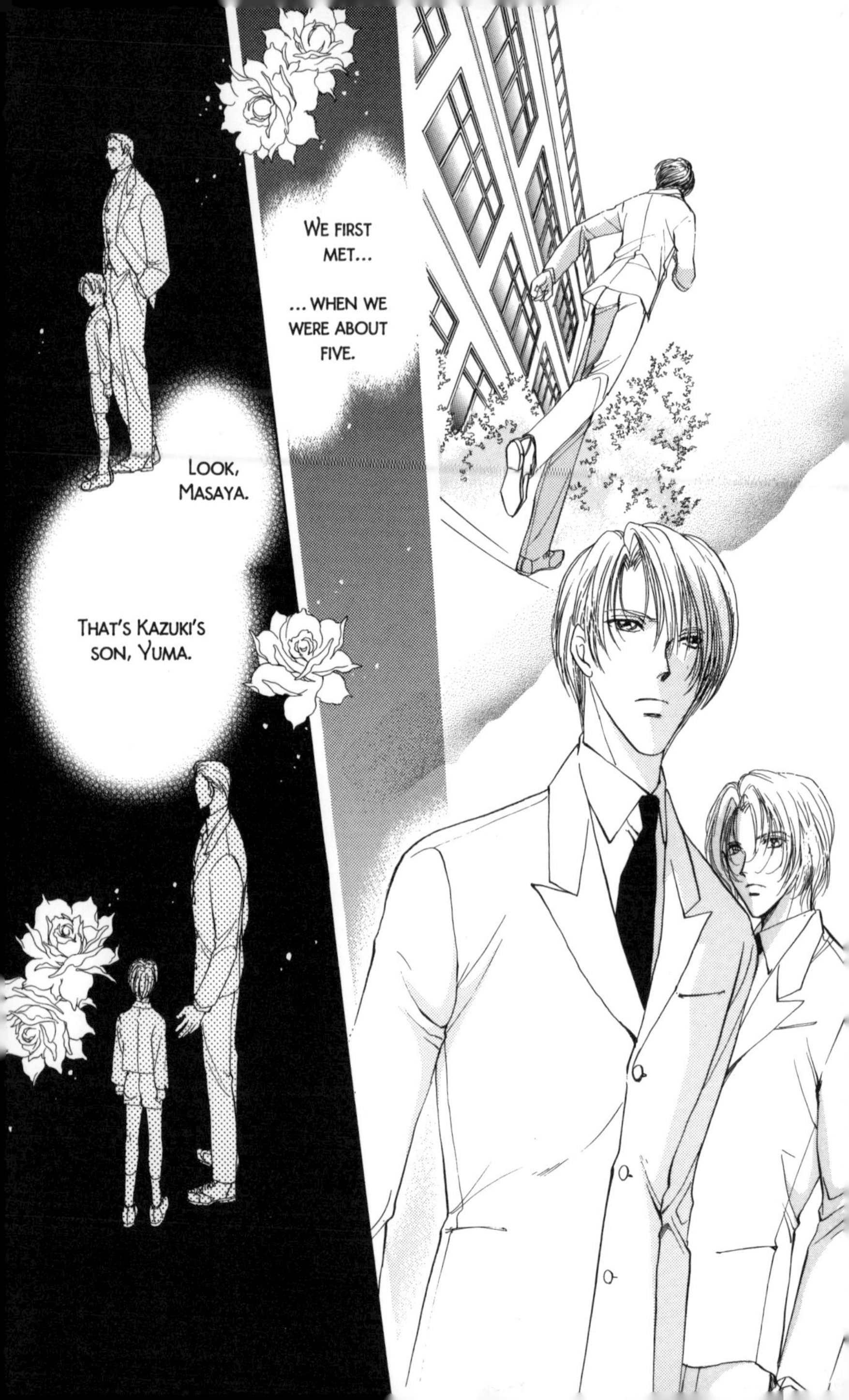
WE FIRST MET...
...WHEN WE WERE ABOUT FIVE.
LOOK, MASAYA.
THAT'S KAZUKI'S SON, YUMA.

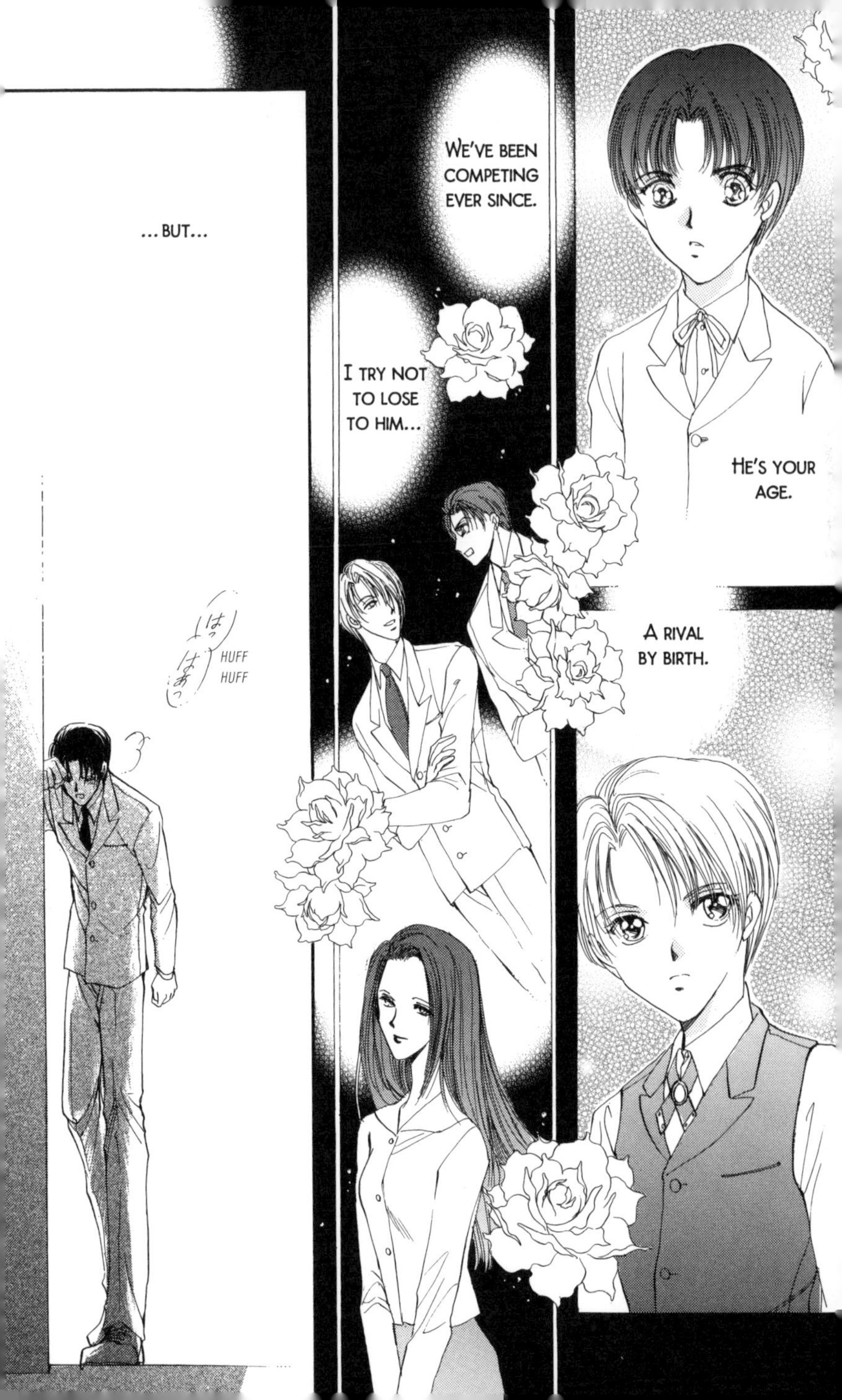
HE'S YOUR AGE.
A RIVAL BY BIRTH.
WE'VE BEEN COMPETING EVER SINCE.
I TRY NOT TO LOSE TO HIM...
...BUT...
はっ はあっ
HUFF HUFF

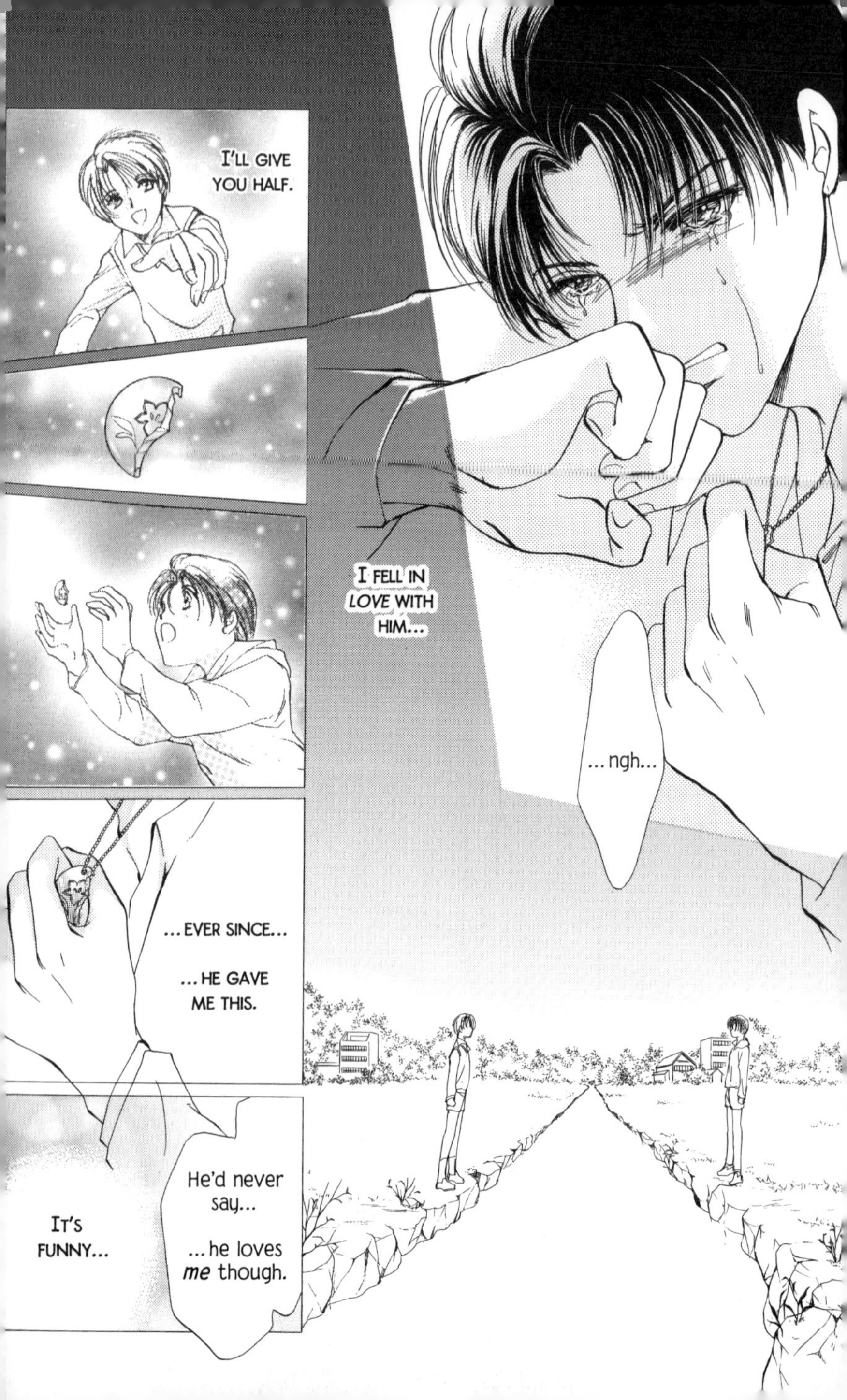
I FELL IN LOVE WITH HIM...
...ngh...
I'LL GIVE YOU HALF.
...EVER SINCE...
...HE GAVE ME THIS.
He'd never say...
...he loves me though.
IT'S FUNNY...

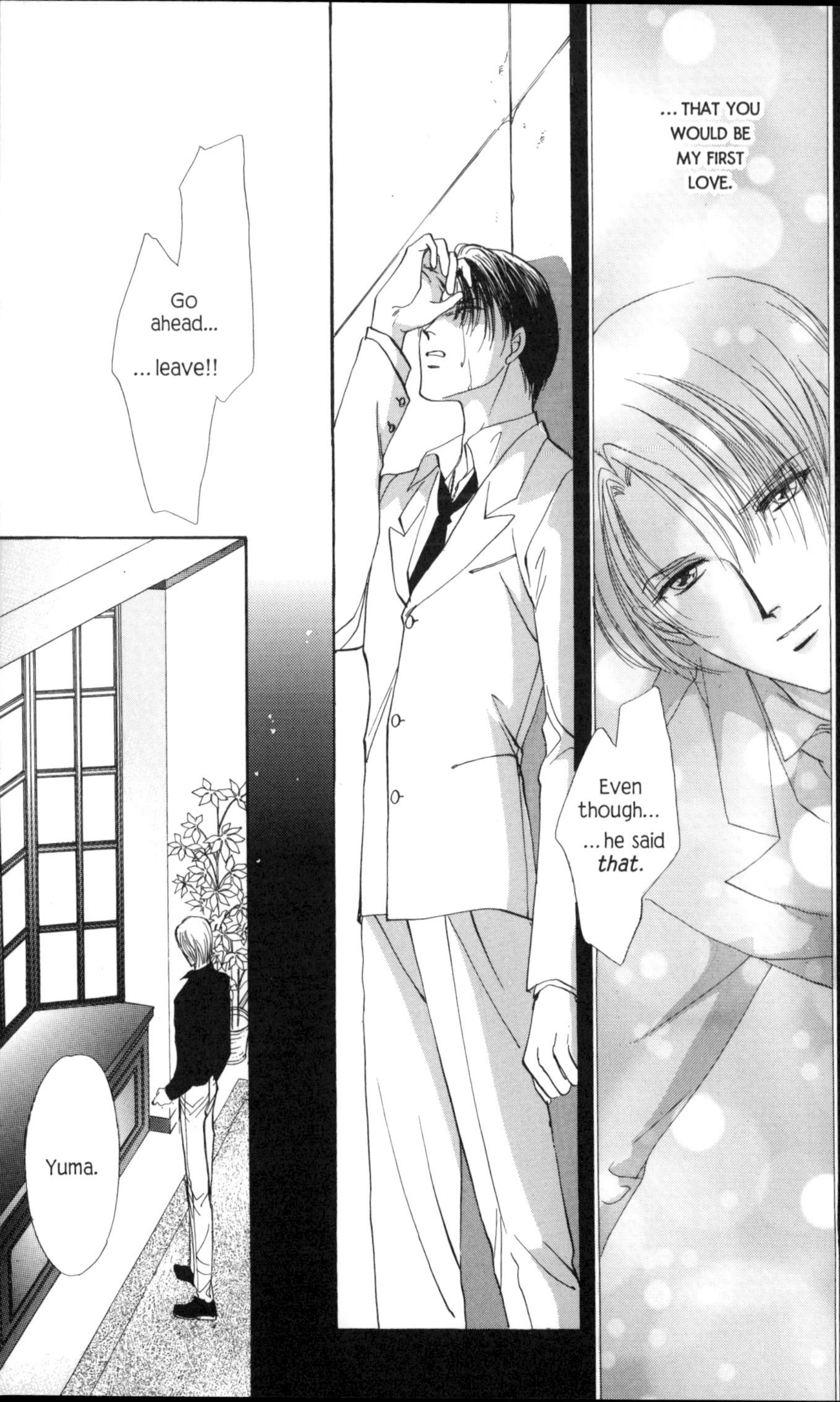
...THAT YOU WOULD BE MY FIRST LOVE.
Even though... ...he said *that*.
Go ahead... ...leave!!
Yuma.

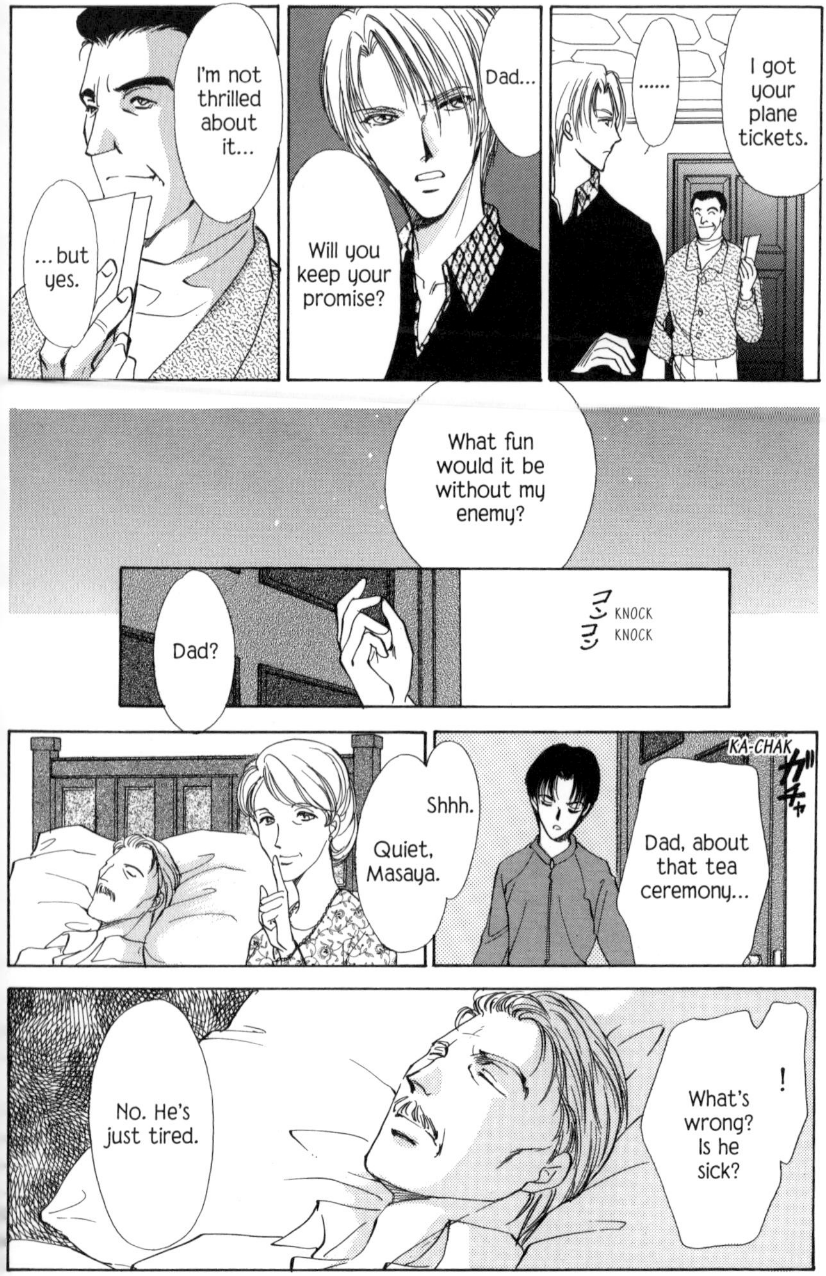
I got your plane tickets.
......
Dad...
Will you keep your promise?
I'm not thrilled about it...
...but yes.
What fun would it be without my enemy?
コンコン KNOCK KNOCK
Dad?
ガチャ KA-CHAK
Dad, about that tea ceremony...
Shhh.
Quiet, Masaya.
!
What's wrong? Is he sick?
No. He's just tired.

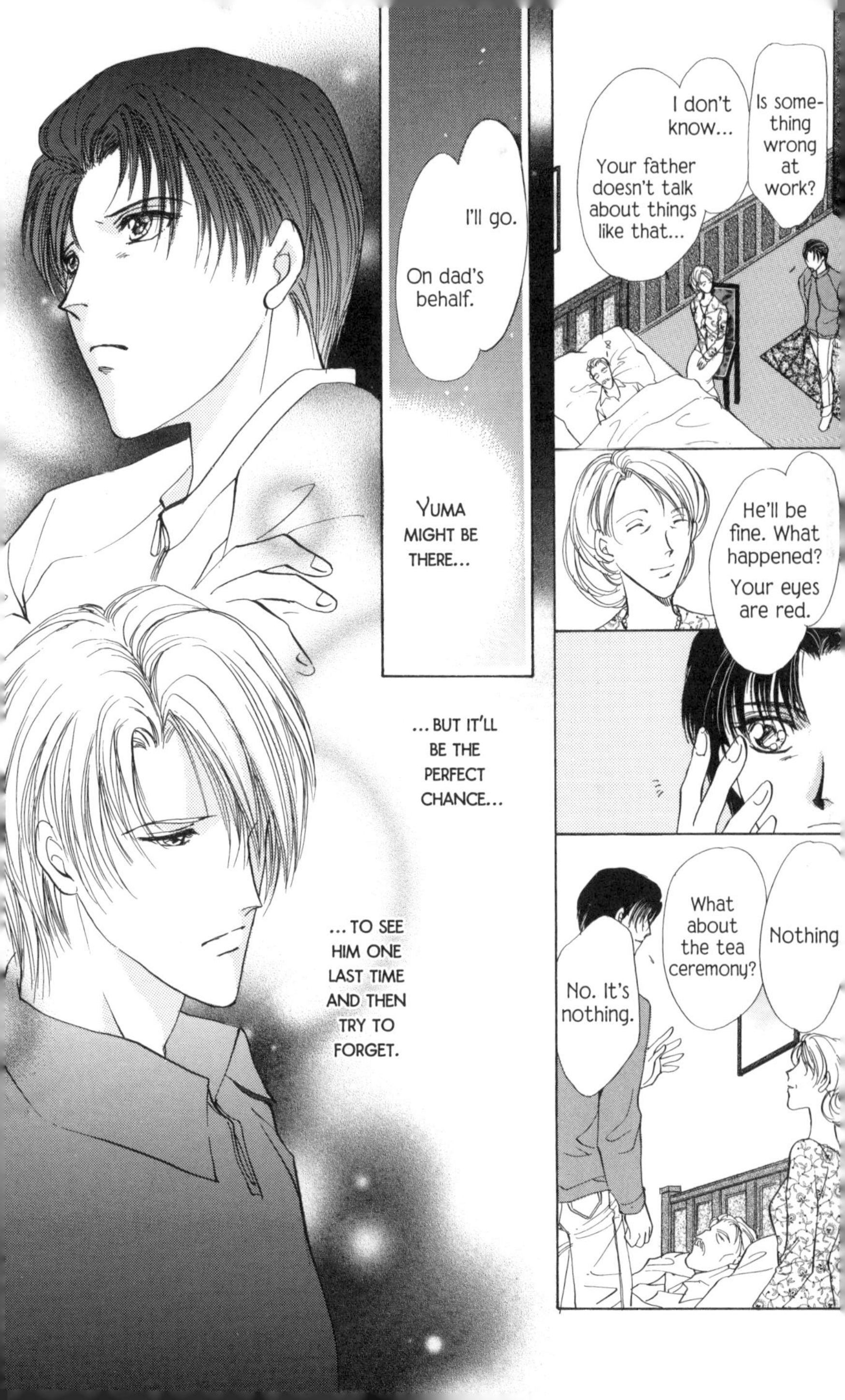
Is something wrong at work?
I don't know... Your father doesn't talk about things like that...
He'll be fine. What happened? Your eyes are red.
Nothing
What about the tea ceremony?
No. It's nothing.
I'll go. On dad's behalf.
YUMA MIGHT BE THERE...
...BUT IT'LL BE THE PERFECT CHANCE...
...TO SEE HIM ONE LAST TIME AND THEN TRY TO FORGET.

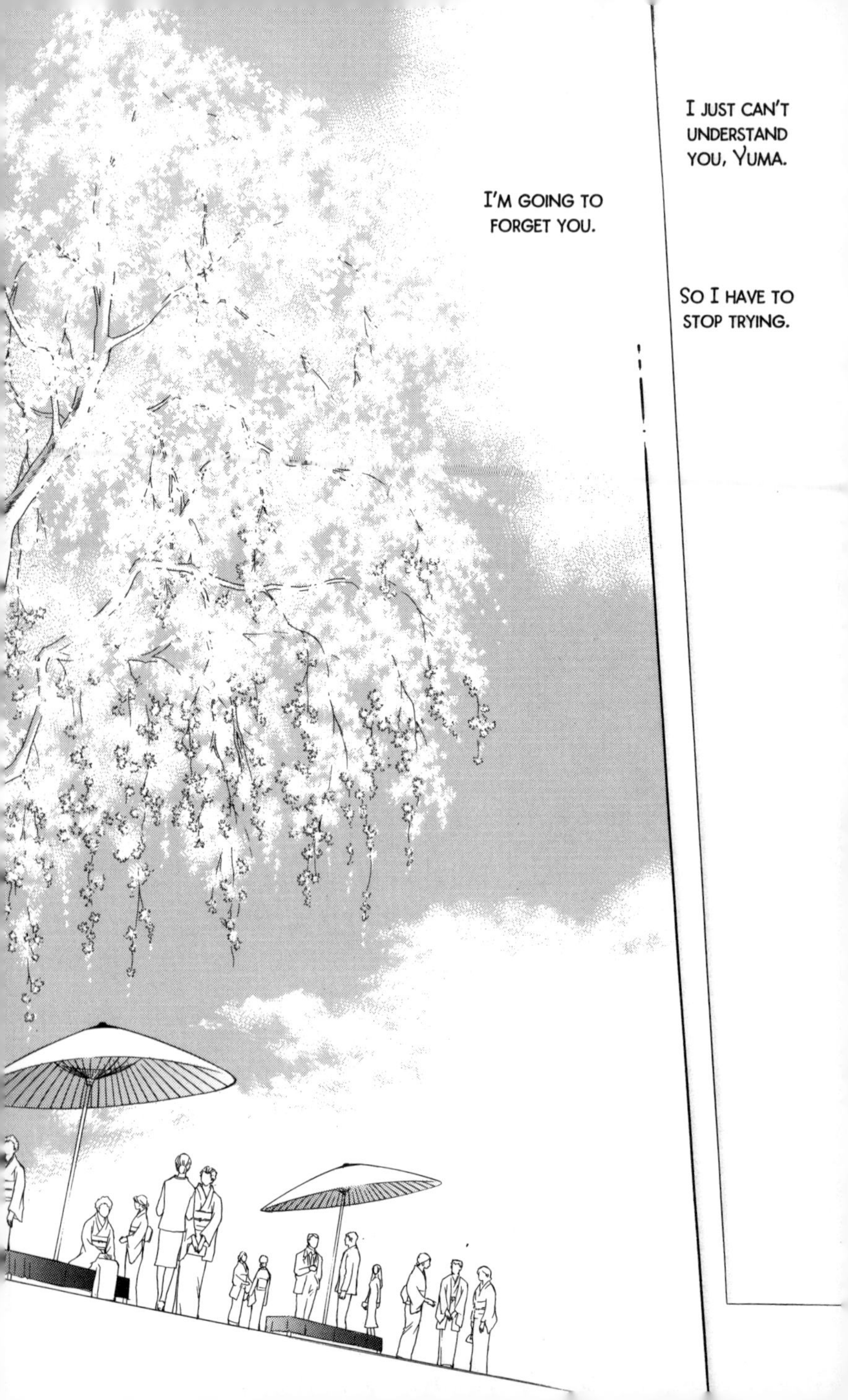
I JUST CAN'T UNDERSTAND YOU, YUMA.
SO I HAVE TO STOP TRYING.
I'M GOING TO FORGET YOU.

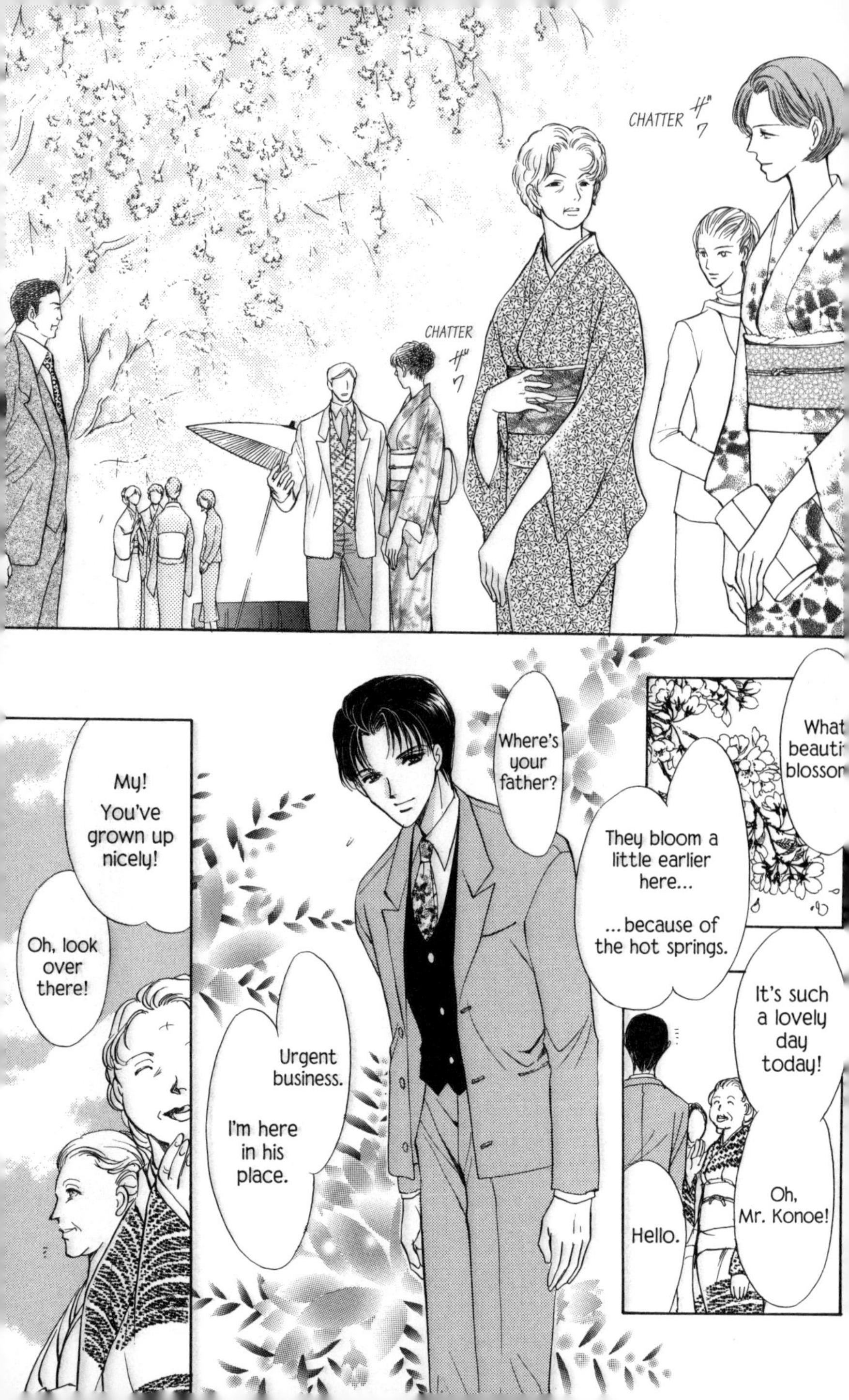
CHATTER ザワ
CHATTER ザワ
What beauti blossom
They bloom a little earlier here...
...because of the hot springs.
It's such a lovely day today!
Oh, Mr. Konoe!
Hello.
Where's your father?
Urgent business.
I'm here in his place.
My! You've grown up nicely!
Oh, look over there!

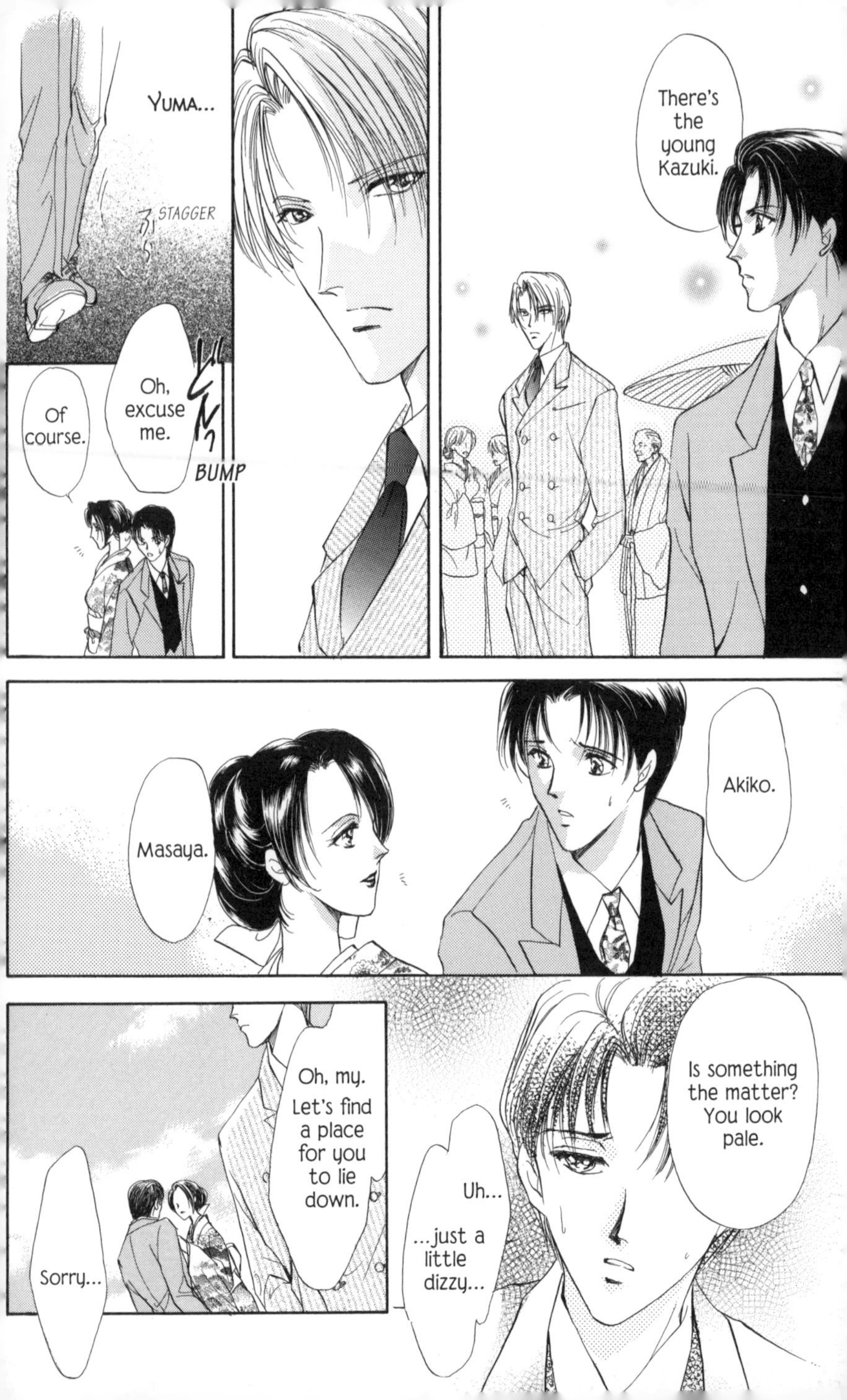
There's the young Kazuki.
Yuma...
STAGGER
Oh, excuse me.
BUMP
Of course.
Akiko.
Masaya.
Is something the matter? You look pale.
Uh...
...just a little dizzy...
Oh, my. Let's find a place for you to lie down.
Sorry...

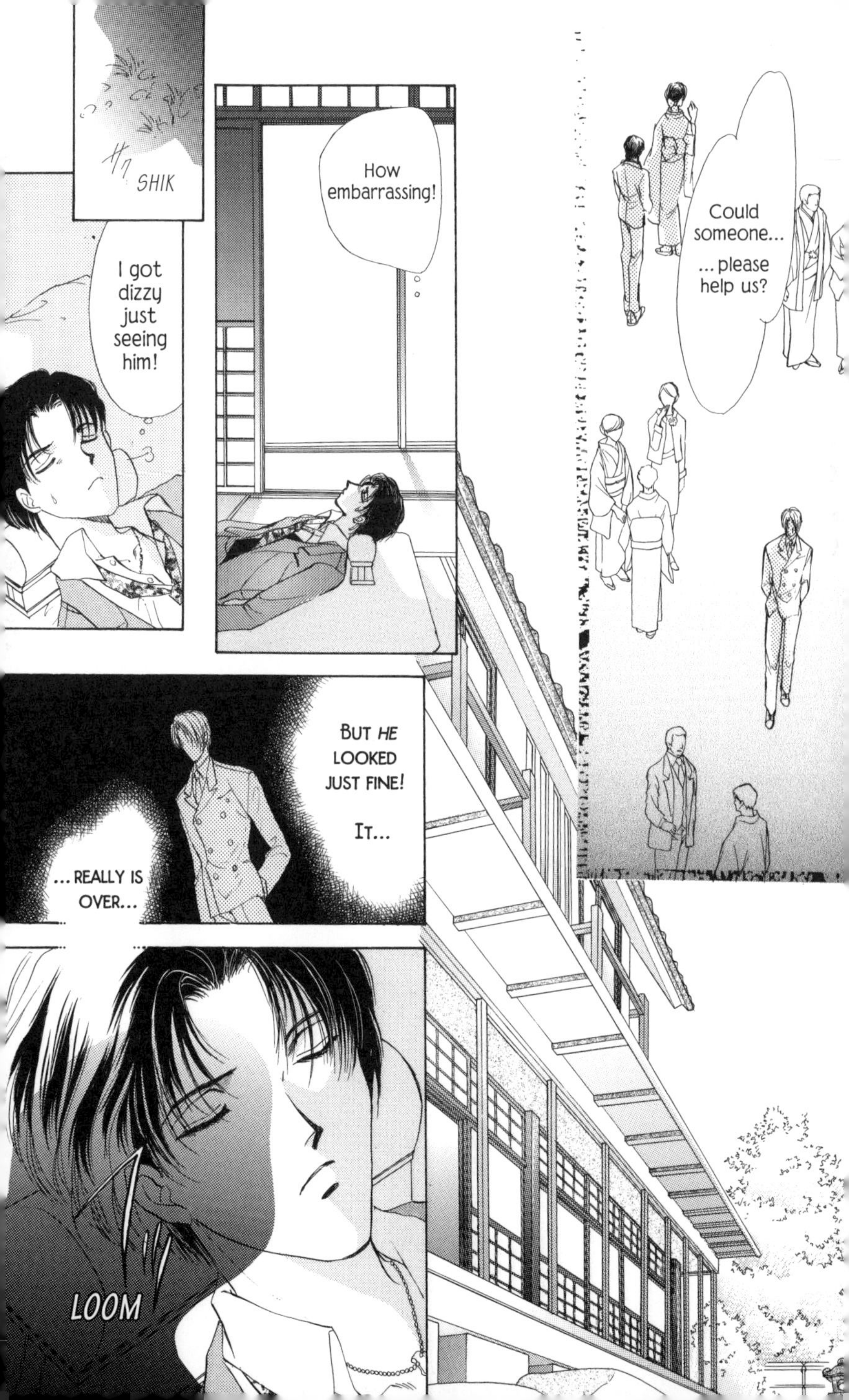
Could someone...
...please help us?
How embarrassing!
SHIK
I got dizzy just seeing him!
But he looked just fine!
It...
...really is over...
LOOM

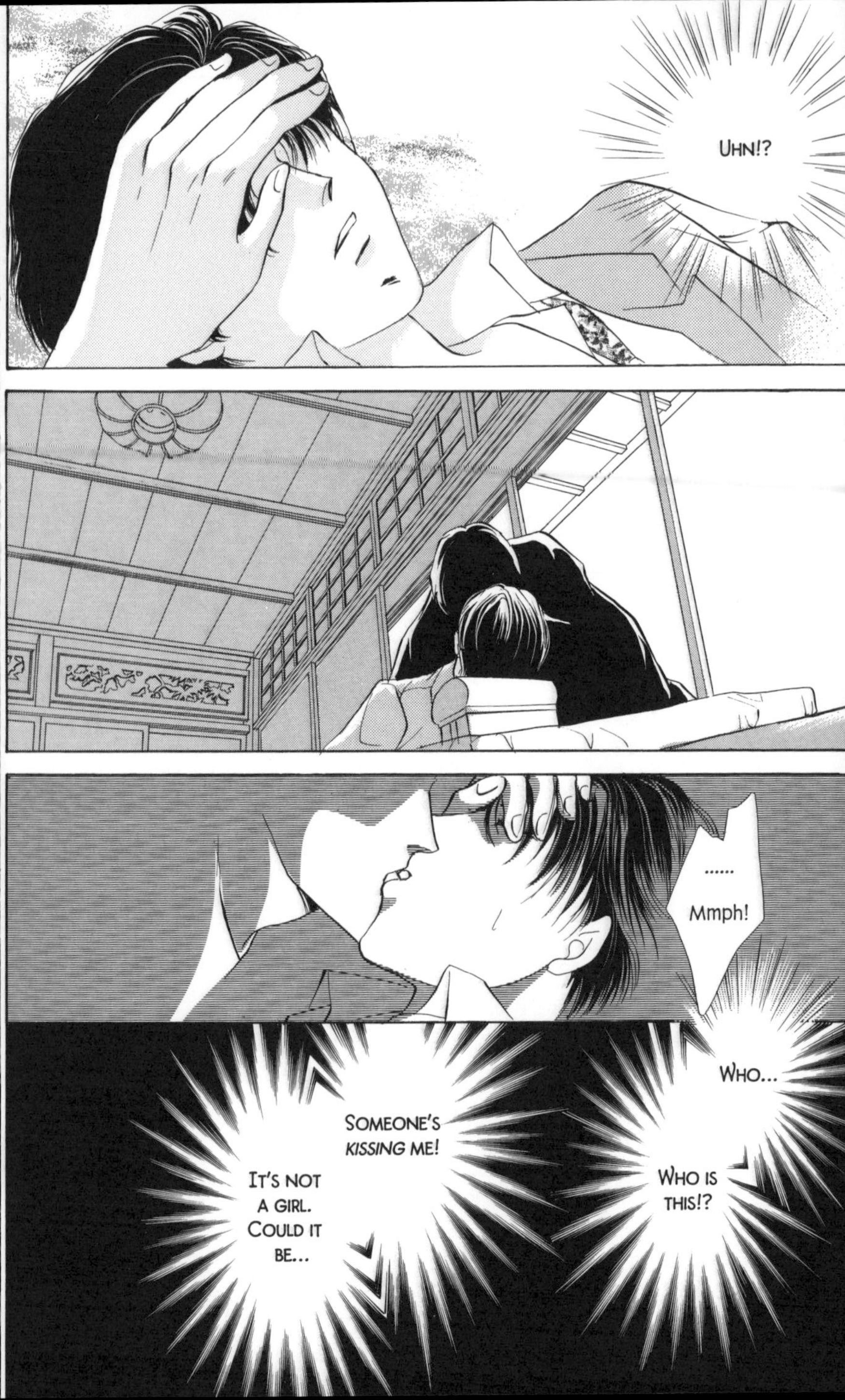
UHN!?
......
Mmph!
WHO...
WHO IS THIS!?
SOMEONE'S *KISSING* ME!
IT'S NOT A GIRL. COULD IT BE...

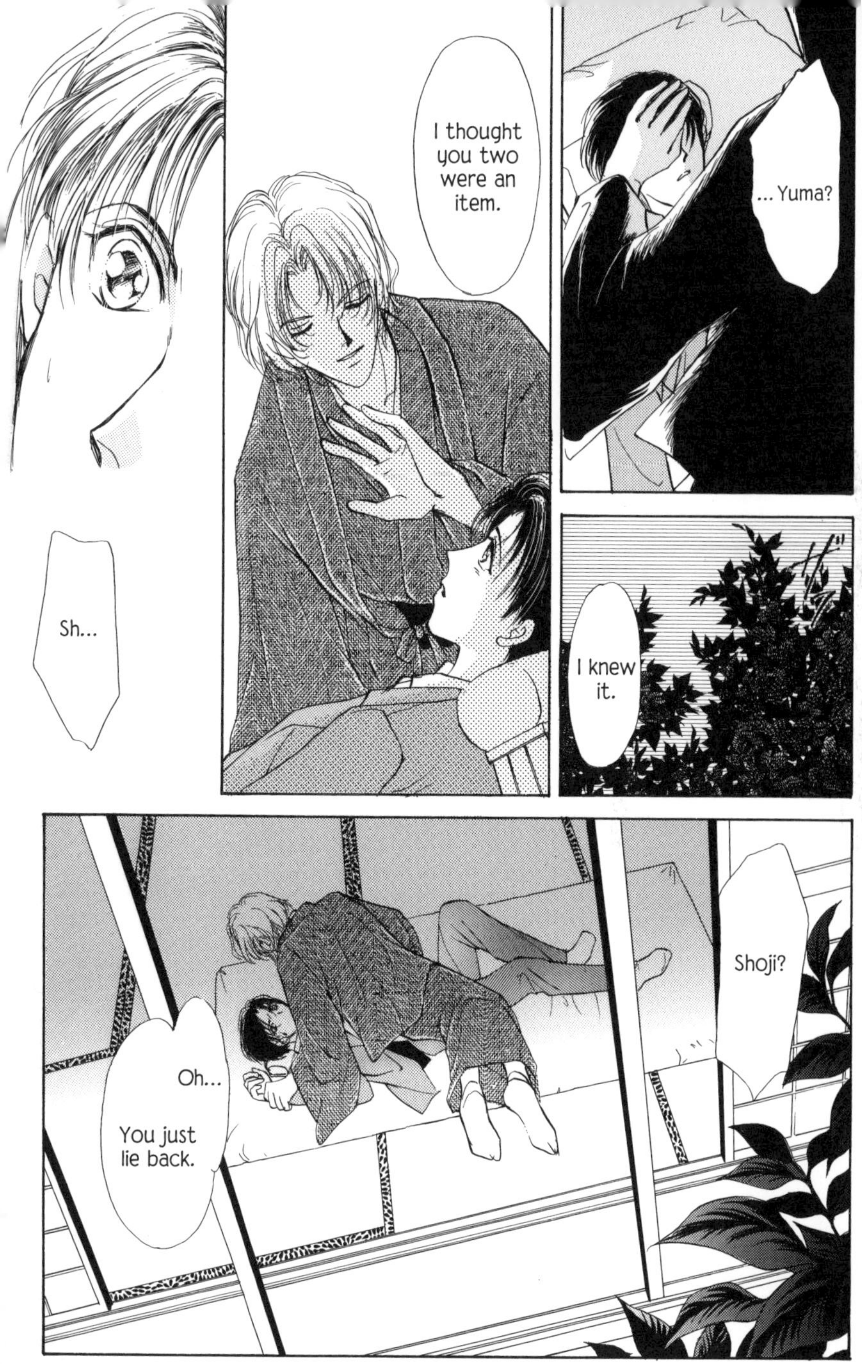

... Yuma?
I knew it.
I thought you two were an item.
Sh...
Shoji?
Oh...
You just lie back.

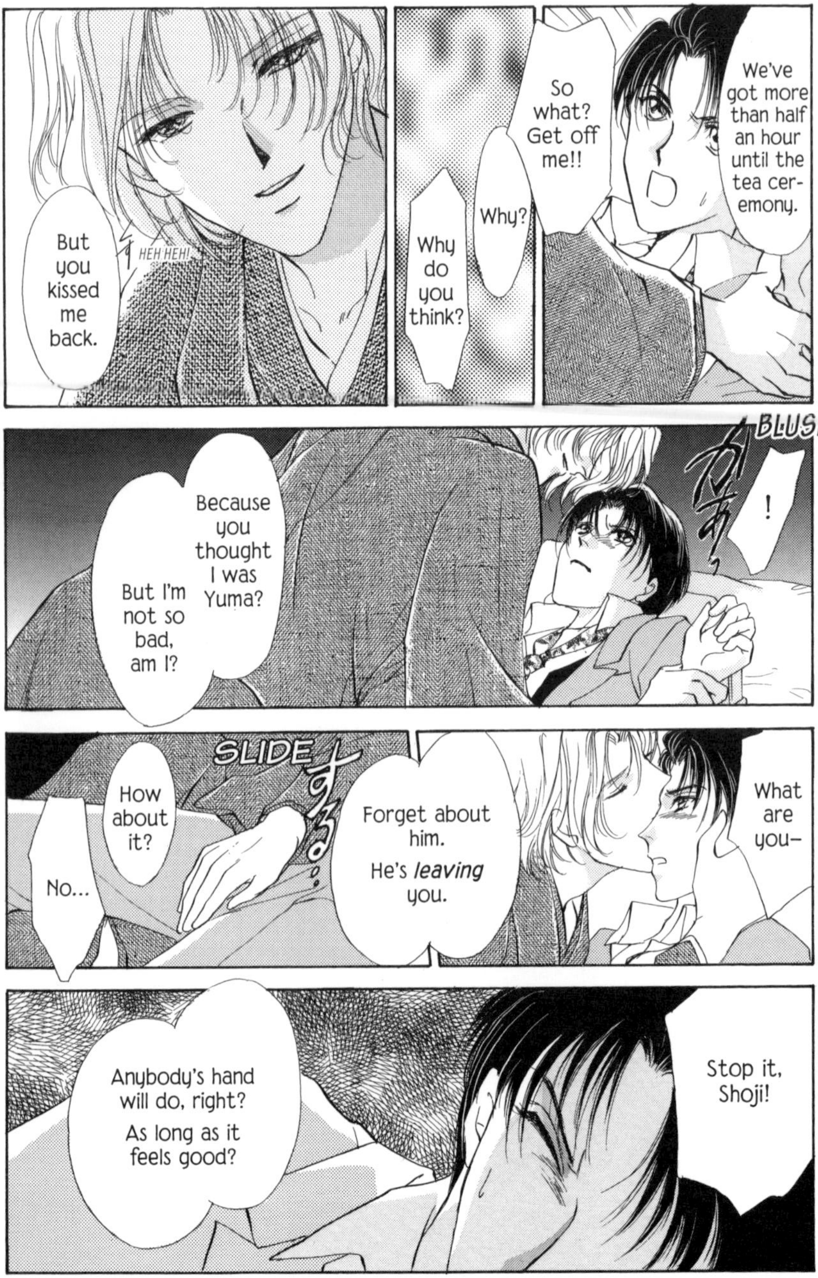
We've got more than half an hour until the tea ceremony.
So what? Get off me!!
Why?
Why do you think?
HEH HEH!
But you kissed me back.
BLUSH
!
Because you thought I was Yuma?
But I'm not so bad, am I?
What are you–
Forget about him.
He's *leaving* you.
SLIDE
How about it?
No...
Stop it, Shoji!
Anybody's hand will do, right?
As long as it feels good?

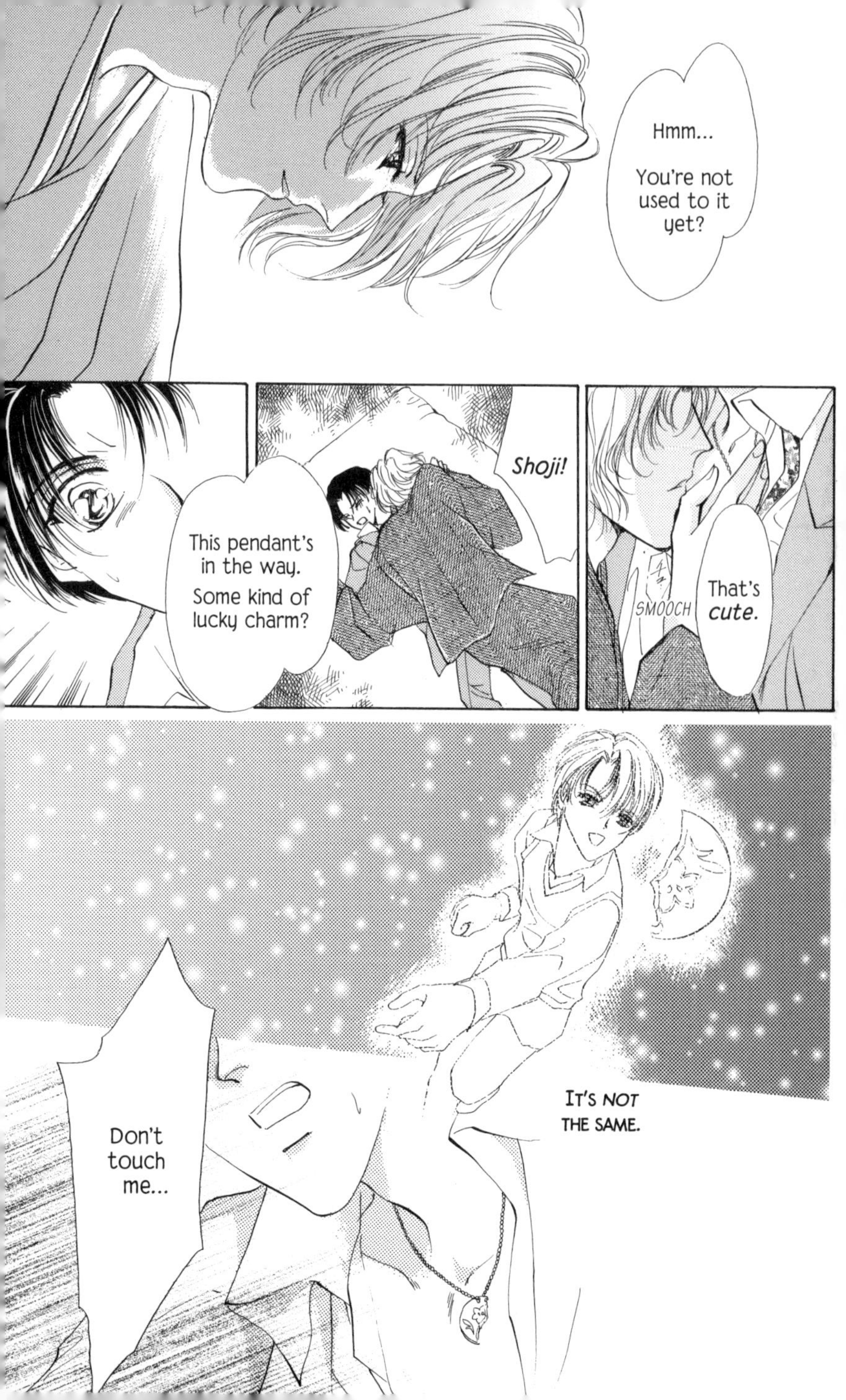
Hmm... You're not used to it yet?
SMOOCH
That's *cute.*
Shoji!
This pendant's in the way. Some kind of lucky charm?
It's *NOT* THE SAME.
Don't touch me...

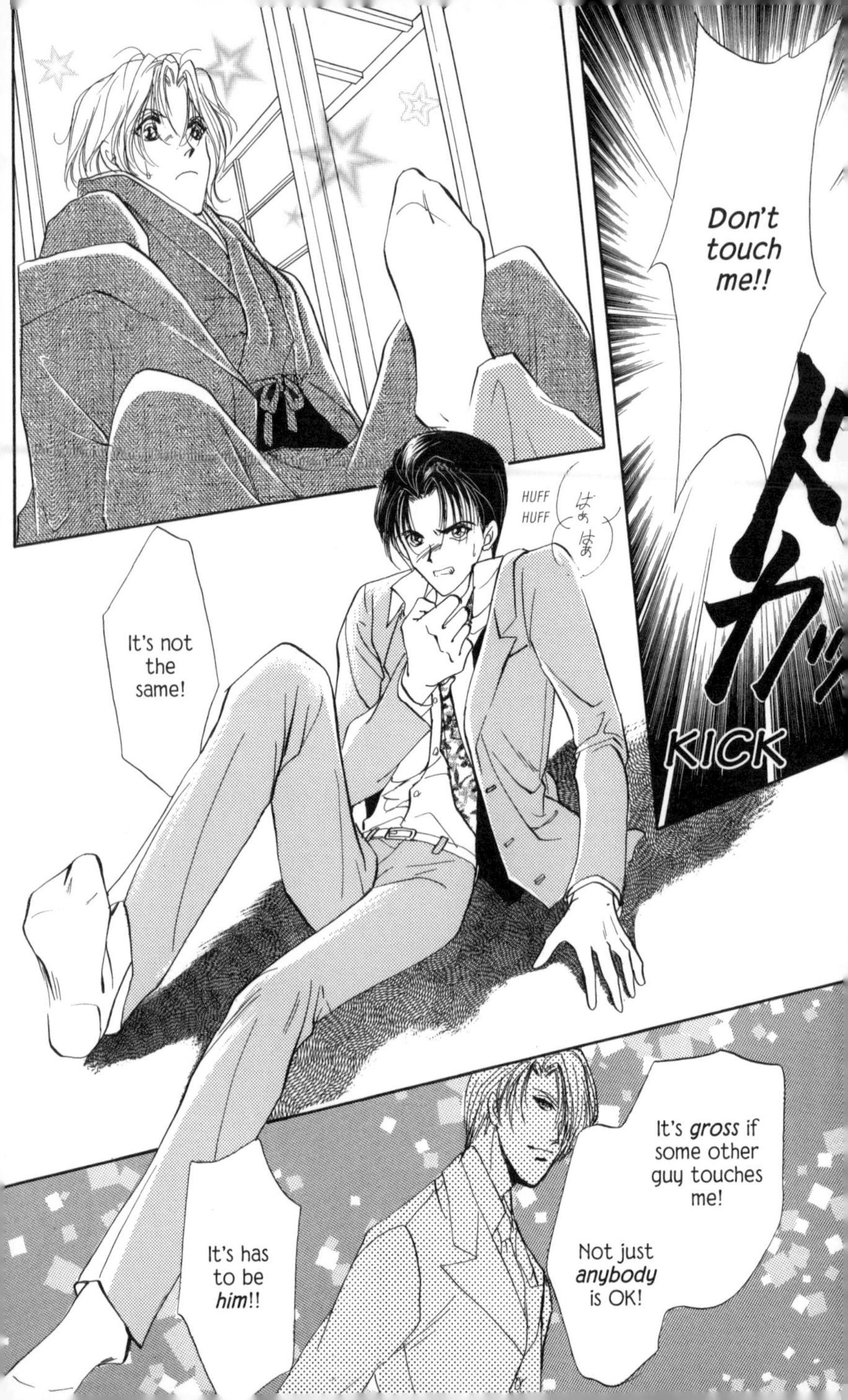

Don't touch me!!
ドカッ
KICK
HUFF HUFF
はぁ はぁ
It's not the same!
It's *gross* if some other guy touches me!
Not just *anybody* is OK!
It's has to be *him*!!

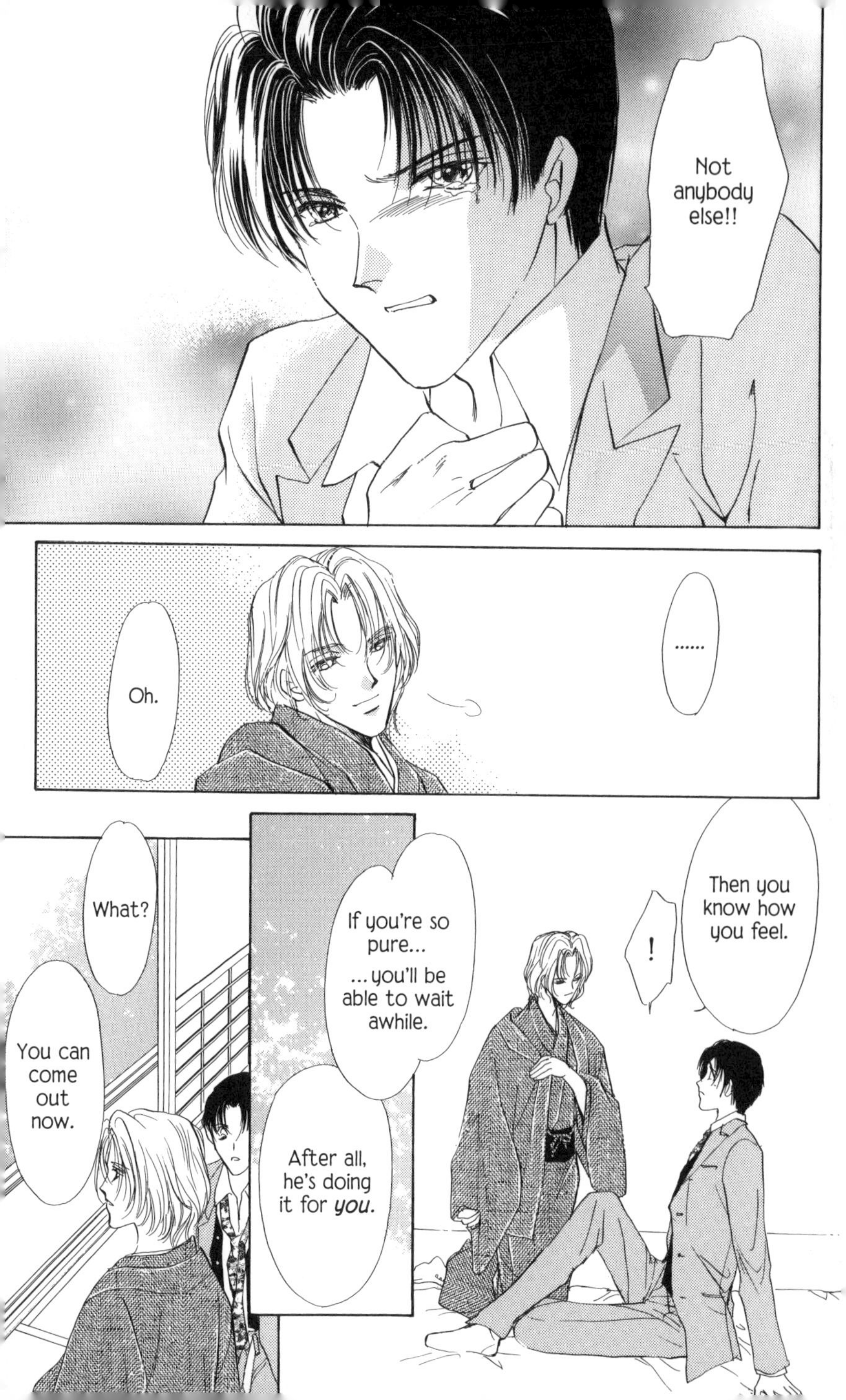

Not anybody else!!
......
Oh.
Then you know how you feel.
!
If you're so pure...
...you'll be able to wait awhile.
After all, he's doing it for *you*.
What?
You can come out now.

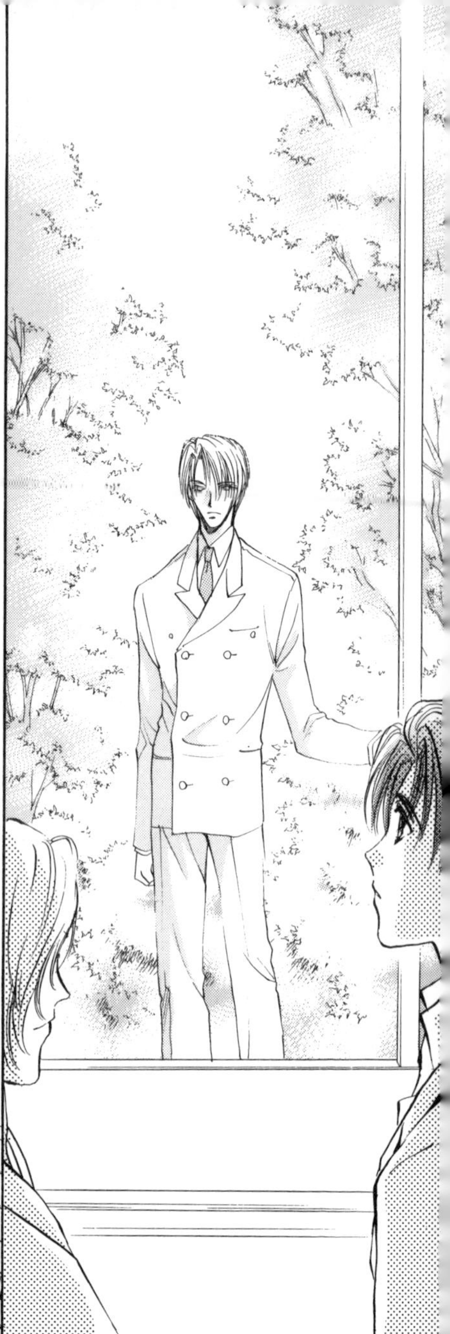

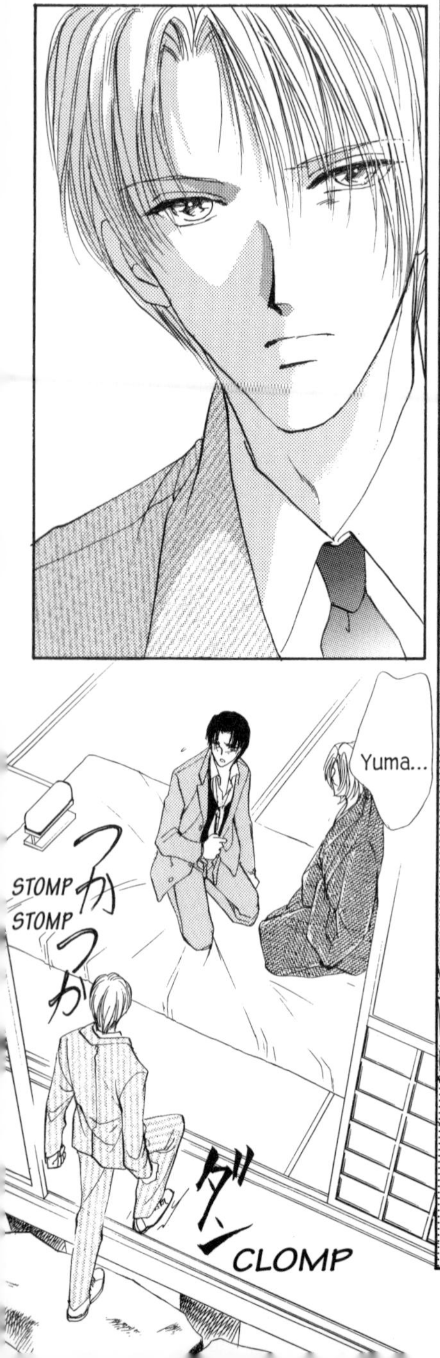
Yuma...
STOMP STOMP
つかつか
ダン
CLOMP

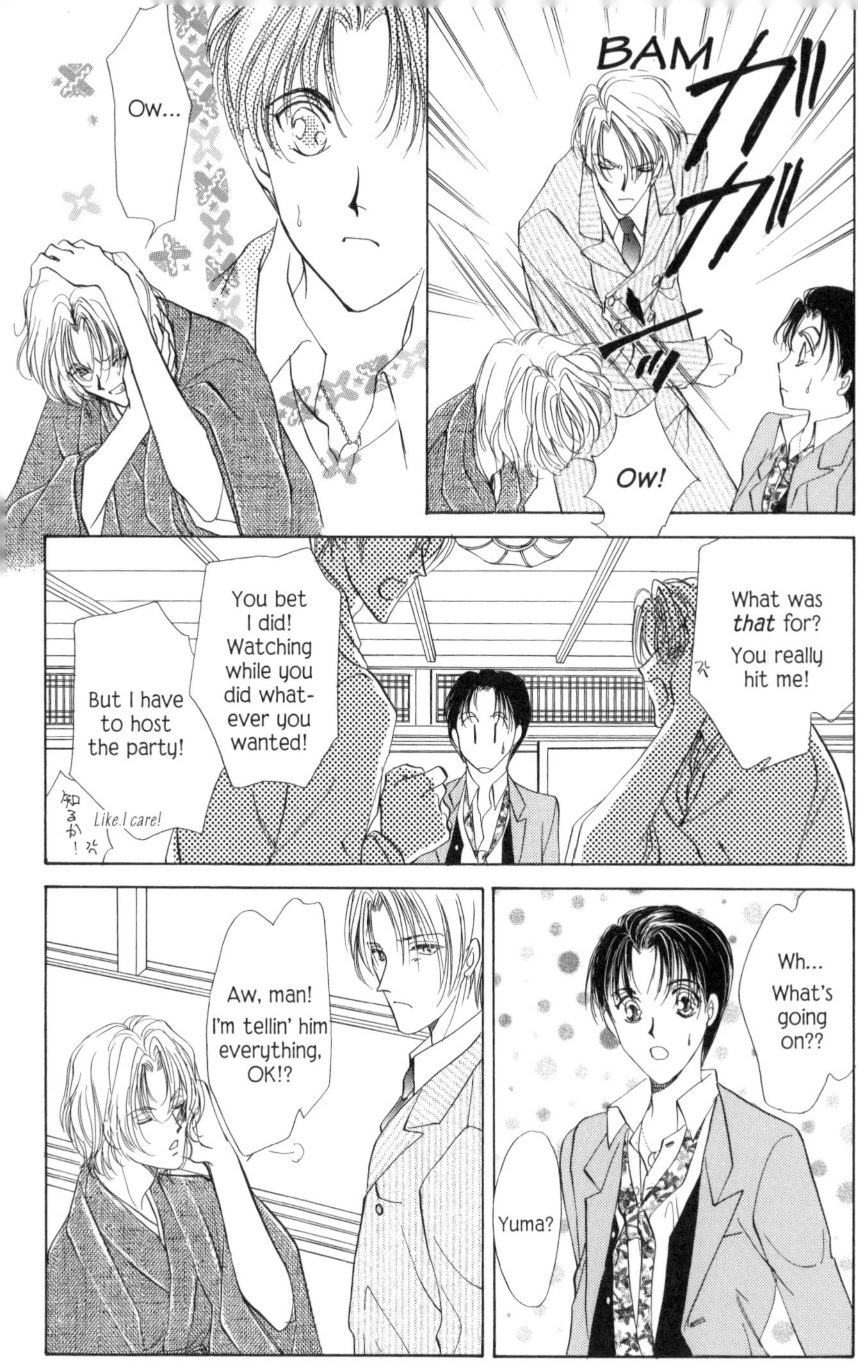
BAM
Ow!
Ow...
What was *that* for? You really hit me!
You bet I did! Watching while you did whatever you wanted!
But I have to host the party!
知るか！
Like I care!
Wh... What's going on??
Yuma?
Aw, man! I'm tellin' him everything, OK!?

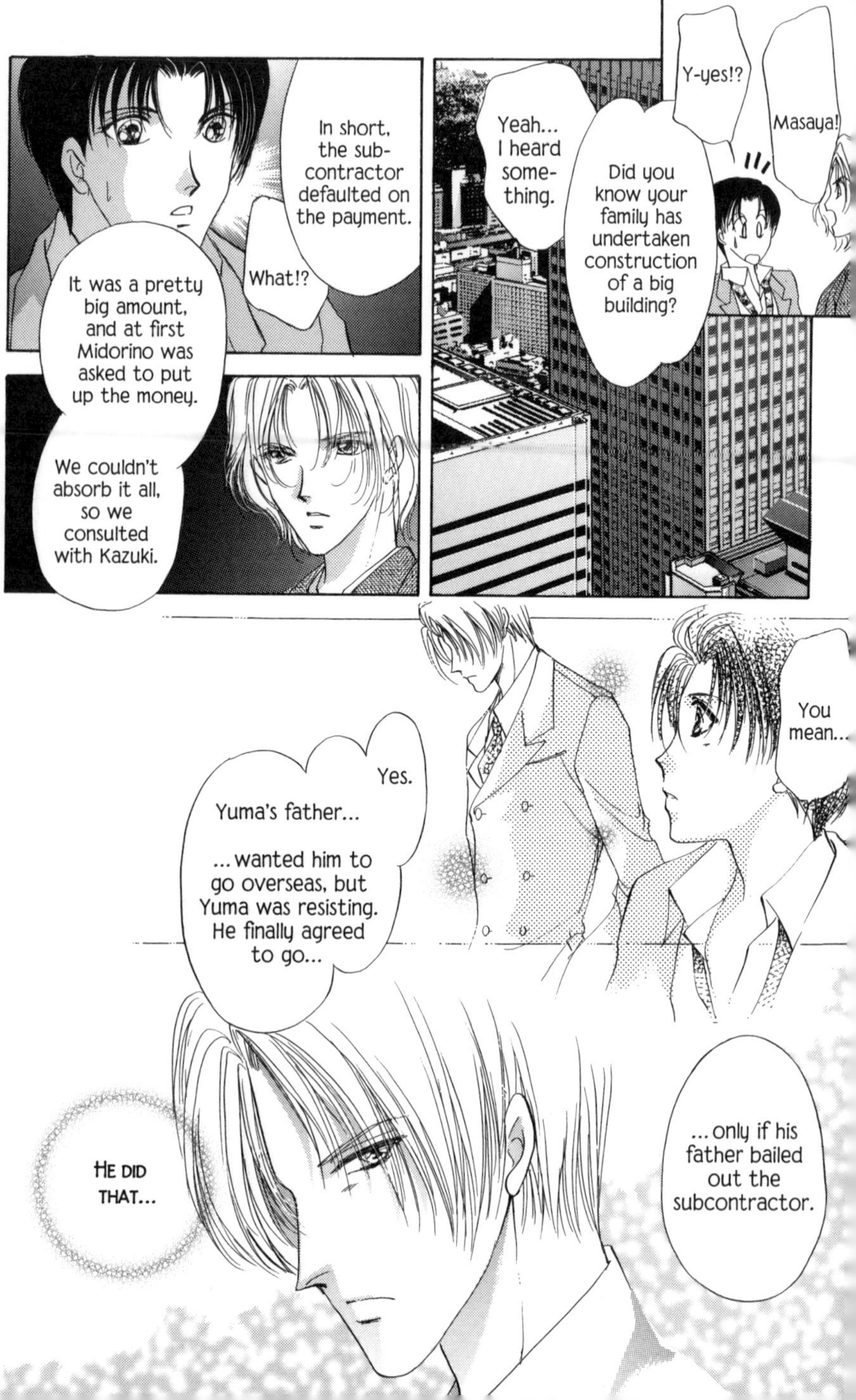
Masaya!
Y-yes!?
Did you know your family has undertaken construction of a big building?
Yeah... I heard something.
In short, the subcontractor defaulted on the payment.
What!?
It was a pretty big amount, and at first Midorino was asked to put up the money.
We couldn't absorb it all, so we consulted with Kazuki.
You mean...
Yes.
Yuma's father...
...wanted him to go overseas, but Yuma was resisting. He finally agreed to go...
...only if his father bailed out the subcontractor.
HE DID THAT...

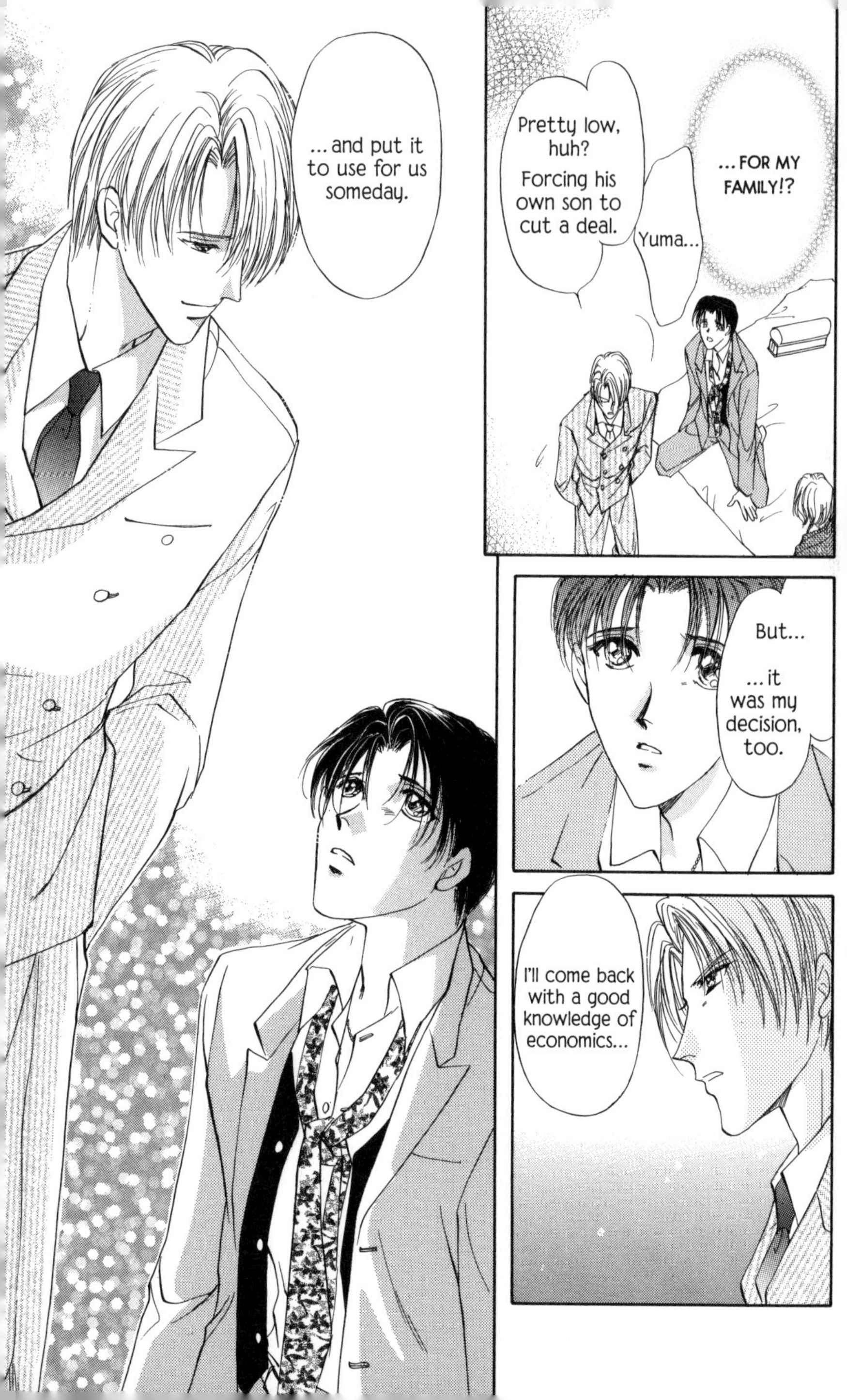
...FOR MY FAMILY!?
Yuma...
Pretty low, huh? Forcing his own son to cut a deal.
But... ...it was my decision, too.
I'll come back with a good knowledge of economics...
...and put it to use for us someday.

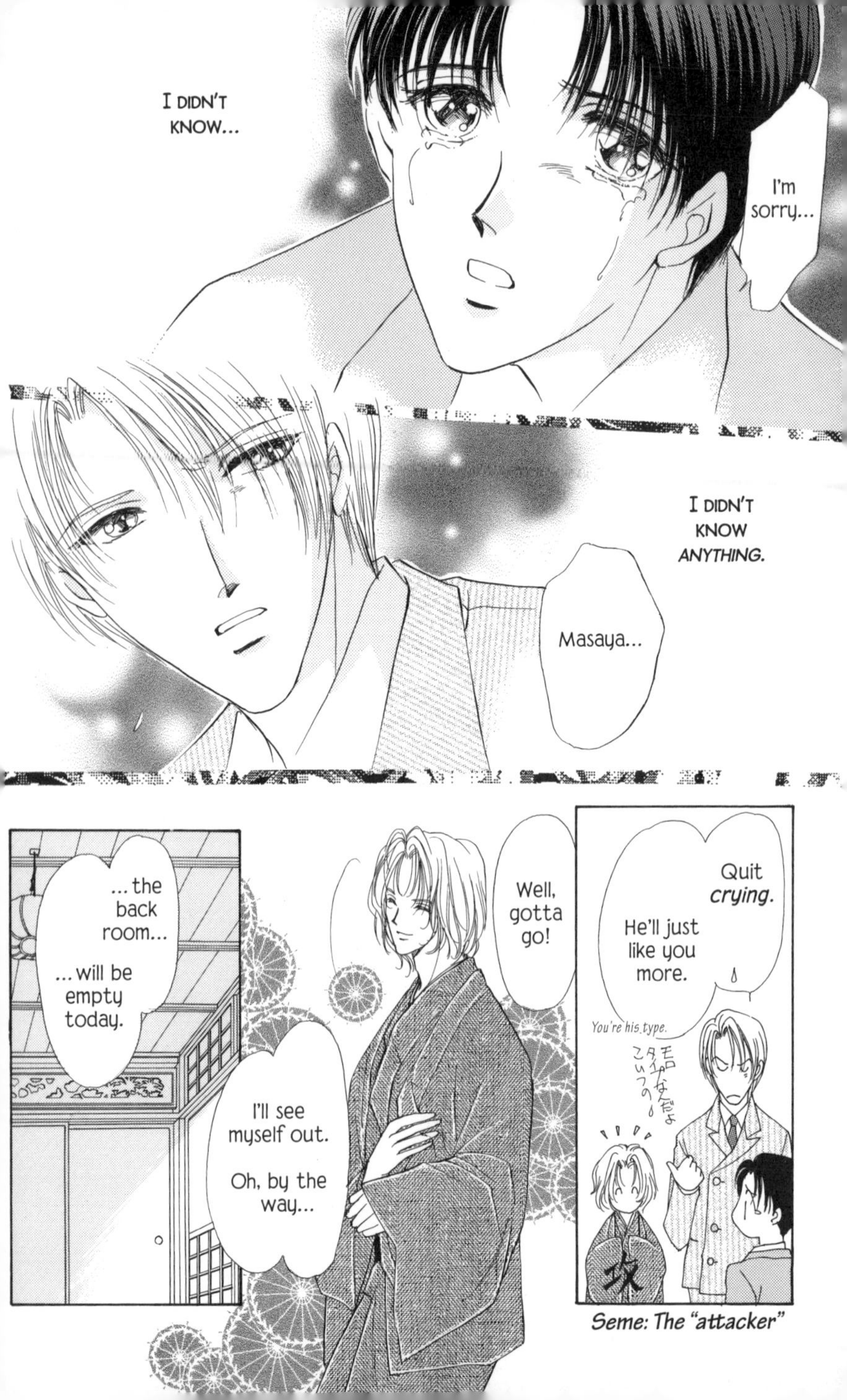
I'm sorry...
I DIDN'T KNOW...
I DIDN'T KNOW ANYTHING.
Masaya...
Quit crying.
He'll just like you more.
You're his type.
Seme: The "attacker"
Well, gotta go!
I'll see myself out.
Oh, by the way...
...the back room...
...will be empty today.

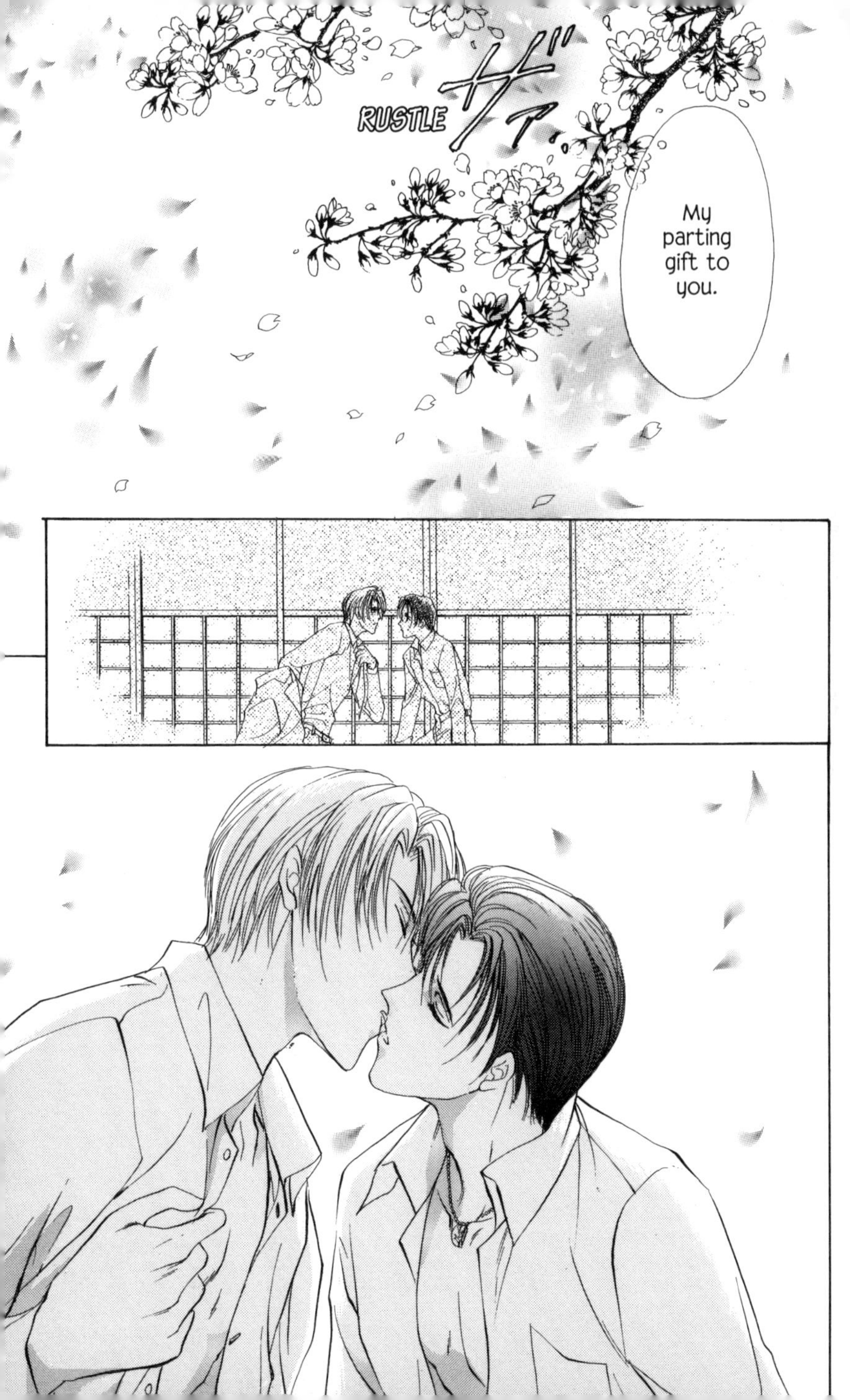
RUSTLE
ザァ
My parting gift to you.

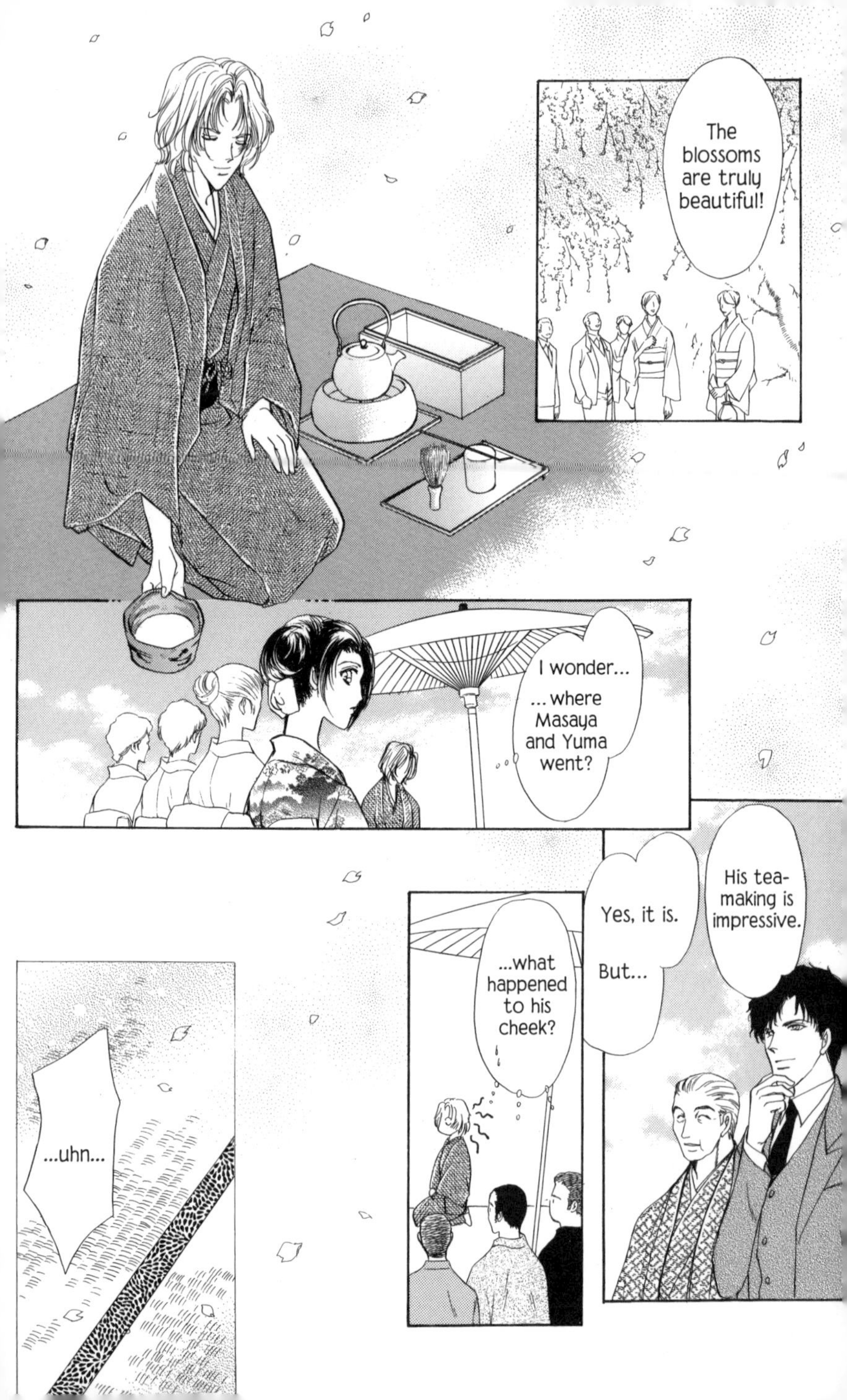
The blossoms are truly beautiful!
I wonder...
...where Masaya and Yuma went?
His tea-making is impressive.
Yes, it is.
But...
...what happened to his cheek?
...uhn...

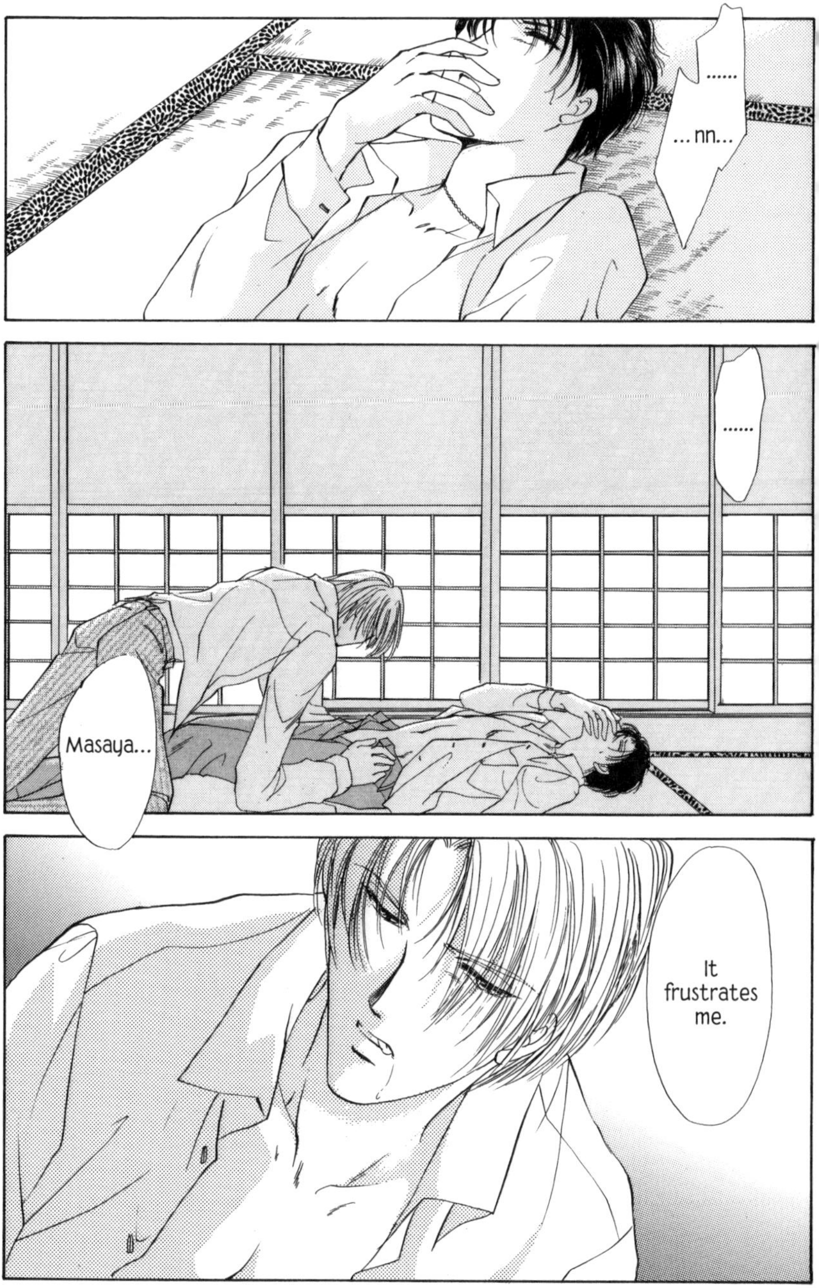
......
...nn...
......
Masaya...
It frustrates me.

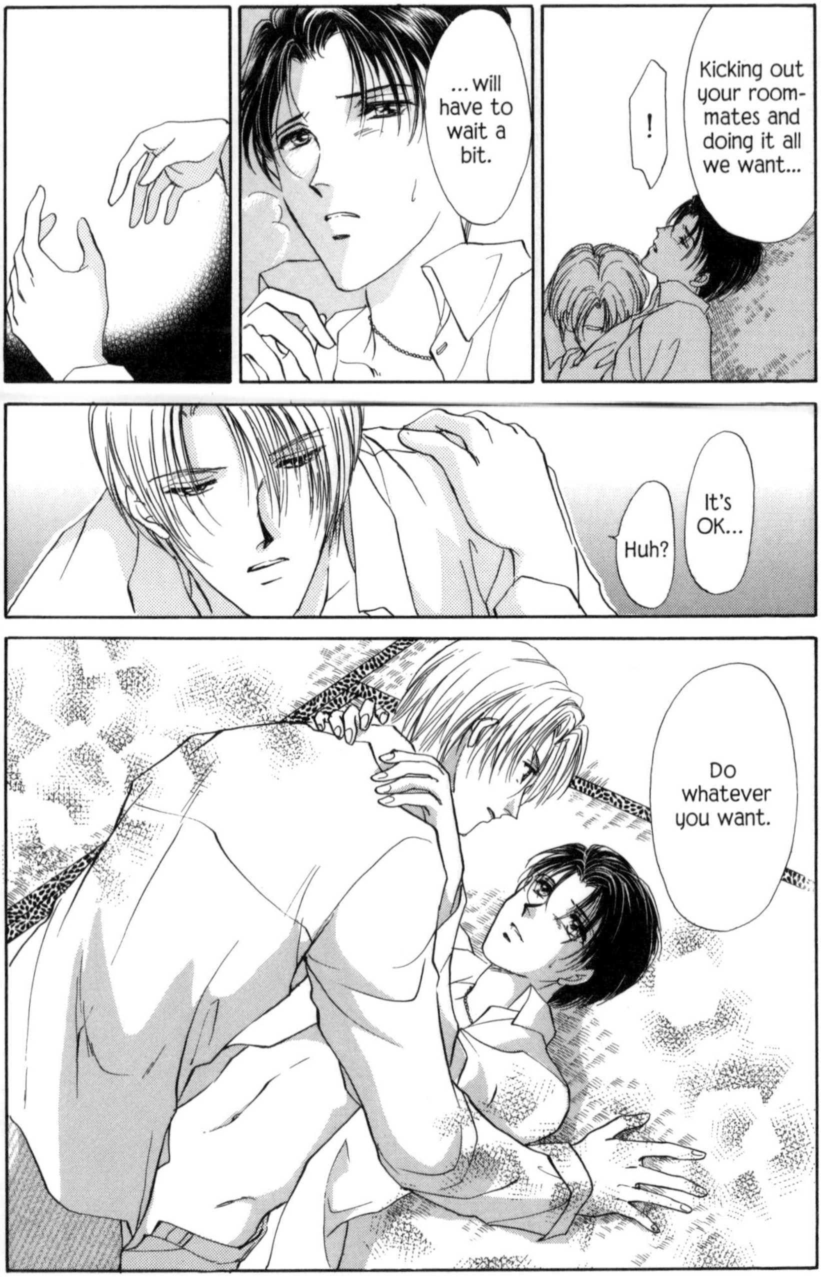
Kicking out your room-mates and doing it all we want...
!
...will have to wait a bit.
It's OK...
Huh?
Do whatever you want.

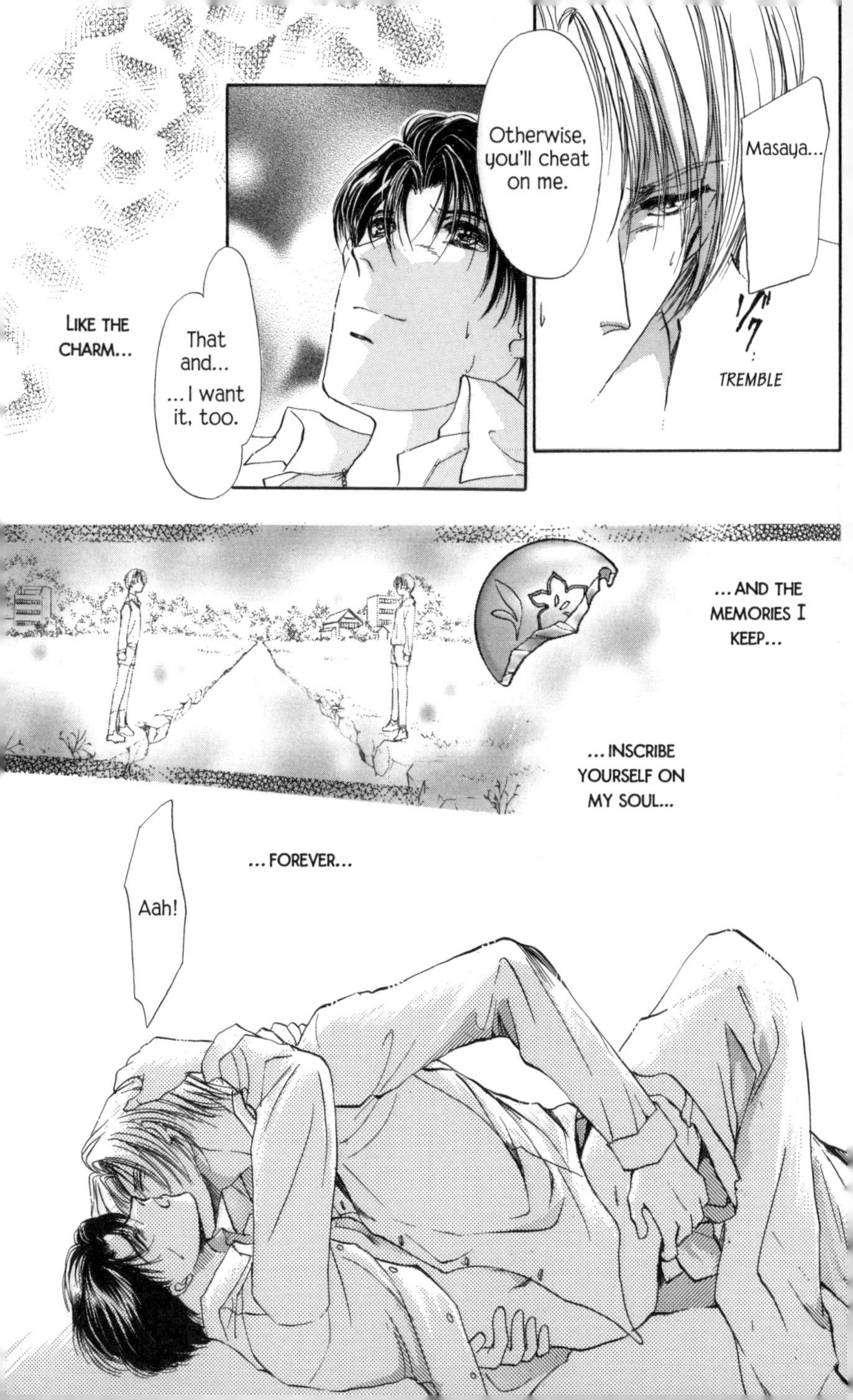
Masaya...
TREMBLE
Otherwise, you'll cheat on me.
That and...
...I want it, too.
LIKE THE CHARM...
...AND THE MEMORIES I KEEP...
...INSCRIBE YOURSELF ON MY SOUL...
...FOREVER...
Aah!

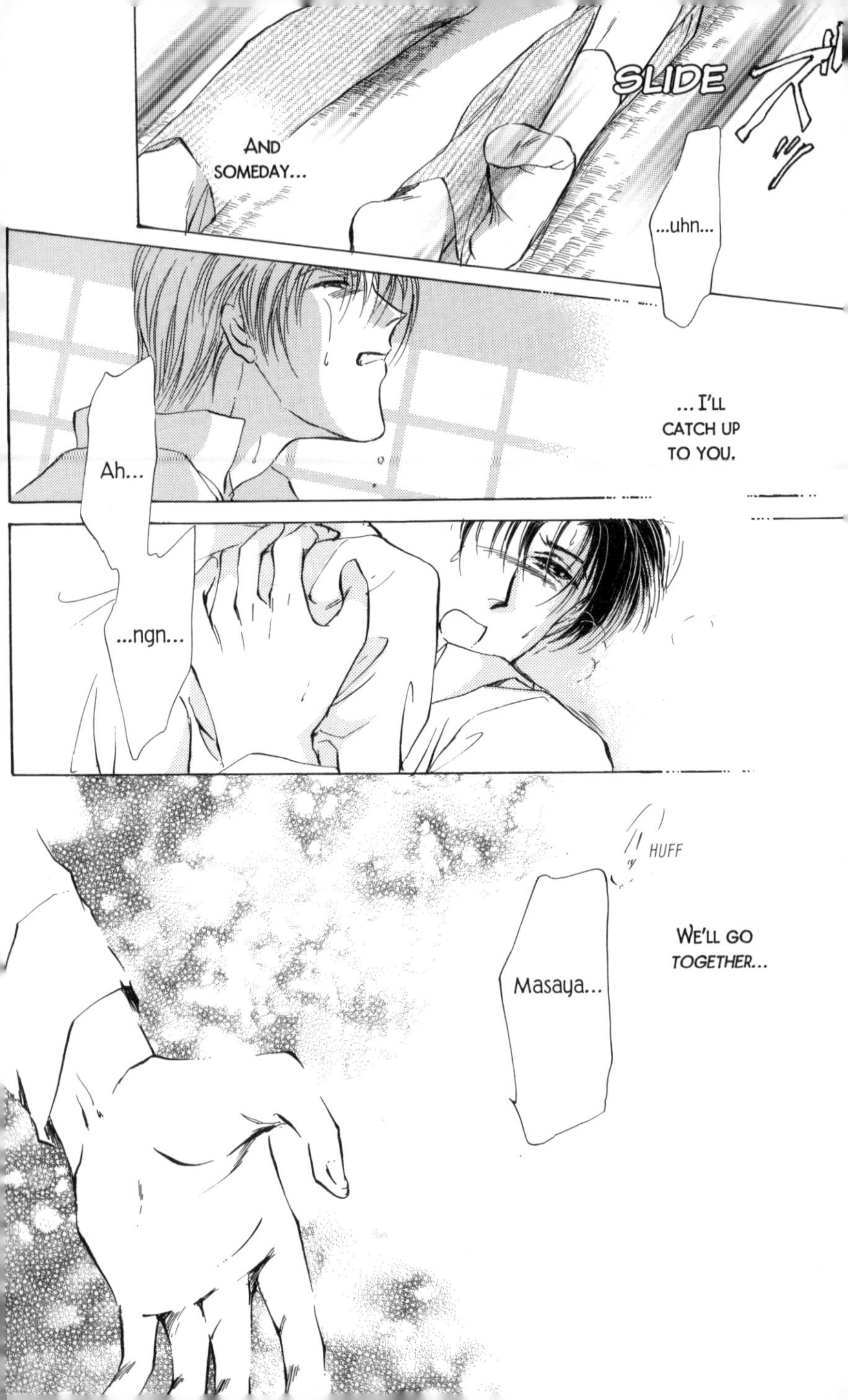
SLIDE
...uhn...
And someday...
...I'll catch up to you.
Ah...
...ngn...
HUFF
We'll go together...
Masaya...

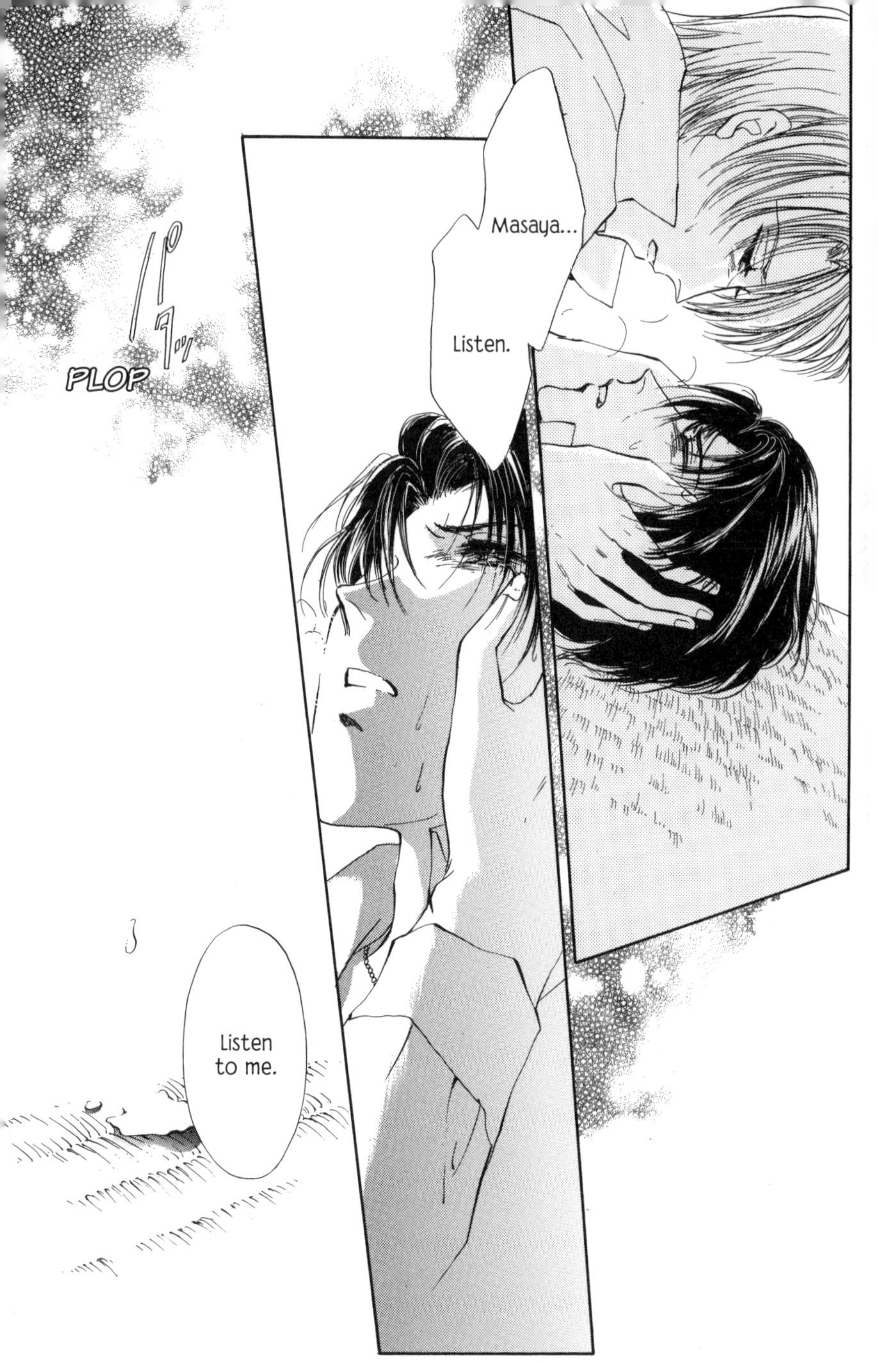
Masaya...
Listen.
パタッ
PLOP
Listen to me.

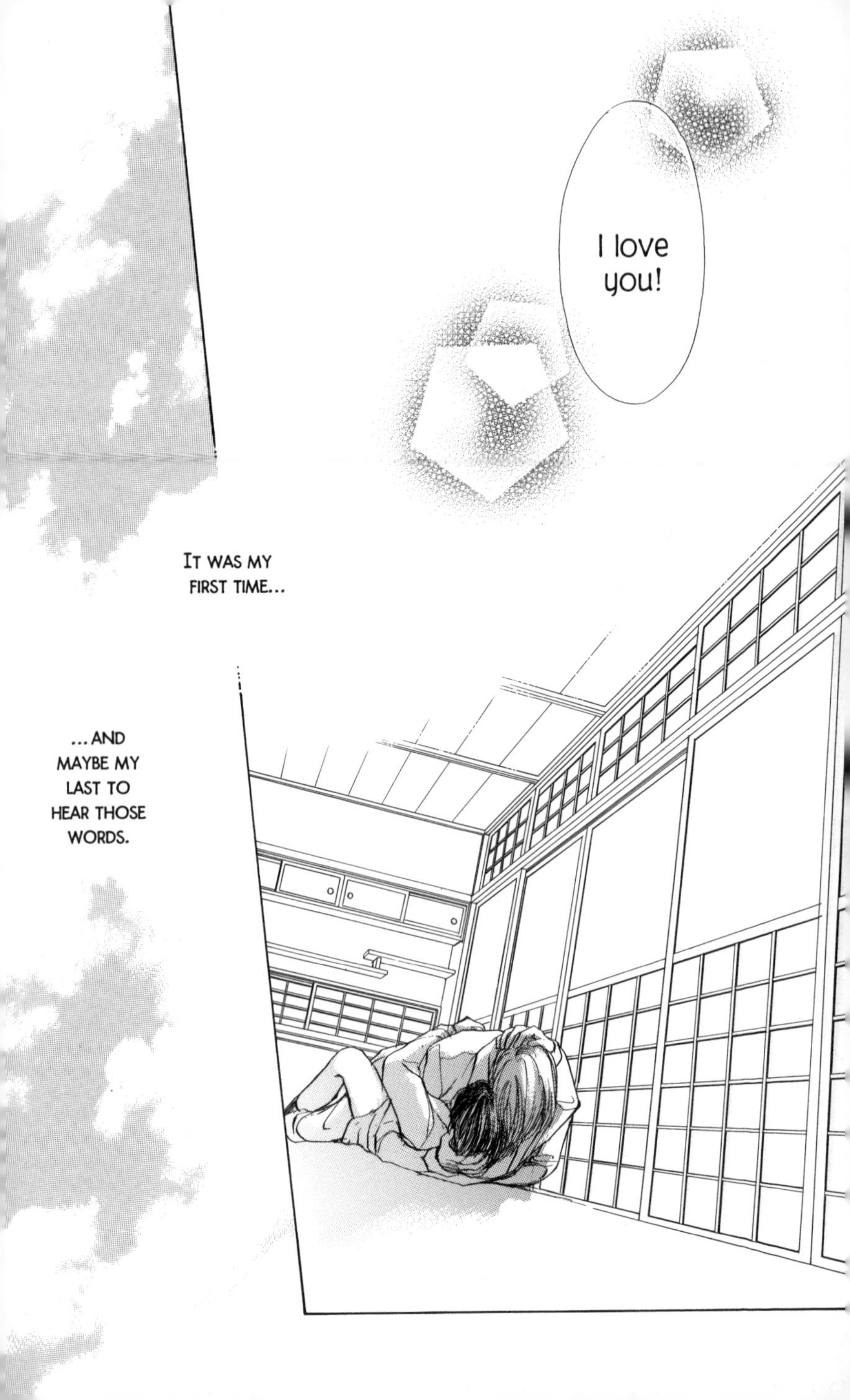
I love you!
IT WAS MY FIRST TIME...
...AND MAYBE MY LAST TO HEAR THOSE WORDS.

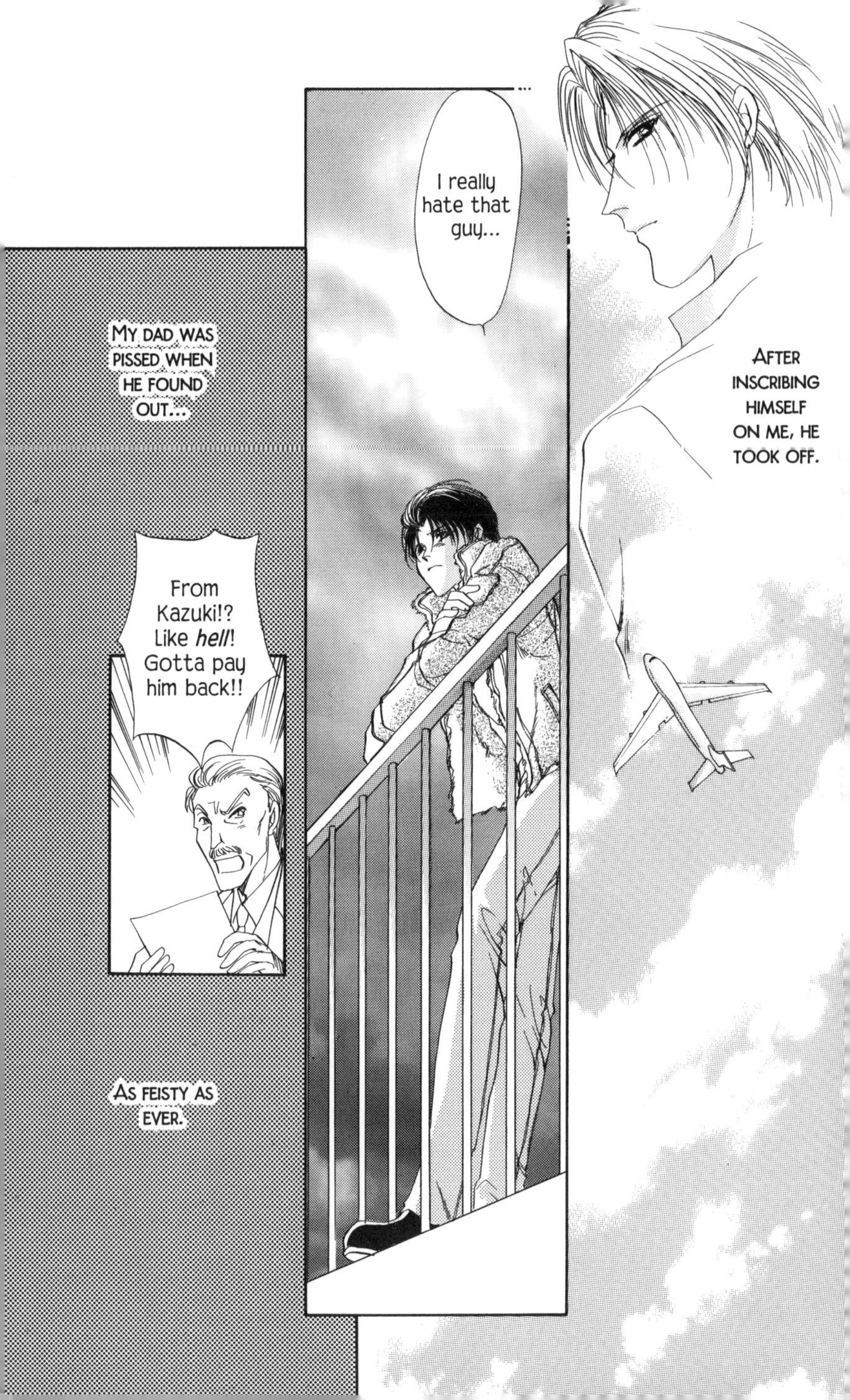
After inscribing himself on me, he took off.
I really hate that guy...
My dad was pissed when he found out...
From Kazuki!? Like *hell*! Gotta pay him back!!
As feisty as ever.

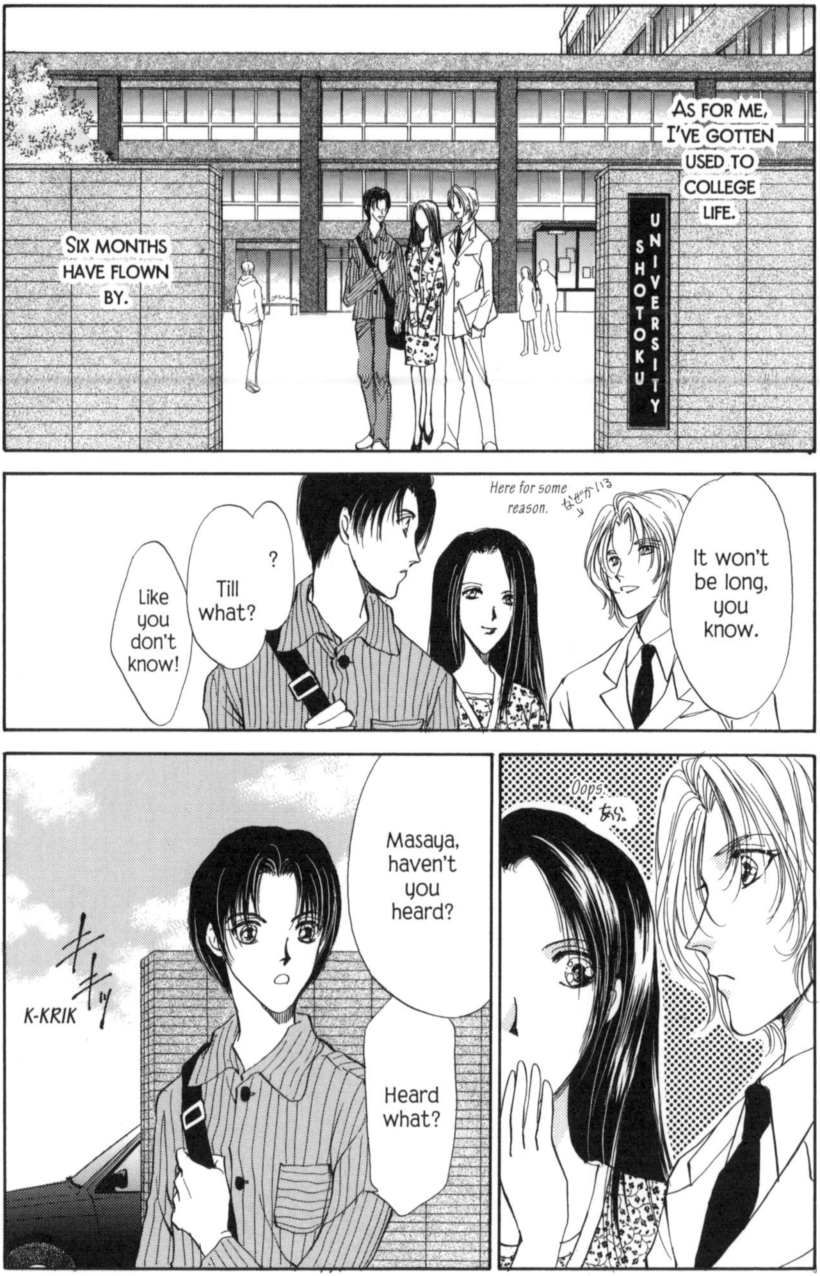
As for me, I've gotten used to college life.
SHOTOKU UNIVERSITY
Six months have flown by.
It won't be long, you know.
Here for some reason.
なぜかいる
?
Till what?
Like you don't know!
Oops.
あら。
Masaya, haven't you heard?
Heard what?
キキッ
K-KRIK

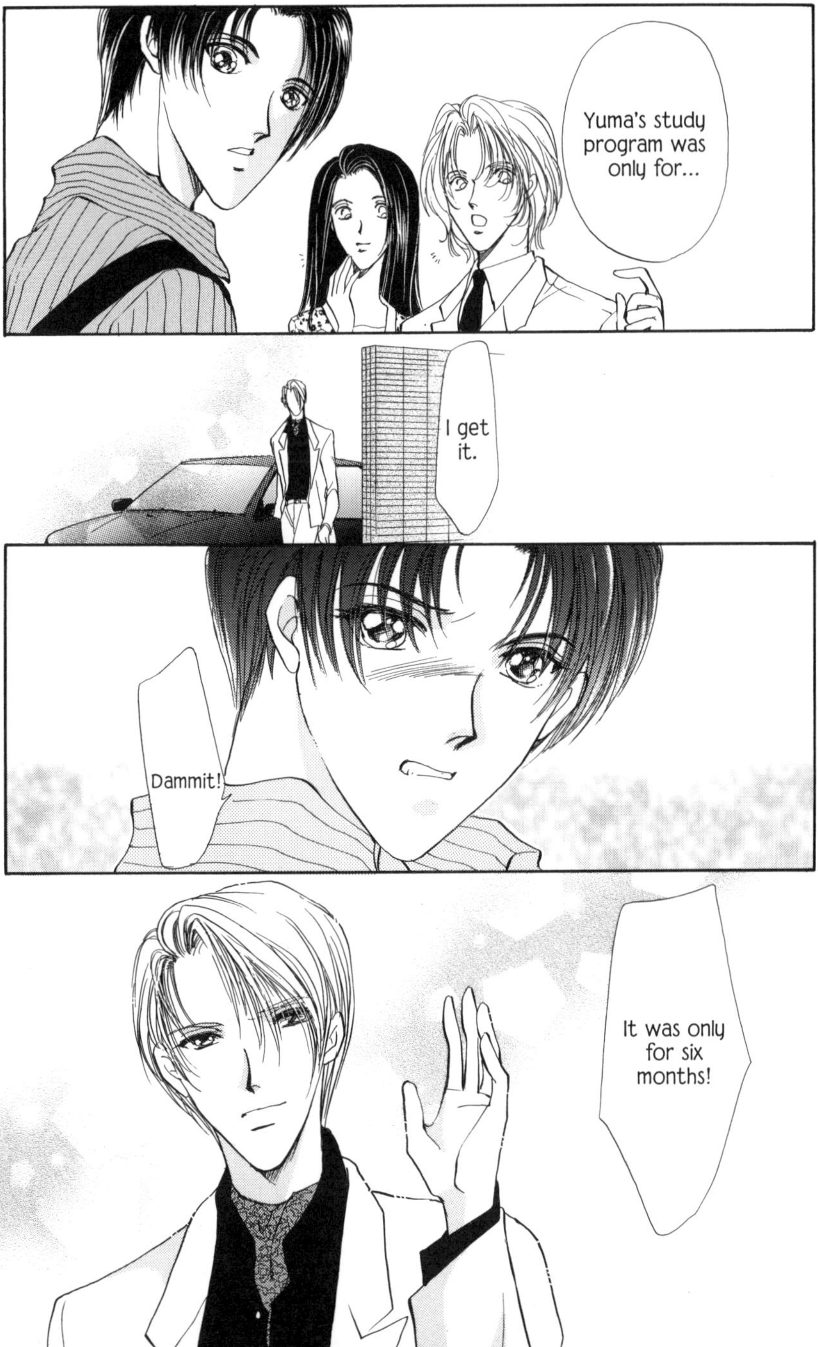
Yuma's study program was only for...
I get it.
Dammit!
It was only for six months!

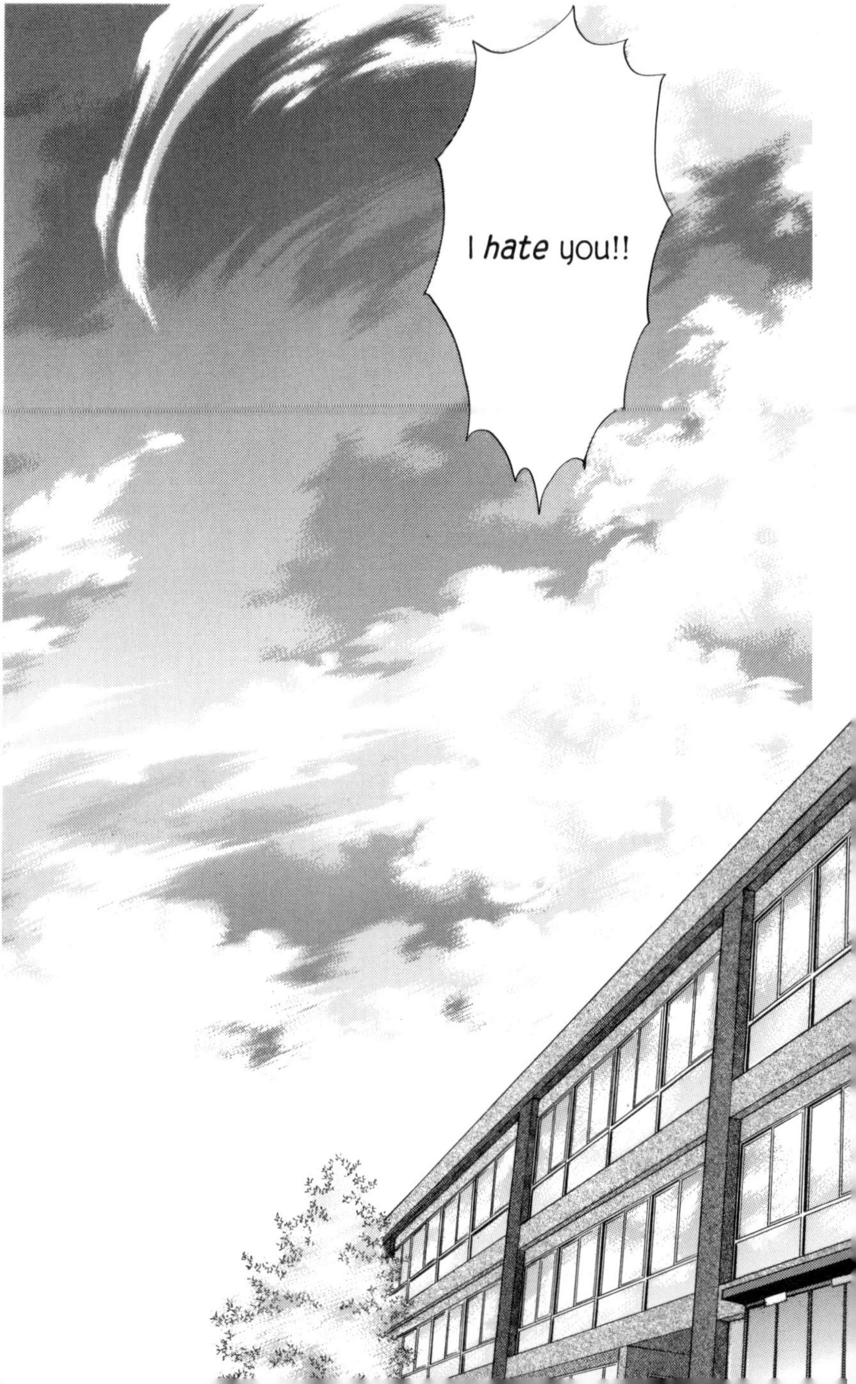
I *hate* you!!

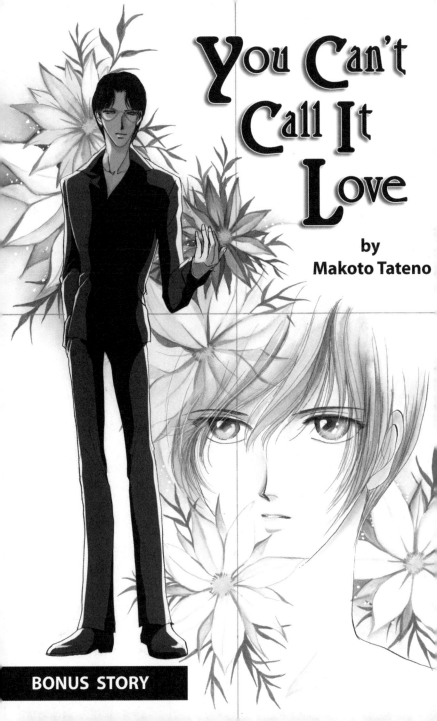

You Can't Call It Love

by
Makoto Tateno

BONUS STORY

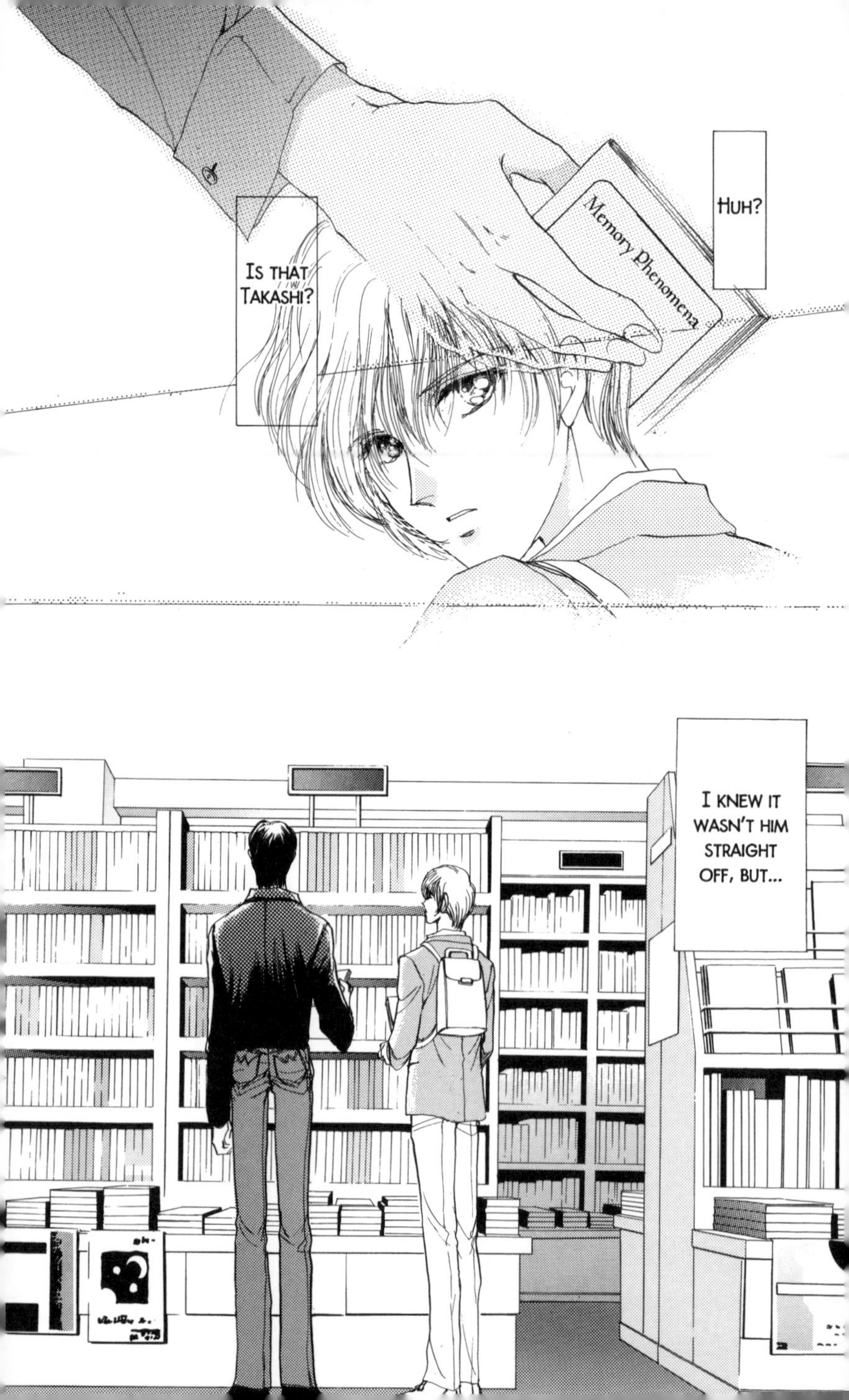
Huh?
Memory Phenomena
Is that Takashi?
I knew it wasn't him straight off, but...

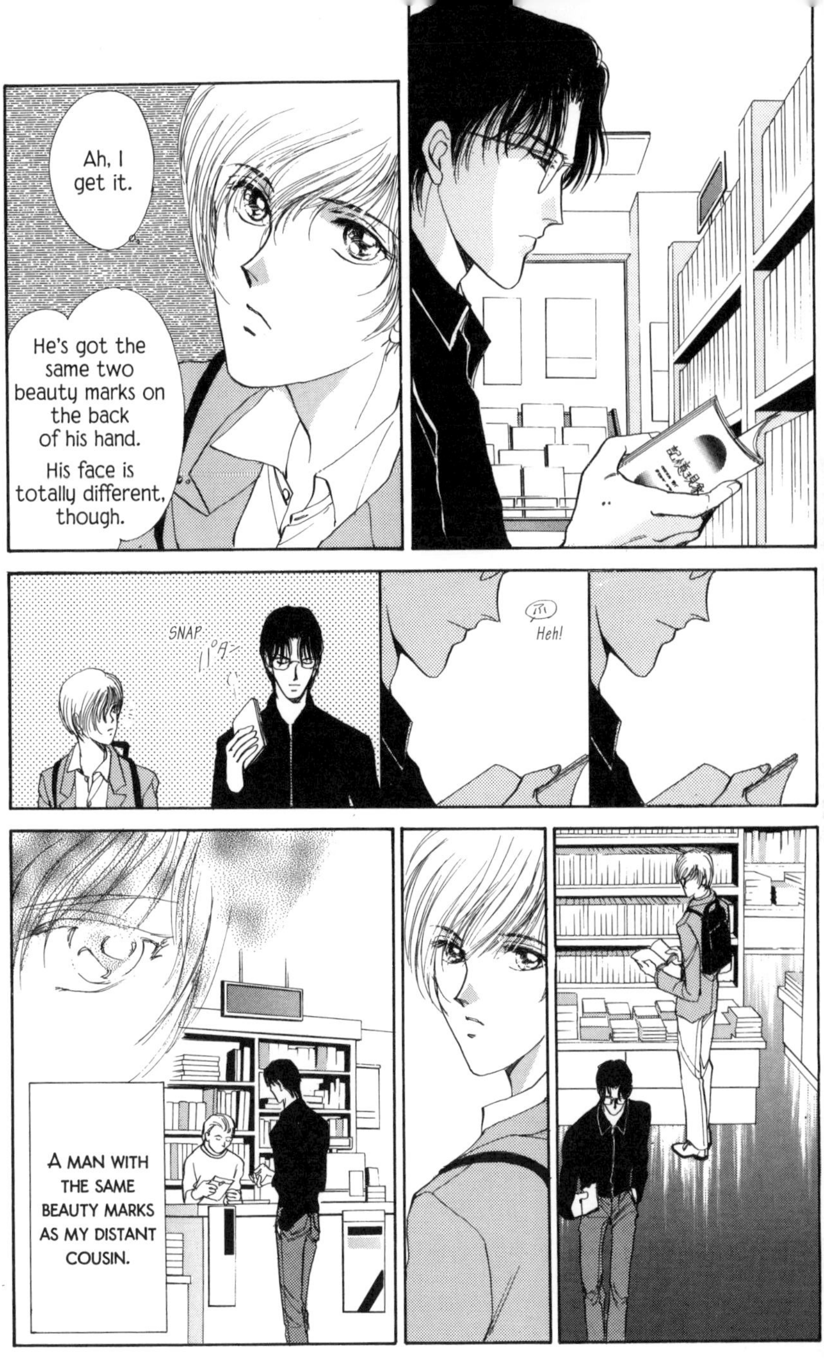
Ah, I get it.
He's got the same two beauty marks on the back of his hand.
His face is totally different, though.
ふ
Heh!
SNAP
パタン
A MAN WITH THE SAME BEAUTY MARKS AS MY DISTANT COUSIN.

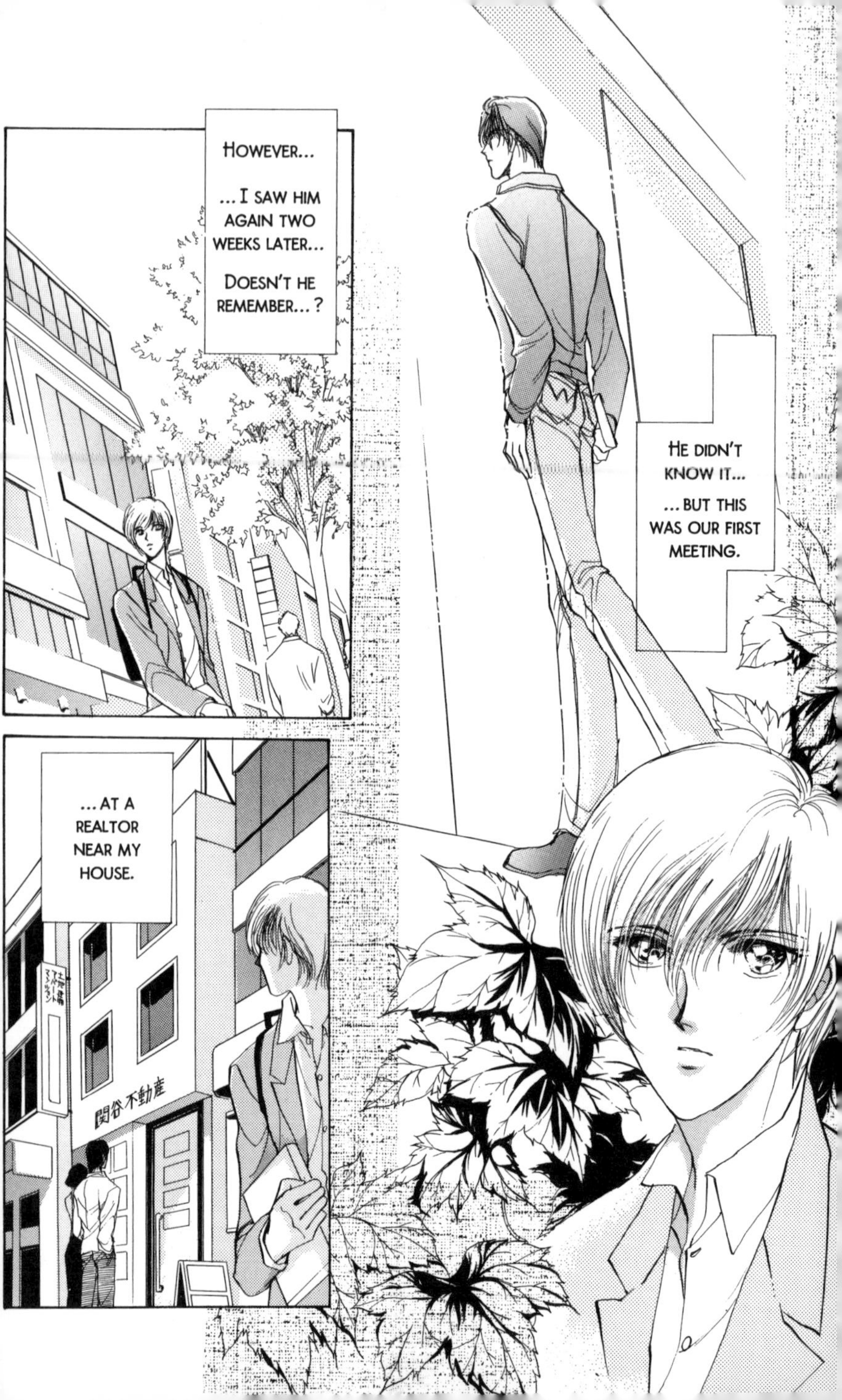
He didn't know it...
...but this was our first meeting.
However...
...I saw him again two weeks later...
Doesn't he remember...?
...at a realtor near my house.
関谷不動産

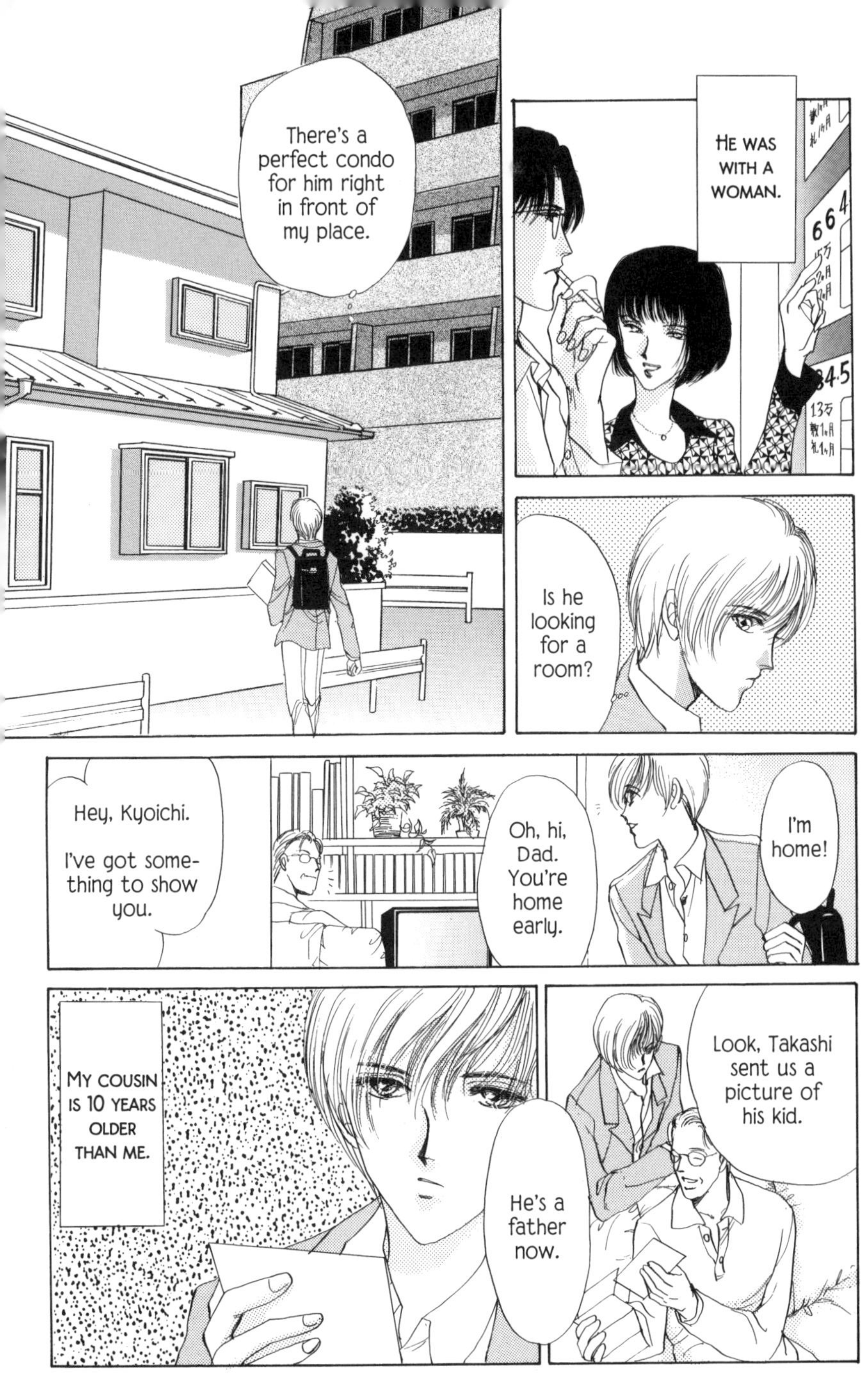
HE WAS WITH A WOMAN.
Is he looking for a room?
There's a perfect condo for him right in front of my place.
I'm home!
Oh, hi, Dad. You're home early.
Hey, Kyoichi. I've got something to show you.
Look, Takashi sent us a picture of his kid.
He's a father now.
MY COUSIN IS 10 YEARS OLDER THAN ME.

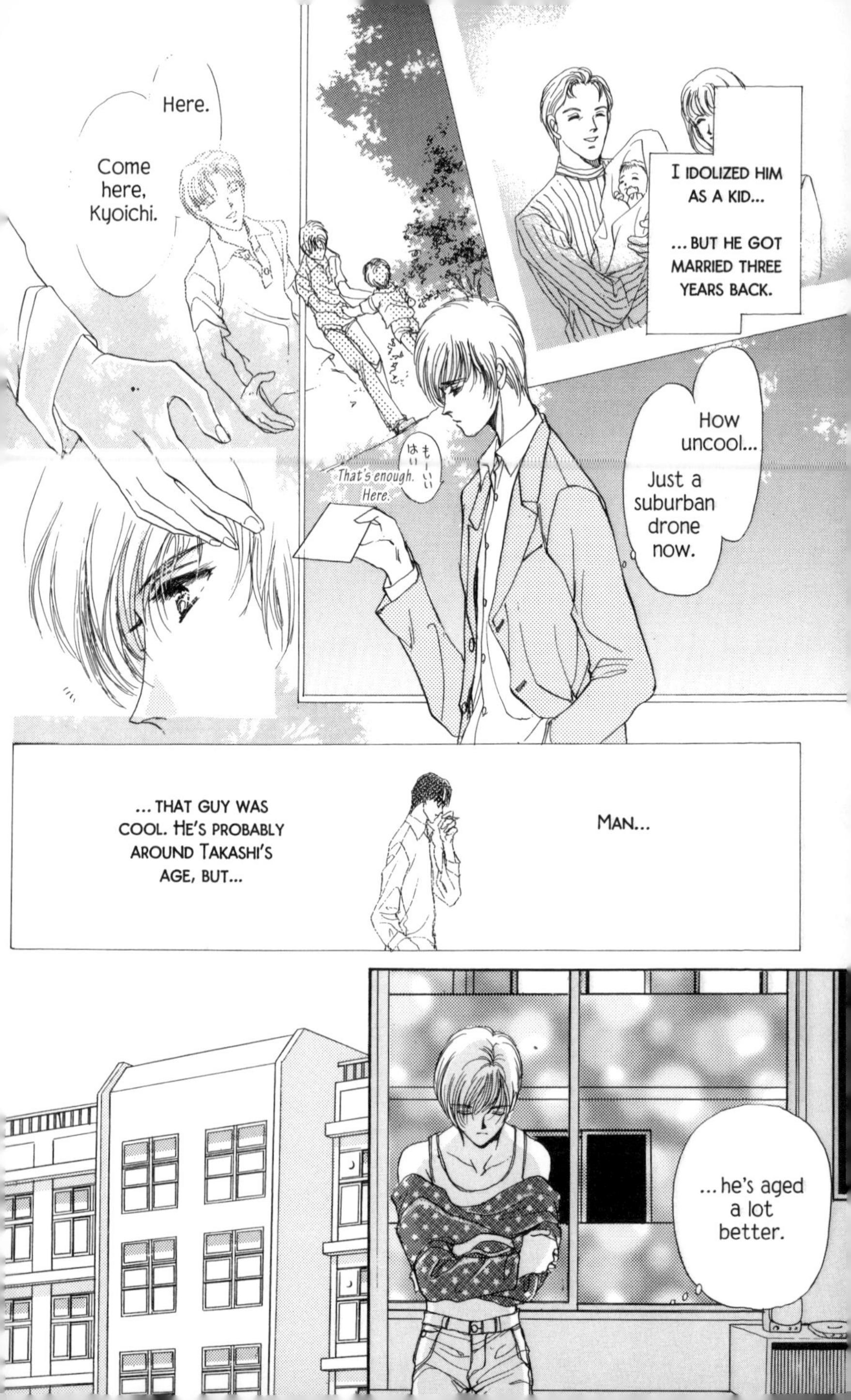
I IDOLIZED HIM AS A KID...
...BUT HE GOT MARRIED THREE YEARS BACK.
How uncool... Just a suburban drone now.
もーいい
はい
That's enough. Here.
Here.
Come here, Kyoichi.
MAN...
...THAT GUY WAS COOL. HE'S PROBABLY AROUND TAKASHI'S AGE, BUT...
...he's aged a lot better.

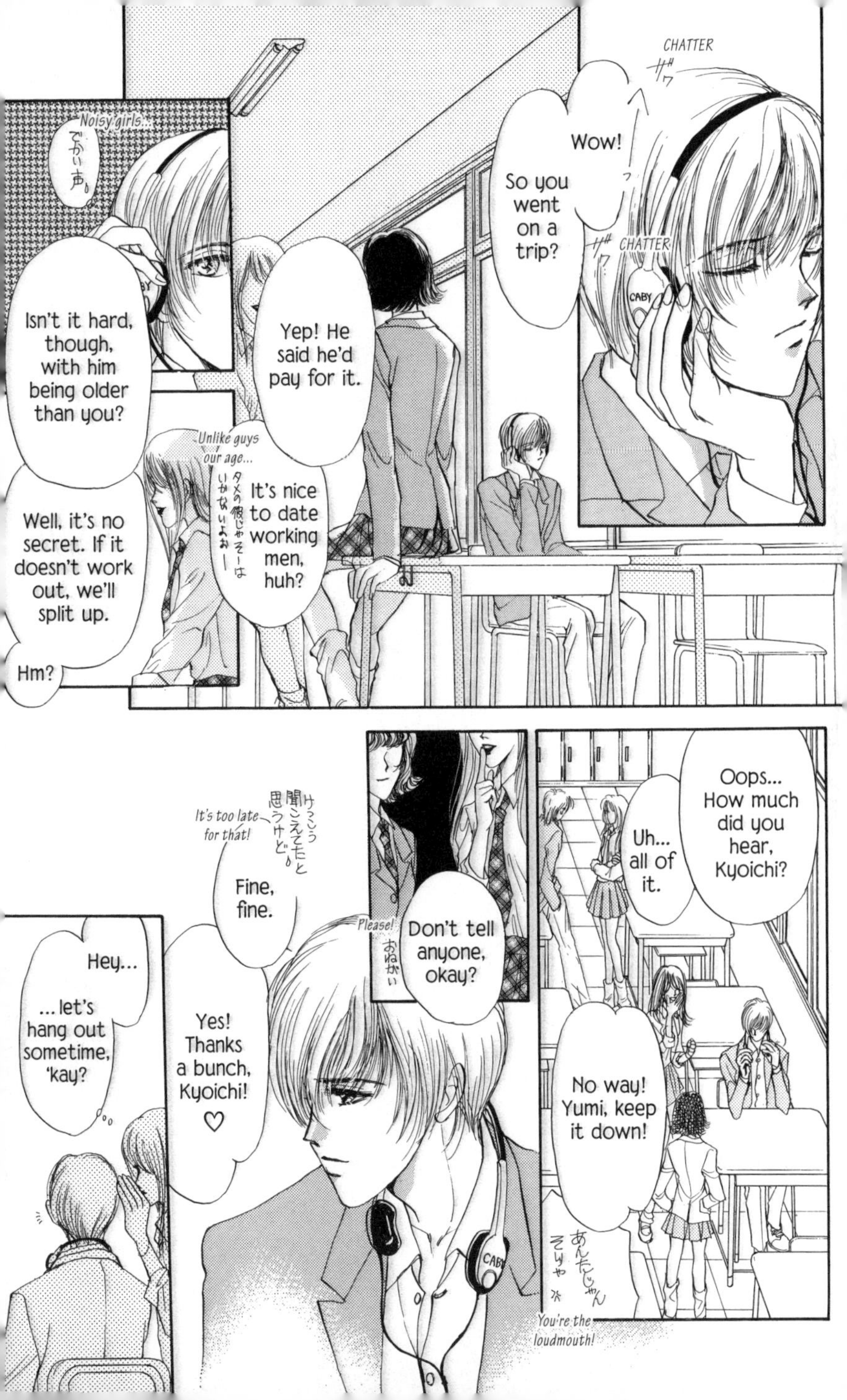

CHATTER
ザワ
Wow!
So you went on a trip?
CHATTER
ザワ
Yep! He said he'd date pay for it.
It's nice to date working men, huh?
Unlike guys our age...
タメの彼じゃそーはいかないよぉー
Noisy girls...
でかい声。
Isn't it hard, though, with him being older than you?
Well, it's no secret. If it doesn't work out, we'll split up.
Hm?
Oops... How much did you hear, Kyoichi?
Uh... all of it.
No way! Yumi, keep it down!
You're the loudmouth!
あんたじゃん そりゃ
Don't tell anyone, okay?
Please!
おねがい
Fine, fine.
It's too late for that!
けっこう聞こえてたと思うけど。
Yes! Thanks a bunch, Kyoichi! ♡
Hey...
...let's hang out sometime, 'kay?

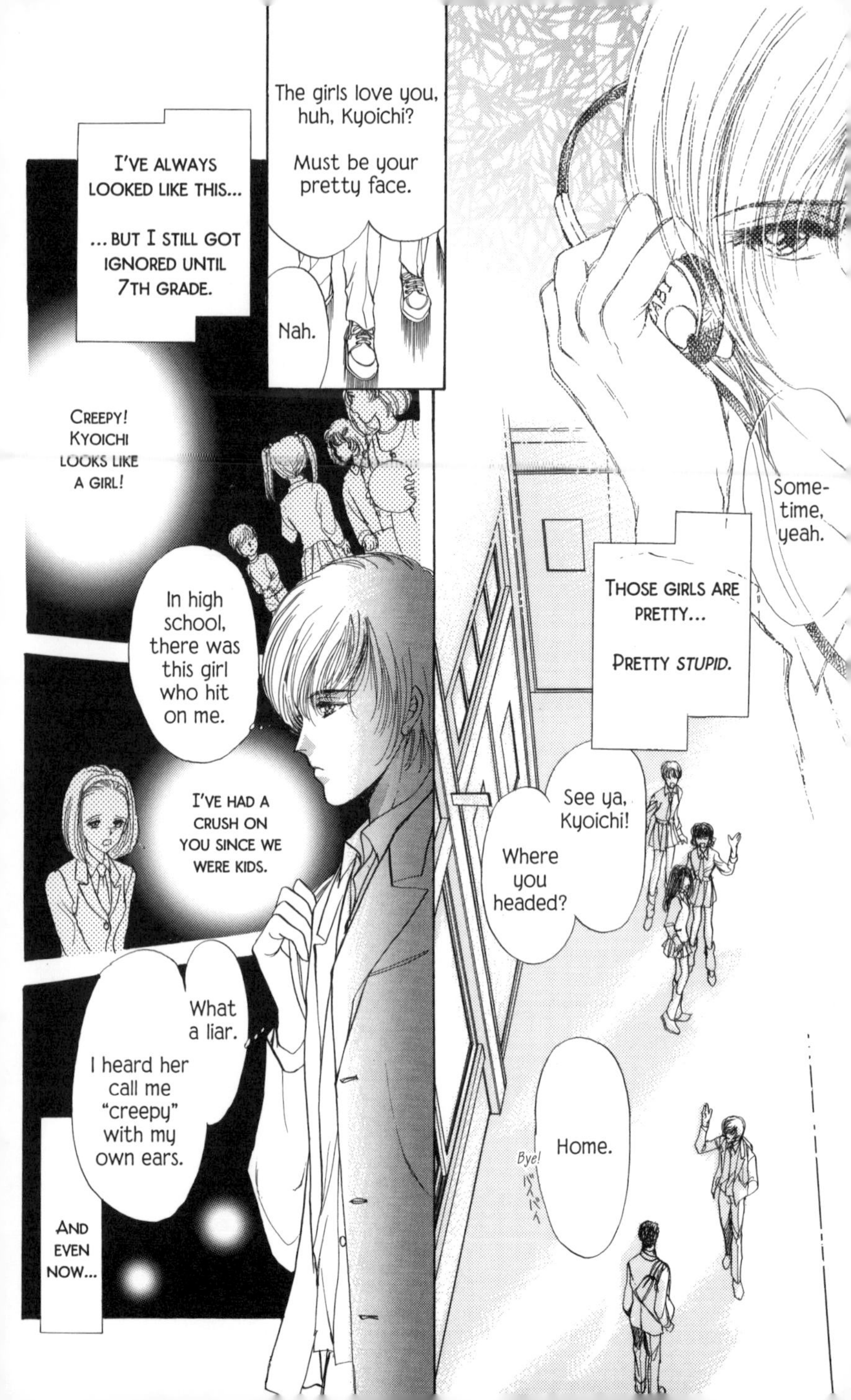
Some-time, yeah.
THOSE GIRLS ARE PRETTY...
PRETTY *STUPID.*
See ya, Kyoichi!
Where you headed?
Home.
Bye!
バイバイ
The girls love you, huh, Kyoichi?
Must be your pretty face.
Nah.
I'VE ALWAYS LOOKED LIKE THIS...
...BUT I STILL GOT IGNORED UNTIL 7TH GRADE.
CREEPY! KYOICHI LOOKS LIKE A GIRL!
In high school, there was this girl who hit on me.
I'VE HAD A CRUSH ON YOU SINCE WE WERE KIDS.
What a liar.
I heard her call me "creepy" with my own ears.
AND EVEN NOW...

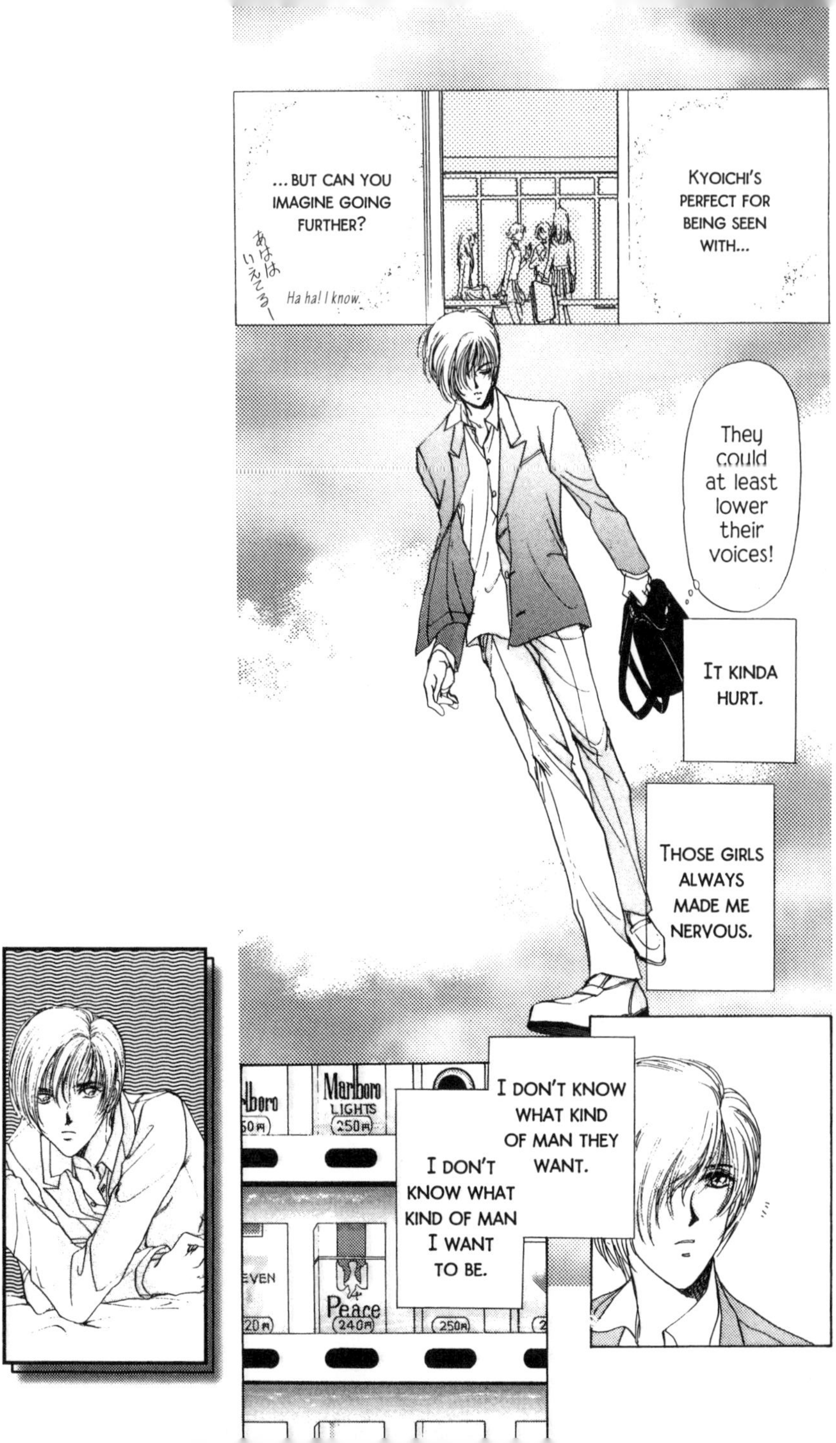
Kyoichi's perfect for being seen with...
...but can you imagine going further?
あはは いえてるー
Ha ha! I know.
They could at least lower their voices!
It kinda hurt.
Those girls always made me nervous.
I don't know what kind of man they want.
I don't know what kind of man I want to be.

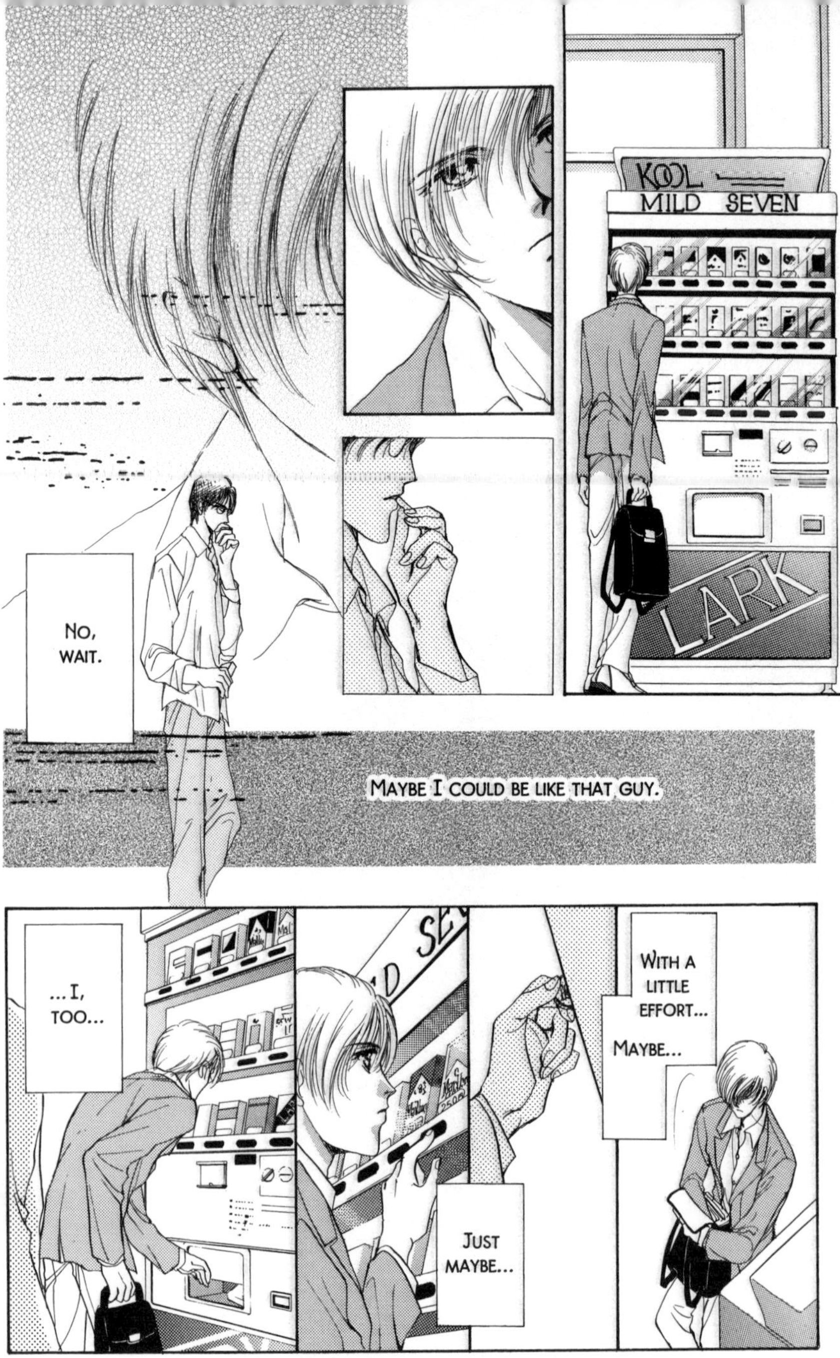
KOOL
MILD SEVEN
LARK
No, wait.
Maybe I could be like that guy.
With a little effort...
Maybe...
Just maybe...
...I, too...

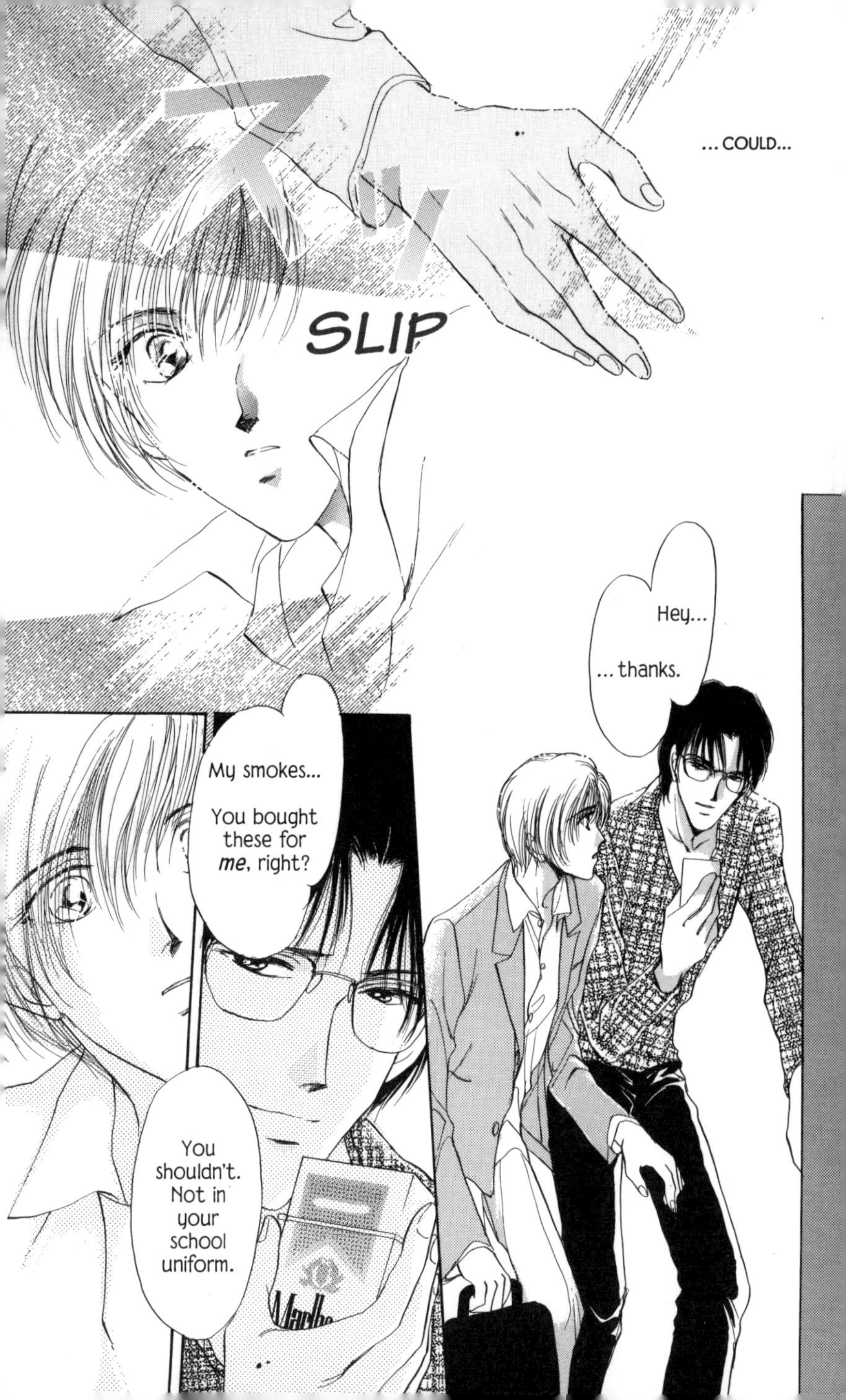
...COULD...
SLIP
Hey... ...thanks.
My smokes...
You bought these for *me*, right?
You shouldn't. Not in your school uniform.

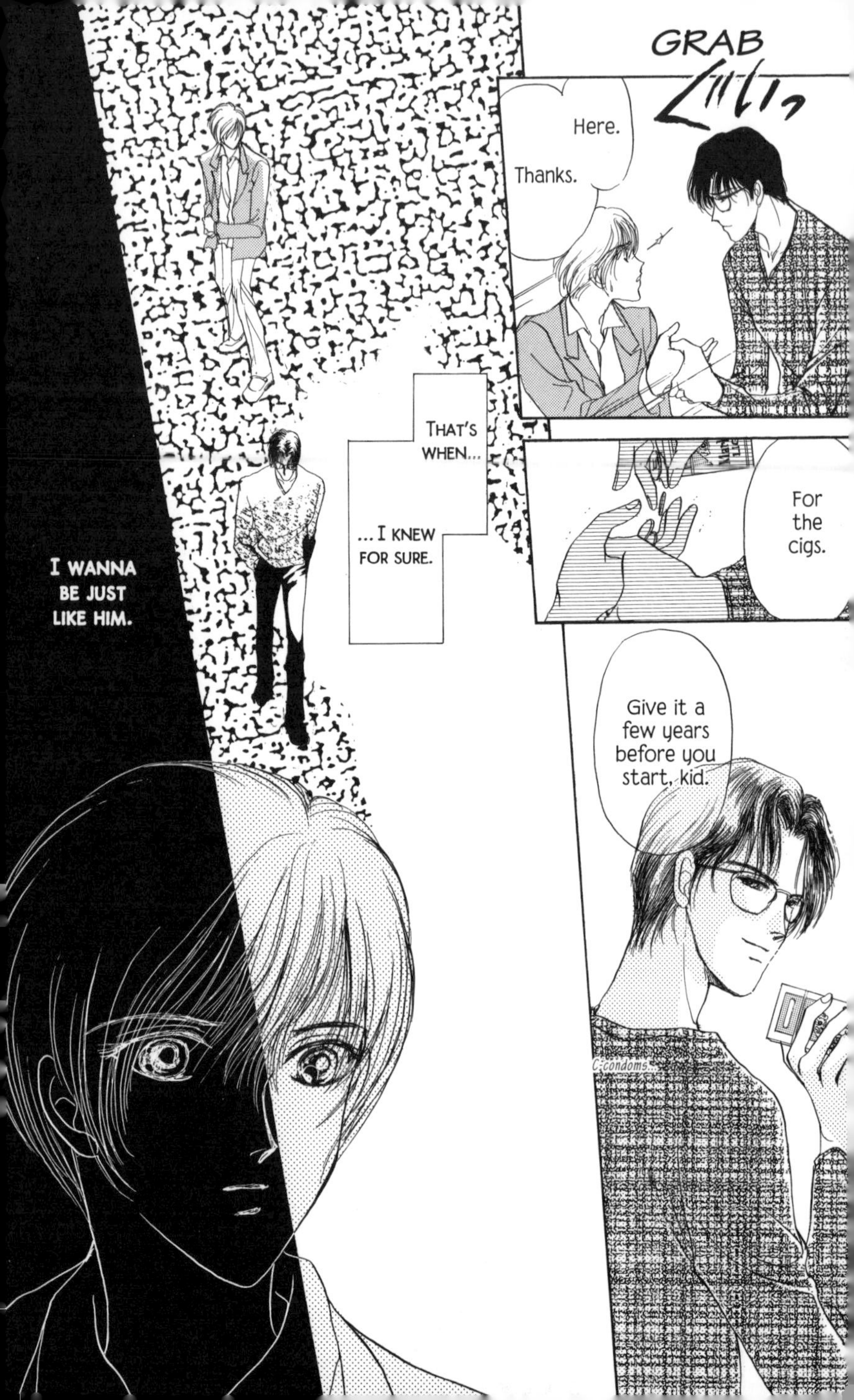
GRAB
Here.
Thanks.
For the cigs.
Give it a few years before you start, kid.
C-condoms...
THAT'S WHEN...
...I KNEW FOR SURE.
I WANNA BE JUST LIKE HIM.

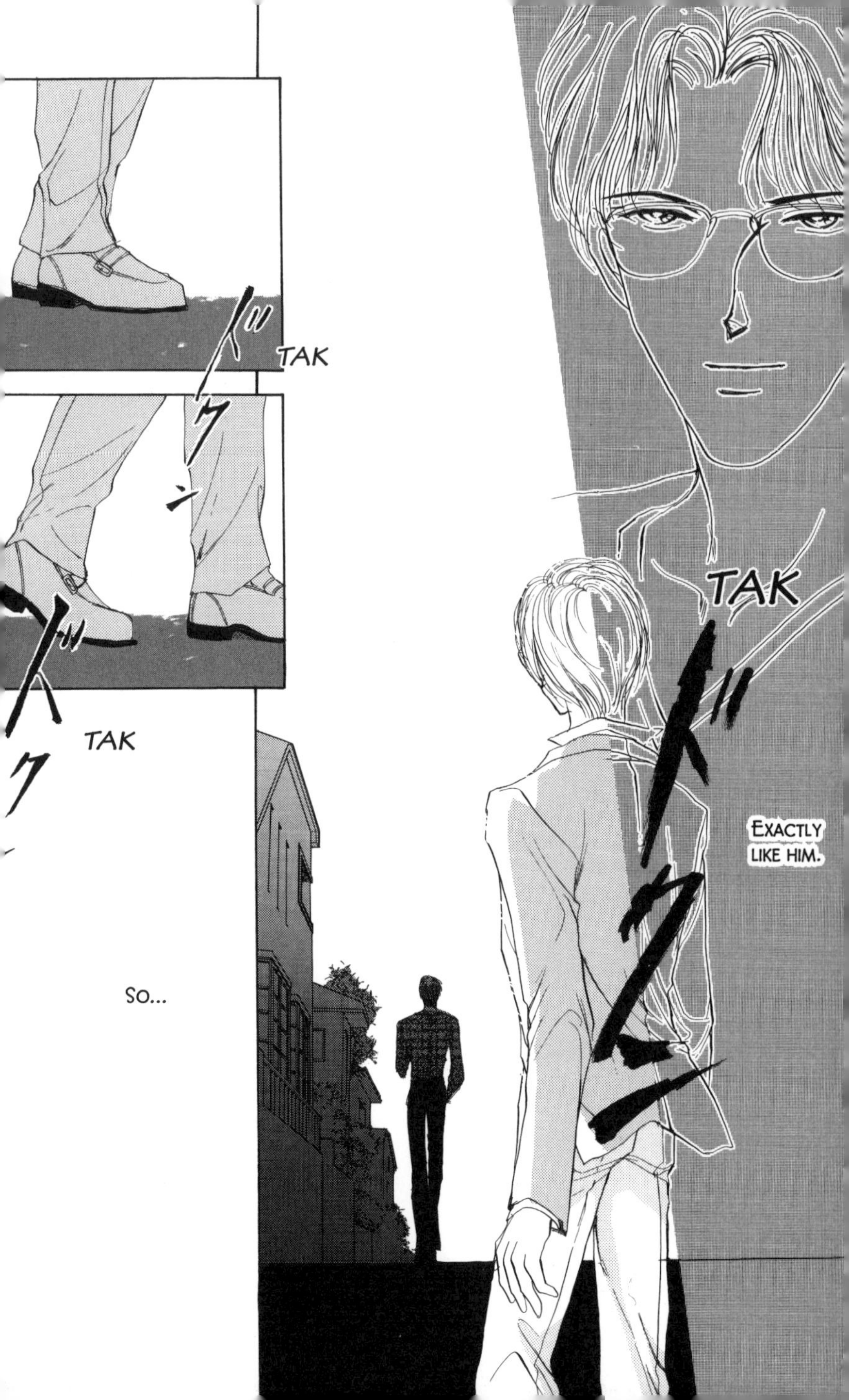
TAK
EXACTLY LIKE HIM.
TAK
TAK
SO...

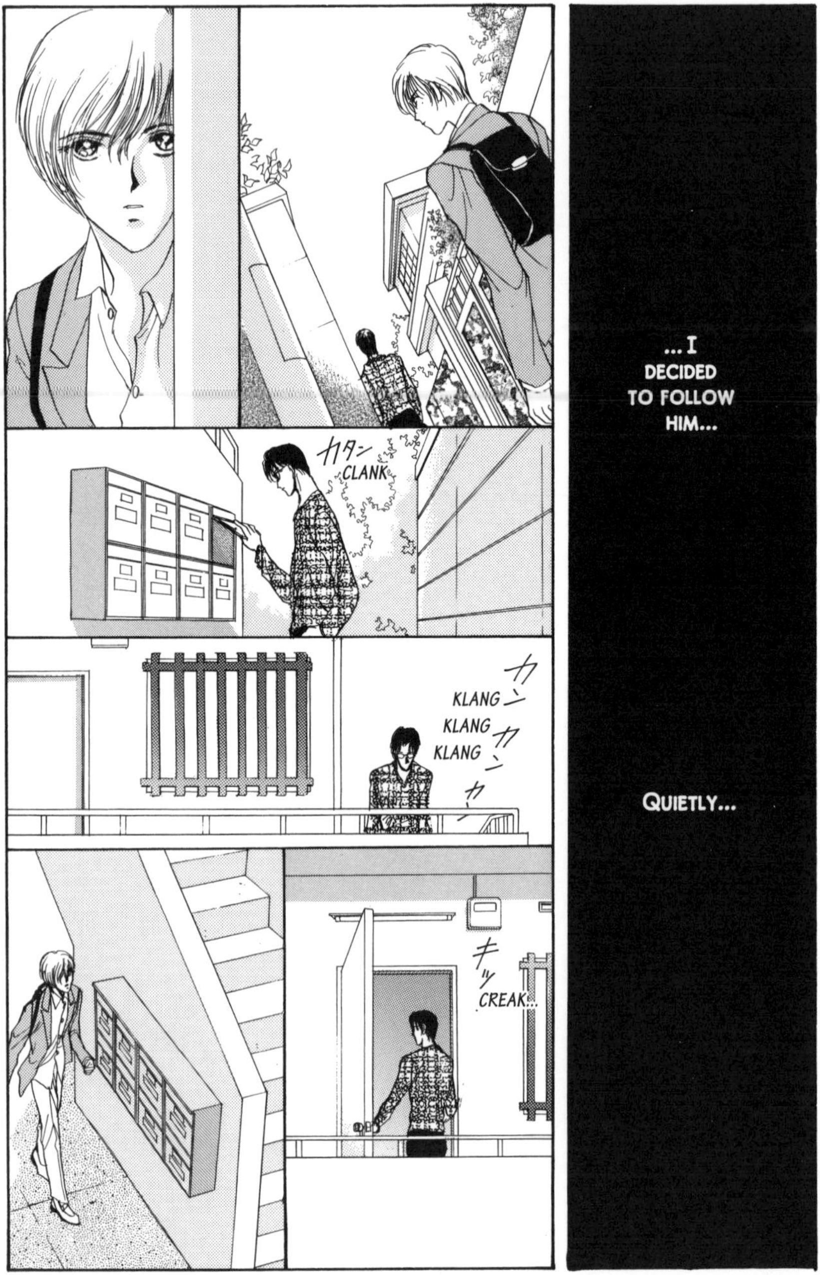
...I DECIDED TO FOLLOW HIM...
QUIETLY...
カタン
CLANK
カンカンカン
KLANG
KLANG
KLANG
キッ
CREAK...

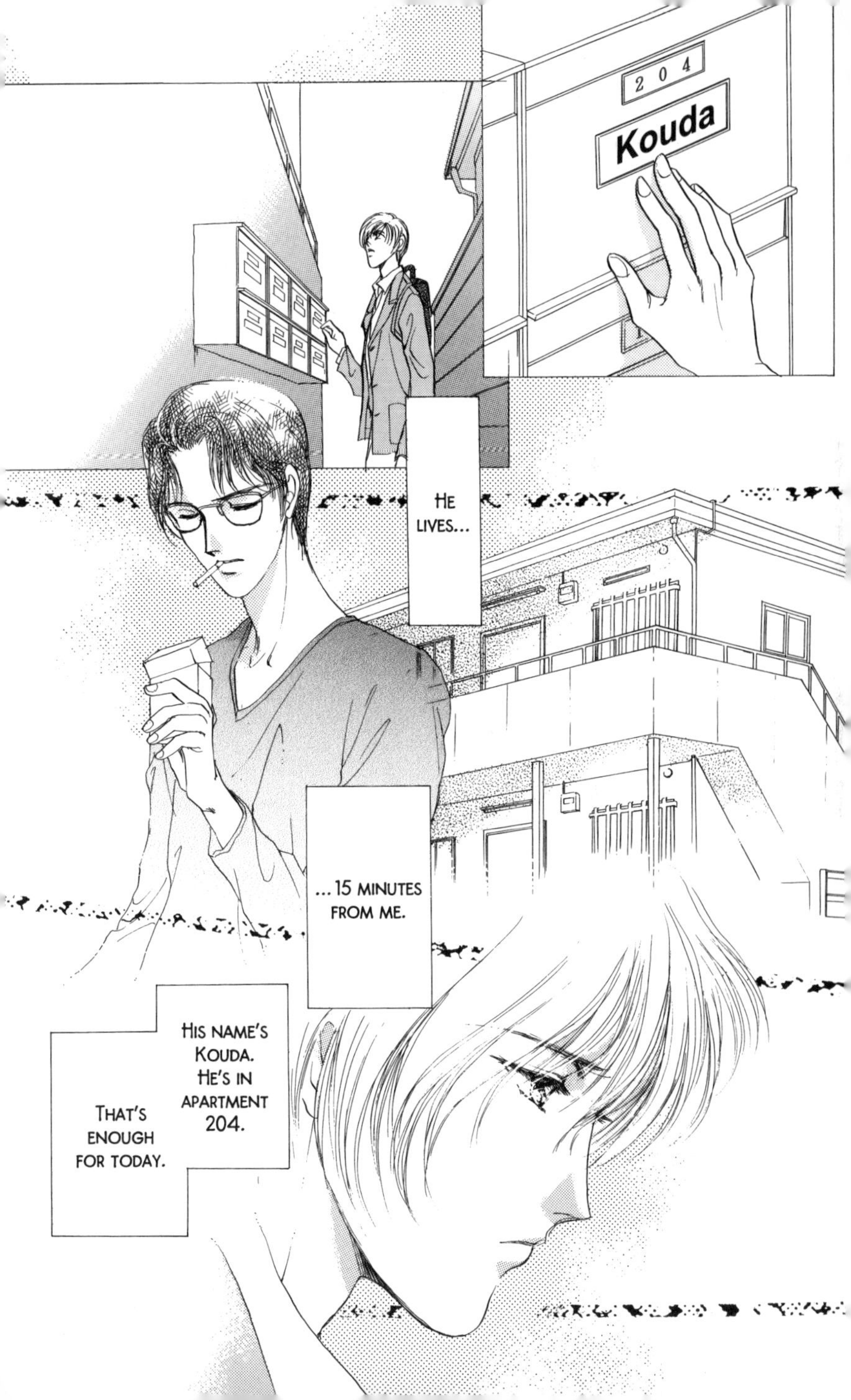
2 0 4
Kouda
He lives...
...15 minutes from me.
His name's Kouda. He's in apartment 204.
That's enough for today.

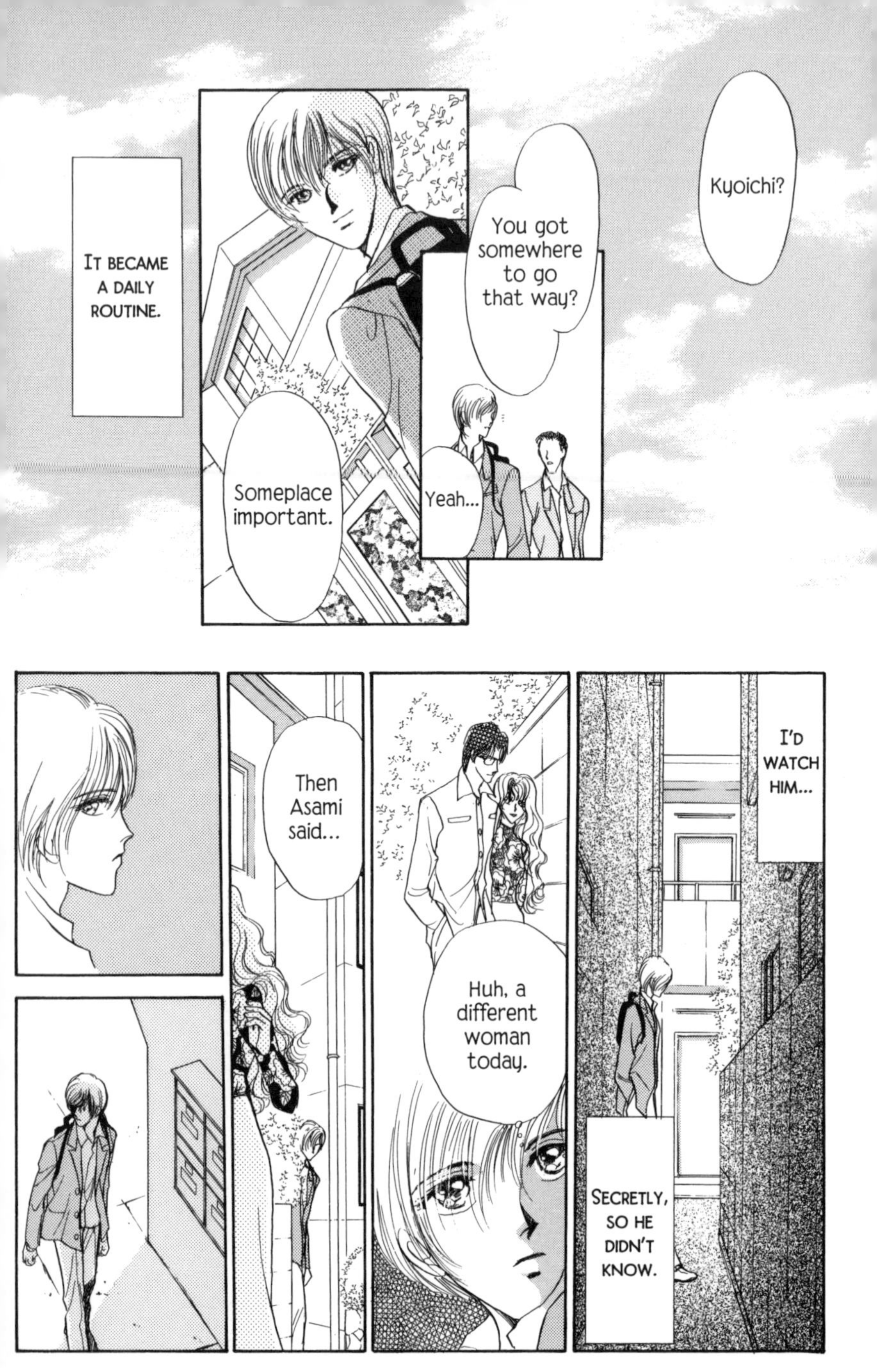
Kyoichi?
You got somewhere to go that way?
Yeah...
Someplace important.
It became a daily routine.
I'd watch him...
Secretly, so he didn't know.
Huh, a different woman today.
Then Asami said...

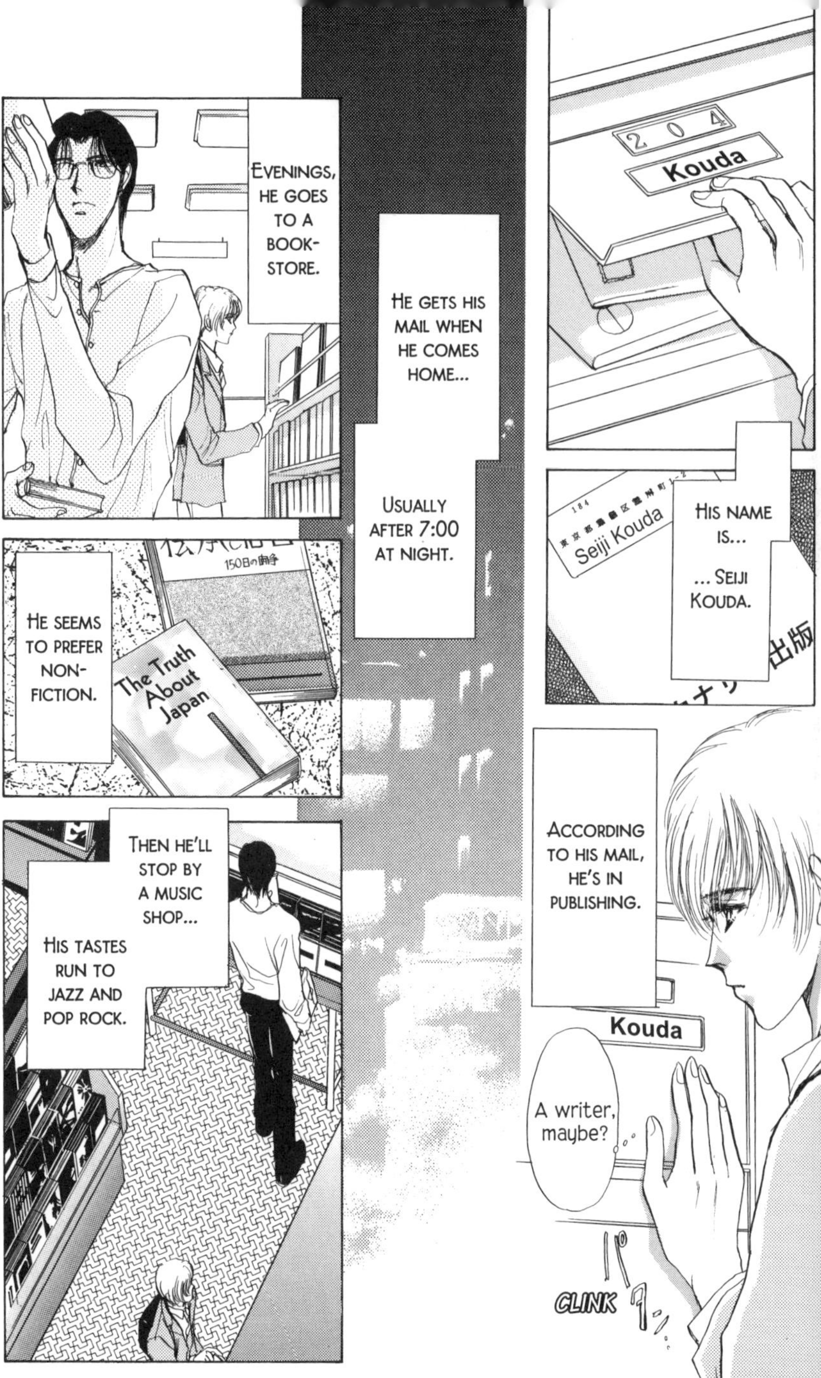
Evenings, he goes to a book-store.
He seems to prefer non-fiction.
150日の闘争
The Truth About Japan
Then he'll stop by a music shop...
His tastes run to jazz and pop rock.
He gets his mail when he comes home...
Usually after 7:00 at night.
2 0 4
Kouda
His name is...
... Seiji Kouda.
Seiji Kouda
出版
According to his mail, he's in publishing.
Kouda
A writer, maybe?
CLINK

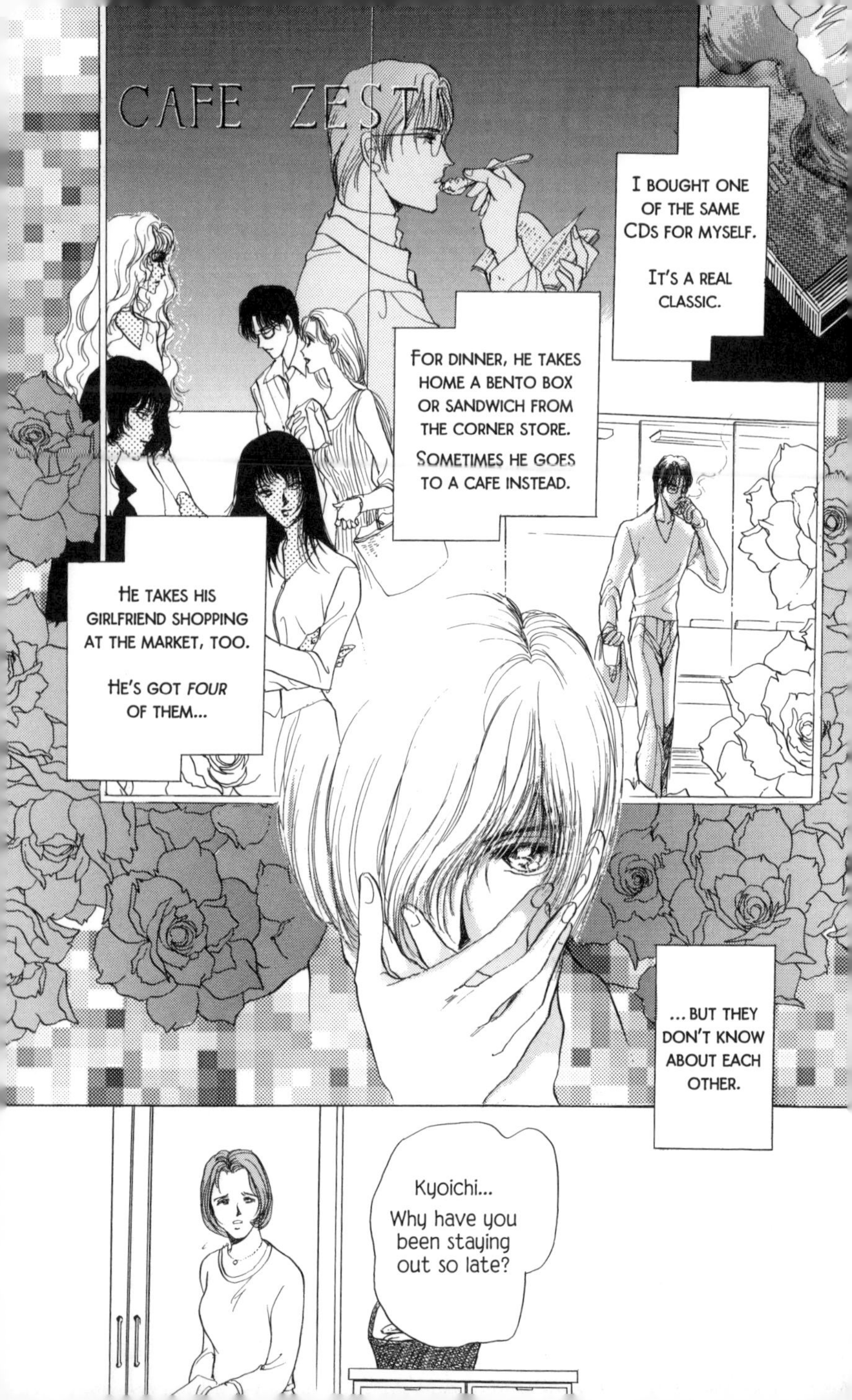
I BOUGHT ONE OF THE SAME CDs FOR MYSELF.
IT'S A REAL CLASSIC.
CAFE ZEST
FOR DINNER, HE TAKES HOME A BENTO BOX OR SANDWICH FROM THE CORNER STORE.
SOMETIMES HE GOES TO A CAFE INSTEAD.
HE TAKES HIS GIRLFRIEND SHOPPING AT THE MARKET, TOO.
HE'S GOT *FOUR* OF THEM...
...BUT THEY DON'T KNOW ABOUT EACH OTHER.
Kyoichi... Why have you been staying out so late?

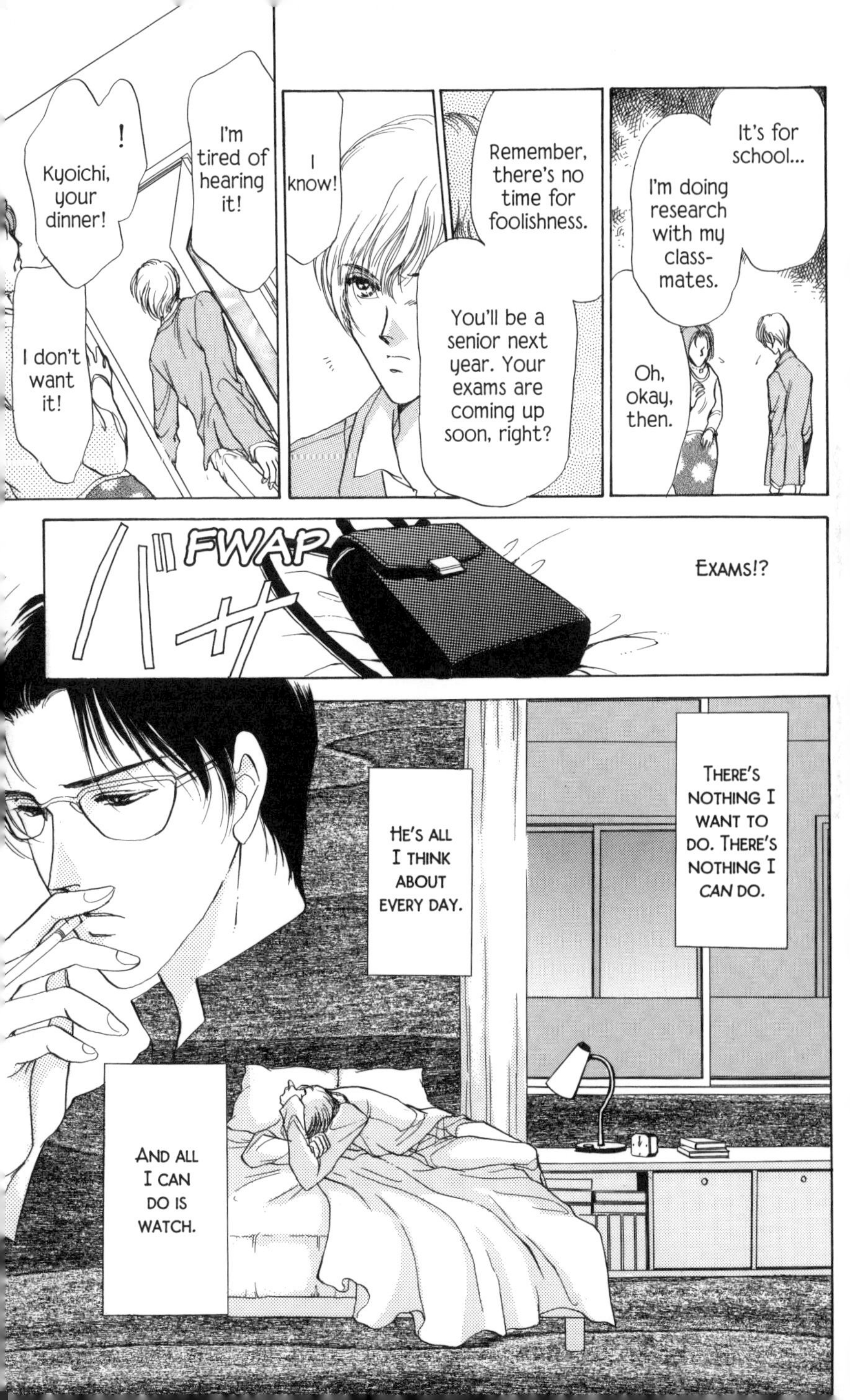
It's for school...
I'm doing research with my classmates.
Oh, okay, then.
Remember, there's no time for foolishness.
You'll be a senior next year. Your exams are coming up soon, right?
I know!
I'm tired of hearing it!
!
Kyoichi, your dinner!
I don't want it!
EXAMS!?
FWAP
THERE'S NOTHING I WANT TO DO. THERE'S NOTHING I *CAN* DO.
HE'S ALL I THINK ABOUT EVERY DAY.
AND ALL I CAN DO IS WATCH.

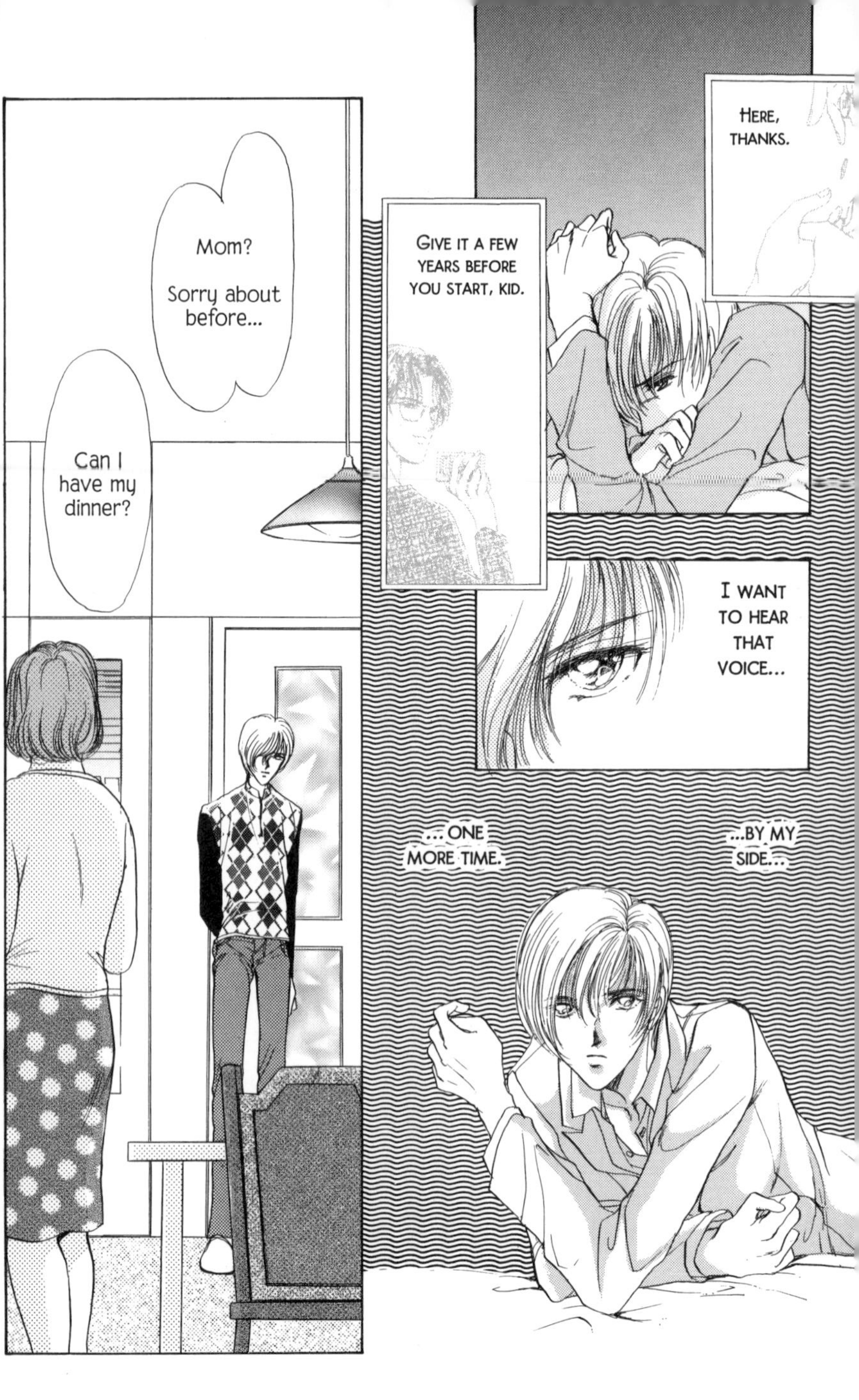
HERE, THANKS.
GIVE IT A FEW YEARS BEFORE YOU START, KID.
I WANT TO HEAR THAT VOICE...
...BY MY SIDE...
...ONE MORE TIME.
Mom? Sorry about before...
Can I have my dinner?

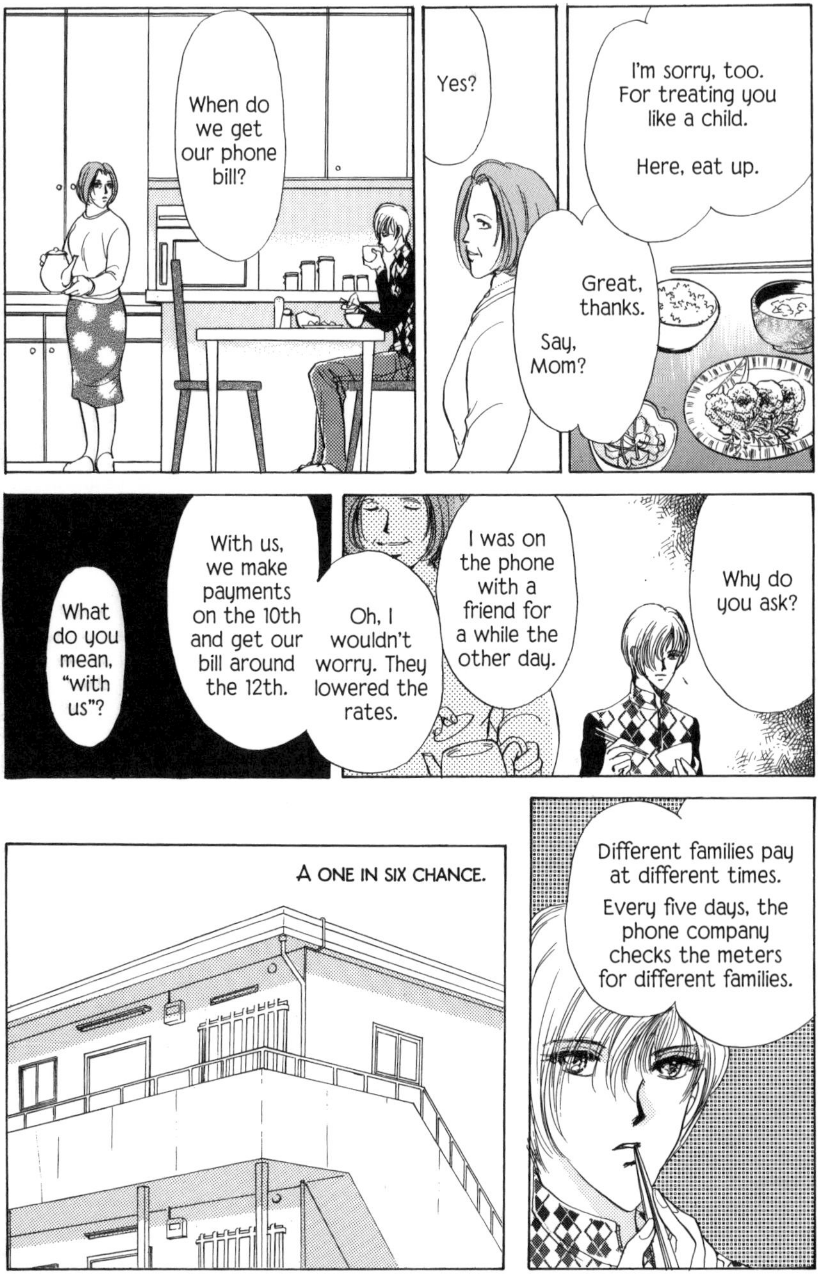
I'm sorry, too. For treating you like a child.
Here, eat up.
Great, thanks.
Say, Mom?
Yes?
When do we get our phone bill?
Why do you ask?
I was on the phone with a friend for a while the other day.
Oh, I wouldn't worry. They lowered the rates.
With us, we make payments on the 10th and get our bill around the 12th.
What do you mean, "with us"?
Different families pay at different times.
Every five days, the phone company checks the meters for different families.
A ONE IN SIX CHANCE.

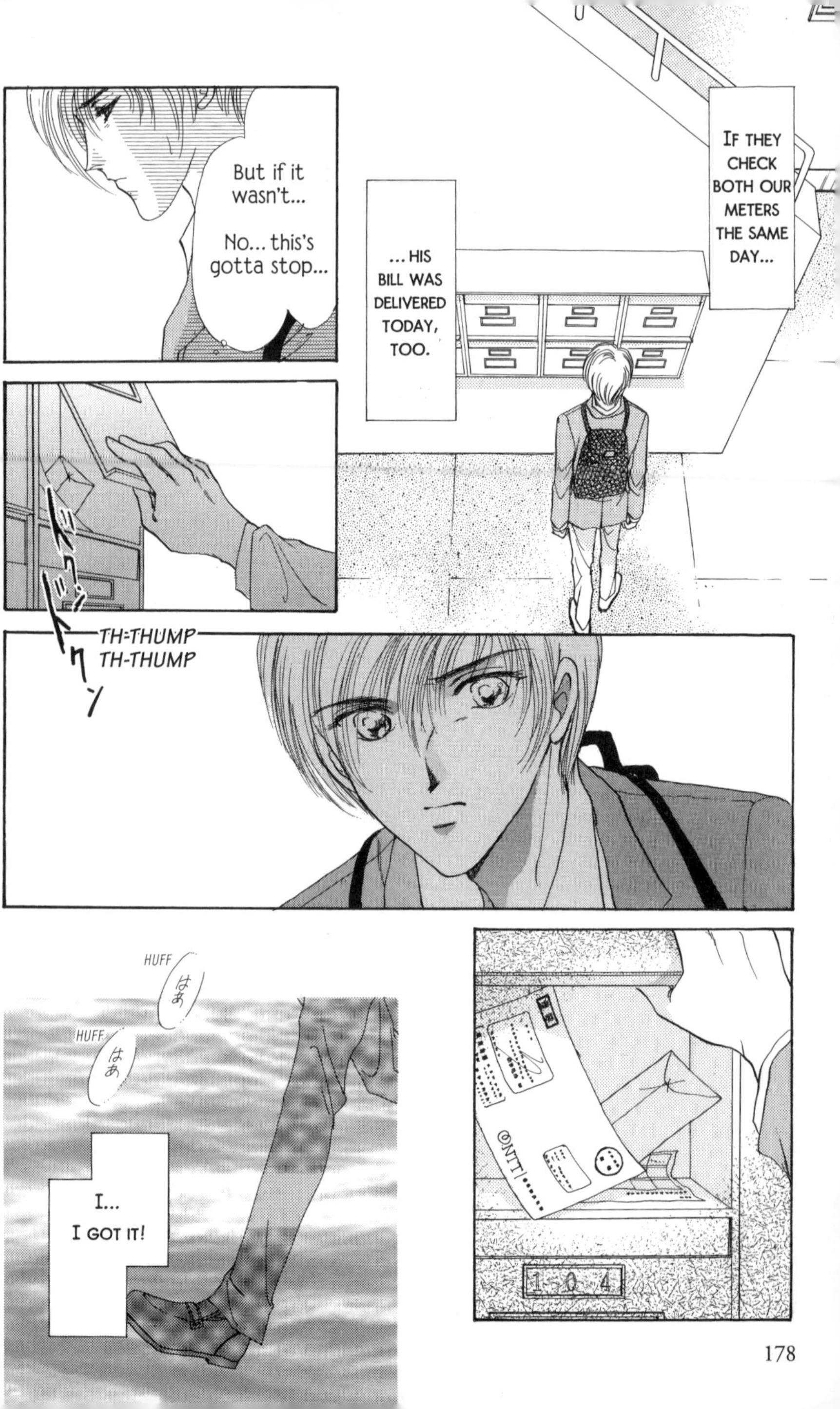
If they check both our meters the same day...
...his bill was delivered today, too.
But if it wasn't...
No... this's gotta stop...
TH-THUMP TH-THUMP
HUFF
はあ
HUFF
はあ
I... I got it!

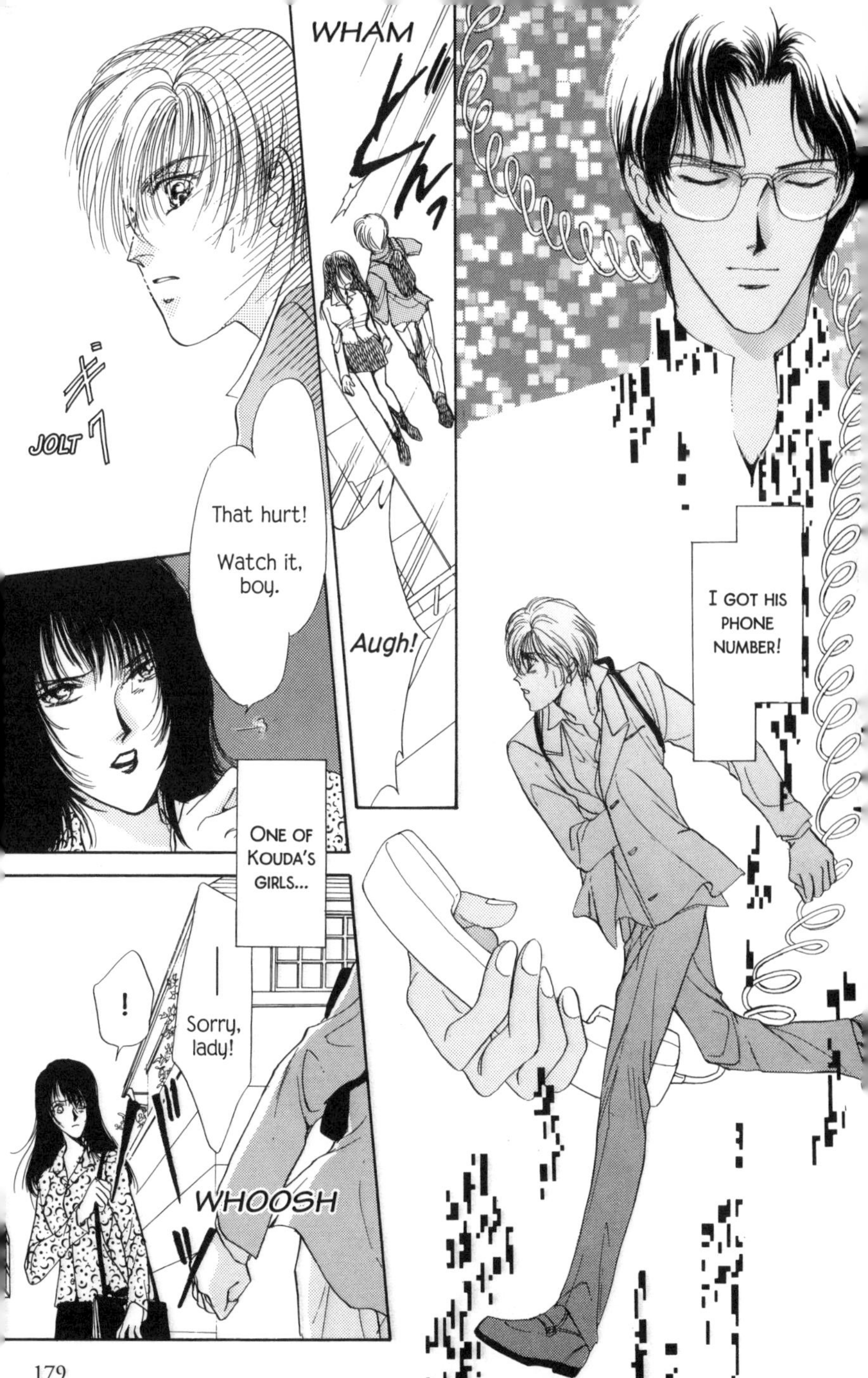
I GOT HIS PHONE NUMBER!
WHAM
Augh!
JOLT
That hurt!
Watch it, boy.
ONE OF KOUDA'S GIRLS...
Sorry, lady!
!
WHOOSH

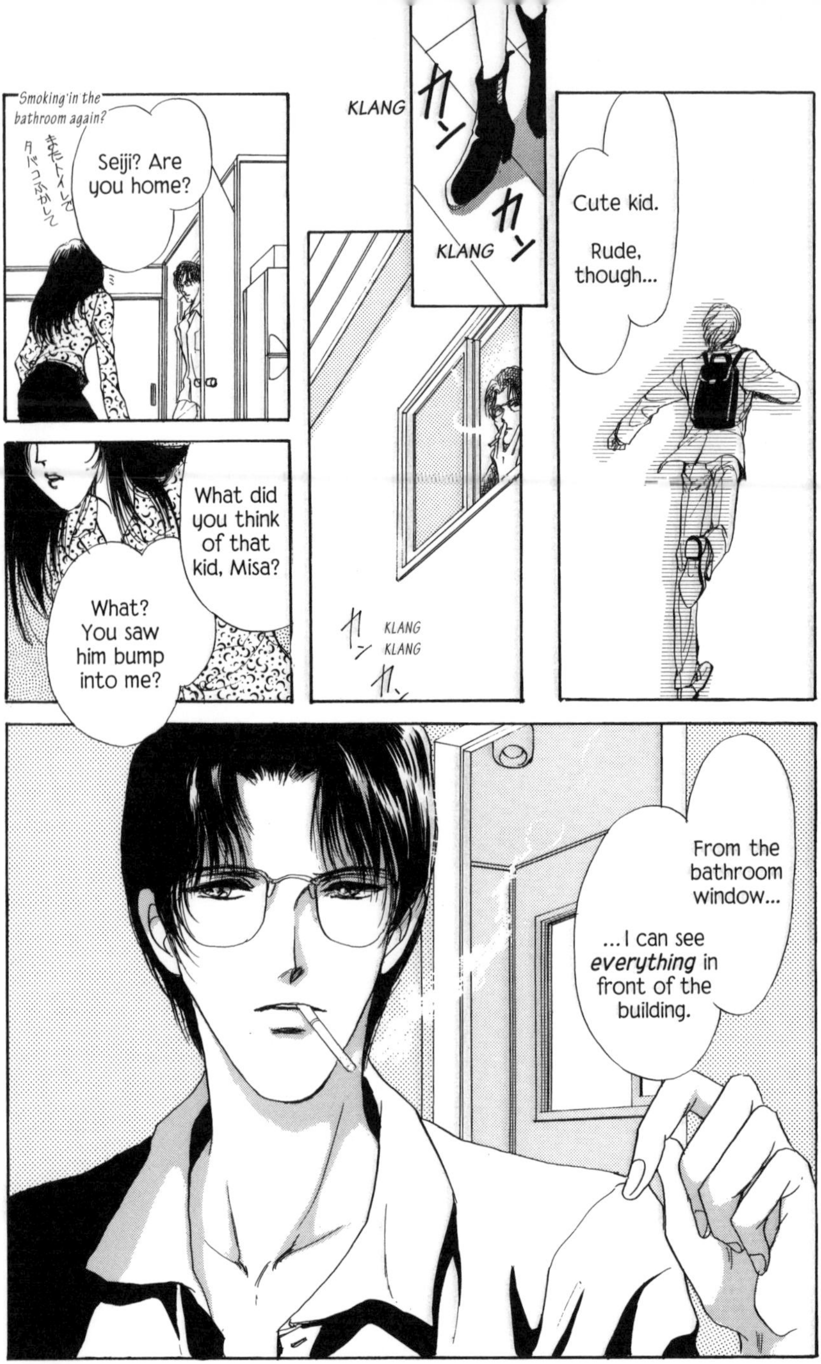
Cute kid.
Rude, though...
カン
KLANG
カン
KLANG
カン
KLANG
KLANG
カン
Smoking in the bathroom again?
またトイレでタバコふかして
Seiji? Are you home?
What did you think of that kid, Misa?
What? You saw him bump into me?
From the bathroom window...
...I can see *everything* in front of the building.

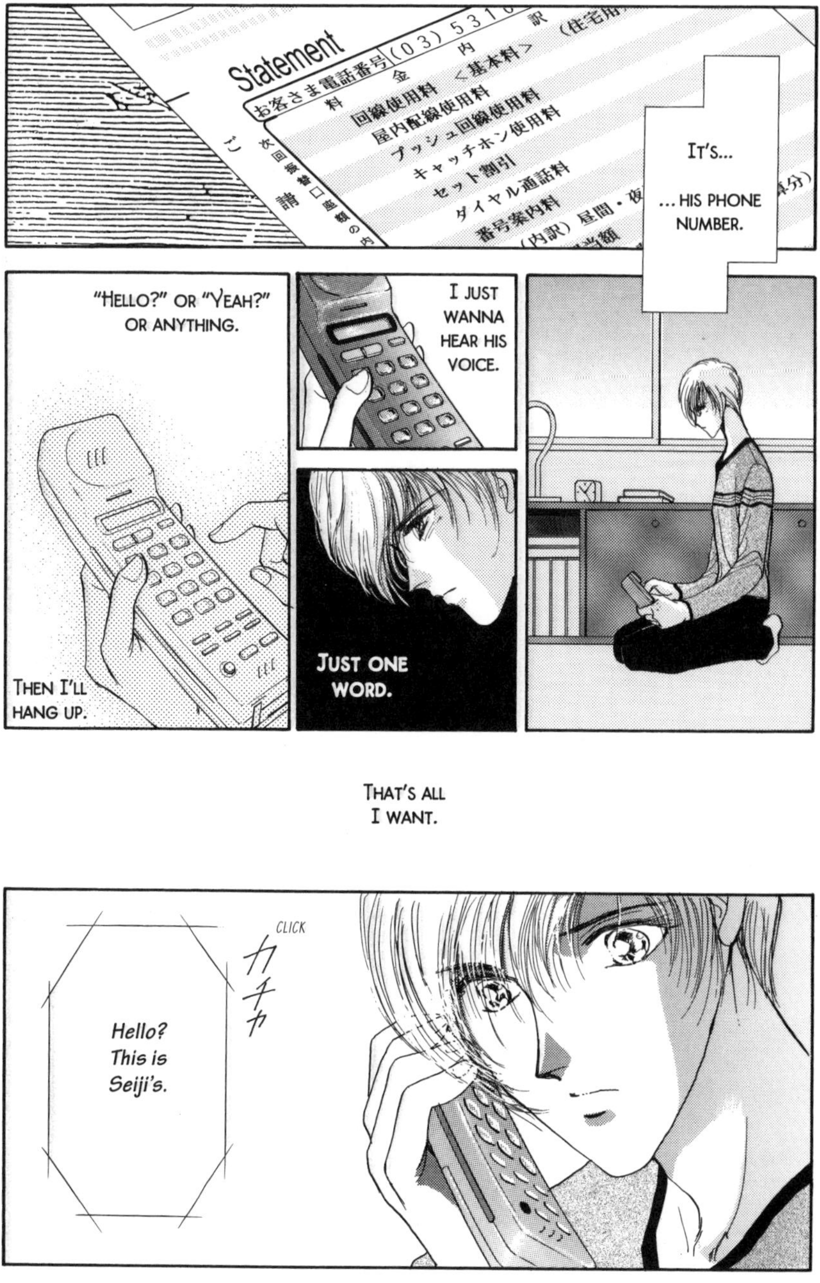
Statement
お客さま電話番号 (03) 531
料金内訳
回線使用料
屋内配線使用料
プッシュ回線使用料
キャッチホン使用料
セット割引
ダイヤル通話料
番号案内料
IT'S...
...HIS PHONE NUMBER.
I JUST WANNA HEAR HIS VOICE.
JUST ONE WORD.
"HELLO?" OR "YEAH?" OR ANYTHING.
THEN I'LL HANG UP.
THAT'S ALL I WANT.
CLICK
カチャ
Hello? This is Seiji's.

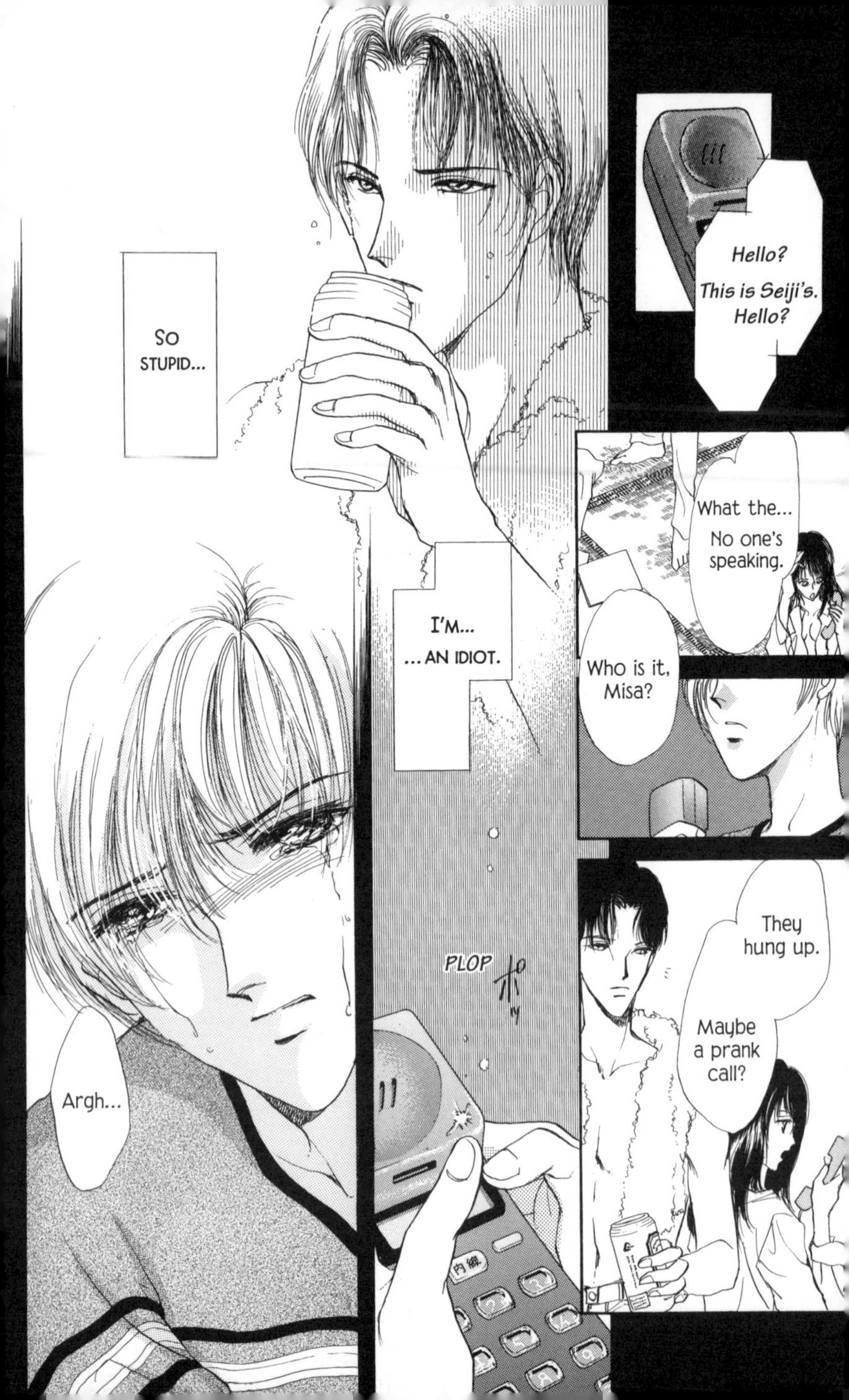
Hello?
This is Seiji's.
Hello?
What the... No one's speaking.
Who is it, Misa?
They hung up.
Maybe a prank call?
So stupid...
I'm...
...an idiot.
PLOP
Argh...

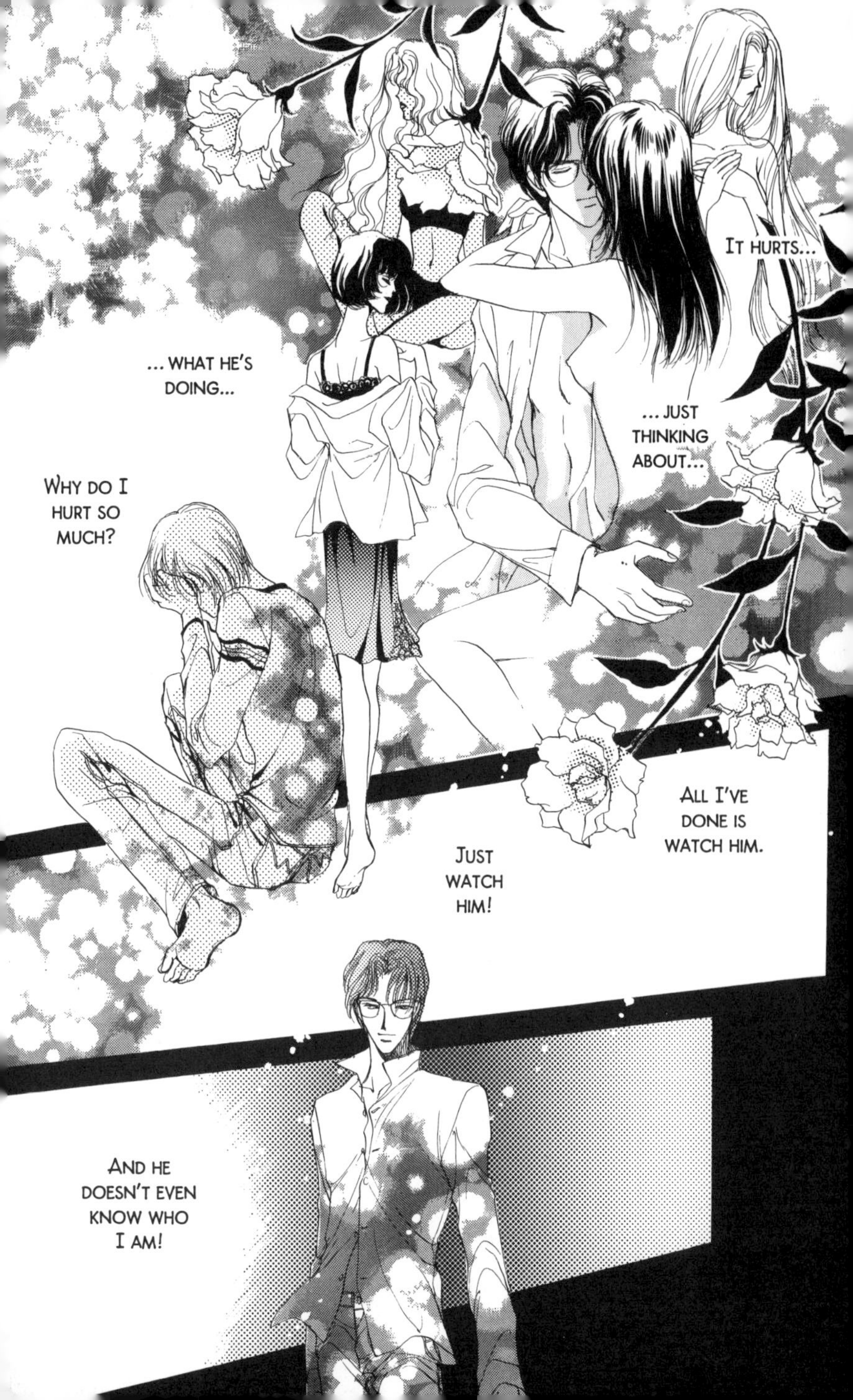
It hurts...
...just thinking about...
...what he's doing...
Why do I hurt so much?
All I've done is watch him.
Just watch him!
And he doesn't even know who I am!

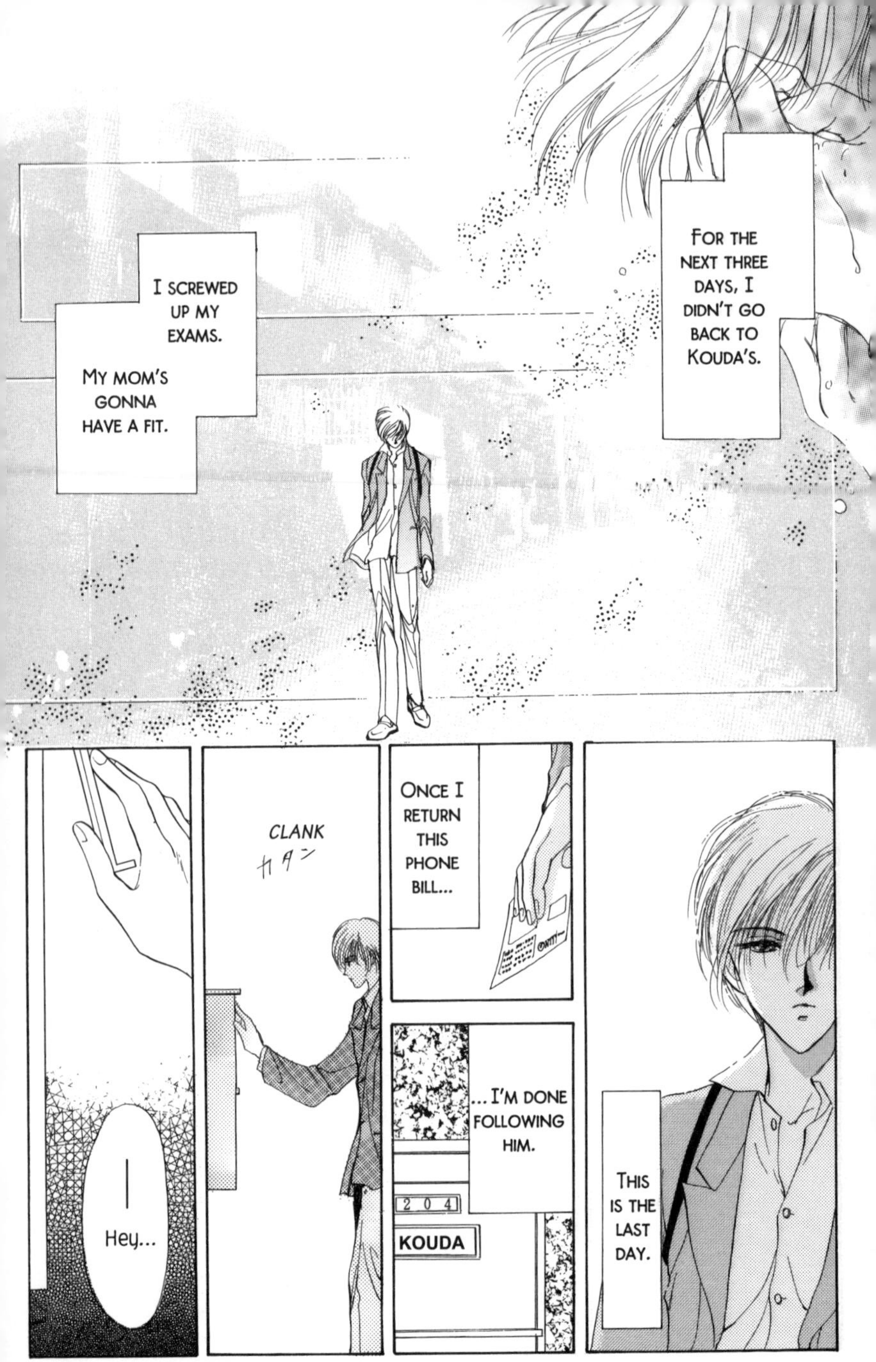
For the next three days, I didn't go back to Kouda's.
I screwed up my exams.
My mom's gonna have a fit.
This is the last day.
Once I return this phone bill...
...I'm done following him.
2 0 4
KOUDA
CLANK
カタン
Hey...

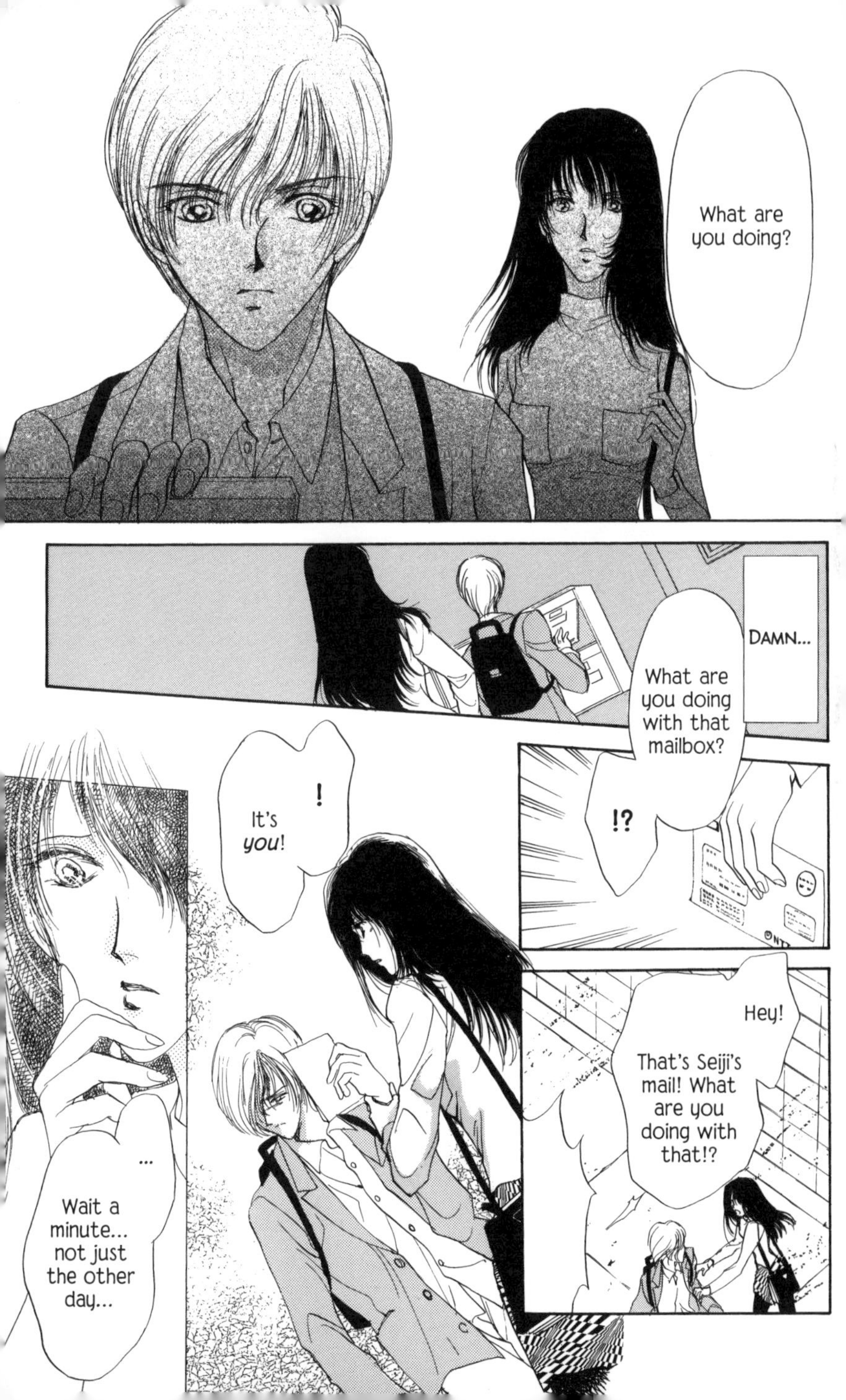
What are you doing?
DAMN...
What are you doing with that mailbox?
!?
Hey!
That's Seiji's mail! What are you doing with that!?
!
It's *you*!
...
Wait a minute... not just the other day...

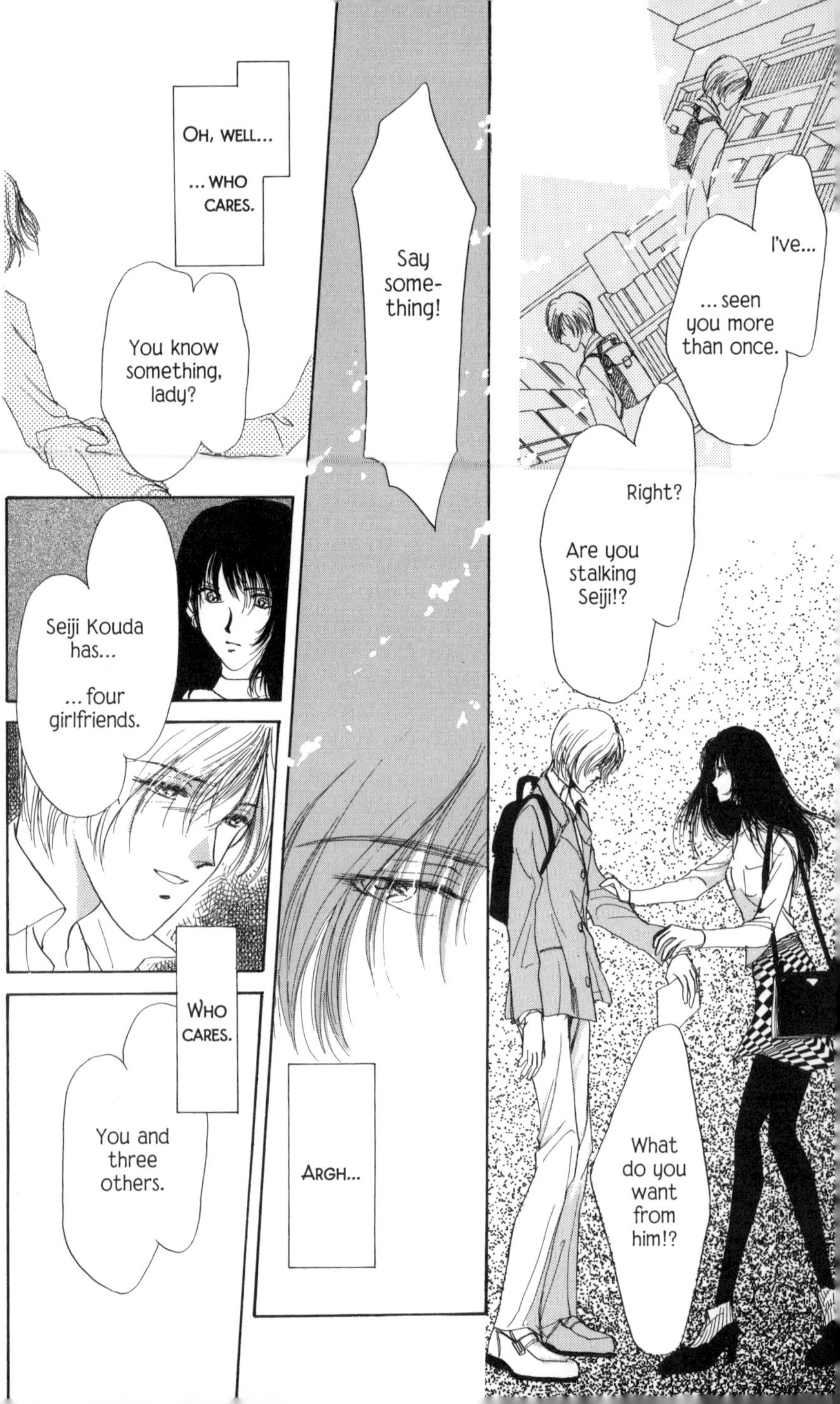
I've...
...seen you more than once.
Right?
Are you stalking Seiji!?
What do you want from him!?
Say something!
Argh...
OH, WELL...
...WHO CARES.
You know something, lady?
Seiji Kouda has...
...four girlfriends.
WHO CARES.
You and three others.

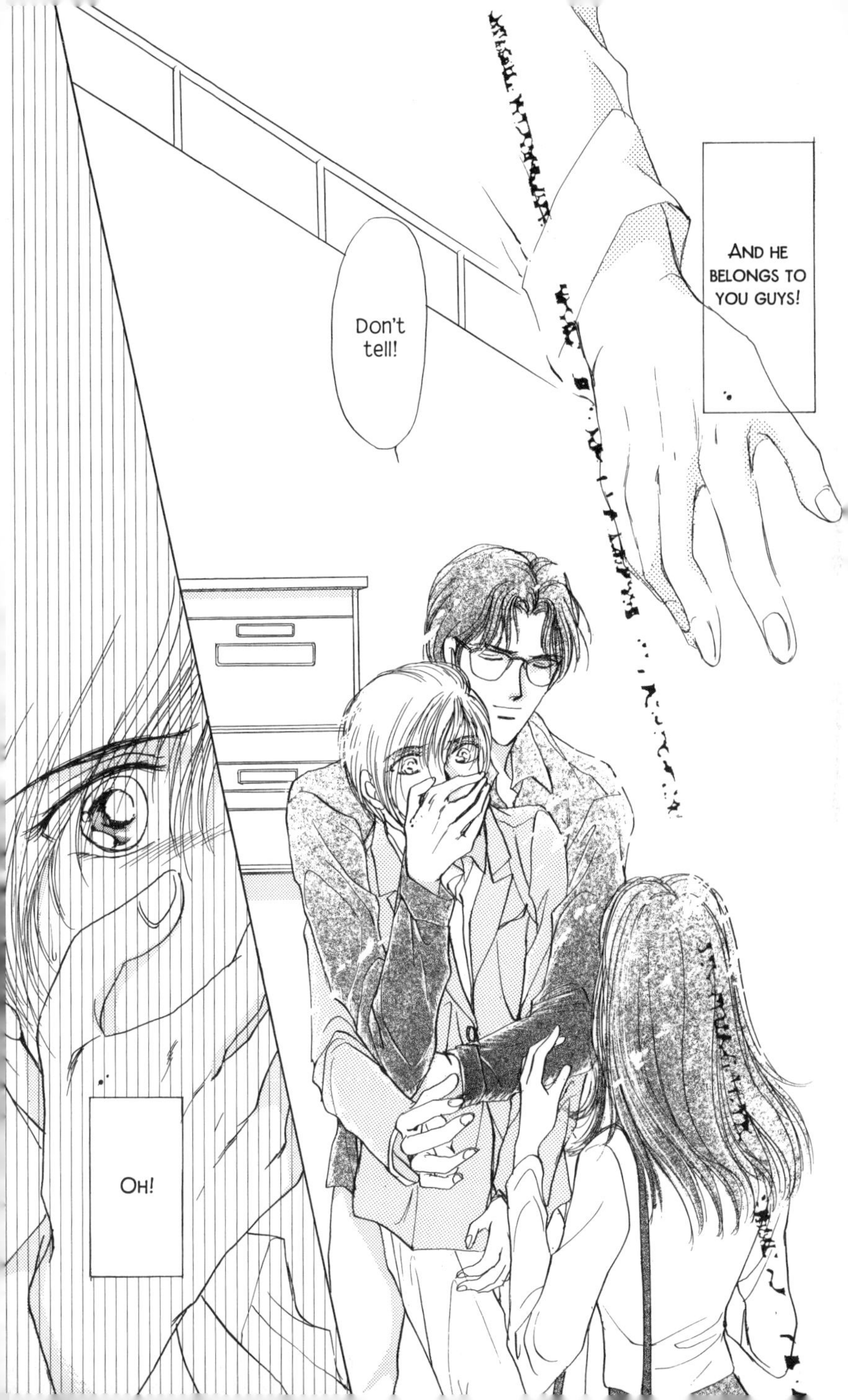
And he belongs to you guys!
Don't tell!
Oh!

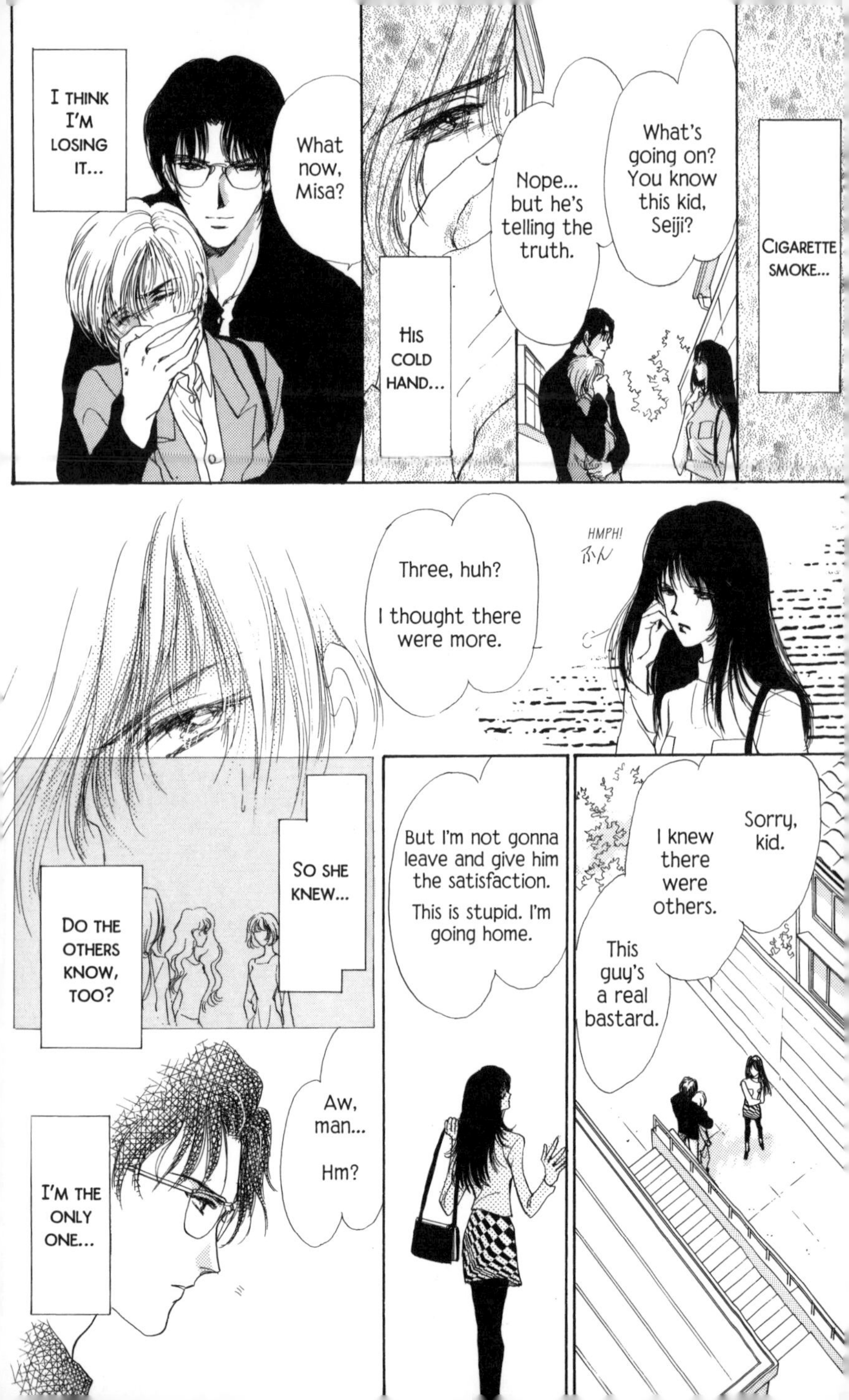
Cigarette smoke...
What's going on? You know this kid, Seiji?
Nope... but he's telling the truth.
His cold hand...
What now, Misa?
I think I'm losing it...
HMPH!
ふん
Three, huh?
I thought there were more.
Sorry, kid.
I knew there were others.
This guy's a real bastard.
But I'm not gonna leave and give him the satisfaction.
This is stupid. I'm going home.
So she knew...
Do the others know, too?
Aw, man...
Hm?
I'm the only one...

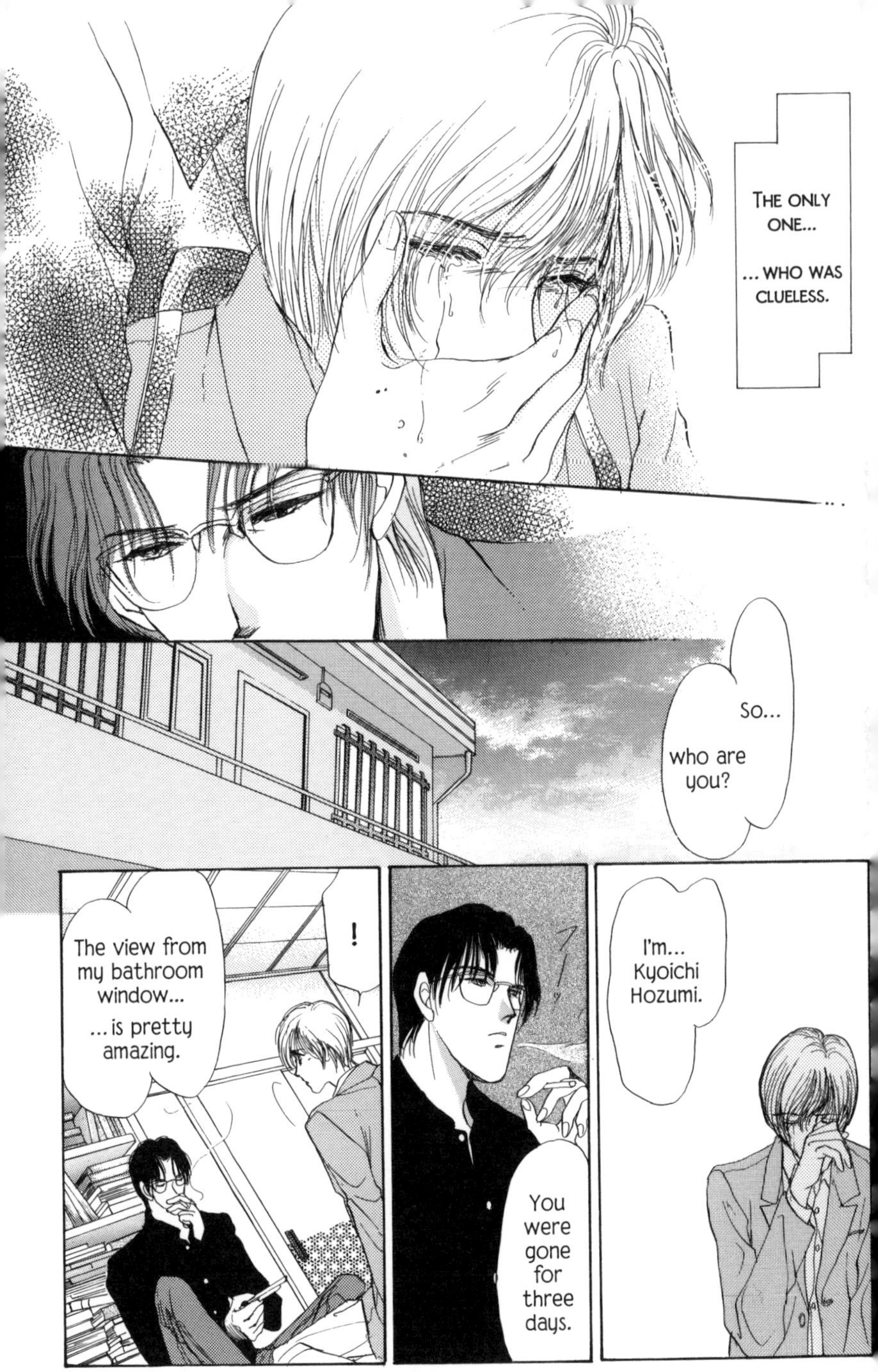
THE ONLY ONE...
...WHO WAS CLUELESS.
...
So...
who are you?
I'm... Kyoichi Hozumi.
You were gone for three days.
!
The view from my bathroom window...
...is pretty amazing.

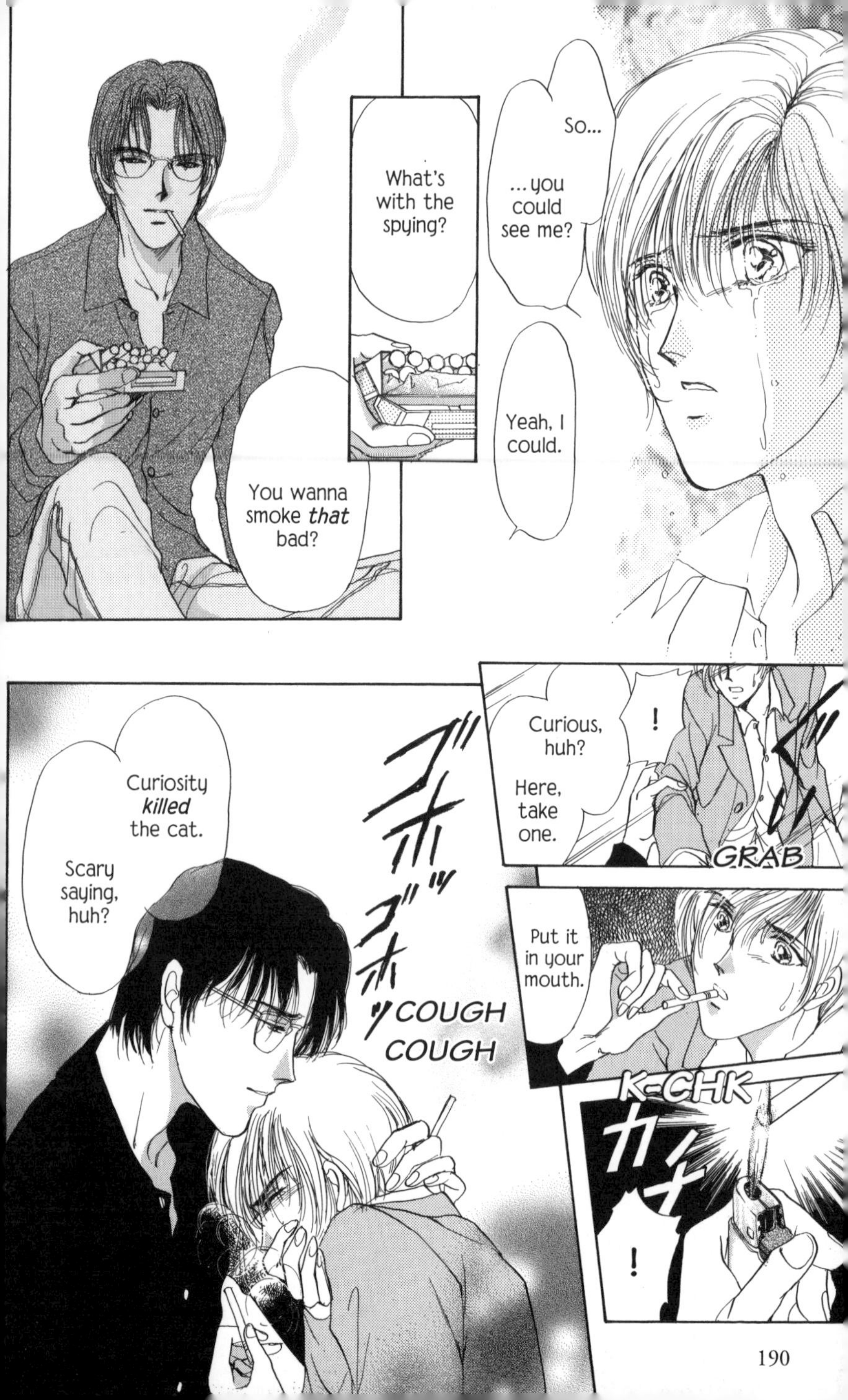
So...
...you could see me?
Yeah, I could.
What's with the spying?
You wanna smoke *that* bad?
!
Curious, huh?
Here, take one.
GRAB
Put it in your mouth.
K-CHK
カチ
!
Curiosity *killed* the cat.
Scary saying, huh?
ゴホッゴホッ
COUGH COUGH

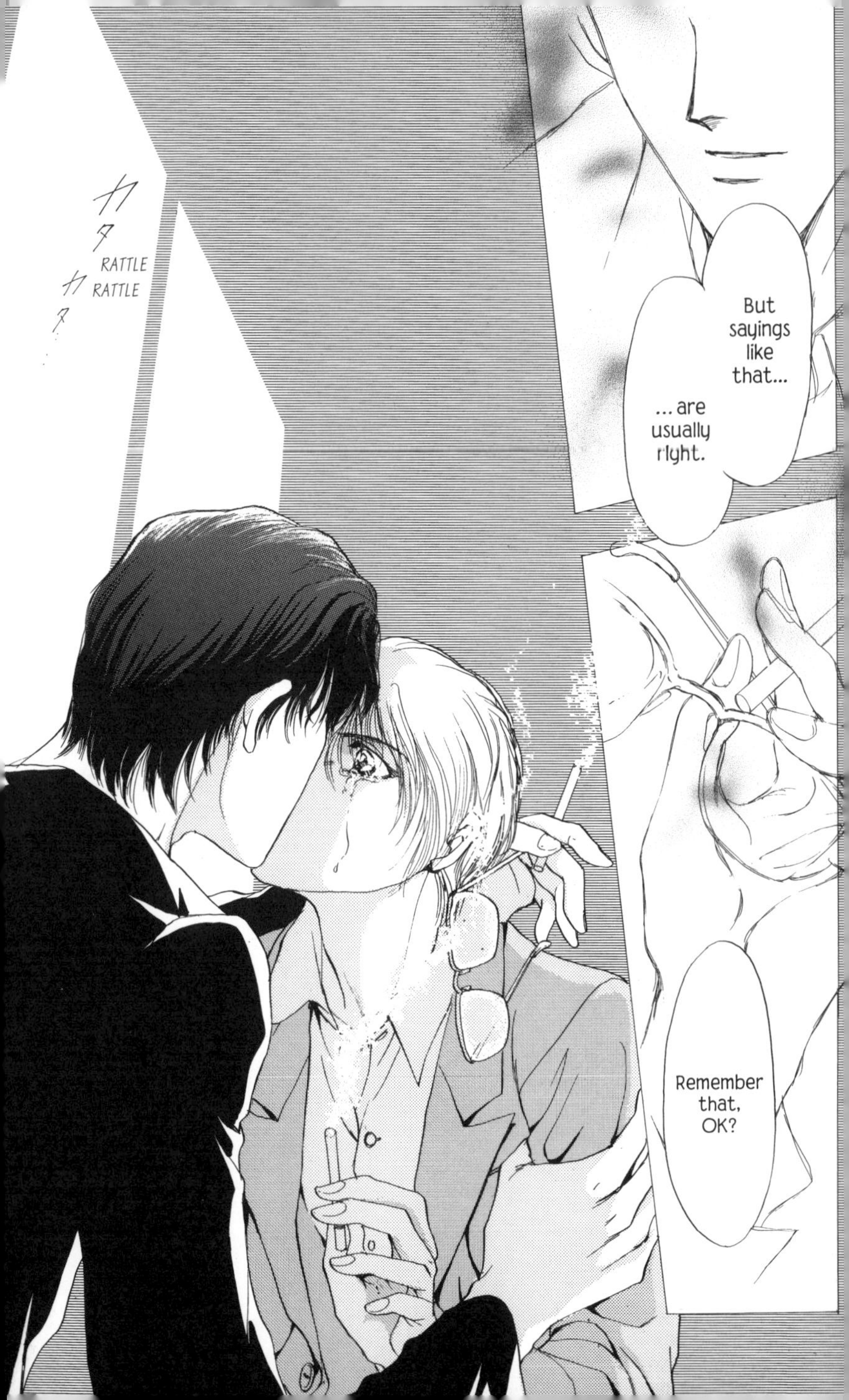
But sayings like that...
...are usually right.
Remember that, OK?
カタカタ
RATTLE RATTLE

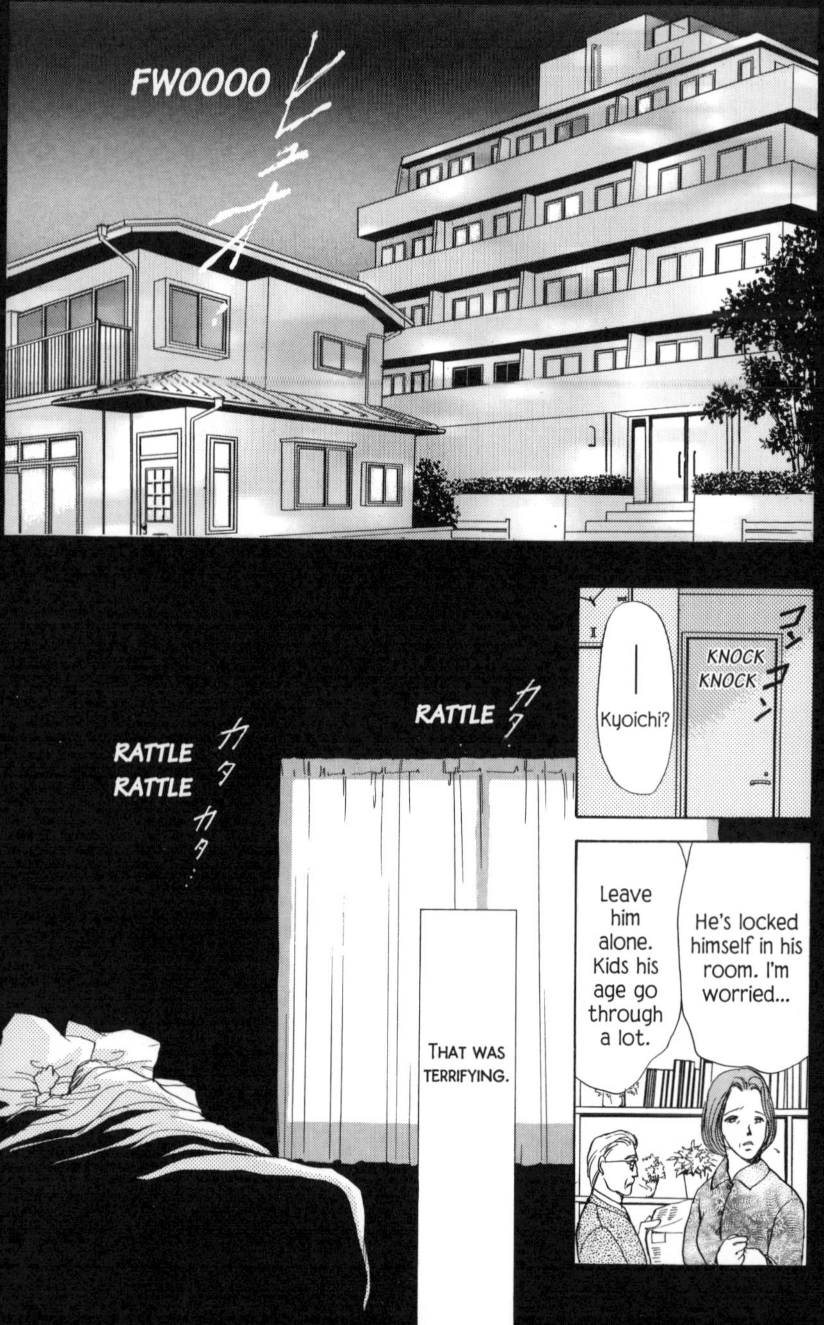
FWOOOO
—
Kyoichi?
KNOCK KNOCK
コンコン
He's locked himself in his room. I'm worried...
Leave him alone. Kids his age go through a lot.
RATTLE
カタ
RATTLE RATTLE
カタカタ...
THAT WAS TERRIFYING.

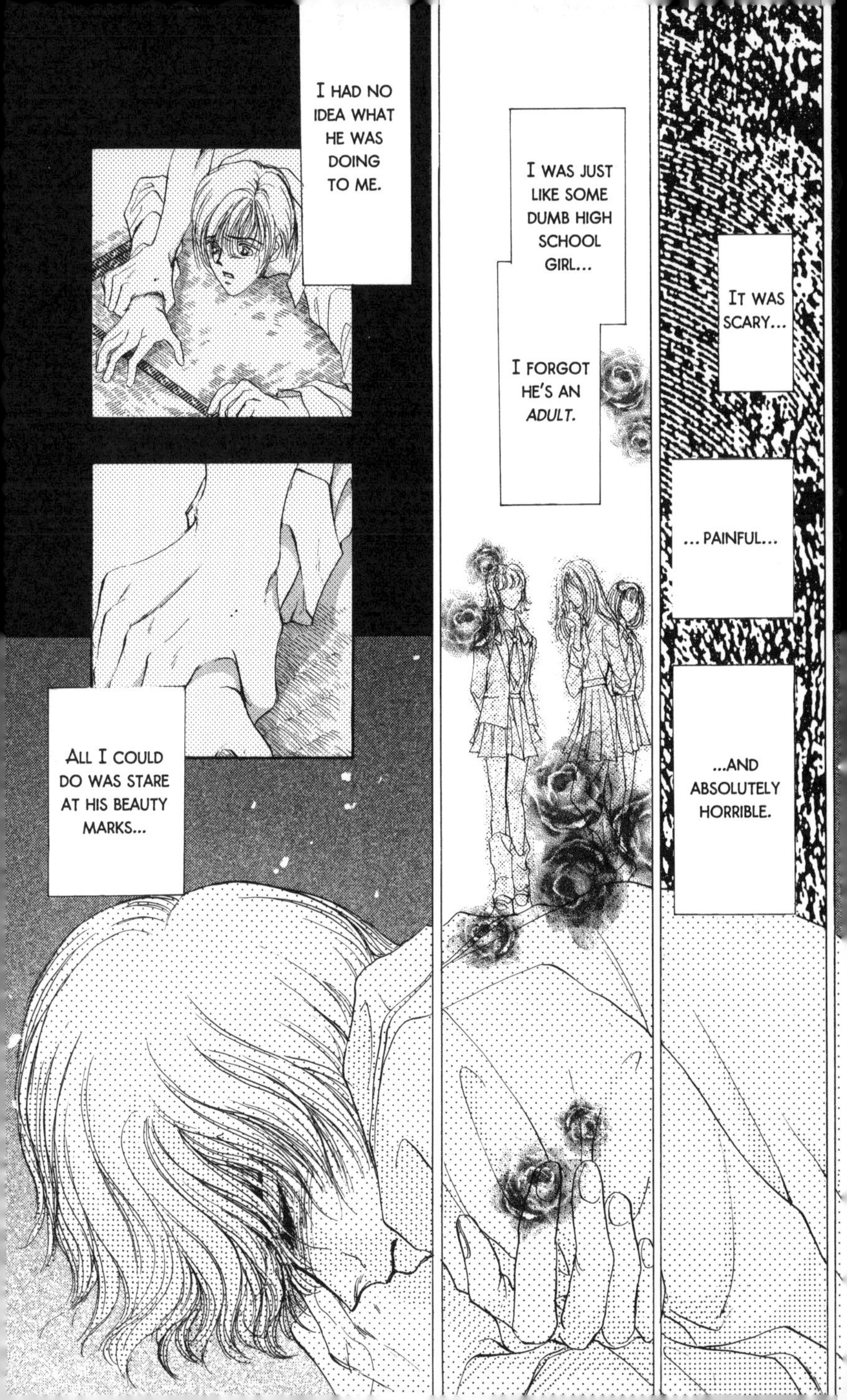
IT WAS SCARY...
...PAINFUL...
...AND ABSOLUTELY HORRIBLE.
I WAS JUST LIKE SOME DUMB HIGH SCHOOL GIRL...
I FORGOT HE'S AN *ADULT.*
I HAD NO IDEA WHAT HE WAS DOING TO ME.
ALL I COULD DO WAS STARE AT HIS BEAUTY MARKS...

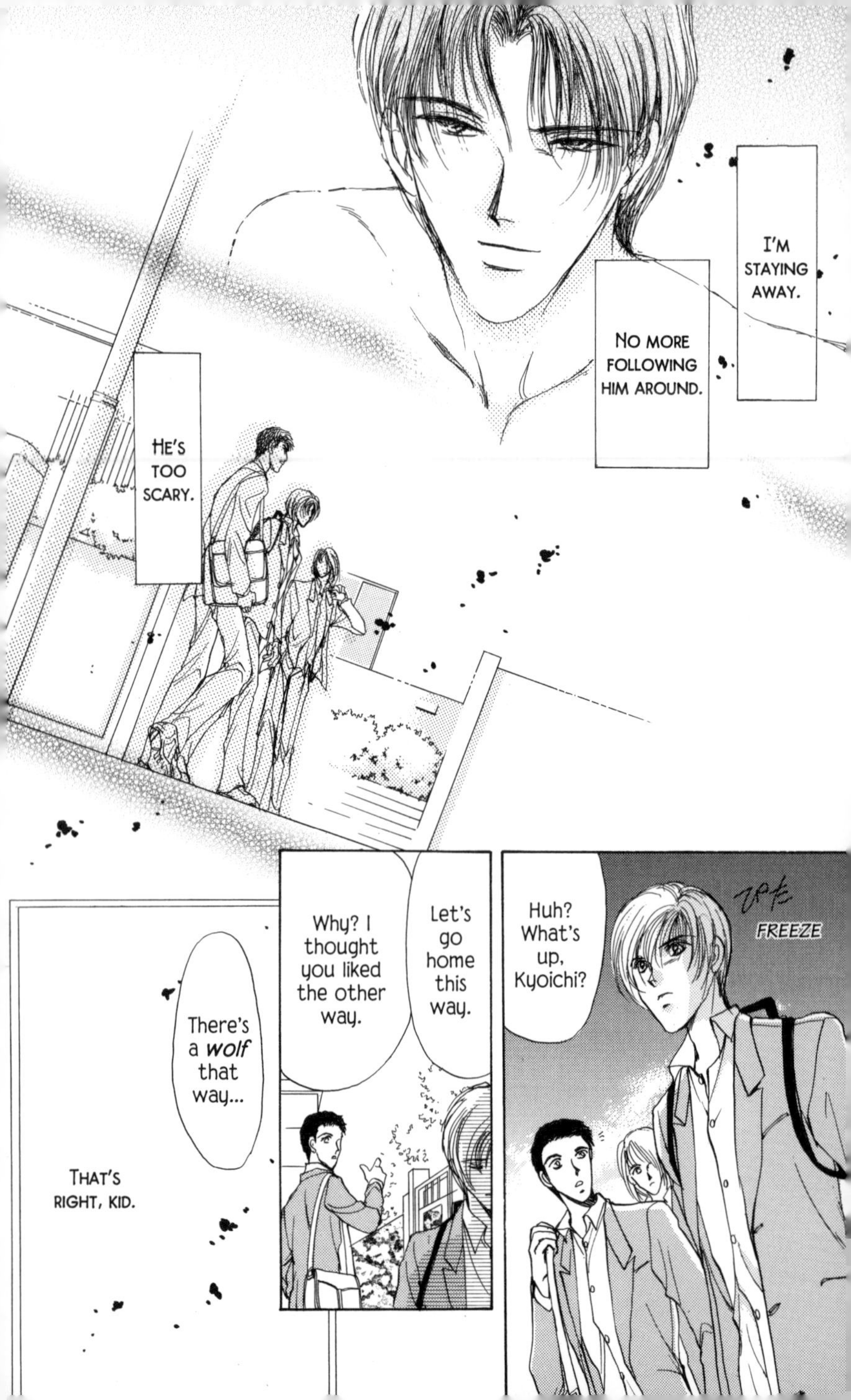
I'M STAYING AWAY.
NO MORE FOLLOWING HIM AROUND.
HE'S TOO SCARY.
ぴた
FREEZE
Huh? What's up, Kyoichi?
Let's go home this way.
Why? I thought you liked the other way.
There's a *wolf* that way...
THAT'S RIGHT, KID.

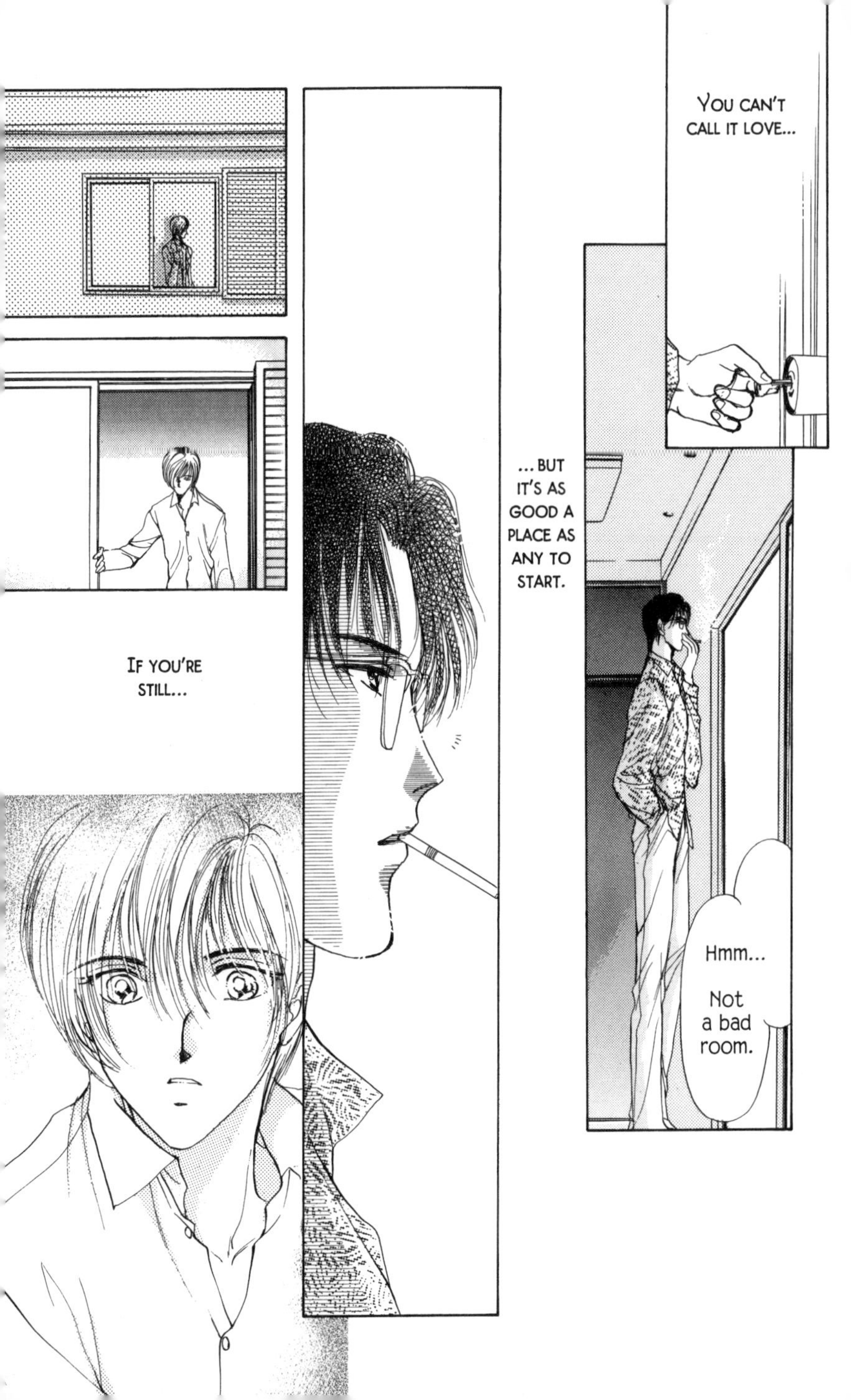
YOU CAN'T CALL IT LOVE...
Hmm... Not a bad room.
...BUT IT'S AS GOOD A PLACE AS ANY TO START.
IF YOU'RE STILL...

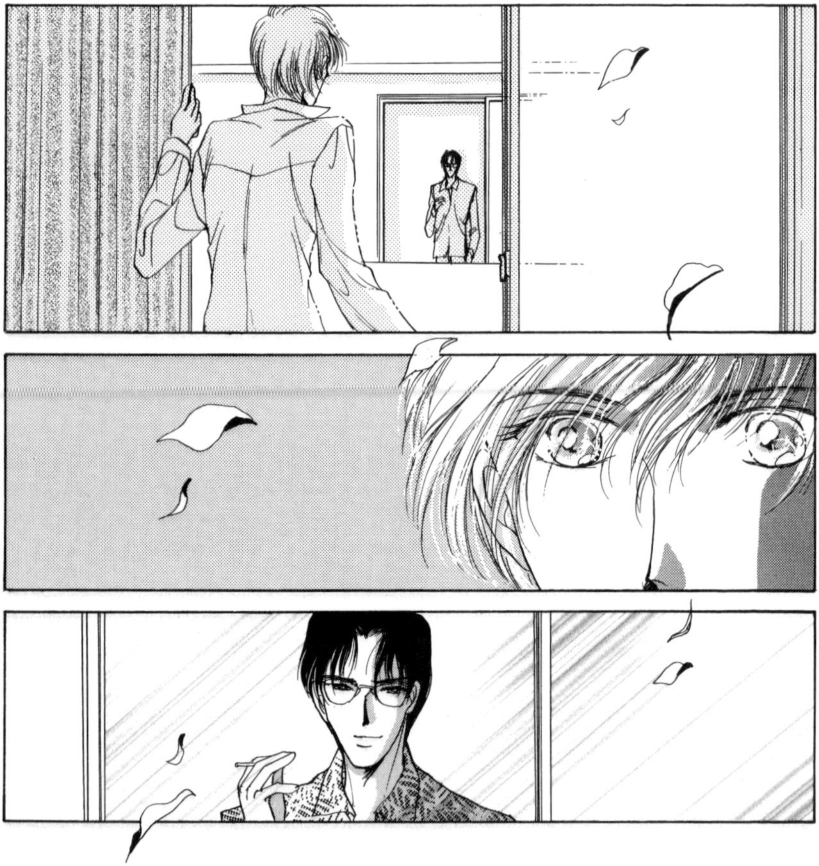

...CURIOUS...

I'M WAITING.

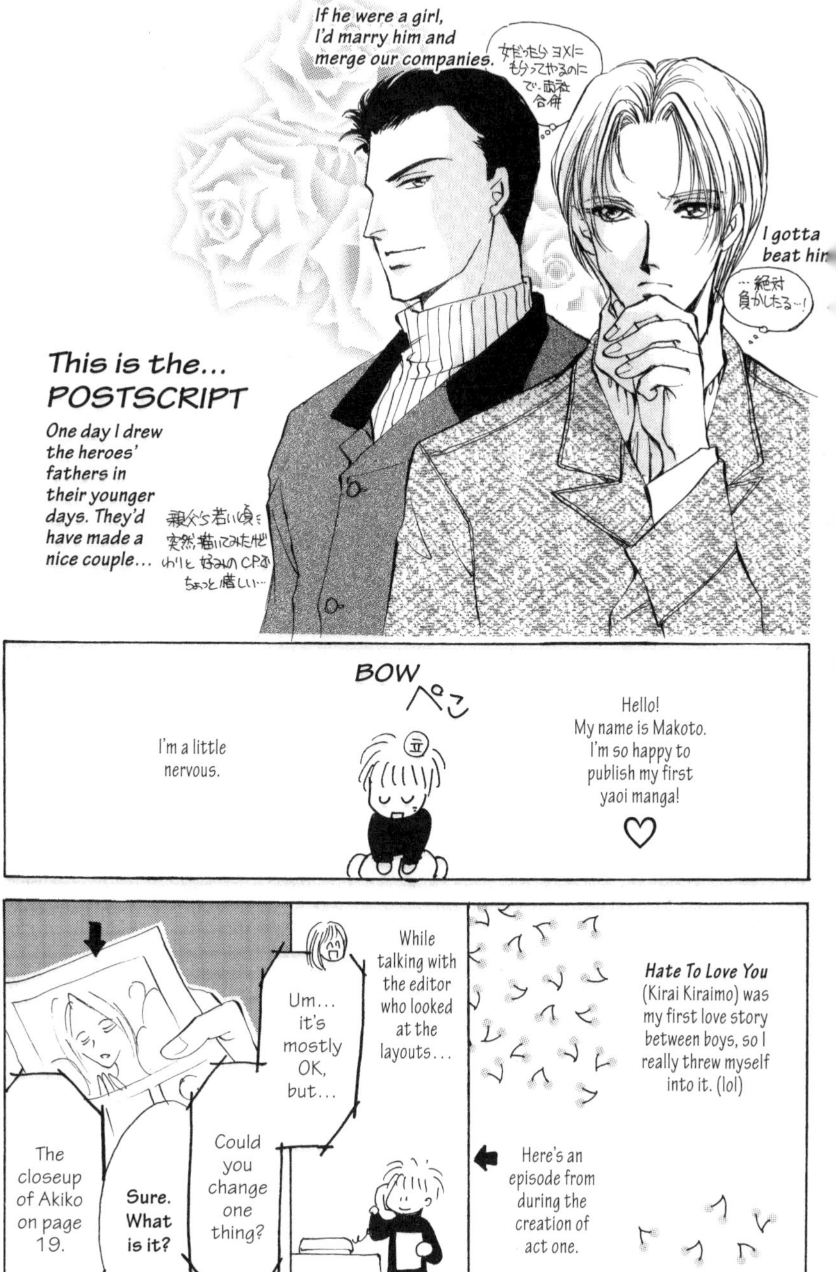

I gotta beat hi
…絶対負かしたる…!
If he were a girl, I'd marry him and merge our companies.
女だったらヨメにもらってやるのにで…両社合併
This is the... POSTSCRIPT
One day I drew the heroes' fathers in their younger days. They'd have made a nice couple…
Hello! My name is Makoto. I'm so happy to publish my first yaoi manga! ♡
BOW
ぺこ
I'm a little nervous.
Hate To Love You (Kirai Kiraimo) was my first love story between boys, so I really threw myself into it. (lol)
Here's an episode from during the creation of act one.
While talking with the editor who looked at the layouts…
Um… it's mostly OK, but…
Could you change one thing?
Sure. What is it?
The closeup of Akiko on page 19.

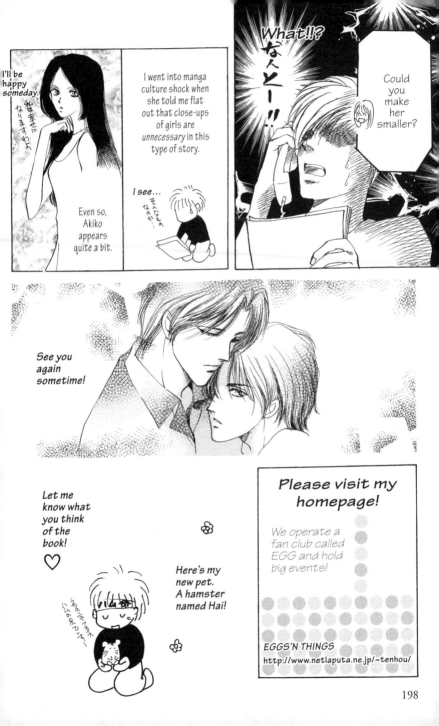

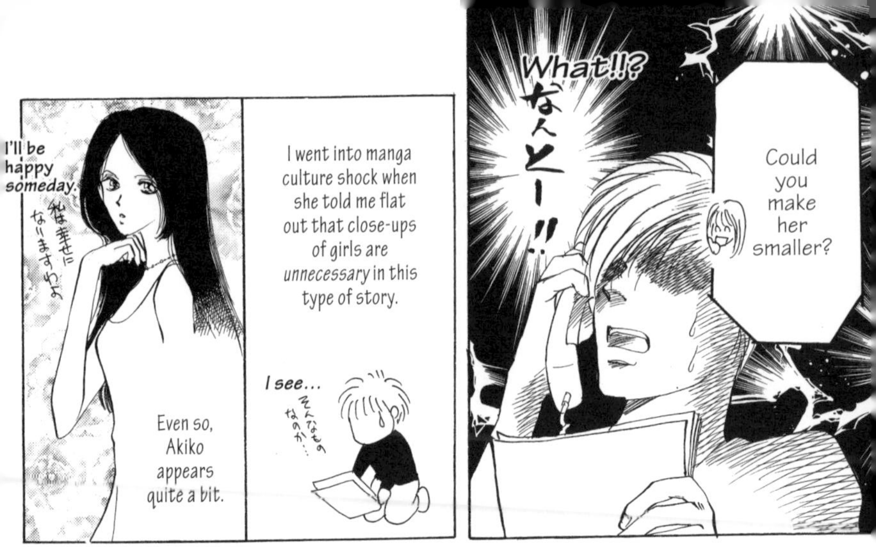
Could you make her smaller?
What!!?
なんとー!!
I went into manga culture shock when she told me flat out that close-ups of girls are *unnecessary* in this type of story.
I see...
そんなものなのか…
I'll be happy someday.
私は幸せになりますわよ
Even so, Akiko appears quite a bit.

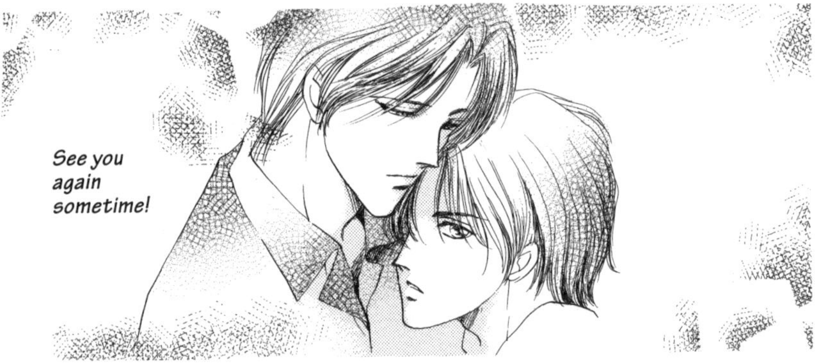
See you again sometime!

Let me know what you think of the book! ♡

Here's my new pet. A hamster named Hai!

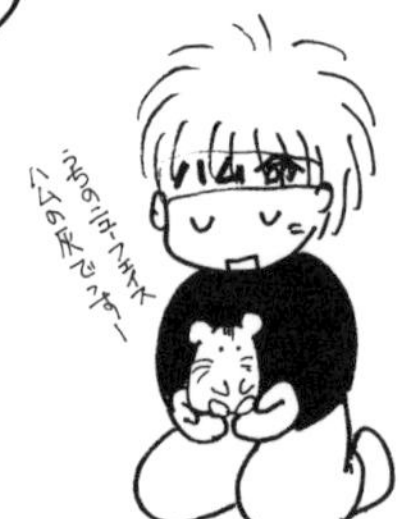
うちのニューフェイス
ハムの灰でっすー

Please visit my homepage!

We operate a fan club called EGG and hold big events!

EGGS'N THINGS

http://www.netlaputa.ne.jp/~tenhou/

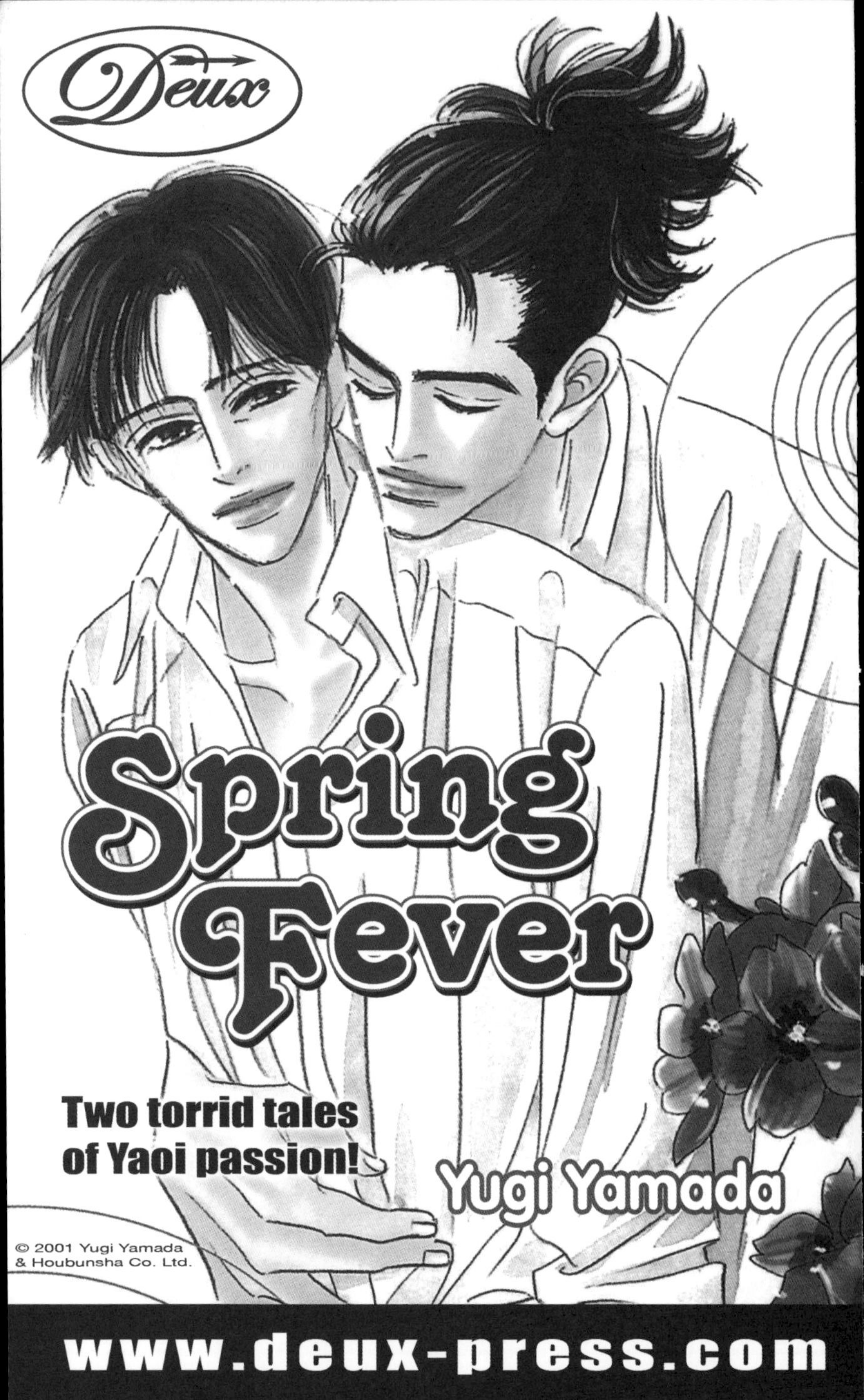
Deux
Spring Fever
Two torrid tales of Yaoi passion!
Yugi Yamada
© 2001 Yugi Yamada & Houbunsha Co. Ltd.
www.deux-press.com

Hate to Love You
Story and Art by Makoto Tateno
Translation: Kyoko Shapiro, HC Language Solutions, Inc.
English Adaptation: W. Church, HC Language Solutions, Inc.
Editor: John Werry
Lettering: Obake Chiizu-chan
© 2001 by Makoto Tateno. First published in Japan in 2001 by Biblos Ltd., Tokyo
as *Kirai Kiraimo.*

You Can't Call It Love
Story and Art by Makoto Tateno
Translation: HC Language Solutions, Inc.
Editor: John Werry
Lettering: Obake Chiizu-chan
© 1997 by Makoto Tateno. First published in Japan in 1997 by Hakusensha, Tokyo
as *Sore wo Ai to wa* in *Hana to Yume* magazine.
English Text © 2007 Deux Press. All rights reserved.
Produced by Goldmund Deux
Publisher: Nobuo Kitawaki
Published by Deux Press
www.deux-press.com
This book is a work of fiction. Names, characters, places, and incidents
are the products of the author's imagination or are used fictitiously.
Printed in China

Where Fantasy Becomes Obsession...